BUSINESS IN THE TRENCHES

Also by David Schroeder
Published by SPW LLC:

The Schlieffen Plan

Tannenberg: Eagles in the East

Galicia: The Forgotten Cauldron

Serbia the Defiant

Romania: Transylvanian Gambit

The 1916 Brusilov Offensive

Gorlice-Tarnow Breakthrough

The Italian Front: 1915-1918

The Western Front: 1914 to 1918

The Grand Campaign

For More Information and Products Visit:
www.businessinthetrenches.com
www.spwgame.com

BUSINESS
IN THE
TRENCHES

DAVID SCHROEDER

Copyright © 2011 by David Schroeder.

All rights reserved. No part of this publication may be reproduced, stored in a retrieval system or transmitted, in any form, or by any means, electronic, mechanical, recorded, photocopied, or otherwise, without the prior permission of the copyright owner, except by a reviewer who may quote brief passages in a review.

Cover artwork by John Rodriguez

Printed in the United States of America

ISBN: 978-0-9828829-0-0

CONTENTS

INTRODUCTION 7

CHAPTER 1: The Schlieffen Plan 11

CHAPTER 2: French Plan XVII 47

CHAPTER 3: British Intervention 87

CHAPTER 4: The Russian Steamroller 117

CHAPTER 5: Victory in the East 147

CHAPTER 6: Folly of the Habsburgs 175

CHAPTER 7: Strategic Confusion 217

CHAPTER 8: Verdun 245

CHAPTER 9: Petain and Nivelle 265

CHAPTER 10: Passchendaele 293

CHAPTER 11: Technology 319

CHAPTER 12: Victory or Defeat 341

SUMMATION: Final Thoughts 373

SELECTED BIBLIOGRAPHY 380

INDEX 381

ACTION FILES

Good and Bad Ideas on How To:

Deal with Subordinates You Didn't Choose 39

Deal with Management Mistakes 43

Formulate Good Business Plans 79

Create a Learning Organization 84

Make Leadership Changes 112

Promote Real Risk Taking 142

Lead an Organization to Success 168

Effectively Use Available Resources 206

Deal with Interdepartmental Conflict 212

Assess and Select Leaders 240

Foster Communication 259

Promote Goodwill that Produces Success 286

Know What's Really Going On 314

Make the Most of New Technology 337

Find the Best Way of Doing Things 369

INTRODUCTION

BUSINESS IN THE TRENCHES

THIS book is about how people make the same mistakes over and over. It is about learning from those mistakes so that you don't make them. It is about how to do better than people did in the past in similar situations.

We live in the most highly pressurized business environment ever. We continually have important decisions to make. You have to make the right call and do it quickly. Failure to make the right decision can spell doom.

The trick is to make good decisions and execute them before the competition does something similar. The problem is to learn how to do this. There is no such thing as a degree in decision making. There are no training classes. There is no secret formula for success. A good decision in one situation can be a bad decision in another.

How do you figure out the right thing to do and get it done quickly? Most people rely on their experience. Unfortunately, it takes a long time to gain a broad base of decision-making experience. Even then, your experience doesn't help when you encounter a new situation.

Where can you look for help? What can help you when you are under extreme pressure? The best way is to look at the experiences of others in similar situations. You can look at what happened because of what they did or didn't do. Similar situations can give you a wealth of insight that your own personal experience may not. This insight will help you avoid the mistakes of the past, help you be decisive when your competition is wondering what to do, and allow you to fully exploit opportunities.

Unfortunately, the history of modern business is actually rather short. You can look back about a century at most. The current environment of intense global competition, of rapidly evolving technology, is a rather recent development in the business world. Business history offers a somewhat meager base of experience to rely on.

True, there are a lot of modern business cases you can read. The great shortcoming with these cases is that you will usually know what the "correct" answer is. You need to know more than just what the correct decision should have been. You need insight into *why* a decision was correct.

Where else can you look for a wealth of lessons applicable to business decision making? It must be an area very similar to the business world for valid analogies. The stories and experiences would have to come from an extremely high-pressure environment, where decisions are needed right away, where the competition stands ready to exploit any weakness. It would need to be an environment where large organizations are locked together in struggles that can last for years, a brutal environment where only the successful survive and thrive, while those who hesitate are thwarted, crushed, annihilated, or absorbed.

The place to look is military history. Stories from military history fit the bill because so much is similar between warfare and business competition. In either environment, achieving goals and objectives is dependent on the decision-making ability of the leadership. No army ever conquered without at least halfway-competent leadership. No company has ever been successful without meeting the same requirement. A well-trained army is useless in the hands of incompetent leadership. A company with the right technologies, in the right markets, and with well-trained and motivated employees is still going to falter if its leaders cannot make good decisions.

Armies at war don't exist as solitary organizations. They battle opposing armies. Each has the goals of occupying the same territory and of hurting the other, yet only one can ultimately win. Each army moves to surprise the other. Each army tries to develop and deploy the latest technology before their competition can. Each looks for alliances. Each attempts to take advantage of the other's mistakes. All of these conditions exist in the marketplace and make the world of military history applicable to business today.

Many business leaders have already drawn the same conclusion. Unfortunately, most histories are just dry collections of facts. You read about what happened one day and then what happened the next. This does not give you insight into why and how specific decisions were made. There is little about what information was available to the leaders at the time and even less information about what influenced them to make their decisions. You need analogies between history and situations faced by the business decision maker of today.

This book fills this need. It is a collection of true stories and parallels to the business world. It presents the stories to provide insight into similar modern situations. It tells not only what happened, but why and how. It details what influenced and motivated the leaders to make the choices they made. It shows you how to do better. It will allow you to avoid common disastrous mistakes.

You will understand that the same tendencies of human nature that exist today existed in the past. The foibles of human nature that created problems for leaders, and the organizations they led, are the same ones that create problems today. The striking similarity between what people did in the past and what people do today (and will do in the future) is plain to see.

You will see people very familiar to you. It will be easy for you to make comparisons between the military leaders of the past and those you work with in business today. The motivations and actions of people throughout history are very similar. The only things different are technology and fashion. The results people produce under the effects of these motivations and influences are repeatable. The same inputs and same actions produce the same outcomes.

This book is *not* about how to use military methods to make a business successful. This book contains stories from military history to help you understand what works and what doesn't in any organization. Too often, the lessons from military history are good examples of what not to do.

The primary purpose here is not to teach history. The purpose is to make pertinent analogies to the present. The stories do not mire down in detail that detracts from making comparisons to business situations. The intent is to show you how the motivations and actions of leaders helped or hindered the organization they led.

This book uses the stories and histories of a great and forgotten war, World War I. Probably the most maligned characters in all of military history are the leaders of this war. People saw these men as the destroyers of their nation's youth. While World War II caused greater overall destruction and loss of life, in World War I the wanton waste seemed to have little or no reason. In the aftermath of this war, people could not understand why so many had died in what seemed to be great battles of mindless futility. They had even less understanding for how those in charge could have used tactics so bloody, so wasteful, and so obviously ineffective.

For many, the questions are "Why were these men so incompetent?" "Why were they put in charge?" "Why were they allowed to stay in charge when they were killing millions without winning?" and, above all, "Why on earth did they continue to use the same methods when they didn't work?"

We should ask similar questions about businesses. We should ask "Why does this particular company fail to improve?" "Why are profits continually so low?" and "Why does this company continue doing the same things when they are not having any success?"

Understanding the reasons for the failures of World War I can help you understand why similar things happen today. The lessons learned from this war will give you the knowledge you need to win victories over your foes in business.

The stories of World War I are in chronological order. Reading will concentrate on one army at a time. You will look at how each particular organization and its leadership dealt with the circumstances they found themselves in. You will learn how to repeat their successes and how to avoid their mistakes.

CHAPTER I

THE SCHLIEFFEN PLAN

"No Plan Survives Contact with the Enemy"

INTRODUCTION

THE starting point for discussing World War I is the German Army's plan for a quick victory. Their plan was extremely bold. It put millions of men and machines into motion. Everyone else could only react to it. As the story of the German plan unfolds, you will see the following main themes:

- Dealing with subordinates you didn't pick
- When your plan discounts the competition's reaction
- The need for common goals
- Mutual support to meet goals
- Changing direction when things go wrong
- Failing to know what's going on
- Personal success versus organizational success

HISTORICAL CASE AND BUSINESS ANALOGIES

The Pre-War Situation

There was intense competition between the great nations of Europe before World War I. Simply put, each country wanted to be more powerful and have more prestige than the others. This country-versus-country competition took many forms. There was competition over who could grab the most colonies. There was competition over who could get the best trade agreements. There was competition over who had the biggest navy. There was competition over who produced the most steel. There was competition over who controlled specific strategic pieces of land. Each country was out to win.

There were bad feelings over who had won in the past and envy about who might win in the future. Every thirty years or so, a war would break out. Then the country that lost would look for revenge. This situation became even more explosive when countries started forming long-term alliances. Counter-alliances sprang up in response. As a result, any outbreak of fighting would guarantee a World War.

Everyone back then expected wars in Europe on a regular basis. Kings and emperors down to their common subjects thought this. Armies and navies did not prepare for wars that *might* happen; they prepared for the war they *knew* was coming. It was just a matter of time. Officers in the German Army would regularly toast *Der Tag*, "The Day" the next war would start. They looked forward to being in another war.

Before World War I, the last big European war was between France and Germany in the 1870s. Germany had won after destroying most of the French Army, capturing the French Emperor, and then taking Paris. The Germans then humiliated the French at the end of this war. They crowned the Prussian King Emperor of Germany at Versailles. They forced the French to pay their cost of fighting the war. They annexed the French provinces of Alsace and Lorraine. All of this caused a lot of French hatred of Germany. The French wanted their lands back. They wanted revenge.

To keep the French in check, the Germans allied themselves with most of the countries France might turn to for assistance. The new German Emperor, Kaiser Wilhelm II, rashly undermined most of these alliances. The Kaiser managed to alienate or antagonize just about every other country in Europe. He wanted to be the most important person in Europe. He wanted to be the undisputed winner of the international "competitions." He wanted to go down in history as the victor of a great war. He either insulted or threatened just about everybody else on the continent. Soon Germany had only one weak ally left, while France formed alliances with both Russia and Great Britain. The Kaiser's words and actions convinced both countries that Germany was their main threat. They all came to believe that war with Germany was inevitable.

The French alliances meant Germany now had potential enemies on both sides. The Russians were to Germany's east while France was directly to the west.

The Schlieffen Plan 13

Added to Germany's difficult strategic situation was the threat of a blockade on vital imports by the British navy. Germany was in a very vulnerable position. [Fig 1]

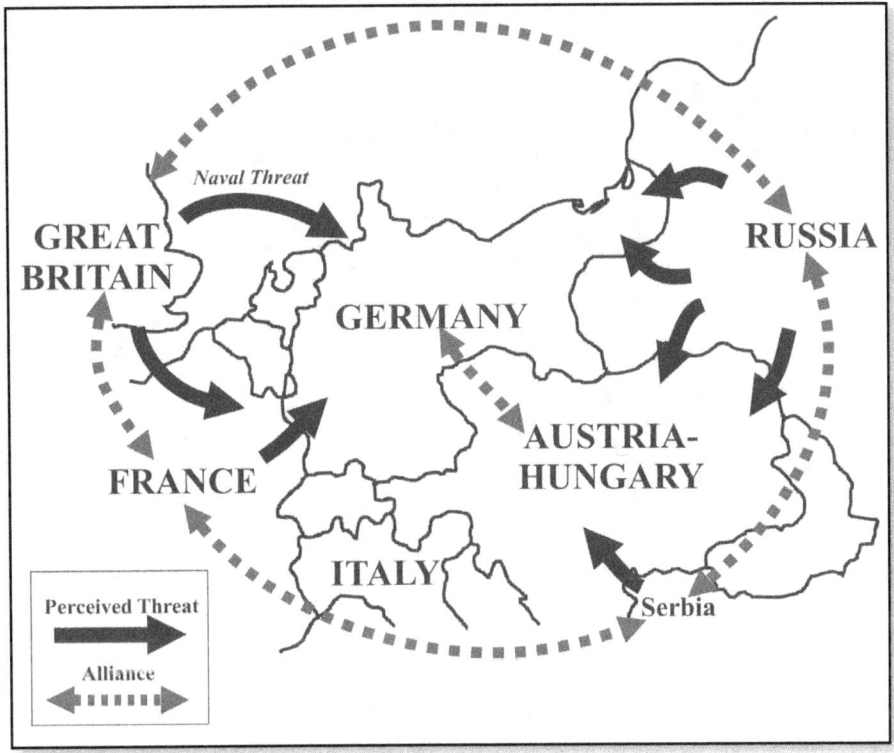

Figure 1. Germany and Austria-Hungary Surrounded by Potential Foes

The German military needed a way to win a war on two fronts, and win it quickly. The Chief of the German General Staff, Count Alfred von Schlieffen, developed the German Army's proposed solution.

The Schlieffen Plan

Schlieffen's plan was to attack France with the bulk of German forces, knocking her out of the war quickly. Only then would Germany shift troops to the east to deal with Russia. The plan would defeat France by moving most of the German Army through the neutral countries of Belgium, Holland, and Luxembourg into relatively undefended northern France. The massive arm of the German Army to undertake this maneuver was the right wing. The right wing would move through Belgium and then around Paris to encircle it. The German generals believed France would give up after Paris fell. The much weaker left wing of the German Army defended the border with France. [Fig 2] An even smaller force defended the Russian border.

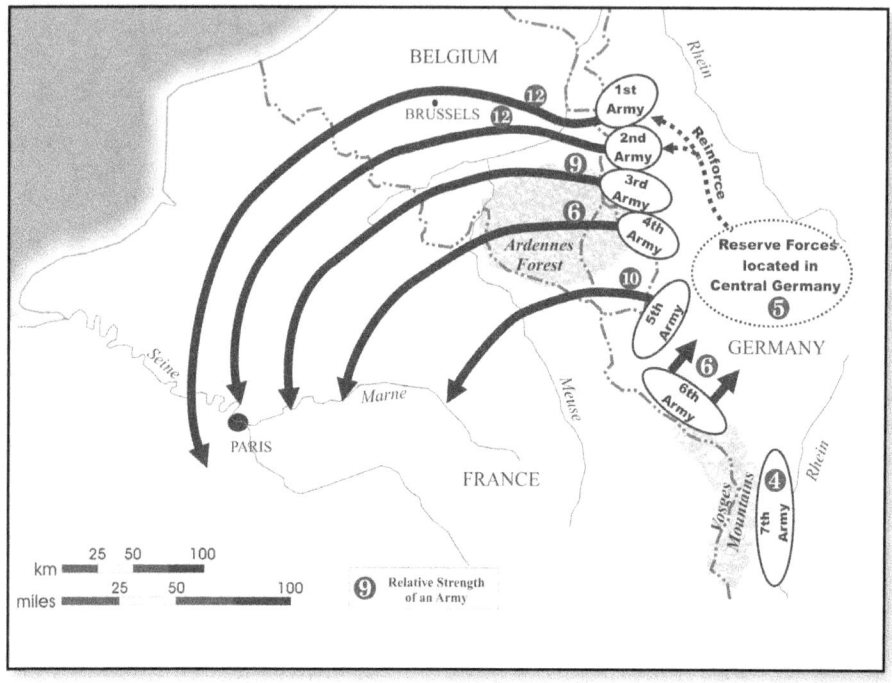

Figure 2. The Schlieffen Plan, Original Concept

German leadership saw violating the neutrality of Belgium and other countries as justifiable, even though Germany had signed treaties guaranteeing their safety. The German Army felt their need to quickly get into the heart of France far outweighed other considerations. After all, armies had traipsed through Belgium for hundreds of years. More battles were fought there than in any other country. Schlieffen gambled that the German Army would defeat France before there were any serious consequences for breaking the treaties. The Kaiser even referred to the treaty guaranteeing Belgium neutrality as a "meaningless scrap of paper."

A number of factors caused Schlieffen to decide on the specifics of his plan. First, even though Germany had the strongest army in Europe, she did not have the strength to defeat France and Russia simultaneously. Second, starting the war by invading Russia would draw the German Army into a long and plodding campaign through the vast Russian interior, similar to Napoleon's experience. Schlieffen had no desire to repeat Napoleon's fiasco. Also, if they invaded Russia, they would still have to hold off the large French Army. The French would attack to regain their lost provinces of Alsace and Lorraine. There just wasn't a way of defeating Russia in a quick campaign. Third, the large Russian Army could only slowly mobilize and could not invade Germany until well after war started. This was because the Russian's rail network was inadequate to move millions of men the distances from the Russian interior to the German border quickly. Fourth, attacking France directly would mean attacking headfirst into strongly fortified areas defended by large numbers of troops. All of these factors combined to drive Schlieffen to devise a plan for attacking France first, and to do so by moving around the French Army through Belgium.

The Schlieffen Plan required the German Army to put as much of its strength as possible into the right wing. Schlieffen's plan accepted great risk. If the right wing failed, the plan would fail, and Germany would find itself in a hopeless situation, with a protracted war on two fronts.

Helmuth von Moltke succeeded Schlieffen as Chief of the German General Staff. Once in charge, Moltke made changes to the Schlieffen Plan. He decided not to invade Holland. He would only move the Germany army through Belgium and Luxembourg on the way into France. He did not maintain the same ratio of forces between the right and left wings. Moltke assigned many newly created units of the growing German Army to the left wing, increasing its strength at the expense of the right. Moltke and his staff considered these minor changes. They just didn't want to accept as much risk on the left as Schlieffen did. Moltke and his staff retained the Schlieffen Plan's grand concept of a sweep through Belgium around the French Army as the best chance for victory. The Schlieffen Plan remained the accepted German war plan.

The War Begins

It didn't take long for some country to find a reason for going to war. The Kaiser's blundering diplomacy made this almost certain. Germany agreed to back their only ally, Austria-Hungary, in punishing Serbia for the assassination of Archduke Franz Ferdinand. Russia then mobilized to protect Serbia. The Kaiser mobilized the German Army in response. The German Army only had one plan, Schlieffen's. There was no plan to just hold off the Russians. Invading Belgium and Luxembourg was actually part of the German mobilization process. Moltke told the Kaiser the plan was unchangeable once mobilization began. In Moltke's opinion, last-minute changes would only produce chaos and delay. After all, the Russians were already moving.

The Germans followed the schedules of the Schlieffen Plan. The German forces that moved against France and Belgium were comprised of seven separate armies. The First and Second Armies were the "fist" of the right wing, which also contained the Third and Fourth Armies. The Fifth Army was the "hinge" between the right and left wings, while the left wing was composed of the Sixth and Seventh Armies. [Fig 3]

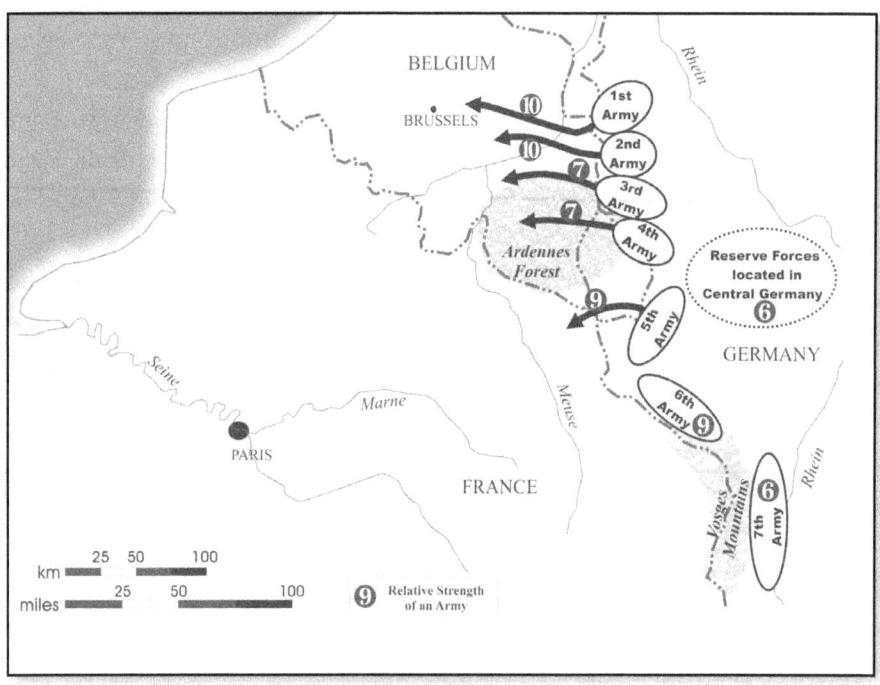

Figure 3. *The Schlieffen Plan as executed, 1-15 August 1914*

Moltke did not have control over who would be in charge of each of his armies. As is usually the case, the leader could not hand pick everyone in important subordinate positions. Some army commanders were already there when Moltke became Chief of Staff. The Kaiser or the military bureaucracy appointed others.

The Schlieffen Plan

ANALOGY 1: INHERITED SUBORDINATES

Leadership selection back then depended on a number of factors. These included skill, political ability, family connections, demographics, and other similar considerations. This method of leader selection is almost the same as it is in most businesses today.

When you assume a leadership position, you are going to inherit subordinates. You can't just place people of your own choosing in every critical subordinate role. You must lead people that you may not want to lead. It is critical that you align their ideas on how to accomplish the organization's goals. You even need to discuss what those goals are in the first place. Set clear expectations. You need to find out what the subordinates think: what they think about where the organization is going and how it will get there. You have to reach consensus with your subordinates about these issues. If you don't do this, people will continue to pursue their own agendas, even if it damages the organization's performance. People act like this all the time.

You cannot just tell people what their jobs are and expect them to act the way you want them to. There is always some resistance by members of an organization against any changes in policies, practices, or direction. You will have to take the time to bring people on board. You must spend time coaching people to get the behaviors and outcomes you want. You also have to assist in the formation of helpful relationships between subordinates. They have to work well together, or results will suffer. If you don't do these things, you will find yourself unable to meet goals and performance targets. People instead will focus on what they want, and they will do so without any regard for the organization and its goals. This is what happened to the Schlieffen Plan.

Understanding what happened with the Schlieffen Plan requires insight into the leaders of the German Army who executed it. Their decisions, motivations, ability to work together, and relationships with their superiors all greatly influenced the outcome of the German campaign in 1914.

The commander of the vanguard German First Army was Alexander von Kluck. Kluck was a hard-as-nails career officer. People who saw him during the campaign said he matched their picture of what Genghis Khan must have looked and acted like. With him at the front of the right wing was Karl von Bülow, also career military, who led the Second Army. Bülow was the same age as Kluck, but looked and acted older. He was more reserved and fastidious than his fire-breathing peer. Supporting these first two armies were the Third and Fourth Armies. Max von Hausen, also a professional soldier, commanded the Third. Duke Albrecht of Württemberg, a political appointee, commanded the Fourth Army at the southern end of the right wing.

Between the right and left wings was the Fifth Army. The German Crown Prince commanded it. Since he was the Kaiser's heir, he was obviously the most politically connected person in the entire army. He had some military training, but he was expected to leave the important decisions to his professional Chief of Staff. The majority of the left wing was in the Sixth Army, led by the Bavarian Crown Prince Rupprecht. Bavaria was a somewhat recent and very important acquisition of the German Empire. Bavaria had its own culture and many privileges of autonomy within the German Empire. Prince Rupprecht was an experienced and competent soldier, but he also wore the Bavarian crown. This was more than enough to get him the job as an Army Commander.

The Schlieffen Plan was worked out to the last conceivable detail. Every unit involved had specific lines of march they were to precisely follow. Units were to reach specified points on the map by specified times each day. The schedule was incredibly exacting. The schedules were meant to pressure mid-level commanders into pushing their men on to the efforts required to make the plan successful. But no plan can take everything into account, and this was also true of Schlieffen's plan. Schlieffen believed that the training and skill of the German officers would allow them to deal with the unexpected. This was counted on to get units quickly back on schedule should anything slow them up.

> ### ANALOGY 2: DISCOUNTING THE COMPETITION
>
> Plans that don't allow for the unexpected are doomed to fail. In the business world, there are a lot of detailed plans just like Schlieffen's. In most cases, these plans contain schedules showing the company marching right along to its goals without any problems. The employees are supposed to quickly and effectively neutralize any problem that arises. On top of that, like the Schlieffen Plan, most business plans tend to discount what the competition will do during execution. The fact of the matter is the competition isn't going to just sit there while you carry out your plan to beat them. They are going to take unexpected action. They are going to counter your moves with moves of their own. They are certainly not going to just roll over and let you have your way.
>
> The great flaw in all too many business plans is not considering the competition's reaction. Poor plans focus only on the movements of the company's own forces. This is not the only thing your plan needs to cover. Your plan needs to deal with both the execution of the plan and how to deal with the competition's reactions. Spend meaningful effort on what you can do to counter the competition's moves. As in chess, you have to think ahead more than just one move.

Execution on the Right Wing

Right from the start, the Germans encountered problems with their plan. The Schlieffen Plan assumed that the Belgians would quickly give up when they saw the huge German armies marching right at them. Instead, the Belgians decided to defend themselves against hopeless odds. The Belgians fought competently and tenaciously, slowing down the German right wing.

The Germans had problems besides the enemy. There were serious communication problems. Radio was in its infancy and was unreliable, and there were not enough radios to handle all of the necessary messages in any case. The armies and their leaders often had to resort to communicating by telegraph or messengers. These methods were very dependent on infrastructure that battles had a tendency to destroy. The result was that each of the armies had trouble communicating with other armies. They also had difficulty communicating with the high command. The senior generals had less and less information on where their people were and what the situation was at the front. This got worse the farther the armies moved into enemy territory. The plan did not anticipate these problems, and the Germans were slow to find solutions. It didn't help matters that supreme headquarters was about a hundred miles from the nearest front line. Even worse, Moltke never left his headquarters to visit any of his subordinate commanders until too late.

Moltke did make a change to improve coordination between the right wing armies. He put Bülow, the Second Army commander, in charge of all of the other right wing armies. Kluck, another right wing Army Commander, felt he should be the one in charge. After all, his First Army was the one out in front, the vanguard of the right wing. Since he was the one moving the farthest and fastest, he felt that all other operations should support his. Moltke did not deal with Kluck's resistance to Bülow's leadership. Moltke just expected Kluck to follow orders.

Bülow had different ideas on the Schlieffen Plan than Kluck did. Kluck wanted to move his First Army as fast and as far as possible. Bülow felt the right wing needed to stay together as a mass, so it could crush any resistance it might encounter. Bülow continually sent messages to Kluck telling him to keep his First Army in contact with his own Second Army. This meant that Kluck's units had to slow down to not race ahead of Bülow's. This was an issue because Bülow's units were dealing with most of the Belgian resistance. Bülow also sent similar messages to Hausen at Third Army to stay in contact with the other flank of his army. In Hausen's case, it was because he was not keeping up with Bülow. Hausen was very confident of victory and was in no real hurry. Hausen was more worried about his personal accommodations, like how big of a house he could stay at each night, than he was with keeping up with the rest of the right wing.

ANALOGY 3: ORGANIZATIONAL ALIGNMENT

Here is an example of a similar dangerous situation in business. Three important departments of a company have a common goal. To achieve this goal, the three departments must work together, coordinating their efforts. This is because no one department has the resources to be successful on its own. Each department encounters various problems, and each has different ideas how to overcome them. The person over all of the departments puts one department head in charge of coordinating efforts. However, the boss does not give the one department head authority over the others. Of course, the other department heads probably feel they should be the one in charge. They don't discuss this openly because they don't want to get into a confrontation with their boss. Instead, they just find ways to cooperate as little as possible. After all, they feel that their own department's goals are more important than those of other departments. The situation gets even worse if a department head has some hidden personal agenda, rather than the goals of the company or even of his own department. All of this is exacerbated by a boss who doesn't want to get involved in personality issues between the department heads, and leaves them to work these issues out on their own. All of this is a recipe for disaster.

The situation just described is all too common. Someone placed under the direction of someone they consider a peer is not going to readily comply with the peer's wishes. This is especially true if they have different ideas about what needs to be done and how to do it. They are going to keep doing what they want to the way that they want to do it. They will do as little as possible to comply with the instructions of the perceived peer. And even this minor compliance is only after a lot of kicking and screaming.

The person in authority over all of the departments must be aware of the difference in opinions about what to do and how to do it in the first place. This person must get the subordinate department heads to reach consensus. The overall leader must get them to align their ideas before sending them off to accomplish set goals. If one of the department heads is to oversee coordination, that person needs some authority over the others. Even after all this, the overall leader must stay abreast of what is going on. The boss must know how the coordination is going and how well the departments and their heads are working together.

Unfortunately for the German Army, Moltke did none of this. Bülow's instructions met with serious resistance by the other right wing commanders. Kluck became increasingly upset that he had to subordinate the actions of his army to Bülow. Kluck did not think Bülow was doing enough to keep up with him. Moltke may have known of Kluck's views, but he did nothing to help work out coordination issues. Moltke never left his headquarters to go and visit any of the involved army commanders. He just read a lot of memos and reports about what was going on.

Moltke may not have cared about the coordination problems. For the first few weeks of the campaign, the right wing was only slightly off schedule. There were no major disruptions because of strains between the three army commanders. True, there had been some delays. The Belgian fortress at Liege did not give up according to schedule. The Germans dealt with this by bringing up the massive Big Bertha howitzers. These famous guns were designed and built specifically to quickly blast such forts to smithereens. But each day the armies of the right wing fell just a little further behind schedule. Moltke focused on other situations instead.

Efforts of the Left Wing

The French executed their pre-war plan of attack while the German right wing was marching through Belgium. The French were determined to regain the provinces of Alsace and Lorraine they had previously lost to Germany. The French attacked the German Sixth and Seventh Armies right after the war started. These attacks were total disasters for the French. They quickly lost tens of thousands of men, and their armies fell back in disarray. The French figured that since the Germans were strong enough to beat them back, that they must be weak elsewhere. So they decided to attack again a couple of days later at a different spot, this time just to the north of Lorraine. The new French attacks aimed at the German Fourth and Fifth Armies. These new attacks went just as badly as the first ones. The French Army suffered substantial casualties again, accomplishing absolutely nothing.

The commanders of the various German armies that repelled these attacks were now brimming with all kinds of confidence. They had totally defeated the main body of the French Army, or so they thought. They were also envious of the successes of the right wing in advancing through Belgium. This was certainly the attitude of Bavarian Crown Prince Rupprecht, commanding the German Sixth

Army. He was not accustomed to taking a back seat to anybody. Now others were overshadowing him. He decided to reach for his proper share of the glory.

A Change of Plan

The Schlieffen Plan intended for the Sixth Army to play a purely defensive role. It was to retreat in the face of French attacks as a ploy. The idea was to entice the French to advance into Alsace and Lorraine, moving them farther away from the right wing in the process. Rupprecht decided against retreating. He wanted to beat the French, not play the part of a coward who ran away from them. He did not care that this was exactly what the plan needed him to do. Since the French appeared beaten and were falling back, Rupprecht proposed even greater deviations from his army's intended role in the Schlieffen Plan. Instead of retreating, or even just staying put, Rupprecht pressured Moltke for permission to attack. He wanted to pursue the French across the border and into France. Rupprecht argued this change to the plan would allow him to encircle the French Army.

Moltke was enticed by this perceived opportunity to achieve even greater success than seemed possible with the Schlieffen Plan. The Schlieffen Plan culminated in taking Paris. If Moltke could now successfully attack with both the left and right wings, he would surround the French Army, achieving one of the greatest victories in military history.

Schlieffen calculated the German Army was only strong enough for one main effort against the French, the right wing. The Schlieffen Plan proposed moving through Belgium in the first place because the French line of fortresses seemed too strong for the German Army to break through. Moltke forgot all about these calculations. He became obsessed with the great victory that seemed within grasp. There was not a lot of discussion about the realistic prospects of Rupprecht's ideas. After all, things seemed to be going better than the plan had predicted.

When Rupprecht made his proposal to Moltke, the right wing was still close to being on schedule. But the right wing had not yet encountered any serious opposition. Moltke saw only the steady progress on the right and victories on the left. Up to now, the German Army was successful everywhere. He did not think of the hard times and difficult fighting the Schlieffen Plan said would come. [Fig 4]

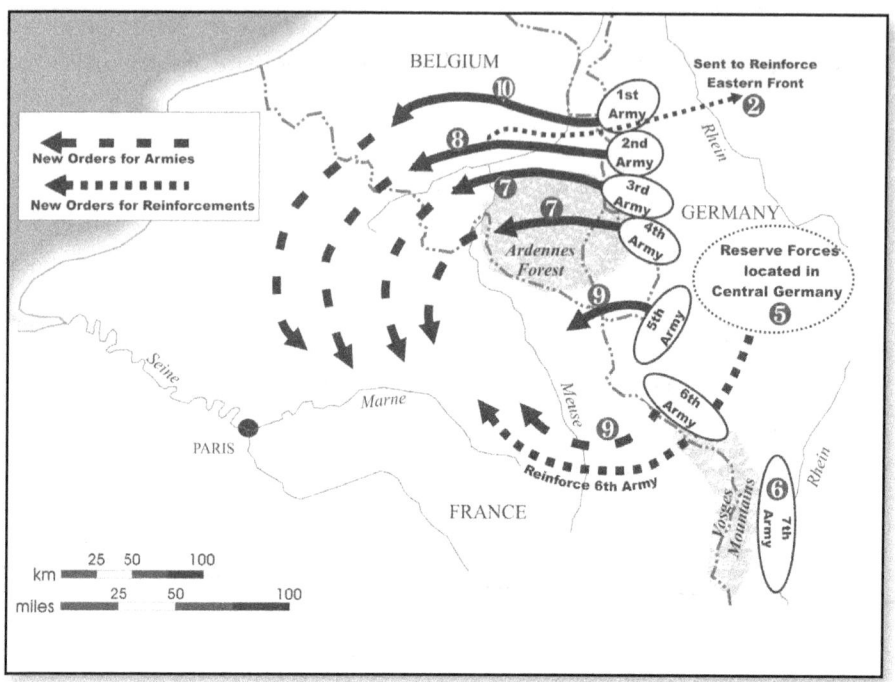

Figure 4. Changes to the Schlieffen Plan

Moltke gave Rupprecht permission to move his army out of its defensive posture and to attack the French. The Schlieffen Plan counted on the left wing to reinforce the right wing as the campaign progressed. Now there would be no such help to the main effort. All of the left wing was now committed to a new offensive. But this was not all. Units coming from inside Germany went to the left wing, rather than to the right. They were to bolster the left wing's attacks, instead of reinforcing the right wing as Schlieffen intended. Resources desperately needed for the future success of the right wing were now committed elsewhere.

> ## ANALOGY 4: PROBLEMS WITH THE LIMELIGHT
>
> The same thing happens frequently in business. Take an ambitious person who does not want a supporting role. Put that person in charge of a business unit with a supporting role. The person works to find ways to increase their visibility within the organization and starts to drain away critical resources from the very units they are supposed to support in the first place. The boss is enamored of the rosy estimates painted by this ambitious unit head. Before, the boss may have thought there were only enough resources to execute the original plan. The promptings of the overly ambitious leader make the boss reconsider. Maybe the boss even thinks things are going well enough to reallocate some resources. The boss moves resources from the main effort into a new project run by the ambitious support unit head. The outcome of these changes is what happened historically.

Moltke cut off reinforcements to the right wing by accepting Rupprecht's proposal. The units of the left wing did not move to other sectors according to the Schlieffen Plan. Nothing from the central reserve went to the right wing either. The right wing would get none of the reinforcements the plan called for. If this wasn't bad enough, a few days later Moltke decided to actually weaken the vital thrust through Belgium and northern France.

Problems Elsewhere

The right wing began to encounter its first real resistance while the new orders to Rupprecht were taking effect. Bülow and Hausen had to fight the French Fifth Army along the French-Belgian border. Meanwhile, Kluck had to deal with the British Army, which appeared along his line of march. These unanticipated battles slowed the German right wing a little more, but it was the winner each time, forcing the French and British to pull back. The Germans continued to move forward.

While the right wing moved into France, something unexpected happened. The Russians invaded eastern Germany. The Germans had incorrectly assumed that Russian mobilization was going to take a lot longer. Dreaded Cossacks were actually inside Germany, in East Prussia, shooting people and burning property. The population was not prepared for this. The civilians panicked. Germans thought their army should be the only one invading enemy territory.

The bad press from the east put a lot of pressure on the German High Command to do something. This was not the only pressure caused by the quick Russian invasion. East Prussia contained the estates of many German nobles and others with connections to the Kaiser's court and inner circle. These influential people used their connections to protect their assets. They let the Kaiser know they expected him to do something to protect their lands and property. Refugees from East Prussia were another problem. Those who fled were showing up in the capital and other cities. The Kaiser and his advisors passed on to Moltke all of these pressures to do something. Couldn't he do something about it? After all, the Schlieffen Plan was working just fine, so couldn't he do something to stop the Russians?

ANALOGY 5: LONG TERM VERSUS SHORT TERM

The influential East Prussians acted just like important shareholders in a business. The long-range plans of the company are under constant pressure by the short-term needs of the shareholders. Those worried about short-term losses usually don't listen to explanations about the long-term benefits of following the company's strategic plan. You have two choices when in this situation. You could ignore the cries of those panicked by the short-term. Or you must redirect some resources to deal with the short-term. This second course means diluting your the main effort. Resources your plan requires will instead go to dealing with the short-term crisis. This greatly reduces the probability of long-term success.

Moltke was hearing panic not just from civilians and the government; he was hearing it from the military commander in East Prussia too. Max von Prittwitz commanded the lone German Army in East Prussia. He was crumbling under the pressure of the early Russian invasion. Prittwitz told Moltke he was going to abandon the province. He wasn't even going to fight a delaying action. The Schlieffen Plan counted on the forces in East Prussia holding off the Russians until France was defeated.

All of these pressures convinced Moltke he needed to do something right away about the Russians in East Prussia. He took substantial forces away from Bülow's army in the right wing. At a crucial point in the invasion of France, he had units from the right wing board trains for the other side of Germany. By the time they got there, the crisis was over. The Germans already in East Prussia won a major victory over the Russians and the province was safe. Moltke had seriously weakened the right wing for a wild goose chase by some of the best units in the German Army.

The Plan Begins to Crumble

The right wing fought a series of battles with the retreating French and British in the days that followed. These engagements took their toll in terms of men, ammunition, and time. The right wing was getting weaker and weaker. It was getting further and further behind schedule. Its commanders moved away from their planned routes as they tried to get around the French and British facing them. The right wing was forced to wheel inward sooner than originally intended because of the changes to the Schlieffen Plan made by Moltke. Instead of moving to encircle Paris as envisioned, the right wing now moved according to Rupprecht's proposals to encircle the French armies.

Meanwhile, Rupprecht was having problems of his own. He was very successful in defeating the initial French attacks, but now his own attacks met stiff resistance. He was getting additional help from units of the central reserve. Even this increase in his army's strength did not get him through the French lines. His army stalled out in front of the French fortress line.

Moltke allowed this situation to continue. Rupprecht's army got permission to attack the French forts, and reinforcements continued to go to him instead of Kluck or Bülow. In all probability, Moltke could not bring himself to admit that allowing Rupprecht's army to attack was a serious mistake. He hoped Rupprecht would eventually break through. But this hope was in direct contradiction with the prewar planning, in which Moltke himself was heavily involved. The Schlieffen Plan authors concluded the only rational hope of victory against France was through the right wing's successful march.

> ## ANALOGY 6: EMOTIONS AND ERRORS
>
> You can't get caught up in the emotions of the moment. Moltke did. He allowed Rupprecht to influence him to do something he knew was a rash overextension of his resources. When it became apparent the deviation from the Schlieffen Plan was not going to work, Moltke did not accept the fact he had made a mistake. He let the mistake continue. This is just like any other leader who cannot admit something they decided to do is not the right course of action.
>
> There are two things that contribute to a leader being unable or unwilling to admit a mistake and to make an appropriate change. The first reason is the ego of the leader. Many people will not face up to the fact that they made an error in judgment. Rather than face reality, such people are perfectly willing to lead their organizations down some path of folly, even when it is apparent to everyone that they are on the wrong path. The second reason is the leader fears if he admits to a mistake, those he leads will question his leadership and judgment. He fears they may think, "If he was wrong about this, maybe he was wrong about other things too." The leader fears such thinking may undermine the confidence the organization needs to have in their leadership. The leader thinks this will do more damage than not correcting the mistake. This is just a rationalization that helps the leader cave into their ego. The reality is the rest of the organization already realizes the leader made a mistake. They will have less confidence in the leader who is unwilling to correct a mistake than they will in a leader who can admit a decision may have been wrong.

A Glimmer of Hope

The right wing of the German Army appeared close to accomplishing its new goal of encircling the French and British Armies facing it. Each of the armies of the right wing now operated under their individual leaders. Resistance to Bülow's leadership role resulted in changing back to the original arrangement. Each army was moving at a record pace across the north of France. The French and British continued to retreat. They stopped to fight a couple of times. In each instance they had to retreat further as the Germans threatened to surround them.

It seemed the Germans might close the trap shut on the retreating French

The Schlieffen Plan

and British forces as the right wing approached the outskirts of Paris. To do this, the German High Command ordered Kluck to move his army behind Bülow's. Kluck was to support Bülow's movements from then on. Up to this point, Kluck was always in the front of the right wing. As the leader of the vanguard, he felt he did not support others; all others were supposed to support him. Kluck did not comply with these orders. Instead of moving behind Bülow, he moved out in front of him. Doing so, he moved the flank of his First Army right past the French forces assembling around Paris. Instead of encircling the enemy, Kluck now made it possible for the enemy to encircle him.

> ## ANALOGY 7: THE LEADER OR THE TEAM
>
> Here is a picture of a leader who cannot subordinate himself to the greater good of the organization. This kind of leader cannot swallow his pride. He cannot move from a position of prominence, where others support him, to give support to others.
>
> You can expect the same kind of self-serving actions by individuals who refuse to support others. Such people think of themselves first, not the best interests of the organization they work for. When a poor leader decides the organization exists to serve them, it is often fatal to the organization.

The Reverse at the Marne

Kluck's rash and self-serving actions made French counterattacks possible. As Kluck's army moved past Paris, the French forces moved from near the city to attack the vulnerable German flank. Kluck had to turn to meet the attack to avoid having the French surround his army. When Kluck's army reversed direction, the weakened state of the right wing was finally revealed. To meet the French attack with sufficient strength, Kluck had no choice but to leave a huge gap between his army and Bülow's. This gave the French and British near this gap the opportunity of getting around Bülow's army too. Bülow had to retreat to stop this from happening. The right wing was stopped. The French and British counterattacks started the Battle of the Marne. This battle prevented the Germans from winning the war. In the next four years of the war, the Germans would never get as close to Paris again. [Fig 5]

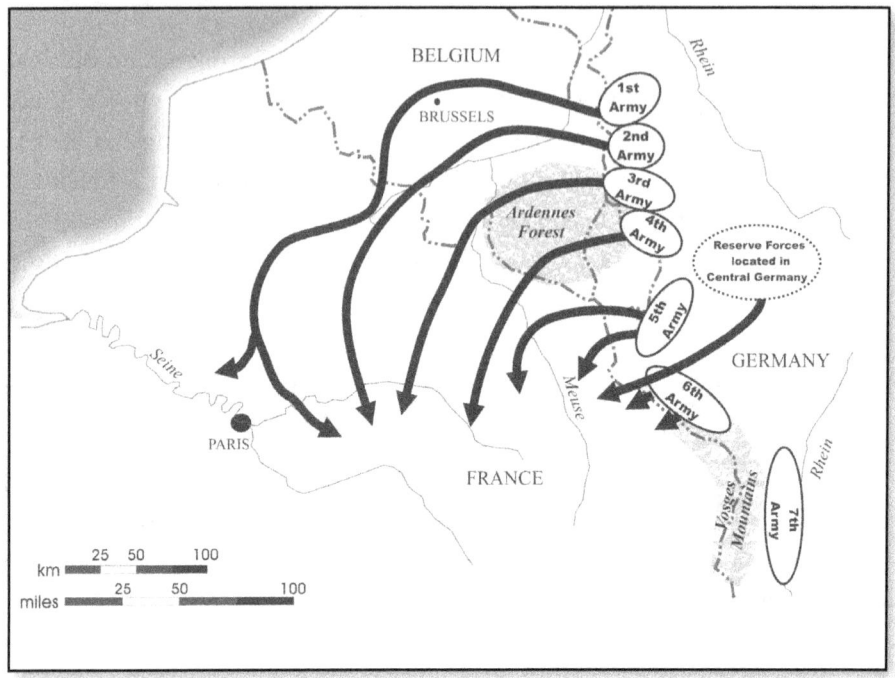

Figure 5. Actual Progress of German Forces to early September 1914

Confusion reigned at German High Command Headquarters while Kluck and Bülow maneuvered their armies. The situation at the front was rapidly changing, and Moltke and his staff were uncertain as to what was really happening. Each army sent back reports putting their situation in the best light, downplaying any problems. Each commander insisted he had decisively beaten the enemy in front of him, and it was only a matter of time before they would achieve complete victory. But even the most recent of the reports at Moltke's headquarters were a couple of days old.

Moltke recognized he did not have an accurate picture of what was really going on, especially what was happening with the right wing. Instead of going to the front himself, Moltke sent a junior officer, a major, as his fully authorized deputy. A major is five ranks below that of an Army level Commanding General. Moltke gave this major authority to act in his name. Moltke even authorized him to give orders to the different Army Commanders. At the front, the major agreed with Bülow's decision to pull back the Second Army to avoid encirclement. He then went to Kluck's headquarters where he ordered the First Army to retreat.

This would reestablish contact with Bülow and protect the First Army from encirclement. These withdrawals ended the forward movement of the German armies. Paris and France were saved.

> ## ANALOGY 8: THE ROSE-COLORED GLASSES
>
> Here is something you see a lot. Senior leadership desperately wants the organization to be successful. So it tends to believe reports saying it is on the road to success while discounting information that may say otherwise. You can also take it for granted that people will almost always report things in the best possible light. They will shout their accomplishments from the hilltops while whispering any shortcomings in the dark. By relying solely on reports, memos, and e-mails, senior leadership may only find out that things are not going as planned when it is too late to do something about it.
>
> Truly insightful leaders must look past reports and gain a clear picture of what is really going on. This doesn't happen by sitting at headquarters or attending a lot of review meetings. You should use multiple sources of information. You should have discussions with customers. You should have discussions with people at the lowest levels of the organization, those who actually produce the product or provide the service. These discussions will give you insight into what is really going on. You need to find and use indices that give you insight on how things are really going, not just how subordinates want you to think things are progressing.
>
> Be willing to intervene if things are not going as well as they should. You may have to reallocate resources within the organization. You may have to make changes to previously agreed-upon schedules. You may need to reassign people in critical roles. You will invite disaster if you do nothing and hope that things will just return to normal.

Once these withdrawals were put in motion, Moltke did finally visit the front lines. All he could do now was approve the movements already taking place. The German Army was no longer positioned to destroy the enemy. The right wing was not strong enough now to push the enemy out of the way. The right wing armies had to move to protect themselves and the gains made so far.

All of this came as a great shock to Moltke and the Kaiser. Up to the start of the Battle of the Marne, everything seemed to be going in the German Army's favor. The Kaiser and his generals believed all of the reports of success. They expected everything to go according to the Schlieffen Plan. Everyone wanted to believe the reports of a defeated enemy. Moltke had some doubts now and then, especially when he noticed that the right wing was not capturing many prisoners. Soldiers of defeated armies frequently surrender. But the right wing was not taking many prisoners as they advanced. Moltke did not want to deal with this information. Enemy armies falling back in good order would mean the plan was not working. Moltke did not want to believe that until he had no choice. After all, he was responsible for the execution of the plan, and he was responsible for modifying it.

Six weeks after invading Belgium and France, the promises of the Schlieffen Plan were unfulfilled. The German Army did not achieve anywhere near a decisive defeat of the French. They had occupied a lot of French territory, but they had not taken Paris. They had killed a lot of Frenchmen, but their own losses were also high. Now the Germans pulled back. They lost the initiative. There was no plan for what to do if the Schlieffen Plan failed. They were now reduced to reacting to threats against their open northern flank. The Kaiser fired Moltke.

The Plan in Hindsight

Why did Moltke do what he did? Why did he make the changes to the plan that strengthened the left wing at the expense of the right wing? Why did he allow himself to be enticed by further changes proposed by Rupprecht once the plan was in motion? While we will never know with certainty, his reasons probably were very similar to the reasons behind similar actions in businesses today.

Moltke lived in the shadow of the renowned Schlieffen. Schlieffen was regarded by the Kaiser and by the establishment as the military genius with the perfect plan, a plan that ensured victory for Germany. Moltke was merely expected to carry the plan out when war came. Like so many others who assume leadership in the shadow of a revered former executive, Moltke probably felt he had to put his own personal stamp on the plan. He had to make some changes to it so that he could say that he improved it. This way he could claim part authorship. This way he increased his influence over the plan and its expected success.

The Schlieffen Plan

> ## ANALOGY 9: "NOW I'M IN CHARGE"
>
> Too often, a new leader comes in and decides he has to make changes. This is done for the very reasons Moltke made his changes. The new leader doesn't want to just appear to be following the lead of some previous leader. They want to show that they have new and better ideas. Their egos require them to show that they have an even better way, that they can achieve even more than the previous leader thought possible.

Moltke had made changes to the Schlieffen Plan before the war even started. He changed the starting locations of many units. Yet these deployment changes were minor compared to the changes Moltke made after the war started. Of these, the change with the biggest impact was allowing Prince Rupprecht to attack with the left wing.

Just as he lived in Schlieffen's shadow, Moltke lived under the shadow of his uncle, also a Moltke. This uncle led the German Army that defeated France in the war of 1870. The older Moltke had encircled Paris, but it was a while before it capitulated, and France had tried to fight on. The younger Moltke probably also wanted to do better than his uncle. When the possibility arose (as far fetched as it might have been) to trap the entire French Army using the right and left wings as encircling arms, he decided to give it a try.

> ## ANALOGY 10: PRESTIGE VERSUS SUCCESS
>
> Thinking more of besting your peers than about achieving your organization's goals is a great trap. When the prize for the leaders becomes personal prestige or showing up prior leaders or their peers, they are following Moltke's example. Their mistaken priorities jeopardize the success of their organization. You and the organization you belong to will both have the greatest possibility of success when you put your personal ambitions to the side and do what will be the best for the organization as a whole. If you don't, you are more of a hindrance to success than a help.

And what about the great Schlieffen Plan itself? Would it have been successful if Moltke had not made the changes and kept the right wing strong? And what if he ensured better cooperation between the generals of the right wing? The Schlieffen Plan entailed huge risks. The plan gambled on a number of things the planners could not be sure of until it was actually executed. There was really no way of knowing for sure if some of the underlying assumptions Schlieffen made were true or not.

There were three such main assumptions Schlieffen made in formulating his plan. First, he counted on Belgium basically rolling over and playing dead. The Germans arrogantly thought their strength would intimidate the weak Belgians. They just figured the Belgians would quickly see it was hopeless to resist and allow the Germans free and unfettered passage through their country.

ANALOGY 11: ORGANIZATIONAL ARROGANCE

The German arrogance has counterparts today. The German thinking is the equivalent of a big company assuming something like, "When we enter the market of tiny company X, and they see how big we are and how many resources we can put behind our push into this market, they will just give up and throw in the towel." The reality is that the tiny company will realize it is in a fight for its life. It will also chafe at the arrogance of the large company thinking they are a pushover. In all likelihood, they will do everything possible to give the large company a run for its money.

The Belgians did not just roll over. They had no intention of following Schlieffen's Plan. Instead, they fought as long and hard as they could, all the while knowing it was hopeless. The plan didn't allow for the time or additional forces needed to deal with stiff Belgian resistance. Of course, the German Army was going to eventually defeat the Belgians, but the idea of the plan was to defeat the French.

Second, the Schlieffen Plan counted on the main opposition, the French, to be both reckless and stupid. It counted on the French attacking into the left wing, while the right wing swung around to their rear. Sure enough, the French started the war by actually doing this. Fortunately for them, they quickly rethought their strategy and made drastic changes to their plans when their attacks went badly. Prince Rupprecht assisted the French in making changes as he counter-attacked instead of retreating according to Schlieffen's plan. The French pulled forces out of their lines facing the left wing and redeployed them to face the right. When they redeployed enough of their forces, they attacked into the right wing and pushed it back.

> ### ANALOGY 12: ORGANIZATIONAL ARROGANCE CONTINUED
>
> You can never count on your competition being stupid. You can maybe hope for it, but you certainly shouldn't plan for it. The competition is probably not going to do what you want them to. It is even less likely to act recklessly and without logic. It may have figured out the same things you have. It sees many of the same opportunities and many of the same risks. It also probably has a pretty good idea of what you are planning to do, and it will use all of their resources to try to stop you. In all likelihood, it won't just sit there while you destroy them. Nor is it likely to go down the particular path you want them to.

The third main assumption of the Schlieffen Plan was the reliance on almost superhuman efforts by the soldiers of the right wing, not just for a day or two but for weeks and even months without a letup. These soldiers needed to march without stopping for hours, from dawn to dusk, day after day, without rest. On top of the seemingly endless marches, they would be in daily contact with the enemy, and would have to fight numerous battles. As the plan unfolded, the drain of the exertions on the soldiers of the right wing slowly became apparent. By the time of the French counteroffensive at the Marne, many of these soldiers were so exhausted that they actually fell asleep during the battle, even when their lives were in mortal danger. This total fatigue was one of the very reasons that a retreat of the right wing became necessary. Many of the right wing troops were totally burned-out.

> ### ANALOGY 13: KNOW THE LIMITS
>
> Know your people's limits. You should expect effort that is "above and beyond the call of duty," but there is a limit. Pass that limit and you will damage individuals and the organization itself. People will begin to leave. New recruits will be harder to come by. You will demoralize the organization by the excessive demands you place on it. And if the goals are not met by the extra effort, the demoralization will dramatically escalate. Such continued extreme demands can put the organization in a downward spiral. Continued demands produce more flight and employee frustration. As more and more leave, the organization finds itself increasingly unable to meet its performance goals. People are pressured to exert themselves even more, and the spiral feeds on itself. The organization's reputation is ruined. Ruined in the eyes of customers whose needs are not met. Ruined in the eyes of prospective new talent that has heard too many horror stories about working there.

The point is, there was more wrong with The Schlieffen Plan than just the changes Moltke made. There were serious problems with the Schlieffen Plan. The only real hope for success lay in duping the French into committing the bulk of their armies against the left wing, even as the might of the right wing approached Paris.

As it was, the Germans got as far as they did because of French folly, but once the French Army realized its mistakes, the Schlieffen Plan was in doubt. As is often the case, it is not the side with the best plans that wins; it is the side that makes the fewest mistakes.

CONCLUSIONS

This was the story of the German Schlieffen Plan. The plan held great promise because of the risks it took. Yet it failed to deliver. A number of important analogies come from looking at why the plan failed. The important lessons from these analogies include the following:

- **Dealing with subordinates you didn't pick**
  Even senior leaders don't get to pick all of their subordinates. Leaders must deal with many they didn't personally pick. You need to work at getting alignment among your subordinates on common goals and how you are all going to work together to achieve them. Goals are only reached when everyone is working together.

- **When your plan discounts the competition's reaction**
  One of the main drawbacks of the Schlieffen Plan was counting on the competition acting a certain way. You cannot base your plans on the competition being slow and ignorant. You cannot devise a plan just from the standpoint of what you and your group will do. Plans must also take into account the possible actions of the competition, no matter how unlikely they may seem. Remember that once you begin to execute a plan, the competition is not just going to sit and do nothing. They are going to do whatever they can to prevent your success. You cannot discount potential reactions. Plans that do not provide for dealing with the competition's reaction are usually doomed to fail.

- **The need for common goals**
  For an entire organization to achieve its operational goals, the entire organization must work on those same goals. Different parts of an organization cannot pursue their own goals if they detract from the desired objective.
  You must ensure that your subordinates are pursuing the objectives of the company, not pet or personal goals. You cannot delegate this responsibility. Do not put someone else in the position of coordinating and guiding the efforts of peers.

- **Mutual support to meet goals**
  Every part of an organization must subordinate itself to the common good. What is good in the end for the organizational whole will also be good for all of the parts. If any part of the organization does things that only benefit it or its leadership, the organizational whole will suffer.

- **Changing direction when things go wrong**
  Be willing to make changes when things go wrong with your plans. Be willing to admit mistakes and make corrections. Do not believe you cannot be wrong, or that your plan is perfect. Deal with the reality of the situation. Understand the situation you are in by knowing what is really going on.

- **Failing to know what's going on**
  Leaders who do not have a clear picture of what is happening out on the front lines are in serious trouble. Have ongoing dialog with customers and with people at each level of your organization. Leaders who stay in their offices at headquarters are blind. They do not have the insight into what is really happening and cannot take proper and decisive corrective action.

- **Personal success versus organizational success**
  When you put your own personal goals ahead of the organization's, you drastically reduce the probability of organizational success. Those who are willing to put aside personal ambition and do what is best for the organization are those with the greatest chance of success.

ACTION FILE

HOW TO DEAL WITH SUBORDINATES YOU DIDN'T CHOOSE

 BAD IDEA #1—Get them all fired or transferred.
Too many managers think the best way to deal with people they didn't select as subordinates is to get rid of them. There are two problems with this line of thinking. First, there is the erroneous belief that they will get to hand pick all of the replacements. Second is the even more dangerous misconception that the subordinates they pick will fix the problems in their department.

Yet many are undaunted. They work to get rid of the people working for them that they didn't choose. They start by emphasizing and even exaggerating all of the faults of their subordinates to their superiors. They spend a lot of time building cases against people they want to get rid of. They constantly look for any mistake or misjudgment. They write all kinds of memos and reports documenting all of the things their undesirable subordinates are doing. They do nothing to correct any of the problems because that would weaken the case for getting rid of them.

The problem with this approach is that no one is leading this part of the organization to success. Instead, the manager is helping it to fail in the short term so they can make the personnel changes they want. This means that a lot of the time and effort the manager should be spending on building a better performing organization is wasted on efforts to get rid of people they did not choose and want to replace.

This misguided course of action has little chance of success. The odds are pretty low that all of the new people will be better than all of the old people. There is also all of the time lost training the new people in their new jobs. There is the loss of experience that goes out the door with the exiting employees. And there is the cost of the time and effort the manager has expended working to get rid of people.

If you want to identify a poor leader, look for someone who has a high percentage of forced turnover in the ranks of their direct reports.

BAD IDEA #2—Bypass them and deal directly with subordinates.

Instead of firing people they would rather not deal with, some poor managers decide to bypass these people instead. Instead of dealing with them, they ignore them and deal directly with people at the next level. These misguided managers ignore input from the "undesired" subordinates. They fail to listen to suggestions or to any kind of feedback from those they wish were not around.

This creates a lot of additional work for the poor manager. They must immerse themselves into all kinds of details. They have to do those things previously done by the person the poor manager is now bypassing.

All of this leads to the poor manager being overworked. They are unable to adequately deal with higher-level issues. They don't have any time because they are not just doing their jobs; they are doing the jobs of the bypassed subordinates, too. Meanwhile, those bypassed are doing little of any importance. The bypassed people get tasks having little or no significance. Their time and talents are wasted.

 BAD IDEA #3—Treat them as losers.

Here is probably the worst idea. Treat the people you think you don't want as losers. Some poor managers do this because, for some reason or another, they cannot get rid of someone they don't like. Nor are they willing to spend the time and effort to bypass them (see the previous bad idea). As a result, the poor managers just resign themselves to their belief that they will get only poor performance from their "undesirables." Acting on these beliefs causes them to become self-fulfilling prophecies. If you decide someone is a loser, they will act like one. Think about it for a minute. If you know your boss has already decided you are worthless, how much effort are you going to put in? Most people quickly decide they are in a hopeless situation. This situation gets progressively worse when the poor manager does little to deal with any substandard work. They do this because they actually expect poor work. And they don't think dealing with the "loser" will do any good. So they do little or nothing in the way of performance management with the person they have branded as worthless. They certainly do not praise anything the subordinate does well. Nor do they spend any time coaching the "loser" on what they could do better. The poor manager just sits there and broods about the "loser's" performance.

The poor manager sees poor performance even when the people they don't like are successful. As a result, the subordinates see they are not going to please the boss no matter what they do, so they stop trying. And then they really do exhibit nothing but substandard performance. Such poor leadership dooms the organization.

 GOOD IDEA #1—Hold initial meetings on direction, goals, and methods.

One of the best things you can do when in a new leadership role is to meet with all of your new subordinates. At this meeting, you need to lead a discussion on the direction of the group. You need to discuss goals for the future and how you will all work together to meet those goals. This is where you spell out your expectations as the new leader and where you and your subordinates work together to spell out their responsibilities and your expectations of them. They should also discuss their expectations of you. This meeting is where you help your subordinates understand what you need them to do. It is also an opportunity for subordinates to tell you what support, help, and direction they need.

There are often serious consequences for not holding this initial meeting. Without it, both the new leader and subordinates will make too many assumptions. All involved may assume what is wanted, what the desired direction of the organization is, what results are expected from current operations, and so forth.

The meeting does take time, and it can be difficult to talk through many of the issues. But it will pay off. It is time well spent that will reward any new leader with improved productivity. It can be the foundation of strong working relationships within the group. Do whatever it takes to have such a meeting whenever you find yourself in a new position of responsibility.

 GOOD IDEA #2 —Sell ideas and vision to subordinates.

The initial meeting you have with your new subordinates is only the first step. Great leaders excel at selling their vision of a better future.

They understand that they need to motivate the group. Only the group, working together, can cause the vision to become reality. You must realize that people will not excel at doing things just because you order them to. Your efforts at selling your vision of the future must continue past the initial stages of taking on a new leadership role. You must continue these efforts the entire time you are in the position.

Selling your vision, your picture of a better future, is what will inspire and motivate the people who work with you. It will drive them (and you) to accomplish the goals that will realize that better future. When people internalize the concepts, plans, and visions of the future, great things happen.

 GOOD IDEA #3—Coach subordinates personally.
Don't think that selling your ideas to your group only means standing in front of people and telling them all about your plans for the future. You have to sell your vision of the future on a personal basis. You can best do this by one-on-one coaching of your subordinates. You need to sell them just like a salesperson. Remember, you will only be successful when they are successful.

You must also reward subordinates for exhibiting the behavior you need and reaching the needed goals. These must be rewards meaningful to the recipient. If not, they will not help motivate the performance you need for the group to succeed.

You must also have negative consequences for performance failure. Just like rewards, the negative consequences must also be meaningful. Otherwise, people will not be motivated to avoid them.

Personal coaching must take place at all levels of an organization. You cannot avoid this task, no matter what level you are at, without risking failure. Nobody is a successful leader without motivating the group to perform. You can't be a successful leader unless you motivate others to better performance. You and your group are in it together. The group will help you only if you successfully motivate them.

ACTION FILE

HOW TO DEAL WITH MANAGEMENT MISTAKES

 BAD IDEA #1—Don't have information systems.

Ignorance is a very common problem with poor leaders. You can't make good decisions when you don't know what's going on. Really bad decisions are based on erroneous or wishful thinking. History is chock full of examples.

You can defeat ignorance by having systems or procedures in place to give you frequent updates on actual performance. If you do not have such mechanisms in place, you will get burned by inaccurate and even misleading information. Not everyone wants you to know what is really going on. People responsible for bad things happening don't want to be held responsible. They certainly don't want you to know what really happened. Other times, people don't realize the information they have is vital to you.

Any situation that leads to misinformed leadership is bad. Too often, the leadership of an organization thinks things are moving along just fine, right up until there is a catastrophe. Then they find out all the pertinent information. Unfortunately, by then, it is way too late to do anything about it.

 BAD IDEA #2—Fail to admit something is wrong.

Another huge leadership mistake is not admitting it when available information points to a problem. There are many reasons why poor leaders may decide that nothing is wrong, or even less than optimal. The most frequent reasons include ego. Poor leaders refuse to believe they could have made the wrong decisions. Another common reason is just plain wishful thinking. They want something to succeed, so they don't believe it when it starts to fail. The poor leader doubts the accuracy of information that is not what they want to see.

In any case, failure to admit that something is wrong leads to inaction. Inaction means that nothing is done to correct the problem. Instead, the organization continues to under perform. It continues to have ongoing difficulties and fails to meet its goals.

Not admitting that there is a problem has other unwanted effects. Information showing that something is wrong won't be as forthcoming in the future. No one wants to go to the boss and point out that something is wrong, only to have it ignored. Even worse is punishing the messenger. If people think that their leaders are not going to take action, then why should they rock the boat? Without accurate information, the leadership ensures its own ignorance of problems the next time around, if there is a next time around.

BAD IDEA #3—Refuse to make worthwhile change.

Not making worthwhile changes is just as bad as failing to admit that something is wrong. Both courses of action ensure nothing meaningful is done to fix a problem. The result is the same, continued poor performance.

The important word in this bad idea is "worthwhile." It's all too easy to make meaningless changes. Meaningless changes don't fix the problem. Yet meaningless changes are tempting because they won't meet much resistance, are usually rather inexpensive, and don't take up too much time. Meaningless changes are worse than doing nothing.

A typical meaningless solution to a problem is an "awareness" initiative. These kinds of programs are supposed to help people become "aware" of a certain problem. Unfortunately, most of these programs do nothing to actually fix the problem.

It is meaningless to educate people about a problem unless you also spur them to correct it. As proof of this, just think of how many people are "aware" that automobile pollution is a problem. Yet how many of those "aware" people do something about it?

BAD IDEA #4—Fail to improve the decision-making process.

You can still have a big problem even if you find out something is wrong in time, are willing to admit it's a significant problem, and take worthwhile corrective action. The big problem is in not changing the processes that led to bad decisions that caused the problem you just had to fix. It is not enough to just fix a problem. You have to make sure you don't end up with similar problems in the future. This is what will happen if you don't correct the process that led to the problem in the first place.

As you deal with a problem, you need to ask the question "How did we end up in this situation?" You need to look at how and why decisions were made that put you on the wrong course. You need to find out what information was and was not available to the decision makers. You need to uncover how and why the decision to go down a particular path was made. You need to change any part of the process that does not survive a thorough evaluation.

 GOOD IDEA #1—Use feedback systems to tell you something is wrong.

Avoid ignorance by having early warning processes in place. These processes are meant to give you early warning of things that have started to go wrong. You need regular and frank updates from all levels and parts of the organization. You can start to fix problems only after you know that something is wrong. Even better is when you can start to take appropriate action when something is not yet a problem, but about to be.

 GOOD IDEA #2—Admit mistakes.

People often say, "It's human nature to make mistakes." It's true that none of us are perfect. Do not think you are the exception. You will make mistakes on a regular basis. Promotion to a higher level does not eliminate mistake making. Recognize this and keep your ego in check. Sometimes, things don't work out the way you wanted them to. Admit your mistakes and then correct them. Things will not get better until you do.

 GOOD IDEA #3—Learn and make changes.

A truly wise person constantly seeks self-improvement. They are willing to learn new things. They then take action based on what they have learned. It is perfectly fine to have strong opinions about what to do and how to do it. But when new information comes to light showing an opinion might be wrong, you need to make changes. Of course, you need to evaluate the validity of the new information. But always be willing to make changes to your opinions.

A lot of people think, "If I change things now, people will think I was wrong before." Look, we have all been wrong about something at some point. Only a fool would continue to do something they know is wrong, unproductive, or damaging, rather than risk temporarily losing face by admitting they were wrong.

Great leaders have a common characteristic: they are willing to learn and try new things. They realize this is how you find solutions and uncover opportunities. Their learning often leads to making changes in how their organization operates. Sometimes, they change how decisions are made. Other times, they may change organizational goals. When people see their leaders acting this way, they will emulate this behavior. This is how an organization can reach new levels of achievement and productivity.

CHAPTER 2

FRENCH PLAN XVII

"Is it Positive Thinking or Wishful Thinking?"

INTRODUCTION

THE principle enemy of the German Army in 1914 was the French. The French Army had aggressive plans for operations when war broke out. These French plans failed miserably. They found themselves reacting to German moves. They were able to capitalize on German mistakes and regain the initiative due to the actions of a few French generals. As the story of the French struggle against the German invasion unfolds, there are good examples of the following issues:

- Dangerous revenge-based strategies
- Inflexible business philosophies
- Overly ambitious strategies
- Failure to learn from others' experience
- The need for quick and effective change
- Risk taking
- The importance of confidence in leadership
- Management changes during a crisis
- Identifying necessary changes

HISTORICAL CASE AND BUSINESS ANALOGIES

The Pre-War Situation

France lost a war to Germany in the 1870s. France lost two provinces along the Rhine, the Alsace and Lorraine, as a result and suffered national humiliation. Prior to their defeat, most people considered the French the world's best army, the keeper of Napoleon's tradition. The Germans, up until then, were just a group of squabbling provinces. They united under Prussian leadership and beat the French decisively. France wanted revenge: it wanted its lost provinces back, and it wanted to regain its lost honor.

> ## ANALOGY 1: THE REVENGE STRATEGY
>
> France based her military strategy after the 1870 defeat on one principle, revenge. Businesses can fall into this trap, too. A company can totally fixate on beating a competitor in a specific product line or in regaining some lost market. Once a company becomes obsessed with this type of goal, it is blind to other opportunities. Too many of the company's resources are committed to gaining some kind of revenge, accompanied by a poor profit outlook. Such approaches usually ruin the revenge-seeking firm.
>
> The leadership of a business must not forget it is there to ensure the future success and profitability of their operations. You must learn from what has happened in the past at the hands of a competitor so that it does not happen again. But when revenge of any sort becomes the motive, it will be detrimental to the business. Better to take your lumps and move on than to wallow in emotions that will cost the business too much, especially when the efforts and resources expended are not worth what you are trying to regain.

In the years immediately following its loss to Germany, the French Army adopted a defensive strategy. The united Germany was stronger than France was. In any future war, France saw it would face the might of the entire German Army. The French constructed a new belt of fortifications along the border with Germany, and their army positioned itself to defend the country from behind this line.

French Plan XVII

The situation for France changed suddenly. In one of the greatest diplomatic blunders of all time, the German ruler, Kaiser Wilhelm II, failed to renew the treaty of cooperation Germany had with Russia. Russia went looking for a new ally and found a very willing and eager one in France. The French could barely believe their luck. Now they had a powerful ally on the other side of Germany. France and Russia could now simultaneously threaten Germany from opposite directions.

Plan XVII

The Russian alliance greatly improved the French Army's position. Now the Germans would have to deal with a possible war on two fronts. This meant the Germans would have to split their forces. For the French, this meant they could start any war against Germany by attacking. The French planned attacks to regain the lost provinces. The offensive action would reestablish the honor and pride France and its army felt they had lost.

The French military philosophy became one of "Attack, attack, attack, and when in doubt, attack." The French felt the spirit and courage of their soldiers would overcome any and all obstacles. They felt the morale of the individual soldier was the deciding factor in combat. The high morale of the French soldier, called *élan*, was a representation of his supposedly superior fighting spirit.

ANALOGY 2: SINGLE MINDED STRATEGY

The French adopted a one-track strategy based on a single tactic: attack. This was the only thing their army was going to do. This was the basis of all their maneuvers. This was the basis of all their planning. Businesses, too, can go down the road of having a single strategy and a single tactic. And when they do, they eliminate their ability to improvise, to find other often uncharted paths to success. This is not because they have opted to do only one thing, but because they have opted to do only one thing *to the exclusion* of doing anything else.

The French military's faith in the *élan* of their men was a prerequisite for promotion in the army. Those who did not believe in the attack were defeatist and labeled unfit for command. Only those with unshakable faith in the irresistible force of attacking Frenchmen reached the highest positions. Those with different views were passed over, or otherwise forced out of the army. The result was an entire leadership structure, from junior officers to senior generals, who were adherents to the accepted doctrine of "attack in all situations."

> ### ANALOGY 3: COMPLIANT THOUGHT
>
> The result of the French Army's philosophy was that it could really only do one thing. They systematically removed the ability to deal with changing situations and to come up with new and innovative solutions. This would prove very damaging when the accepted doctrine was discredited. This can happen in the business world. If an organization takes steps, actively or passively, to stop promoting people because they do not totally accept the prevailing corporate philosophy, it will find itself blind when that philosophy becomes invalid.
>
> Not "if" but "when." The difference is important. This is because just about any operating philosophy or methodology eventually becomes obsolete. The company must change to adapt to changes in its environment. If it only has people who can think in a specific way, those people will be either unwilling or unable to deal effectively with the changing situation. It will continue to try the same things over and over again, even in the face of repeated failure. This is exactly what happened to the French as the war dragged on for years.

The French military adopted Plan XVII prior to the outbreak of war in 1914. Plan XVII was based on revenge. It was based on the single principle of *attack*. Plan XVII was not as detailed as the Schlieffen Plan was. The primary goal was to recapture Alsace and Lorraine by quick and decisive offensive action. The French then planned to move across the Rhine River.

The commander of the French Army at the start of the war was General Joffre. He was sure he would be the commander of the army during war with Germany, and he was sure that he would win it. He firmly believed that attacking into Germany was the right course of action, and he disapproved of anyone below him not having this attitude. Even worse in his sight were commanders

French Plan XVII   51

who would not attack aggressively. He had approved Plan XVII, and he believed its success would be his crowning achievement. He would of course be hailed as the savior of France when it worked.

France mobilized according to their Plan XVII. By doing so, it was as if they arranged to have all of their forces at the front door, while the Germans were poised to enter through the back. While the French moved against the Germans in the south, the Germans would be marching into France from the north. It is almost impossible to conceive of a worse initial plan for the French. This is the situation their arrogance and their misguided faith in the "spirit of the attack" placed them in. [Fig 6]

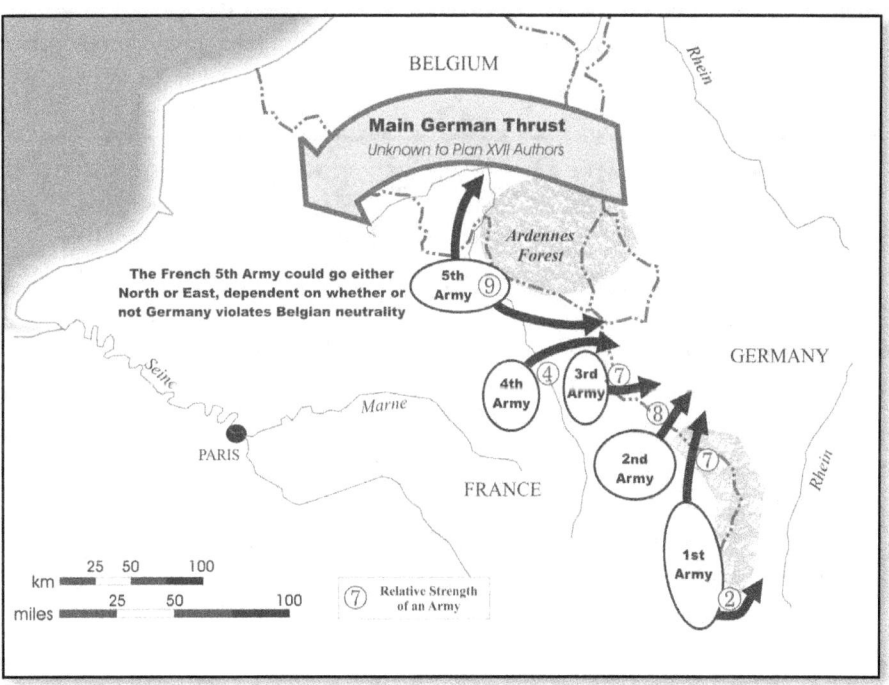

Figure 6. French Plan XVII, Original Concept

The War Begins

The French mobilized five separate armies at the start of the war. The preponderance of their strength was at the southern end of the line. The French First Army was southernmost and was to attack into Alsace. This would mean attacking across the most rugged terrain between Switzerland and the English Channel, the steep and densely forested Vosges Mountains. Just to the north of the First Army, the French Second and Third Armies were to attack into Lorraine. The Fourth Army was to act as a reserve, to back up any success, or to help extend the line if needed. The French Fifth Army would move to screen the border with Belgium and attack any German forces that might try to move into France from that direction.

While German forces started into Belgium, the French Army prepared to retake Alsace and Lorraine. The French discounted Belgian reports of massive numbers of invading German troops. They thought the Belgians were a bunch of incompetents. They saw the Belgians as inferior troops with inexperienced leaders. The French thought the Belgians were exaggerating things in a panicked state of mind. The French also discounted the Belgian reports because they showed the Germans doing things contrary to what the French wanted them to.

> ## ANALOGY 4: FAILURE TO ADMIT FAILURE
>
> Why did they do this? For the same reason modern leaders cannot be persuaded their plans are unrealistic. They made those plans. If their plans were misguided, they would have to admit that they were wrong, made a mistake, or worse. Few and far between are leaders that can swallow their pride and change a plan they have already committed to. Most have this difficulty even when they receive credible information that their plan is flawed.
>
> Not only would the leader have to admit making a mistake, they would also have to confront the accepted philosophies of their peers. You get to the top by believing in the correctness of the organization's philosophy behind its plans. To question it would be to question the beliefs of almost every other leader. Most organizations will expel the person who abandons the accepted way of thinking.

In fact, for some time prior to the start of the war, the French had received intelligence about German war plans. There were comments the Kaiser had made about traipsing through Belgium. There were articles in German military periodicals alluding to their plans. There was even information provided by spies inside the German High Command. The problem was that if these reports about German plans were true, the French Army would have to adopt an

French Plan XVII

initially defensive stance. The leadership of the French Army just refused to do this. The desire to attack was strongly entrenched in their organizational culture. They wanted to believe their plans for attacking across the German border would be successful, so much so that they discounted all information that could force them to abandon their Plan XVII attacks.

The head of the French armies prior to Joffre tried to change the French war plans. General Michel proposed changing back to a defensive stance to fend off a strong German blow through Belgium. He was treated as a heretic. Other French generals thought he had lost his mind, his nerve, or both. He was fired and put out to pasture. The French military's culture of the attack was so strongly entrenched that not even its leader could change it.

And so, as the German right wing started to pour into Belgium, the French launched the first of their attacks. In the very south, the French retook the city of Mulhouse in Alsace. German forces in the area quickly moved around them on three sides. In danger of being surrounded, the French retreated.

The French continued to execute Plan XVII. Millions of French soldiers, clad in dark blue wool coats and bright, crimson red pants, marched forward. With bayonets fixed at the end of their long bolt-action rifles, they moved across the open farm fields of the countryside towards an unseen foe. The French attacks quickly developed into disasters. The fields were soon covered with the broken corpses of the valiant and colorful army. The attacks produced the same results: huge numbers of dead and wounded. The French infantry, wearing bright red pants visible for quite some distance, marched towards German positions defended by machine guns and supported by quick-firing artillery. They were massacred. The Germans then attacked the dazed and demoralized survivors, throwing those still alive back across the border.

Tactical Deficiencies

World War I is full of stories of bad ideas and obsolete practices. French infantry in colorful uniforms attacking fortified positions is one such story. Why did the French march their troops into machine guns? Did they just not know any better? And why were the French wearing red pants that made them almost perfect targets?

First, about the machine guns: It is true that the French Army did not have experience attacking anybody with machine guns prior to World War I, but plenty of other countries had. Machine guns had already been used to deadly effect. This was the case in the war between Russia and Japan a decade earlier. Machine guns also played a prominent role in Balkan wars. The Balkan wars had barely ended the previous year. The French Army had reports from observers in each of these conflicts. They even had these weapons themselves.

The reason they did not take the reports on the effects of machine guns into account is very basic. They just did not believe they would suffer the same effects from these new weapons. They stubbornly clung to the belief that their situation was different. What happened elsewhere was not going to happen to them. After all, those other situations involved inferior troops from backward countries—countries without inspired leadership; armies that did not possess a truly great fighting spirit. Such troops would have problems against new weapons they thought, but not the French Army.

ANALOGY 5: FAILURE TO LEARN FROM OTHERS

Unfortunately, this is a very common story. Leaders are either unable or unwilling to see the analogy between what happened somewhere else and what is about to happen to them. The resounding cry of "Our situation is different" is all too frequent. People give many reasons for saying this. They think because the situations are not exactly the same that the outcome will not be similar. They don't want the outcome to be similar if the outcome is potentially disastrous.

Too often, people and organizations fail to learn until they experience something themselves. Too often, they believe their situation is unique, or that their methods and practices are different enough from others that they will not encounter similar problems. Only when it happens to them do they begin to question their thinking—and only after they fail to achieve some important goal. Only when defeat stares them in the face do they begin to think that they might be wrong. It is far better to learn from the mistakes and experiences of others than to learn from your own. One of the greatest lessons from World War I is what happens to you when you fail to learn from what is happening to others around you.

There was plenty of opportunity for the French Army to learn about the effects of new weapons like the machine gun. At least ten years before the French learned about machine guns the hard way, information on the new weapon was available from reports on the Russo-Japanese war. It wasn't just the French who failed to learn the lessons. It was every major power in Europe. Even the Russians failed to learn the lessons and to make changes to their tactics. The point is that armies did not make changes until after they had brutal experience themselves. Only then did they start to deal with the fact that their tactics were outdated. Even then, it took them years to develop, accept, and implement changes to their way of doing things.

The next issue is why the French were wearing bright red pants. Remember that the French military leadership believed they would be successful because of the fighting spirit, *élan*, their soldiers had. They believed this fighting spirit partially came from the look of the uniforms the soldiers wore. Everyone in the French Army was very proud of how well they looked on parade. The leadership felt that changing the uniform would hurt the morale of their fighting men and would thereby reduce the chance of successful attacks.

There were plenty of examples showing that colorful uniforms were a bad idea. The British Army had traded in their red uniforms. Instead of the red that they had worn for centuries, they now wore a new color developed in India, khaki. It blended into scenery and made for much less of a target. The Germans no longer wore bright-colored uniforms like Prussian blue. They now wore a new color specifically designed to be unnoticeable in the countryside of Europe. They called it *Feldgrau*, German for "field grey." Even the Austrians abandoned their traditional white uniforms for muted blues and grays.

To the French, the red pants were part of their heritage and tradition. Others could throw those things aside, but they could not. It was a part of their organizational culture they were not willing to discard. If they had, it may have called other parts of their military philosophy into question. They were not going to allow that to happen.

Launching the Attacks

General Joffre unleashed Plan XVII at the start of the war. The attacks by the French First and Second Armies were unsuccessful. Attacking units from these armies took huge losses. In some cases, the units were so badly shot up they practically ceased to exist as fighting formations. This was not supposed to happen. But Joffre didn't look into the reasons why the attacks failed. To him the reasons were simple enough. He thought the leaders of the attacks were either incompetent or did not attack with enough vigor. He believed the soldiers did not want victory enough to achieve it. That maybe the Germans were stronger than anticipated was a minor consideration. Joffre believed his troops and officers should overcome any obstacles placed in their way.

Since the French First and Second Armies had shown that they could not achieve results, Joffre now looked to the soldiers of the French Third and Fourth Armies. Joffre felt these two armies would have an easier time because he did not expect them to be opposed by that many Germans. He thought that since the Germans in the south were stronger than expected, and since some Germans were in Belgium to the north, they must therefore be weak in the center. So Joffre ordered his Third and Fourth Armies to attack the German center. [Fig 7]

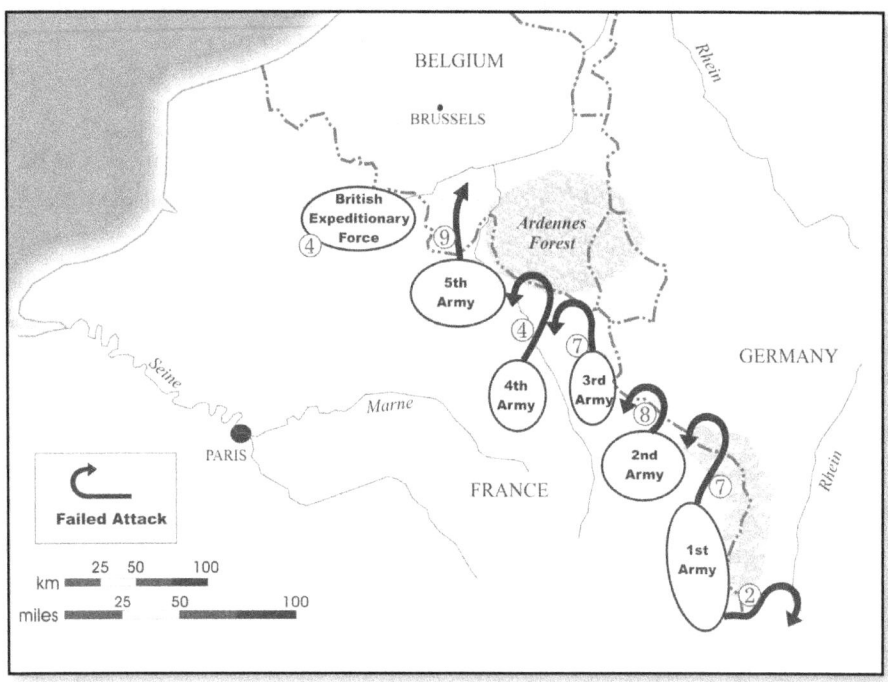

Figure 7. French Plan XVII, Execution and Results

Once again, long lines of French infantry rose up to march toward the Germans. Officers in braided uniforms, pointing the way to the enemy with their swords, led the way. Their faith in *élan* was not yet shaken by bloody experience.

These new attacks went just as badly as those of the First and Second Armies did. There were no gains. There were no breakthroughs opening the way into Germany. There were no defeated enemy units. There were just more French dead and wounded lying untended in the fields and forests, and more divisions of the French Army ceased to exist as effective fighting units. Once again, Joffre placed the blame on those involved in the attacks. There was no questioning the viability of Plan XVII. There was no questioning the basis of French tactics or strategy.

ANALOGY 6: NEED FOR RAPID CHANGE

All of the Plan XVII attacks happened over a relatively short period of less than two weeks. This is how long it took to expend a major portion of the French Army's available resources. In war, outcomes are decided rather quickly. It was once a bit different in the business world. In the business environment of the past, a company might have a couple of years to look at and analyze their efforts. It had plenty of time to make incremental changes to procedures and practices. This is no longer the case. Business organizations are now in an environment that closely resembles warfare. In this kind of environment, the failure to quickly exploit opportunities, or deal immediately with a crisis, can have serious and long-term negative consequences. Look at what happens to companies that fail to quickly recall defective products from the marketplace, or those that alienate customers because their Internet servers are down for awhile.

Crisis to the North

At the northern end of the French line was the only French Army that had not yet attacked. This was the Fifth Army. Joffre ordered this army to move into southern Belgium while the other French armies attacked. This was done to protect the northern flank of the French from the Germans now in Belgium. Yet this movement of the Fifth Army put it right in the middle of the German right wing's line of march. This French Army was to launch attacks against any Germans it encountered, just like all the other French armies.

General Lanrezac commanded the French Fifth Army. He had some real concerns about his orders. He put more weight and validity on Belgian reports about the German right wing than others in France did. As he looked at the situation, he began to believe that the bulk of the German armies were indeed marching through Belgium. Lanrezac also realized that once he moved forward as ordered by Joffre, his army would be directly in the path of overwhelming German forces.

Lanrezac was very vocal in protesting his orders to move forward and launch attacks. He told Joffre repeatedly that it was inviting disaster. Lanrezac told Joffre his estimates of the numbers of Germans moving against him in Belgium. Lanrezac even quoted to Joffre reports from Joffre's own intelligence section about German strength in the area. He also pointed out that Germans moving around him to the north and west could outflank his positions. There were no French forces of any consequence north of Lanrezac's. The British were supposed to show up there, but they were a small force, and Lanrezac's staff had yet to hear from them. Joffre did not believe the reports of German strength in Belgium. The French believed they had accounted for all of the German front line troops and felt there could be few left to operate in Belgium. The problem was that the French believed the Germans were using the same organizational model that they did. The French Army had strong opinions about what kind of troops should or should not be on the front line. Both the German and French armies contained troops of three different classes. Those of the top class were "active." This class comprised soldiers in units on active duty prior to the outbreak of war. They spent day after day doing drills and going on maneuvers. They were expected to bear the brunt of fighting. Below the "active" class were troops of the "reserve" and "territorial" classes. Units of these lower classes were made up of a cadre of officers and some sergeants on active duty, while the rest served only a couple of weeks or so with the military each year. The rest of the time, these part-time soldiers had civilian jobs.

The French military establishment felt reserve and territorial troops were worthless in the front line. The French felt that once troops left active duty and returned to the softness of civilian life, they would lose their fighting spirit, the *élan*, on which French hopes of victory were pinned. Therefore, in the French Army, the reserve and territorial troops were garrisons in the rear areas. They intended that only the divisions of their active class would be in the front lines. Since the French Army felt this way about their reserve and territorial troops, they felt that everyone else would feel the same way about their own second and third class units.

The reality was that the Germans had reserve units in the front line right alongside their active units. This dramatically increased the size of German front line forces. The German planner Schlieffen did this because it was the only way to create the massive right wing his plan needed.

The French had a hard time accepting the fact that the Germans were using reserve units on the front lines. The reality of what the Germans were doing was clouded by their active and reserve formations using the same unit designations. When the French captured a German soldier, and that prisoner reported that he was from the Fourth Corps, it might mean he was from the Fourth Active Corps, or it might mean that he was from the Fourth Reserve Corps. When French intelligence counted up all of the formations the French Army had already come up against, it assumed only a few active class German divisions were left over and thus could be in Belgium. Based on this assumption, they concluded the Germans in Belgium were nothing more than a feint meant to distract them.

ANALOGY 7: ACCEPTED ASSUMPTIONS

The way the French military leadership thought about reserve troops is an example of a great trap in management thinking. You cannot presume that just because you see things a certain way that everyone else sees things the same way. You must think about what your opponent could do with the resources available to it, not what you would do with those assets. This myopic mindset will only result in the competition surprising you with what it does next.

General Joffre released most of the Fifth Army from its original orders due to pressure from Lanrezac and others who held similar views. Joffre did respect Lanrezac's intellect and was prepared to grant him some latitude. He allowed Lanrezac to move farther to the north, but he was still to attack according to the spirit of Plan XVII. Joffre was more than a bit perturbed at Lanrezac for his change of heart. Lanrezac was expected to carry the offensive spirit as a senior commander. Joffre now saw him as an annoyance, a "non-team player" in today's terms.

The Germans showed up in front of the French Fifth Army almost twice as strong as Joffre expected. Lanrezac found his army under attack by two strong German armies, each of which was more powerful than his own. Yet he was still under orders to attack. Out on the front line, individual French units did move to attack when they made contact with the Germans, but Lanrezac did not attack with his army as a whole. He saw this course of action as too dangerous. At about this time he also learned that the French Fourth Army, to his immediate south, was pulling back after its own failed attacks. On his other flank, the British had arrived, but were also under heavy pressure, by yet another strong German Army. [Fig 8]

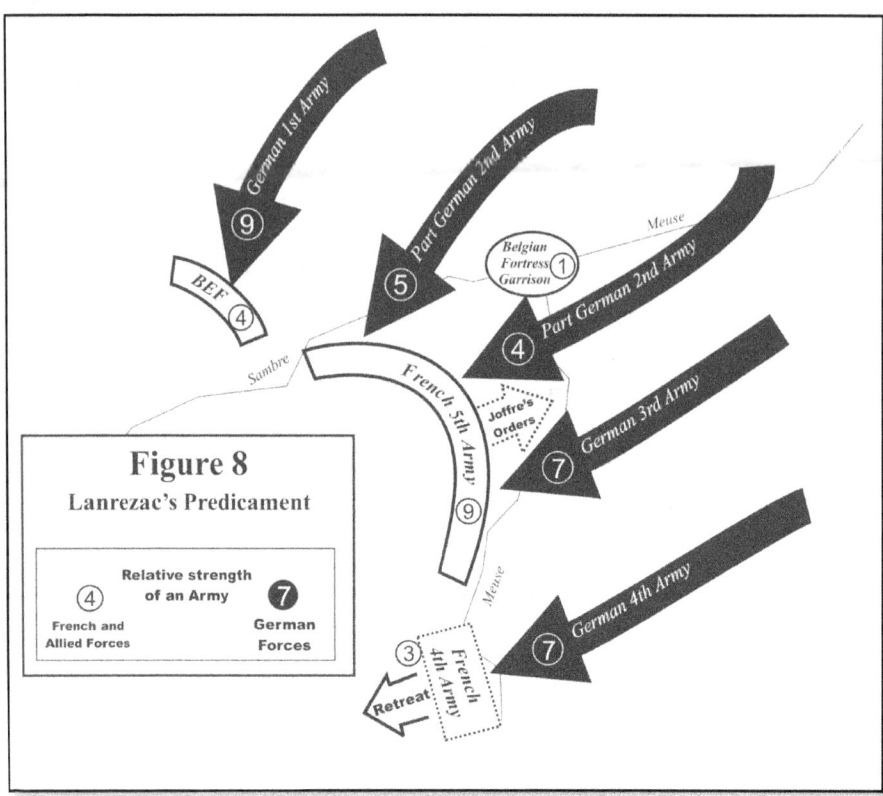

Figure 8. Lanrezac's Predicament

Lanrezac saw that his army was the only one astride the path of the main German effort. He also realized that if he attacked, or even stayed put, the Germans would probably surround his forces. On his own initiative, he ordered his army to retreat. He knew that Joffre would brand him a coward for doing so. Lanrezac knew he would be blamed for failing to attack and undermining Joffre's plans.

ANALOGY 8: THE TRUE RISK TAKER

You hear a lot in the business world about the need to take risks. Risk taking is proclaimed as a valued skill for all business leaders. The statement, "We want people in positions of responsibility who are willing to take risks!" is often heard. Lanrezac's story is a real example of taking a risk. In most of the examples of risk taking in history, people take risk by *not* complying with the orders of their superiors. Risk taking is not just going out on a limb. Real risk taking is going out on a limb when your superiors already told you it's not a good idea. Real risk taking flies in the face of accepted theory and practice. True acceptance of risk is doing something contrary to the expressed desires of your bosses. This may mean "attacking" when it is not authorized. Or, it may mean falling back to protect important resources from destruction. In either case, real risk taking means going against the accepted way of doing things, and if it fails, the risk taker knows for sure that he will take the blame.

Lanrezac put the needs of his country above his own personal career goals. He pulled his army back from a perilous position. His intention was to save his army, to save it to fight on for France. He knew that retreating would incur the wrath of his boss. He knew he would be branded a defeatist. Yet, he made the decision based on the good of the army and France, even though he would suffer personally.

> ## ANALOGY 9: THE TRUE HERO
>
> A true hero is someone who willingly suffers for the good of others. There are not many people out there like Lanrezac. Few place the needs of a group over their own desires for advancement and gain. Yet isn't this trait something any organization would want a lot of? Instead of encouraging this type of behavior, most organizations squash people who exhibit it like bugs. How often do you hear of someone saying to the boss, "This course of action is wrong, and I am going to do something else instead" and it turns out well for that person?
>
> It takes a truly great leader to see the value of such risk taking behavior by subordinates. Such a leader, instead of punishing the insubordination, is willing to praise the quick actions of the subordinate and admit to others that it was the right thing to do. The reason such leaders are rare is that such action involves admitting not that the subordinate was correct, but that the leader was wrong. There are few indeed who are willing to swallow enough of their pride to do this, or who have enough confidence in themselves to not see the subordinate's actions as a threat to their position and authority.

All of the French armies were retreating as Lanrezac pulled away from the oncoming Germans. The French First and Second Armies retreated to the line of fortresses in their rear. Here they stopped and held off repeated attacks by the Germans under Prince Rupprecht. The other French armies retreated to a line between the French fortresses and Paris.

Abandonment of the Plan

Joffre began to take units away from the control of the First, Second, and Third Armies as they retreated. He formed two new armies, the Sixth and the Ninth, from these units. The new armies also received reserve units from the rear areas. The Ninth Army filled the gap that opened up between the Fourth and Fifth Armies as they fell back. The Sixth Army was formed just to the north of Paris. [Fig 9]

French Plan XVII

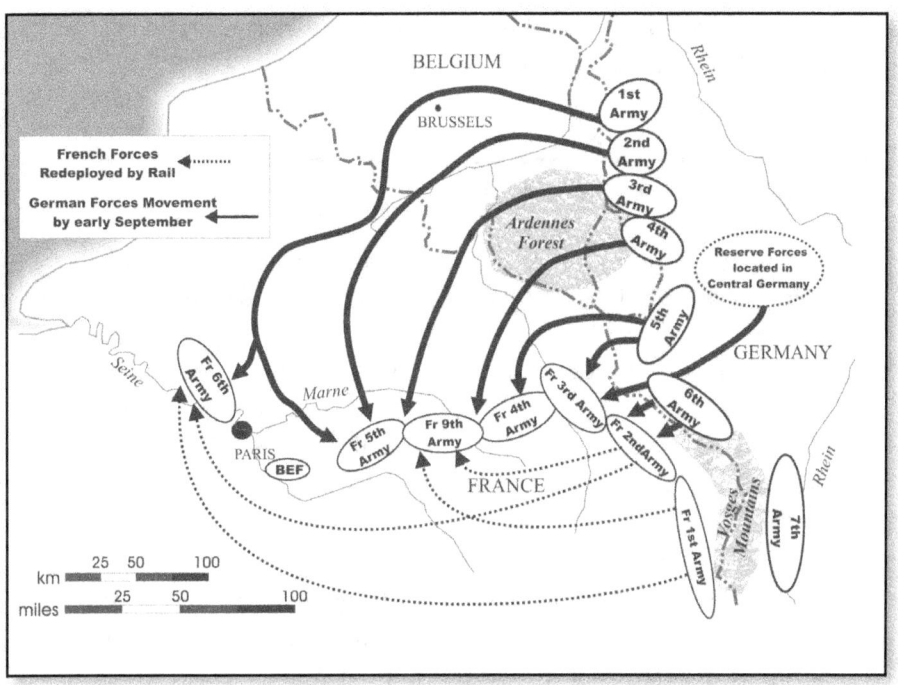

Figure 9. French Redeployment

Joffre abandoned Plan XVII. His intention now was to retreat until the French Army could reestablish a solid line. Then it would resume attacks against the enemy. Forming such a line was not easy because each army was retreating under German pressure. Units were often out of contact with the friendly forces on each side. Sometimes, headquarters had no idea where a particular unit was for a couple of days. The start date to resume the offensive had to be postponed repeatedly. The French retreated to a new line farther to the rear with each postponement.

Joffre was committed to begin the new attacks sooner than he wanted. This was due to the actions of another general. Once again, a French general took the initiative to do something before he had orders to do so.

This time it was not Lanrezac, but Gallieni. He was once Joffre's superior. He was retired due to his age before the war started. Early on, the French government asked Joffre to have Gallieni at his headquarters. The politicians were worried something might happen to Joffre. If so, then Gallieni could take over. Joffre didn't like this idea. He didn't want his old boss hanging around his headquarters. It could undercut his authority. People might start asking Gallieni his opinion about Joffre's plans and orders.

> ### ANALOGY 10: INSECURITY
>
> Joffre's misgivings about having Gallieni at his headquarters are a good example of common behavior by someone new to a senior leadership position. The new leader is worried about having total control over the organization. He views any appearance or unsolicited advice from the previous leader as interference. He thinks that if the old leader shows up, people might turn to him or her for ideas, or even decisions, rather than come to him. Obviously, this is due to the insecurities of the new leader.
>
> One of the best places for a newly promoted person to get ideas and advice from is the person they replaced. Too many would never consider doing this. Sometimes the old boss was fired for incompetence or some nefarious practice. But the vast majority did not leave their positions due to such problems. The previous leaders are still a rich source of ideas and advice. If you judiciously receive and review this advice, it can help you avoid past mistakes and allow you to build on what your predecessor learned during their tenure.

Joffre was the insecure type, so he prevented Gallieni from hanging around at Supreme Headquarters. Gallieni was in retirement at the start of the war. As the Germans moved through Belgium and then into France, the government asked Gallieni to command the Paris garrison. He felt the city was inadequately defended and called Joffre for more troops. Joffre wouldn't even talk to him on the phone. He had subordinates tell him there were no troops to spare. Gallieni was left to deal with the situation with only what was on hand.

The Perfect Opportunity

The newly created French Sixth Army was pushed back as it was forming up north of Paris. It retreated towards the city and was placed under Gallieni's control, but Joffre retained final approval authority over its operations. Joffre did send a few more divisions to Paris, due to continued pressure from Gallieni and the government.

French Plan XVII

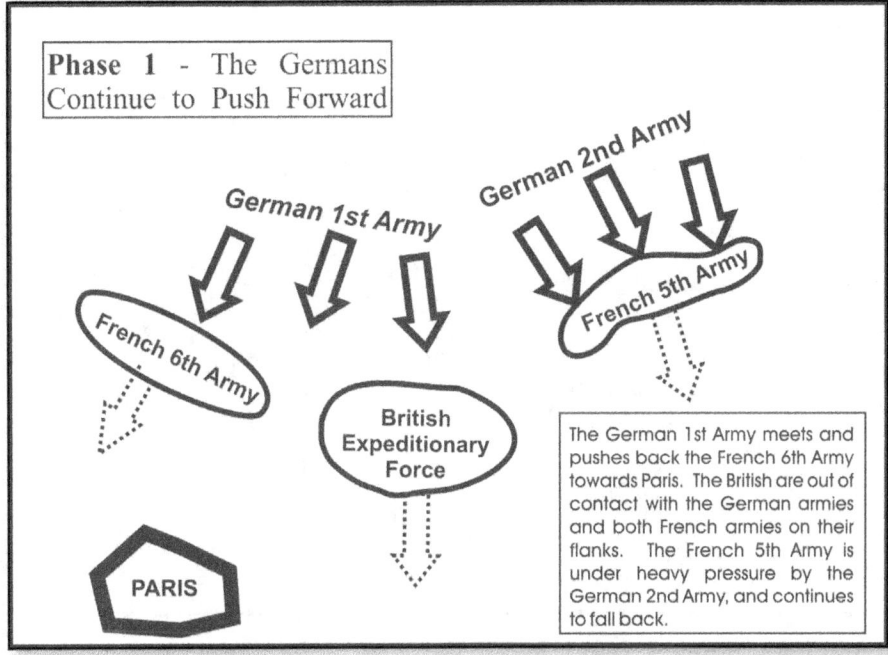

Figure 10. The Opening of a Gap, Phase 1, 30 Aug - 6 Sep 1914

The Germans under General Kluck pushed the French Sixth Army back. [Fig 10] As the French pulled back, Kluck concluded he had eliminated this new French Army as a fighting force. Kluck now felt there were no threats to his army. He then moved his command, the German First Army, in front of the German Second Army. Kluck did this to keep his army in the lead while the Germans attempted to encircle the French Fifth Army. By doing this, he exposed the flank of his army to the French in and around Paris. [Fig 11]

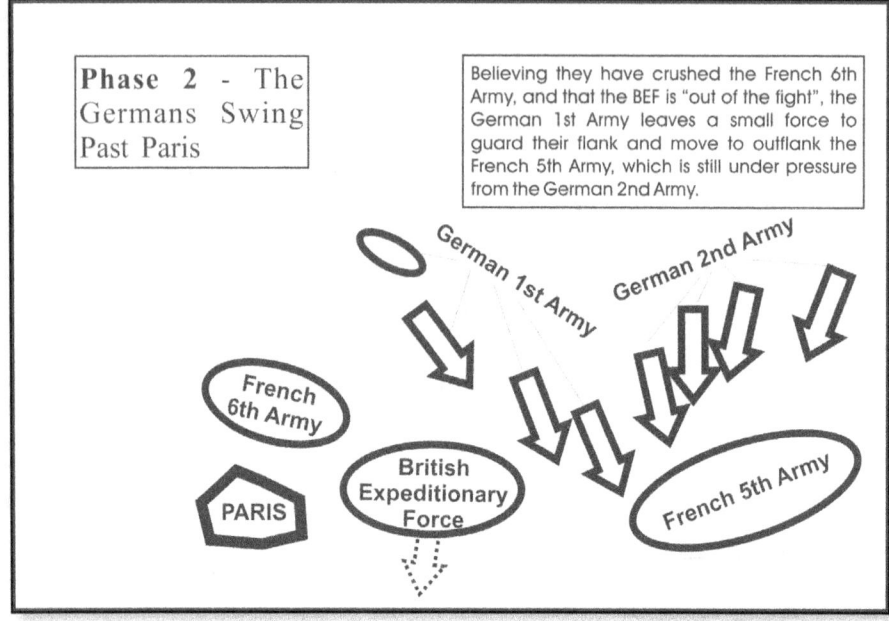

Figure 11. The Opening of a Gap, Phase 2, 30 Aug - 6 Sep 1914

Gallieni saw the opportunity, if he acted very quickly, to hit Kluck's army in its vulnerable flank. If Gallieni waited, Kluck could possibly redeploy. He might reinforce his flank or face more troops against Paris. Gallieni knew he did not yet have Joffre's approval to attack. He knew that Joffre wanted to wait until all his forces were ready to attack simultaneously. Further, Gallieni knew that he would need the support and assistance of others armies for his own attack to be successful. The other French armies would need to support his attacks with attacks of their own. This way the Germans could not send units from other areas to reinforce Kluck. Gallieni also needed the support of the British Army. It was between Paris and the French Fifth Army. From their positions, the British could move against the other flank of Kluck's army. [Fig 12]

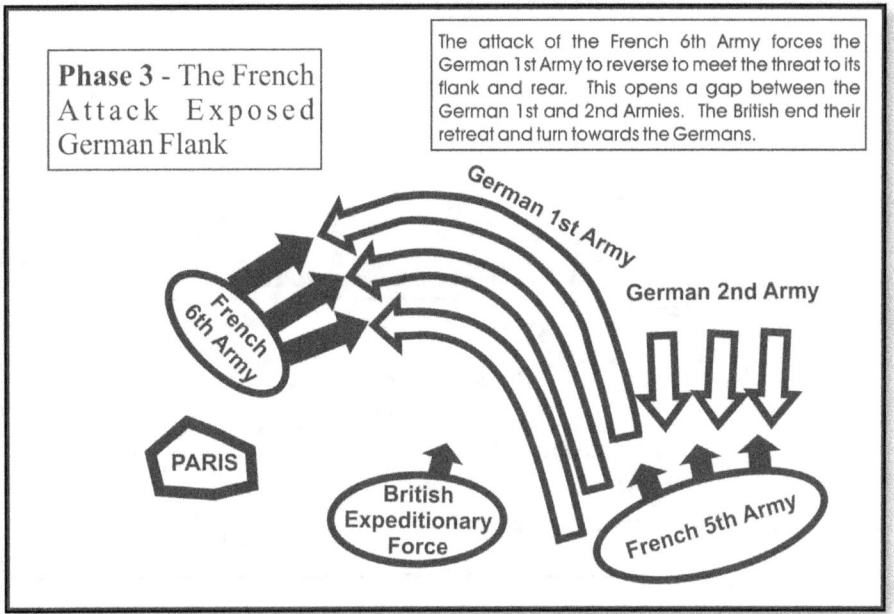

Figure 12. The Opening of a Gap, Phase 3, 30 Aug - 6 Sep 1914

Gallieni forced his boss's hand to ensure Joffre's support and thereby the support of the other French armies. Gallieni's attacks gave Joffre no choice but to support him. If Joffre did not support Gallieni by ordering the other armies to turn and attack, Gallieni's forces would be out on their own. The Germans could easily turn against them.

Joffre did want to turn around and attack the enemy. He just wanted more time for his armies to get in some rest from the long retreats before attacking. But Gallieni tipped his hand. Joffre weighed the options and decided to support Gallieni. The French launched attacks all along their lines.

The French armies' attacks started the Battle of the Marne. This battle marked the closest point the Germans got to Paris in the course of the entire war. The French attacks near the Marne River caught Kluck's German First Army off guard. As Kluck's army turned around to meet Gallieni's, he opened up a gap between his forces and those of the neighboring German Second Army. Both German armies had to retreat to seal off this gap, and this eliminated the threat to Paris. [Fig 13] Their success in the Battle of the Marne meant that France could fight on.

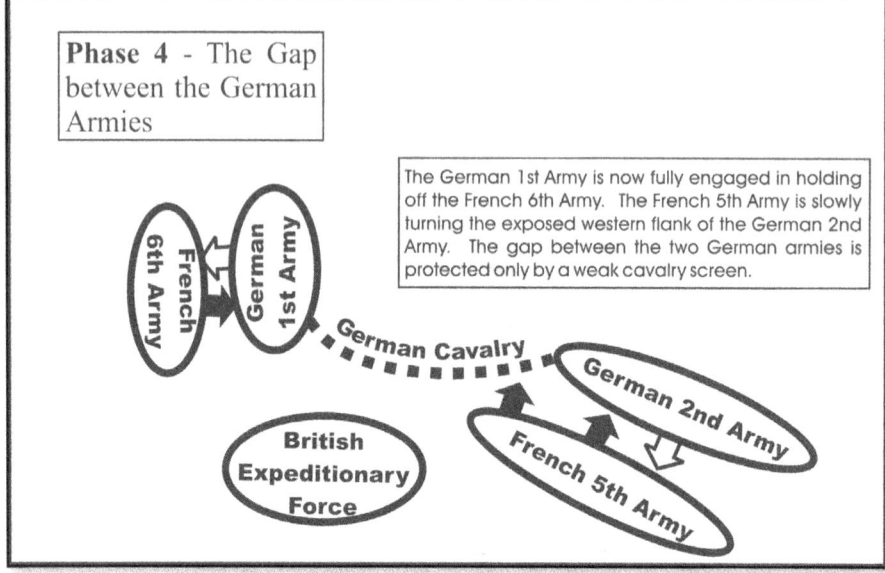

Figure 13. The Opening of a Gap, Phase 4, 30 Aug - 6 Sep 1914

ANALOGY 11: DEPARTMENTAL MYOPIA

A poor leader's myopic view, looking only at the immediate consequences to their own area of concern, can easily create disaster. When leaders react to a crisis situation only by covering their own behinds, they are acting just like Kluck did at the Battle of the Marne. You cannot place some other part of the organization in jeopardy to save only yourself and your department.

Always keep the big picture in mind. You can't just look at the short term and how your department will get out of the immediate crisis. You must consider the long term. Look at the consequences of your possible reaction to the business as a whole. In the end, your area will not be "safe" if the entire business has problems due to your shortsighted reaction.

ACTION FILE

HOW TO FORMULATE GOOD BUSINESS PLANS

 BAD IDEA #1—Count on the competition doing something stupid.

Any plan to beat the competition needs to consider what they might do in response. They are probably going to come up with a counter initiative for every initiative in your plan. They will also have initiatives and plans of their own. Too often, these include things your plan didn't anticipate.

In any case, the competition will do things aimed at preventing your organization from reaching its goals, just as you are attempting to beat them. A plan that doesn't consider what the competition may do is only half a plan. A plan that counts on the competition being blind or stupid is even worse. Such poor plans are based on advantages you probably won't have. In the vast majority of cases, they are not going to stand there and let you trounce them without doing something about it. A common military principle is "never underestimate the enemy." Too few business plans take this into account.

Of course, the competition may pleasantly surprise you with some flagrant mistake. Maybe they will fail to counter your plan until it is too late. Maybe they will embark on a bad plan of their own. In such cases, you should count your lucky stars because that's what happened; you got lucky. Good plans are never based on luck.

 BAD IDEA #2—Plan for unrealistic performance.

Too many plans count on achieving performance that past experience shows is unrealistic. Do not count on your organization far exceeding what has been done by similar businesses in similar situations in the past. Yet poor plans make the mistake of overpromising what the business will do. An example of overpromising is a plan that counts on the business having interim results like "returns of 25 percent in the next fiscal year" when a common return in the industry is more like 7 percent. Plans

Kluck's conduct in creating the French opportunity is illuminating. Kluck reacted to the French attacks by only dealing with the threat to his particular army. He didn't react to the threat posed to German forces as a whole. This is evident when you look at the size of the gap he left between his army and Bülow's Second German Army.

Kluck acted only on the peril to his own army. His moves to save the army he commanded imperiled first the neighboring Second Army, and then the entire German Army in France.

Leadership under Pressure

A lot of rather uncomplimentary things about General Joffre have come out up to this point. Aside from the faults already discussed, he did have some very important strengths. He did quite a number of things right. Joffre's decisions after early mistakes allowed the French Army to recover from the Plan XVII disasters. He did indeed save France from defeat. But he had not yet produced victory. Victory and "saved from defeat" are two different things.

What good things did Joffre do? First, and probably the most important, is that no matter what happened, no matter how bleak the outlook, Joffre did not lose his cool. He never panicked. He never even came close to doing so. He never lost faith in himself, or in the eventual success of the French Army. You cannot underestimate the amount of strain, stress, and pressure placed directly on Joffre. The destiny of millions was in his hands. The very existence of his nation weighed in the balance. His decisions would become a part of history that people would read and debate for hundreds of years. Few business situations come anywhere near to this amount of pressure.

Most people would crack under the strain of such pressure. There are plenty of historical cases where commanders placed under similar pressures actually hid, leaving important decisions to their staffs. They didn't make any decisions at all. Others sat around in some sort of stupor, not knowing what to do, or even what to say. Reverses or reports of failures entwined them in a mental world of defeat and despair that totally incapacitated them.

Joffre did not act like this at all. He exuded confidence no matter how bad the news was. He kept a constant daily schedule. He never exhibited any signs of panic. He never talked or mused about catastrophe. He never did anything frantic or ran around yelling at people. Instead, he calmly dealt with the reality of the situation.

> ## ANALOGY 12: LEADERSHIP OPTIMISM
>
> You cannot overemphasize the importance of an optimistic leader. Leaders must realize that everyone they meet, the entire organization they lead, gets their confidence from them. If the leader starts to show any sign whatsoever of despair, defeatism or, worse yet, panic, the entire organization will have the same feelings. Rumor and lack of information will even exaggerate these feelings.
>
> Such demoralization is the beginning of the end. People start to flee to find security elsewhere. Work isn't done or is done poorly as people's minds are caught up in worries about their personal situation. The good of the group is no longer anybody's concern. Everyone's goal becomes how to find his or her own way out of the situation before it gets worse.

The French Army of 1914 responded to its commander's optimism. The army did not falter during the retreat. Few French soldiers surrendered to the enemy that seemed so unstoppable to the rest of the world. The vast majority were willing to stick it out. And when they were asked to turn around on a moment's notice and attack, the French Army did so, believing they would win.

Leadership Changes

Optimism was an important part of Joffre's leadership. Another important part was his willingness to replace subordinates who did not share his optimism, or who broke under the pressures of real war. Joffre promptly replaced them. In Joffre's case, promptly meant they were gone the next day, if not sooner. He replaced some for pessimism. But mostly he replaced subordinates for incompetence or the inability to deal with the strain of combat. During the campaign of 1914, Joffre replaced about half of the generals of the French Army in the field. In all of military history, no other supreme commander replaced so many senior officers so fast.

If you think such measures were rash and overly harsh, you must remember the speed with which events were happening. Battles were won or lost in the space of hours. Indecision or worse behavior by a senior commander could have disastrous consequences under such conditions. Some of the replaced generals had actually hidden or run away. Some didn't report where they and their units were for days on end. That's right: for a couple of days at a time, the whereabouts of some divisions were unknown by the rest of the army. True, some of the sacking was not warranted or justified; yet, on the whole, it did improve the French Army.

> ### ANALOGY 13: MAKING LEADERSHIP CHANGES
>
> As business leader, you will have personal relationships with the people whose performance you judge. Of all the things a leader has to do, replacing someone who is a personal friend, someone you have worked with for years, whose family you know, who you've shared experiences with, is one of the hardest things you will ever have to do. But you have to do it when it is warranted. You must put the performance of the organization and its welfare as a whole above the needs of personal relationships. Obviously, the person replaced will take it personally and, in all reality, won't want to be friends anymore. They will probably hate you. You have to be willing to live with such malice, to put your personal feelings aside, and do what is best for the organizational whole. You must do this to protect the organization and give it the best chance at success.
>
> Too often, leaders are not replaced even when it is apparent they are damaging the very organization they are meant to serve. Some get chance after chance to change and improve. And, after the passage of what is often a considerable amount of time, when still nothing has changed, when there is still no improvement, the person is still kept on. There are many reasons given to justify this. "It would really disrupt the organization to change things now; no one is ready to fill his shoes." Or, "They mean well and are trying very hard; things will turn around soon." Unfortunately, these reasons rarely turn out to be true.

It is important to note that Joffre personally knew many of the people he sacked. He would have spent time with them during his career in various units or on different assignments. He would have known many of their wives and families. This is an important point. He was not just replacing names on an organizational chart. He was firing people, knowing they would be personally crushed by losing their commands. He knew they would see him as someone who quickly forgot what they had done for him in the past.

In Joffre's case, he just did not have the time to wait and see if things would get better for a certain person. He needed almost immediate improvement. The Germans were not going to wait for French generals to get better at their jobs.

Joffre was able to replace people, even close friends. The other heads of national armies were not, and it hurt every one of them and their armies. Joffre held his subordinates to a set of standards. He decided to replace people when they didn't meet those standards.

Yet one of those replaced by Joffre was Lanrezac. Based on what Lanrezac did, this seems quite unfair of Joffre. Lanrezac's opinion of Joffre went downhill fast during the retreat from Belgium. This is putting it quite mildly. More and more, Lanrezac was very vocal about the fact that he had no faith in Joffre's ability to lead the army. Based on what Joffre had asked him to do, he did have some justification in such opinions. From Joffre's point of view, Lanrezac did not possess the "offensive spirit" expected of his commanders. Lanrezac had other significant problems. A big one was his relationship with the British commander.

Lanrezac was to coordinate his operations with Sir John French, the British Army field commander. The British Army was operating on Lanrezac's left. The relationship between Lanrezac and French started poorly and got worse, much worse. Initially, each wanted the other to help their own commands, usually by having the other put their army in danger. Then, each of them did things best described as "self-optimization." They each operated under the principle of "to heck with the other guy and what he plans to do." Soon, neither man trusted the other. They had about as bad opinions of each other as of the Germans.

Joffre replaced Lanrezac with d'Espérey prior to resuming the offensive. D'Espérey was a Corps Commander under Lanrezac. He had shown ability and initiative before and during the retreat of the Fifth Army. He possessed the "offensive spirit" Joffre was always looking for. Lanrezac's retreat saved the Fifth Army from encirclement and annihilation. But based on his experiences so far in the war, Lanrezac was hesitant to attack. The change in leadership put the Fifth Army under the control of someone without this hesitancy. D'Espérey aggressiveness and willingness to attack in chaotic situations contributed significantly to French success in the battle of the Marne.

Joffre did something else important for the French war effort. He did not fixate. He did not stick to unattainable goals. Prior to the war, the French strategic goal was to regain Alsace and Lorraine. The immediate objective of Plan XVII was to achieve this goal. The initial French attacks were launched directly across the border into these provinces. These attacks failed miserably. Joffre launched additional attacks after the initial failures. These, too, were disastrous for the French. But he did launch them into areas he believed were less strongly held by the enemy. He didn't try to repeat the same thing.

Too many times, the commander of a failed attack decides to try the same thing over again against the same location. He convinces himself that his original idea on where to attack was correct. He decides the previous attack failed because it wasn't done correctly. So the next time maybe he uses more men or fires a longer artillery barrage before the attack starts. But in the end, he is attacking the exact same place where the enemy previously defeated him. Such attacks are doomed to failure. The proof of this is the history of World War I.

By repeating an attack that failed, the opposition has a clear picture of where you are going. Their morale is higher because they just beat you back. They know where the weak points in their line are because of the experience they just gained from the last attack. They usually have not only replaced the men they lost in the last attack, but probably received reinforcements as well. All of this means they are *much* stronger when the same attack comes the next time. Rather than increasing the chance of success by attacking again, the second attack is even less likely to succeed.

Joffre could have easily fallen into this trap. He could have reinforced the French First and Second Armies after their initial attacks failed and had them go right back into the Alsace and Lorraine. Instead, he tried the next attacks with other armies in other places, hoping to find the weak point in the enemy line. Unfortunately for him and for his armies, there were no weak points. The point is that he continually looked for alternatives to the original strategy and plan. He abandoned Plan XVII when it didn't work.

When the true strength of the German Army and the reality of their right wing's advance became clear, Joffre made drastic changes to French strategy. He took troops away from the armies positioned to retake Alsace and Lorraine. He was willing to completely reject the plan he so strongly supported before the war. Joffre used the forces stripped from the Alsace/Lorraine area to build up new armies. He placed the new armies to resist the German right wing's thrust into France. When the opportunity presented itself, these armies threw the Germans back. France would have lost if Joffre had not made these drastic changes and radically redeployed his forces. Had Joffre stuck to his original plans and intentions, the Germans would have won.

> ## ANALOGY 14: STRATEGIC INFLEXIBILITY
>
> Businesses can make the same kind of mistakes. They try the same strategy repeatedly, even when it doesn't work. Their leaders are convinced they have the right ideas. They blame their subordinates for faulty execution. Sometimes they just blame bad luck. Then they try the same thing over again, maybe with a small change or two. They just won't accept the fact that their plan and even its underlying ideas were wrong. They keep at it until their business is in ruins. The competition repeatedly thwarts the faulty strategy. You will doom your business when you never seriously question the wisdom of plans that fail. You must seriously look at the actual results your plans and strategies produce when executed. If they have failed, you need to consider alternatives for the next time, or you will doom your business to additional failure.

Of course, Joffre had help in deciding on the new course of action. Lanrezac's actions assisted. It made the magnitude of the German right wing's strength visible. It preserved a French Army for later use. Gallieni's pleas for assistance in the defense of Paris also helped. It forced Joffre into dealing with the threat to the capitol. Had it not been for Gallieni, Joffre might have actually abandoned Paris to the advancing Germans. Gallieni also helped by forcing Joffre's hand on the moment to attack, the moment when the enemy presented a golden opportunity.

Later in the war, Joffre no longer had the assistance of brave leaders willing to have different opinions. Joffre was unable to adapt to the realities of the deadlock of trench warfare. He was unable to find other options, to innovate, to look elsewhere for opportunities. Joffre can claim a lot of the credit for saving France from defeat, but he was unable to adapt to the changing conditions of the war. The French government replaced Joffre when it became clear he could not produce victory.

ANALOGY 15: LISTENING TO SUBORDINATES

To a large degree, Joffre's success was due to the actions of his subordinates, subordinates Joffre did not initially support. This is often the case in the business world, too. Your success is very dependent on the assistance of your subordinates. If you are willing to use this assistance, and reciprocate by helping the subordinates, you will greatly increase the likelihood of success. A truly great leader is willing to listen to the ideas of others and to change course based on valid evidence presented by competent subordinates. You will march down the path of folly if you don't.

CONCLUSIONS

This was the story of the French Army and its operations at the beginning of World War I. The French Army in this period had both success and its share of failures. French pre-war plans failed. Yet the French Army stopped the German invasion. In the end, the French leadership dealt with an apparently catastrophic situation and found opportunities for success. The stories of what worked and what failed provide analogies to modern business life. The most important of these lessons deal with the following:

- **Dangerous revenge-based strategies**

    Never base your strategy for the future on getting even with a competitor. Focusing on revenge will blind you to other opportunities. You limit your organization's possibilities for growth when you concentrate on getting even for things that happened in the past. Focus on the present, the future, and the lessons of the past. Get over what happened. Get on with finding ways to be successful now and in the future.

- **Inflexible business philosophies**

    Almost any strategy, tactic, or philosophy in business will become outdated or invalid. Always focus on what is working and what is not. You must be willing to change things that are not working. You will need ideas from those with unconventional thinking to do this. If you jettison people who challenge the accepted ways of doing things, or hinder those who do not always agree with current practices, you will doom the organization. If all of the leadership thinks the same way, and is unwilling to even consider that their way of doing things may no longer work best, the organization will not be able to adapt.

- **Overly ambitious strategies**

    Leaders must work to find the best balance between stretch goals and reality. It is a good idea to have goals that seem out of reach. Just don't put the business's existence on the line by trying to do something unrealistic with the resources available. This is a good way to invite disaster. Good leaders find a balance between lofty aspirations and the realistically attainable.

- **Failure to learn from other's experience**
  Just about everyone thinks their situation is unique. Most think that bad things that happened to others are not going to happen to them. Unfortunately, this is not the case. The best way to learn is not from your own experience, but from the experience of others. Remember, you are no better than they are. Remembering this will open your eyes to all kinds of potential problems.

- **The need for quick and effective change**
  In military history, changes made in the course of a day, an hour, or even minutes, win battles and wars. It's the same way for business today. Slow and incremental approaches to change will leave you in the dust. Constantly look for changes to make, and be willing and able to make those changes *quickly*.

- **Risk taking**
  Risk taking is not just going out on a limb. It's often going out on a limb without approval. Leaders too often crush such risk-taking spirit, even when it produces spectacular results. They do this because lauding the risk taker means having to admit they were wrong. Great leaders put the organization and its success ahead of such egotism.

- **The importance of confidence in leadership**
  Good morale starts at the top and flows downhill. Any organization is doomed if the rank and file sense the leadership does not have faith in the future. Leaders need to remain upbeat and confident at all times. They need to exude confidence in the organization and in the direction it is going. If leaders act depressed about the future, everyone else will feel even worse. Then people will flee. This will mortally wound any business.

- **Management changes during a crisis**
  Organizations require leaders who produce results. It is often necessary to replace people in senior positions who are not productive. Friendship cannot get in the way. Such decisions must be based on the good of the

organization. The sooner such decisions are made, the better off everyone will be. Things will not get better by waiting to make such changes. Procrastinating will just put you even farther behind the competition.

- **Identifying necessary changes**

    Very little of what an organization does or produces is sacred. A successful organization constantly evaluates the effectiveness of everything it does. If something is not as effective as it could be, then change it. Make such changes as quickly as possible. Find out what is working and what is not. Go with what works. Have ongoing discussions within the organization to help make such evaluations. The path to failure is to keep doing the same thing, in the same way, over and over.

based on such wishful thinking are often put forward by a new executive eager to show they have aggressive plans and goals for the future.

The problem with such grand visions is that people will actually expect the business to deliver what the plan promised. They are not going to care that the plan was just meant to "energize" the organization with some "pie in the sky" goal. They want to see the promised results. If they don't see those results, they will take actions of their own. The effects of these actions are rather undesirable, like a drastic drop in the price of the business's stock, or the removal of the leader whose plan didn't deliver what it promised.

BAD IDEA #3—Count on flawless execution of the plan.

Few, if any, plans are flawlessly executed from start to finish. Plans that require perfect execution are pretty well doomed from the start. A common military axiom holds that "no plan survives contact with the enemy." You should expect things to go wrong with your business plans as well.

This does not mean that plans are worthless. What the axiom means is that you cannot put a plan into action and just sit back and wait for the desired outcome. You have to carefully watch the plan's execution. You will need to make continual adjustments to the plan. For example, if one group falls behind schedule, you may need to provide additional resources so they can catch up. Or you may need to find ways to make up the lost time in other parts of the schedule.

You may have to deal with problems the plan didn't anticipate. In fact, you should pretty well count on this. Of course, the best way to deal with problems is by being proactive. Always have procedures in place to help identify and deal with situations that could occur before they ever do. But there will still be unanticipated issues you will have to deal with. This is why military planners have reserves, resources held back for emergencies. Businesses should have reserves, too.

BAD IDEA #4—Plan for success just through current practices.

Most people are aware by now that organizations that fail to change, that fail to innovate, are going to die. You can improve any product or process or service. If it isn't improved, it becomes obsolete. To continue to compete in the future, your business will have to change what it is currently doing.

You can't allow resistance to change to stifle your business. Don't allow others to quash efforts just because they are "not our way of doing things." There is always room for improvement. Improvement requires change. Any organization that continues on auto-pilot will eventually run into an unexpected mountainside.

 GOOD IDEA #1—Stretch performance, yet allow for minor mistakes.

Plans should require your organization to stretch outside of its comfort zone. You need to set goals at the start of the new endeavor that appear out of reach to many. Trust in the abilities of the group to rise to the challenge. They will gain new skills and abilities as the project moves forward. They will begin to deliver what they may not have expected themselves capable of before.

Yet the stretch needs to be realistic. Rely on the experience of your leadership. Consider the experience of other companies in similar endeavors. Do not think that just because you are now in charge, your group will quickly accomplish what everyone else found difficult or impossible.

Recognize that flawless execution of any plan is next to impossible. Be ready to change things as you encounter obstacles. Find additional resources to overcome unanticipated problems. Be willing to make adjustments to the plan. Constantly tweak it as you gather information on results.

 GOOD IDEA #2—Anticipate the competition's moves.

Too many plans are made without considering the competition's reaction. If you cut prices, they can cut prices. If you move into some new market, they might too. Consider what they might do and plan to stay one step ahead of them. Good chess players don't just look for the next good move; they think many moves ahead and consider what the opponent will do (or could do) in response to each of their moves. Use the same thinking, and you will have better business plans.

GOOD IDEA #3—Use surprise and ruses.
One of the holy grails of military planning is surprise. Surprise in battle cuts overwhelming odds down to size. Surprise in warfare makes the otherwise impossible achievable. Surprise stuns the enemy, and they don't know how to react. Phenomenal victories are possible through surprising your foes.

Surprise does not mean the competition has no clue about what you are doing. It means they know about it too late to take effective counteraction. Military strategists use feints and ruses to surprise the enemy. The idea behind feints or ruses is to make the enemy think you are or are about to attack a location when you are really going to attack elsewhere. In business, you can do this by leading your competition to believe you are about to embark on some endeavor when you really have no intention of doing so. Most businesses are so worried about what their competition even might do that they will put all kinds of resources into meeting perceived threats. This leaves the competition with less to deal with your real efforts when they become apparent.

 GOOD IDEA #4—Have a strategic thrust.
Good plans are pointed in a specific direction. Do not attempt to do everything and be everywhere at the same time. By trying to be everywhere and do everything, your business will end up being nowhere and accomplishing nothing. Going in too many directions at the same time will leave you with multiple diluted efforts. You will waste your resources in losing battles on many fronts while you fail to gain significant success anywhere.

A respected military strategy axiom is "concentration of force." This axiom says that you should put the overwhelming preponderance of your resources into your plan's main effort. Do not reduce the strength of your main punch by dispersing your resources to many different points on the front line. Put as much as you possibly can into the main effort.

Concentrate on the specific area where you can be most successful. Do not dilute your efforts. Put everything needed into the push to accomplish the main strategic thrust. Do this even if it means not funding or otherwise resourcing other less important projects. To achieve stunning success, you need to not just fight the competition but aim to overwhelm them in critical areas. Point your company at the strategic point most important to your future.

ACTION FILE

HOW TO CREATE A LEARNING ORGANIZATION

 BAD IDEA #1—Learn only from your own experience.
It's said that experience is the best teacher. An even better teacher is someone else's experience. When you learn from some else's experience, you don't have to go through all the pain and frustration they did. The same lesson that goes for individuals applies to organizations.

Arrogance is the main reason organizations fail to learn from the experience of others. Organizational arrogance is when the group thinks it is better than other groups. Organizations with this problem think things like, "We would never suffer the same poor results that the XYZ company did, because we are better at [insert whatever fits here] than they are." The only way you get better than the competition is to *not* do the same things that got them into trouble. Be wise, learn from what has happened to others, and act on that knowledge.

 BAD IDEA #2—Fail to find analogies to your situation.
We often mistakenly think no one has ever had to deal with the same problems we face. While some portion of our problem may be new, 90 percent or more is similar to something that already happened to someone else. This is the power of understanding history and why the stories of what others did, and what happened as a result, can provide you with a wealth of insight.

The old saying is that "Those who forget the past are doomed to repeat it." You should constantly be looking for analogies and lessons to help you overcome the problems you currently face, or will probably face in the future. Use case study discussions and other similar methods to help you to understand what others experienced. But don't just stop with learning about what happened to others. Apply the lessons to yourself and your business's situation. Continue the learning by discussing "How are we doing similar things today?" and "What can we do differently to avoid having a similar painful experience ourselves?"

BAD IDEA #3—Believe you are unique.

Some fail to learn from what happened to others because they believe their situation is unique. They believe the perceived "uniqueness" of their situation will insulate them from the problems others experienced. They don't learn because they think what happened to others could not possibly apply to them. Never delude yourself into thinking you are in completely uncharted territory.

There is very little that is entirely new. You can learn from situations that aren't exactly the same as yours. Look for situations similar to yours. Learn from the applicable parts. Don't reject the experience of others just because all the conditions are not exactly the same as yours.

GOOD IDEA #1—Watch for evidence that change is needed.

Organizational learning is a continual process. You can never stop and say "Okay, we are done learning now." You cannot rest on the laurels of even recent success. If you've beaten your main competitor, you still cannot stop learning and looking for ways to improve. Learning how to continually do things better must become an essential part of your organizational culture. It must be part of everyone's personal philosophy. Reading, listening, taking courses, observing, and discussing are all important to the learning process. But it's not enough just to know more. You must constantly look for ways to apply what you have learned. Constantly think about "What is the lesson?" in conjunction with "How can I apply that lesson here?"

When the organization learns, it will identify things needing improvement. People who are continually learning are not satisfied with the status quo. They want to make things better. You need to encourage and support them in changing things and thereby improve productivity.

GOOD IDEA #2—Evaluate the validity of other's changes.
Continuous improvement is the name of the game. You have to look both internally and externally for ideas. Encourage ideas that come from your own organization, regardless of the source. Recognize best practices and quickly disseminate them to the rest of the group. Also, look at what others are changing. Use benchmarking and other ethical intelligence gathering to study what is going on at the competition.

Don't just blindly copy what others are doing. Analyze each potential change you are considering before implementing it. Just copying what others are doing may put you on the wrong path too. Think about what your mother told you. "If everyone was jumping off of a cliff, would you do that too?" Make sure you are not jumping off of a cliff. Make sure any change is worthwhile. You only want to make changes that will produce positive results. Evaluate everything.

 GOOD IDEA #3—Be willing to change anything.
The only ideas you should quickly dismiss are ones that are either unethical or illegal. You should have no sacred cows. You should have no limits on what you might consider. Don't wait for failures and missed targets to tell you something is definitely wrong. Go ahead and make changes when the indications are clear enough.

The truly great organization quickly and effectively liberates itself from anything that holds it back. It will even change its own culture if necessary. The successful organization can throw away from one day to the next any policy, practice, procedure, or belief impeding its progress. Only a handful of organizations throughout history have been able to do this. Why not be one of them?

CHAPTER 3

BRITISH INTERVENTION

"The Fewer Men, the Greater Share of Honor"

INTRODUCTION

GREAT Britain decided to assist France and Belgium in defending themselves against Germany. The plan for the small British Army, the British Expeditionary Force (BEF), was to occupy a quiet sector of the front, freeing up French units for fighting elsewhere. Unfortunately, the British quiet little sector was directly in the path of the German Army's main body. The British were blocking the route of the German right wing to Paris. The British Army and its leadership were unprepared for the critical position they found themselves in. The following important business themes are covered by exploring the tale of the British Army in 1914:

- Problems with popular business strategies
- Leaders in new environments
- Elitist criteria in leadership selection
- Pitfalls of strategic alliances
- Conflict in upper echelons
- Internal conflicts and finger-pointing
- Combative executives

HISTORICAL CASE AND BUSINESS ANALOGIES

The British Policy

Great Britain's traditional foreign policy was to stay out of conflicts on the continent unless one of the participants was upsetting the balance of power. Great Britain would stay neutral, unless somebody was becoming too powerful. If that was the case, they would get involved. Great Britain would then form alliances aimed at restricting the "upstart" and would become militarily involved if necessary.

Great Britain could be selective about its involvement on the continent because it is an island nation, and they were *the* dominant naval power. "Britain rules the waves" was the status quo at the start of the twentieth century.

Great Britain's strong navy could prevent any invasion of their country. This was not the only service the Royal Navy provided to the defense of their country. Great Britain is not self-sufficient in either food or important raw materials for her industries, and her industries need to ship their products to foreign markets. Thus, the country is dependent on both imports and exports, all of which move on ships. To protect her trade and her needed imports, the Royal Navy protected her merchant fleet. A threat to the British merchant fleet was a threat to British national existence. Any threat to British domination of the seas alarmed both the British government and public.

Great Britain's involvement in World War I was a direct result of bad decisions made by the German Kaiser, Wilhelm II. His bad decisions threatened what the British cared about most.

The Arms Race

Kaiser Wilhelm decided to threaten British naval supremacy. He read a very popular and influential book, *The Influence of Sea Power on History*, by the American Admiral Mahan, which stated that only nations with mastery of the seas controlled their own fates. The Kaiser wanted Germany to control every aspect of its fate. He also had a giant inferiority complex and did not want Germany to be second to Great Britain in any way. The Kaiser bought into the premise of the book. He decided to launch a major shipbuilding program for the German Navy.

> ## ANALOGY 1: POPULAR PROGRAMS
>
> This is a pretty familiar story. The head of a business reads a popular book. The latest theories of the author captivate his imagination. He sees the heads of other businesses embracing these ideas, so he becomes even more convinced that he should do the same thing. His staff may point out problems with these ideas, but that doesn't dissuade this leader. A lot of resources are then committed to projects arising from these latest theories. The business has to deal with a major disrupting and confusing change in direction. Resources are siphoned from other areas for the new programs, slowing or stopping proven and productive projects.

Like the leader following this common path of folly, the Kaiser did not think through the consequences of his naval construction program. He never really thought through the question "What do I have to gain by doing this?" or "What might the consequences of this new program be?" The Kaiser made this monumental mistake because it was the "popular" thing to do. However, it was not the right thing to do. Building battleships was a drain on Germany's limited resources. Naval operations were not a core competency of the German military. The massive expansion of the German fleet disrupted the plans of the German Army, and it seriously damaged German relations with Great Britain.

The Kaiser's advisors pointed out that building a big navy would seriously antagonize the British. They also pointed out it was unnecessary for Germany to have much of a navy. Building a large navy would mean diverting funds from the expansion of the German Army. The Schlieffen Plan relied on expanding the army to the fullest extent possible.

Kaiser Wilhelm dismissed all of the logical arguments and sound advice. Instead of using all available funds to expand the army, significant funds went to building battleships. Instead of more army divisions, personnel went to man these ships.

Of course, the British reacted to the German naval buildup as a direct threat to their survival. In the past, the British had a rather benign view of Germany. Now they saw the Germans as rash, inflammatory, and aggressive. The British began to move to thwart German power.

By 1907, there was a full-blown naval arms race between the British and

Germans. Whenever the Germans launched a battleship, the English public demanded at least one or two more. When the British started to build more battleships, the Germans would follow suit. Neither side would back down or slow the massive naval build up.

This naval arms race affected British foreign policy. The British decided to find non-German friends in Europe. They turned to France, Germany's traditional enemy. In the face of German saber rattling and battleship building, Great Britain forgot that France had also been its traditional enemy.

Before the British smoothed things over with the French, it would have taken the British Army months to move a small force to the continent and have them ready to fight. Now that Great Britain saw Germany as an enemy, they arranged to land their army in France. They worked with the French on plans and coordinating measures for their army. Previously, it would have taken months to get the British Army to the continent and have it ready for action. The prewar agreements and coordination with the French reduced this to a couple of weeks at the most.

The British Expeditionary Force

The French, of course, were delighted to have the assistance of yet another great power. The French already had an alliance with the Russians. Now both the Russians *and* the British would support them in fighting Germany. French and British staffs made detailed arrangements for a British Expeditionary Force (hereafter the BEF) to come to France at the start of the war. These staffs planned for and prepared the port facilities, railroad cars, rail lines, and encampment areas well in advance. The BEF had a place in the French line. It was to cover the northern flank of the French Fifth Army, between the end of the French line and the English Channel. It was to cooperate with the French Army and its operations as spelled out by the French Plan XVII. [Fig 14]

The British selected Field Marshal Sir John French to lead the BEF in France. Sir John was subordinate to the supreme head of the British Army, Field Marshal Lord Kitchener. Only the British Army sent to France was under Sir John's control.

Sir John rose to prominence in the British Army during the Boer War in South Africa at the turn of the century. The Boer War revealed the incompetence of an awful lot of senior British generals. Anyone who showed any degree of

British Intervention 91

competence, and actually produced some success in this conflict, far outshined his peers.

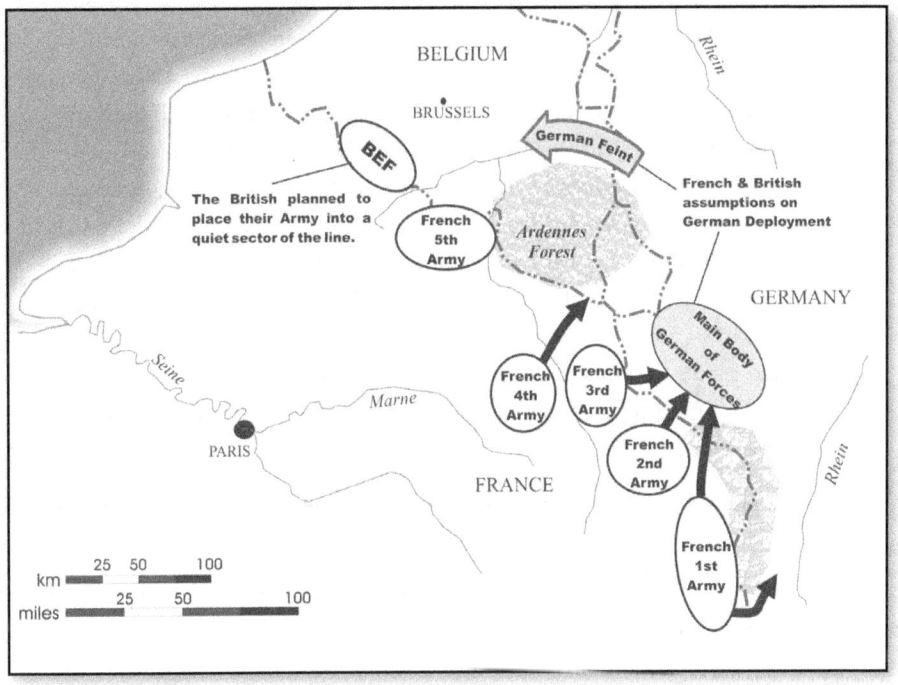

Figure 14. Original British Assumptions and Plan for BEF Deployment

Sir John was a cavalry officer. He rose to the command of the British cavalry in the Boer War. The Boer War ranged across the vast and wide-open spaces of South Africa. Here, the cavalry could go wherever it wanted to. It was the one branch of the army mobile enough to cover the great distances involved in fighting this war.

The Boer war was very different from war in Europe between major powers. In South Africa, combat units were relatively small. They were like ships on the vast ocean of South African territory. In the Boer war, each side had thousands of soldiers. In Europe, each side would have millions of soldiers. In the Boer war, most army units could go wherever they wanted to. In Europe, there were so many soldiers that units were shoulder to shoulder, from one end of the line to the other. In Europe, there would be little room to maneuver.

> ## ANALOGY 2: AURA OF SUCCESS
>
> Success in one situation does not guarantee success in other, very different, situations. Sir John was successful in an environment completely different from what he would face in France. It is a false assumption that someone successful under a given set of circumstances will always be successful. The circumstances and situation specific to the success are overlooked. Businesses want people who are "successful," so they find a "successful" person and often put them in an environment very different from the one where they worked so well. The result is predictable problems for the new leader, because they have to deal with unfamiliar conditions and constraints. It is always a good idea to find out not only if someone is "successful" but also to find out what made them so. Similar conditions will give the person the greatest chance of repeated success. Putting them in a very different environment often results in their trying to repeat earlier successes with tactics often unsuited to the new environment.

It was no coincidence that Sir John had a background as a cavalry officer. The cavalry was the premier branch of the British Army. In the pecking order of the different branches (infantry, artillery, cavalry, engineers), the cavalry was on top. In stratified British society, cavalry officers were on the highest rung of the ladder. British Army culture certainly held that the best officers were from the cavalry.

This belief strongly influenced decisions about leadership in the British Army. The BEF initially going to France consisted of five divisions. There were two infantry divisions in each of two corps and a cavalry division. The commanders of both of the corps, the cavalry division, and the overall BEF commander, were all cavalry officers. Even Lord Kitchener, head of the British Army, was a cavalry officer. The entire senior leadership of the British Army consisted of cavalrymen.

ANALOGY 3: ELITISM

This type of elitism is a common problem in business. Business leaders think their background is a fundamental part of what made them successful. This is true. What isn't true is that this background has a better probability of making someone successful than a different kind of background. Because people think their backgrounds made them successful, they think it will make others successful. This is flawed logic. Yet leaders often fall into the trap of preferentially selecting subordinates with the very same background they have. As the leader moves up in the organization, these subordinates move up with them. This is how too many businesses end up with everyone in senior leadership having the same or very similar backgrounds.

The "golden" background can be any one of many forms. It could be attending the same school the leader did. In this case, the leader makes it a point to try to hire people from that particular school. These people continue to receive special treatment when it comes to promotions within the company.

Instead of an alma mater, the "golden" background could be a specific professional discipline. The business leader might view their functional background as the one best suited for positions of great responsibility in the company. This discipline could be research, or manufacturing, or sales, or accounting, or something else seen as vital to success. In this case, the tendency is to find subordinates from the same functional area. The simple fact that since the leader came from a particular functional area and most of the people they know and are comfortable with are from that area too only magnifies this tendency. The leader spent years working with these people, and they trust them.

Another frequent "golden" background is working on a successful, high visibility project in the company, usually a project the senior leader was personally involved in. They have come to see it as the perfect example of a well-run project. They view those who worked with them on this particular project as having the skills necessary for advancement.

In bad cases, the "golden" background necessary for advancement has more to do with something completely unrelated to the business, like the ability to play golf, than with anything else. In the worst of cases, the "golden" background has to do with race, gender, or religion.

> In every case, the use of an elite background as a prerequisite for increased responsibility has severely detrimental effects on any business. It leads to a homogonous leadership, where all the decision makers have the same view of problems. Because of this, they will look to the same common areas for solutions and will have a rather narrow view of the business, trends, competition, and possibilities. Frequently, elitism results in the selection of someone with inadequate skills and abilities for a crucial position.
>
> The "golden" background litmus test for promotion also leads to good people leaving the company. They are the ones without the desired background. They see that they cannot get ahead, that they cannot meet their personal goals. So they leave. And where do they go? Either they go to one of your competitors, or they start their own company. Either way, you lose. There are no positive effects of elitism in any organization.

The British Army suffered the effects of elitism many times over in the course of World War I. The background that produced the leadership of their army, cavalry experience, was next to worthless in the mud and trenches of the war. The cavalry played little or no role in operations in France and Belgium. The beliefs of the cavalry officer, theories never discarded by the British in the war, led to most of the disasters they and their army would suffer.

Great Britain Declares War

Great Britain did not automatically enter the war in August 1914. No one attacked or invaded Great Britain. The British had never signed formal treaty papers with the French. They were a signatory to an agreement (along with France and Germany) that guaranteed the neutrality and sovereignty of Belgium. When German units crossed the border of Belgium, Great Britain had a valid reason for declaring war on Germany. The Germans invaded Belgium according to the schedules specified by the Schlieffen Plan. This invasion was reason enough for the British government to commit its army to the conflict.

Lord Kitchener gave Sir John his orders concerning the BEF on the continent. The various instructions given to Sir John were potentially conflicting. He was to cooperate with and assist the French, yet he was to ensure the protection and preservation of his force. Sir John's interpretation of his orders was that he should view the preservation of his little army as his highest priority. In his opinion, he would only cooperate with the French if he was reasonably sure the BEF was in no great danger.

> ## ANALOGY 4: PITFALLS OF JOINT PARTNERSHIPS
>
> The British high command acted very much like many organizations that enter into some kind of partnership or joint venture. The partnership could be internal to a larger company, such as when two divisions must work together on a common goal, or the partnership could involve an outside party, such as a supplier. In both cases, the separate organizations make agreements about how they will cooperate. Both sides specify what they will allocate to the joint endeavor. Behind the public scenes of agreement, other attitudes often prevail. Frequently, the leadership of one, if not both, of the involved organizations wants the other side in the venture to take the majority of the risk. It also wants the other side to put up the lion's share of the resources necessary for the project. Both sides may say they will cooperate on the joint project, but if the assets allocated to the venture appear to be at risk, either side's priority may revert to protecting what it put in, rather than the overall success of the project.

In August 1914, the BEF mobilized in England and was quickly on its way to France. The BEF got across the English Channel, unloaded from its transport ships, and packed onto French trains rather quickly. This was due to all of the arrangements made in advance for French port facilities and railroads. In only a few days, the BEF was well on its way by French trains to its assembly areas in the northeast of France.

One of the most senior British generals died during the train trip from the ports to the front. General Grierson, one of the two corps commanders of the BEF, died of a heart attack. Sir John, as the commander of the BEF, felt that it was his prerogative to pick Grierson's successor. He wanted to promote General Plumer into the job. As you might expect, Plumer was a cavalry officer.

Lord Kitchener had other ideas. Instead of Plumer, Lord Kitchener surprised Sir John by appointing General Horace Smith-Dorien to the vacant post. Unlike all the others, Smith-Dorien was an infantry officer. Sir John did not like him, and he resented Kitchener making personnel decisions in "his" army.

Rather than try to work with Smith-Dorien, Sir John from the outset adopted a rather bad attitude about one of his two most important subordinates. He felt that Smith-Dorien was not competent and would constantly question his orders. Sir John had these views of the man even before the BEF was in contact with the enemy.

> ## ANALOGY 5: PREDESTINATION
>
> General Smith-Dorien found himself in a common situation. He became a critical subordinate to a superior forced to accept him in that role. It is common for leaders to get subordinates they did not personally pick. Most people are able to deal with this. Some create a big problem out of this. The problem is when the leader decides that this person is not up to the job, even before they start to do it. Sometimes, such poor leaders may even tell them things like, "I wanted someone else for the job," or "I don't think that you can do this job, and I have no confidence in your abilities," or "I have heard that you are difficult to work with, and I want you to know that I won't tolerate any of that here!" This is a horrible way to start a new working relationship. The person starts an important job knowing their new boss has no faith in them. The new person is almost predestined to fail. Without the support and encouragement of their superior, they begin their job at a distinct disadvantage. It gets even worse when the poor leader actually acts on these prejudices and threats. In their eagerness to prove the new subordinate is not the right person for the job, they actually undermine the performance of the organization.

Sir John was certainly to blame for taking such a jaundiced view of his new subordinate. Additional blame for this terrible situation in the British chain of command lies with Lord Kitchener. He certainly knew that Sir John was against the choice. Maybe he promoted Smith-Dorien over Sir John's objections just to show who was in charge. This is a common action. The problem was that Kitchener did very little, if anything, to ensure that the working relationship between the BEF commander and his new corps commander got off to a good start. Nor did he intervene in the situation once it became clear that Sir John had no confidence in Smith-Dorien and acted as such. When Smith-Dorien showed up to take command of his corps, Sir John told him to "prepare for combat with the enemy." Smith-Dorien asked if he was to attack or to defend. Sir John told him to shut up and obey orders. Unbelievably, Sir John never answered his question! Sir John hindered Smith-Dorien's job performance. He put the half of his army under Smith-Dorien at a distinct disadvantage. Sir John's attitude about his unwanted subordinate turned into vague instructions. It was a portent of worse things to come.

ANALOGY 6: LIMITS TO PROFESSIONALISM

The bad relationship in the BEF command structure had an underlying cause still common today. There is an expectation that senior leaders behave in a professional manner at all times in their personal dealings with the others. The expectation is that they can ignore personal dislike of a peer, subordinate, or a superior and still get the job done. Lord Kitchener probably had this expectation of Sir John. It is not unreasonable to expect people to work through any personal difficulties they may have with each other. But you have to do more than just expect this from people.

You must realize that personal relationships *do* affect the ability of an organization to function. The vast majority of people, including senior executives, are *not* going to work around personality conflicts. They will, unfortunately, do things to get people they don't like into trouble. They may even hamper organizational success so the person they don't like fails. This is serious and damaging.

You must constantly look for the possibility of this going on. You need to intervene personally. You need to make your expectations clear to those with real or even potential relationship difficulty. You cannot allow such problems to damage the performance of the organization.

Into Action

The BEF moved forward and took its place on the extreme left of the French armies. Its neighbor was the French Fifth Army commanded by General Lanrezac. The plans of both the French and British armies called for the close cooperation between the leadership of the BEF and the French Fifth Army. They were the only armies the allies had for operations in the northern part of the front. The initial plan was for both armies to move aggressively into Belgium. [Fig 15]

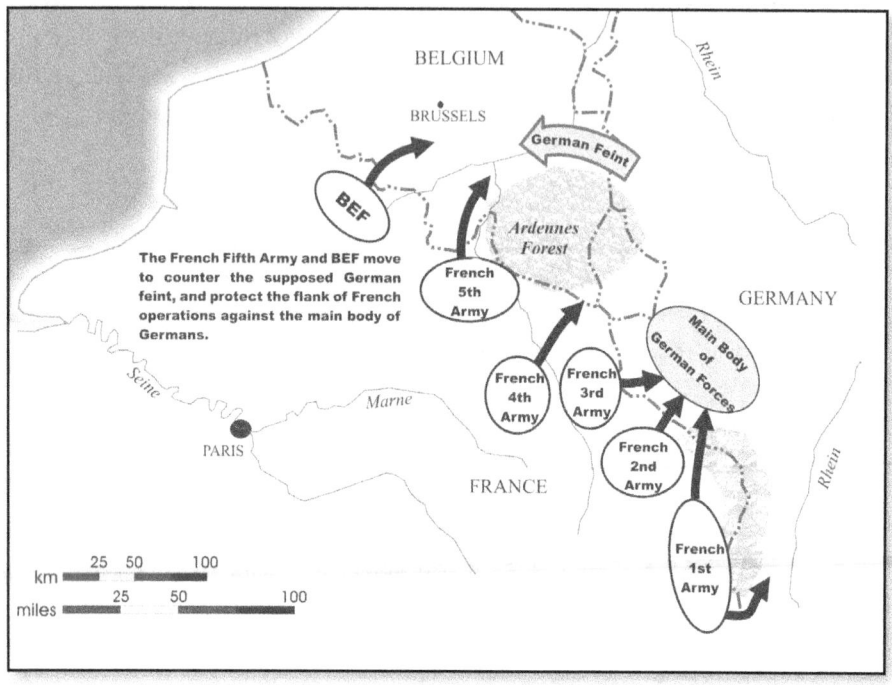

Figure 15. French and British Plans for Movement into Belgium

Before the BEF moved into the front line, Sir John met with both senior French leaders. He met with both the French Commander in Chief, General Joffre, and with the French Fifth Army commander, General Lanrezac. In each case, Sir John listened but didn't promise much. Sir John was "stand-offish" with Joffre. He was more abrupt with Lanrezac. Sir John would not push his force forward into what he viewed as a dangerous and unclear situation. This is exactly what Joffre was pressuring Lanrezac to do at the time. Lanrezac wanted the British to move forward with him.

Sir John wanted to maintain his independence from the French Army. He was not going to allow any of the BEF to be under French command. Further, he was not going to take orders from a French general about when and where to go. His priority was primarily the safety and security of the BEF. He would consider cooperation with the French only after the safety of the BEF was ensured.

Sir John could get away with this less than helpful attitude because there was

British Intervention 99

no unity of command among the allies on the western front. The British would not place their forces under the orders of a French general, even if it made sense to do so in terms of the big picture. The result was that Sir John and his French ally Lanrezac got into serious disagreements about who should be doing what at the very moment neither could afford to do so.

> ### ANALOGY 7: UNDEFINED LEADERSHIP
>
> This is the same situation seen when groups under different bosses work on a combined project without a clear leader. With no clear picture as to who has final decision making authority, the people at the top of the pecking order are going to spend most of their time posturing and trying to make sure that they are the one with the most influence. They work together on decisions only with the time left over from the power struggle. Even then, the decision they will want to make is the one that is best for them and the piece of the pie they control. It does not matter to them if it is the right thing to do for the group project or not.

Instead of working together, both the BEF and the French Fifth Army moved forward independently. Each decided to "do their own thing" in their assigned areas of responsibility. As a result, neither could support the other in the battles that shortly took place.

The BEF moved toward the Germans. They made contact near the Belgian city of Mons. The BEF's movement placed it right in the middle of the route that the German right wing was to take on its way into France. The British sent the BEF to France only to play a minor assisting role in the great French offensives called for by their Plan XVII. Instead, the BEF found itself right in the path of the largest and most powerful group of German armies. [Fig 16]

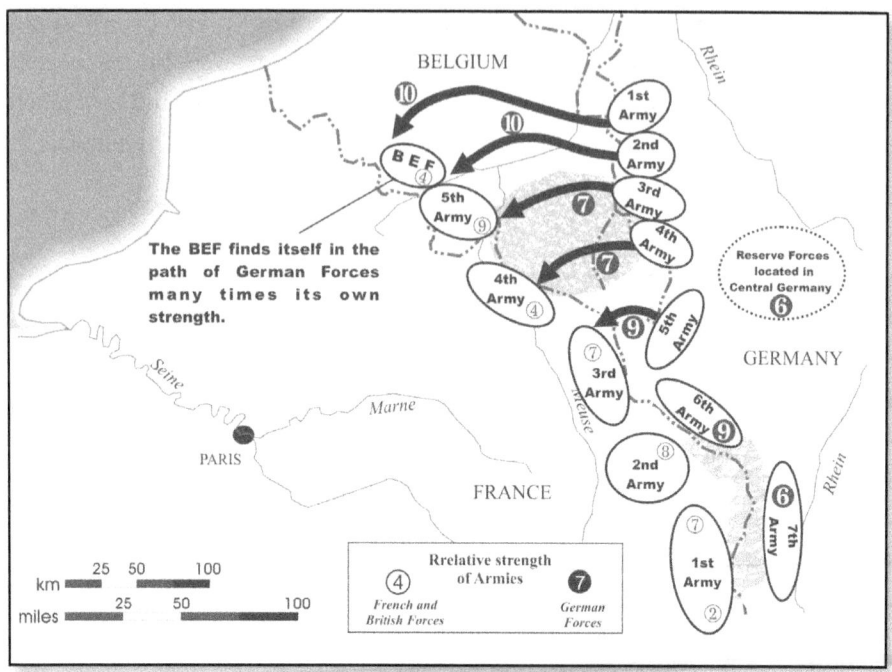

Figure 16. The Reality Facing the BEF

The German First Army that advanced on the BEF's positions was the most forward of the large armies that made up the German right wing. The professional soldiers of the BEF held off the initial German attacks at Mons, but the Germans had enough men to move around the edges of the British positions, making them untenable. This was partly possible because the French Fifth Army was pulling out and retreating back into France. While Sir John did little to help Lanrezac, he expected Lanrezac to help him. The reality of the situation for Sir John was that Lanrezac's French Army was retreating while the BEF was under attack by the German Army.

Both Lanrezac and Sir John felt betrayed by the other. Each blamed the other. Both told their superiors that the other's behavior forced them to move their forces even further to the rear. Each lost faith in the ability of their ally. Each stopped sharing information with the other. Both of them made plans that put no reliance on the other to do anything. To some degree, both lost sight of who the real enemy was.

> ## ANALOGY 8: FINGER-POINTING
>
> This is an example of what happens when there is a breakdown in coordination between separate parts of an organization. Some part sees another part as the source of its problems. "We can't achieve our goals because the XYZ section is creating problems for us…" is the lament at top-level meetings. More and more effort goes towards showing superiors the error of the other group's ways. Finger-pointing between the different groups becomes an accepted part of the organization's culture. Teamwork, ideals of working towards a common goal, of achieving things in the best interest of the organizational whole are lost in the infighting between these feuding groups. There are absolutely no positive outcomes from a situation like this. It can only cause damage. Over time, it will get worse and worse, until it ultimately causes a catastrophic failure.

The British placed a lot of faith in the competence of the French Army and in France's ability to execute their war plans. The BEF was supposed to be a minor player on a quiet part of the front. It was mostly a show of support by the British for the French. Its job was to free up French units for the big Plan XVII attacks.

Now, the leadership of the BEF was looking at a drastically different picture. Instead of occupying a relatively quiet place along the front, they were in the hottest spot. The British believed the French when they reported only weak German forces in Belgium. Instead, they found out by direct experience at Mons that they were up against the strongest of German armies. On top of that, the French offensives failed. Everywhere, the French armies were retreating in disarray. More and more reports of French reverses came in. The French Army was losing badly.

Staring into the Abyss

This is not what Sir John had signed on for. He was now facing the real possibility of the Germans annihilating the BEF with their massive right wing. He was responsible for the BEF. The British government had entrusted it to his care. The BEF was the only army Great Britain had. Losing it would be an unprecedented national catastrophe.

With this in mind, Sir John was determined to save his army at any cost. There was even less cooperation and coordination with the French. Sir John felt that if the French Army was going to lose, he and the BEF were not going to be a part of their defeat. He put the BEF on a course not only to get out of the current danger, but also to retreat out of it even faster than the French could.

The only thing that slowed Sir John was that his soldiers could not march that fast. At one point, contrary to orders from BEF headquarters, Smith-Dorien's corps turned to face the enemy. Smith-Dorien felt that Germans were about to turn his flank and cut off the entire BEF. He turned his corps to protect the way further to the rear. The corps acquitted itself well in the ensuing battle of Le Cateau and resumed the retreat the following day. The action probably saved the BEF from encirclement by the Germans.

Sir John was incensed at the action. He blamed Smith-Dorien for putting the BEF in danger. He blamed Smith-Dorien for failing to retreat as ordered. He made a habit of blaming Smith-Dorien for any action he took.

The British had less and less contact with the enemy as they retreated farther to the rear. Reports came in to BEF headquarters from subordinate units that the army was out of danger. Senior British officers, including both corps commanders Haig and Smith-Dorien, felt that the time had come to turn about and face the enemy. The BEF commander rejected these views. In fact, Sir John sent a report to Lord Kitchener spelling out that his force was badly beaten and that he intended to make for the safety of the coast, leaving the French to fend for themselves.

To make things worse for the French, the retreating BEF was between their Fifth Army and the new Sixth Army that Joffre was forming to the north of Paris. If the BEF left, it would leave a wide gap in the front lines between these two French armies. The Germans could easily take major advantage of such a gap. They could encircle Paris and the Sixth Army, or move around the flank of the Fifth. Sir John did not see this as his problem. His priority was to save the BEF from the mess he saw them in. [Fig 17]

British Intervention

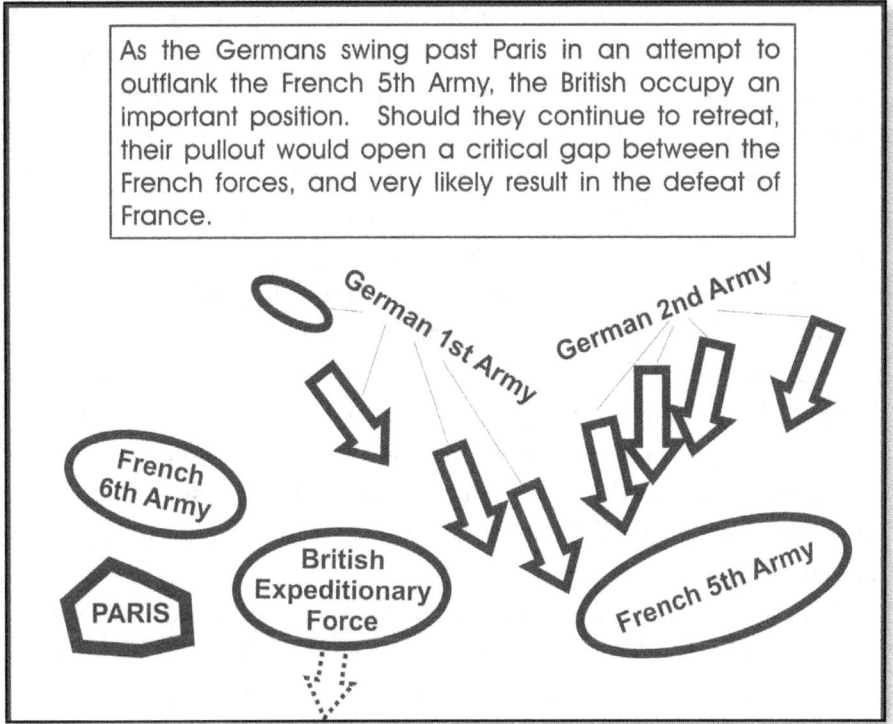

Figure 17. Critical Position of British Expeditionary Force

Back in London, Sir John's report on the BEF's situation and the intention to retreat all the way to the coast alarmed Lord Kitchener. He decided to go to France and talk with Sir John personally. He wanted to make it clear that he did not want to abandon their allies in their moment of greatest need. Lord Kitchener met Sir John at the British embassy in Paris. While the discussion between the two resulted in a slowdown in the pace of British retreat, it did not stop it. It became evident Sir John was not very receptive to Lord Kitchener's directions.

Well before the Battle of the Marne, it was clear to all involved that Sir John was not going to cooperate with the French. Also obvious was his intent on pulling the BEF back to a safe area, even if that meant abandoning his allies. All of this was clear within a couple of days after the fighting at Mons. Sir John told his staff that he wanted to move the BEF hundreds of miles from the front to an easily defensible French port. There, the British Army could quickly re-embark for England when it wanted to.

The question at this point is why Sir John was not relieved of his command. He acted contrary to the wishes of his superior. He was not cooperating with the French. It was obvious to everyone on his staff that he was demoralized and beaten. Yet Sir John remained in charge of the BEF. Lord Kitchener had come to talk to him, but that intervention did not fix the problems. Sir John continued as before. There were no other interventions. His inadequate performance continued. Why was he not sacked?

Sir John was well known within British Army and government circles as someone with a bad temper, an irritable nature, and given to wild mood swings. Sir John received the command of the BEF primarily because he was a hero of the Boer War. He had done well while most of his contemporaries proved themselves muddling incompetents. It was felt Sir John had the proper background for commanding the BEF. He was both an aristocrat and a cavalry officer. For some reason, his personality, and the effect it would have on his performance, was not an issue.

Once things started to go badly for the BEF in France, it was clear Sir John was in over his head. Yet the government and the army tolerated his substandard performance. His superiors hoped he would learn quickly on the job, and start doing better. The problem was that there was no time to learn, and Sir John was not someone considered teachable anyway. He didn't get along with the French generals. He viewed them as personal inferiors because they had commoner backgrounds.

Lord Kitchener did nothing besides his trip to Paris to talk to Sir John. Sir John's performance after this meeting was pretty much the same as it was before.

No one confronted Sir John directly because of his bad temperament. Everyone treated him deferentially even when all had lost faith in him. People just could not deal with his bad side. Rather than deal with it, they avoided it. No one wanted to get into a big argument with the man about what the BEF should do on the battlefield. No one wanted to deal with the shouting, screaming, yelling, and foot-stomping rages that a serious discussion with Sir John would probably produce.

ANALOGY 9: DIFFICULT PEOPLE

There are plenty of people out there with bad tempers, reputations as "hard to get along with," disrupters of meetings. These people are simply jerks, and many of them hold positions of great responsibility within companies. They get to such lofty positions for the same reasons Sir John came to lead the BEF. These people may have shown some degree of skill in the past in a lesser function. They may have some kind of background that qualifies them as elite within the business environment, or they may have some special technical skill. But in all of these cases, as with Sir John, people already know they have explosive personalities.

In spite of their behavior, they are still promoted to positions of increasingly greater responsibility. The hope and belief is that they will change. Their superiors hope they can repress the undesirable behavior and yet exhibit the wanted skills and abilities. Maybe their boss thinks they can control the bad behavior by their presence or by coaching. Unfortunately, this is all wishful thinking. People come as a complete package. You don't get to choose only the parts you want. You get the good and the bad together. You have to deal with both.

People can change. It is possible for someone with a bad temper to find ways to control it. This just needs to happen *before* receiving greater responsibility. If not, you may actually reinforce the bad behavior. In many cases, people with this problem actually think it is good behavior, which helps to produce results. You need to correct such erroneous thinking.

Once it became clear that Sir John had performance problems, no one above him wanted to deal with them. This is common in the business world as well. Very few leaders will deal with the performance of people who are combative. They shy away from any action or comment they think might lead to some kind of confrontation. They are afraid to deal with it. It is amazing how pervasive this attitude towards combative people is, even when the very existence of the organization is at stake.

The meeting between Lord Kitchener and Sir John in Paris is an example of the typical counseling session held with a combative person about performance issues. The general course and outcomes of such counseling sessions are repeated all too often in the business world.

Here is an example. A subordinate takes action counterproductive to what the leader wants to accomplish. At first, the leader decides to sit on the sidelines and wait and see if things get better on their own. They don't. So the leader takes the first tentative step in addressing the problem by talking to the subordinate. They don't want to be too harsh, so the message about current performance is sugar coated. The message usually begins with an introduction such as "John, you are a really great guy and I appreciate all that you've done, but I wish that you could do better at...." The message usually ends with another pulled punch. It goes something like, "You have been doing a great job up until now, and I don't really want to meddle in the details of how you do your job. I know you will be able to find a way to get past this little problem."

Dealing with problems by such methods is leadership cowardice. The leader is afraid to get into some kind of confrontation with the subordinate, so they don't come right out and say what they mean. They fail to communicate the severity of the current situation and the urgency with which they want the problem addressed. In a lot of cases, the subordinate hears only the praise in the superior's message. They don't understand what the problem is. Many who get such weak messages will do nothing about it. This is because the leader ends the message by telling the subordinate to "keep up the good work" and then backs off addressing the problems on a recurring basis.

Lord Kitchener failed to impress on Sir John the extent of his disapproval regarding the movements of the BEF. He failed to spell out to Sir John what his expectations were for cooperation with the French Army. There were no consequences for Sir John's performance. His poor performance continued. No one did anything about it.

The French Armies turned around to face the Germans at the Battle of the Marne. When they did this, the British were still moving away. Joffre had tried to get Sir John to cooperate with the attacking French Armies, but to no avail initially. The British Army began to turn around only after the French attacks were well underway. The BEF slowly moved forward as the French attacks created a gap between the German First and Second Armies. The BEF was right in front of the gap between these two enemy armies. Suddenly, there were no Germans

British Intervention

in front of the British Army, only open fields. The BEF then moved forward, but cautiously.

Lost Opportunity

Had the BEF coordinated its movements with the French forces to either side of it, it could have moved much farther into the gap between the German armies. There were only a few German cavalry patrols in the gap, nothing else. The BEF was virtually unopposed. Aggressive BEF action might have surrounded the German First Army. The BEF would have outflanked the Germans, putting them in serious peril. [Fig 18] If the Germans lost their First Army, they might have had to retreat out of France entirely. But this did not happen. The Germans had time to pull back and adjust their line. They closed the gap. They no longer threatened Paris, but the Germans had not yet lost the war.

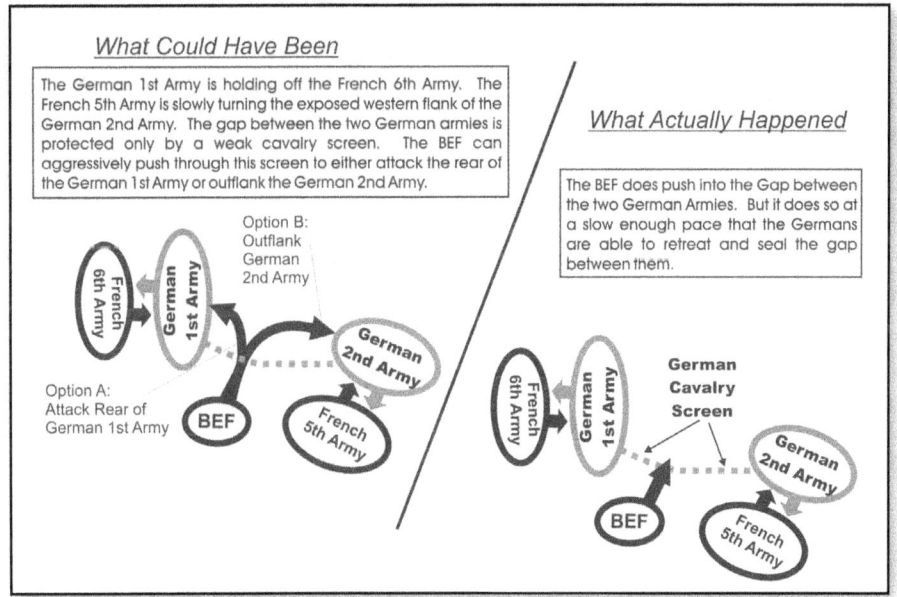

Figure 18. Options Available to the BEF for Advance

Sir John stayed in command of the BEF, even though everyone else thought he was doing a pretty miserable job of it. Sir John remained in charge of the British armies in France until the end of 1915, almost a year and half after the missed opportunities of the Battle of the Marne. By that time, he had managed to get Smith-Dorien sacked for failing to carry out an order. Interestingly, Smith-Dorien's replacement was not willing to follow the order either.

Sir John finally went too far. It surfaced that he was trying to get Lord Kitchener fired. It seems Sir John wanted total control over the BEF. This was too much for Lord Kitchener and the government. Sir John's replacement was General Haig, another cavalry officer with society connections. Unfortunately, things did not get much better for the British Army in France.

CONCLUSIONS

This was the tale of British leadership at the start of World War I. Sir John French's tenure as commander of the British Army in France is largely forgotten, eclipsed by the much larger operations of Haig and eventual British victory. British victory was not a foregone conclusion, because of what happened in August and September 1914. Sir John created serious command issues. The BEF under his command failed to exploit one of the greatest opportunities for victory ever presented to a modern army. The story of the BEF in 1914 under Sir John's leadership provides numerous analogies to the business world. The most import of these include:

- **Problems with popular business strategies**

    You must base your business strategies on logic and reason. You should not embark on a path just because "everybody else is doing it" and fear that you will be left behind if you don't. You have to weigh the tradeoffs involved in adopting any new plan or strategy. You can only make intelligent decisions about changes in strategic direction by the systematic and logical consideration of the possible benefits and risks of a new idea. Don't do something just because others are.

- **Leaders in new environments**

    Success in one set of circumstances does not guarantee success under different circumstances. You must consider more about a potential leader than just how successful they were in the past. You must also consider the *how* and *why*. Think about this, too: are the methods they used in the past applicable to the environment they will be operating in? If not, maybe you need to consider someone else.

- **Elitist criteria in leadership selection**

    Don't base leadership decisions on some kind of elitism. Elitism can take many forms. It usually only considers one part of a person's background. Elitism might consider only the school they went to, what department they were in, what their functional background is, or what their golf handicap is. It's worse than elitism if such decisions consider ethnic background or gender.

Elitism, besides being morally wrong, leads to an organization's leadership having a very limited skill set. Such leadership will have problems adapting to change or dealing with crisis. Elitism also creates retention and morale problems when it is used as criteria for promotion consideration.

- **Pitfalls of strategic alliances**

   In any alliance, you must be aware of the fact that your partner wants to enjoy all of the rewards after you put up most of the resources and take most of the risks. It's best to hash out such things before embarking on the alliance.

- **Conflict in upper echelons**

   Personality conflicts are problems at *all* levels of organizations. Such conflicts can spiral out of control. When this happens, personal vendettas become more important than the organization's needs. Everyone needs coaching in handling personality conflicts. *Do not* assume that people at or above a certain level are always going to handle things in a professional manner.

- **Internal conflicts and finger-pointing**

   Most organizations still do not function as teams. Many *do* function as leagues, with individual department teams trying to win the championship by beating the other teams in the league. Too often, the parts of an organization forget who the real enemy is and fight among themselves. This is always great for the competition. When you see finger-pointing instead of true group problem solving, you are seeing this type of self-defeating behavior.

- **Combative executives**

   People with combative personalities frequently get away with poor performance. Superiors and especially peers are usually unwilling to deal with the issues if they think the other person will lose their temper or do something else drastic or unpleasant. You cannot allow combative people to get away with this. If anything, they require more counseling and more coaching than others do. You must deal with all performance issues, no matter what the personality of the person concerned. If you don't, you are telling everyone that poor performance is okay if you are a jerk. Do not send a message like this due to leadership cowardice. You need to handle this, no matter how ugly it might get.

ACTION FILE

HOW TO MAKE LEADERSHIP CHANGES

BAD IDEA #1—Base decisions on friendship.

The old saying goes "It's lonely at the top." You have to make this sacrifice to succeed at the top of any organization. The leader's ultimate loyalty must be the organization's success. This means that you must put the success of the organization above your friends.

The organization will suffer whenever you hire, promote, or fire based on friendship. When you do this, you are not using performance criteria for making personnel changes. You are only deluding yourself if you think you will get what you need from a person because you have some kind of special relationship with them. Friends also believe they have some kind of special protection. They think they won't be held accountable for substandard performance because of their friendship with you.

You send a dangerous signal to the organization when you make leadership selections based on friendship. The signal is that the way to get ahead is to concentrate on building personal relationships with superiors, *not* through performance. As a result, people will spend more time trying to be friends with their bosses than working on achieving the best possible performance.

BAD IDEA #2—Allow too much time for someone to improve.

Friendship can seriously hinder organizational effectiveness if it has too much influence. This happens when a friend is given extra time to come around. Rather than take appropriate and timely action for substandard performance, the friend gets additional time to try and improve. This places the needs of the friend above the needs of the organization and its customers.

People tend to make this mistake for two basic reasons. First, we do favors for our friends. They get breaks, advantages, and rewards we don't give others. This is one of the ways we show people they are truly our friends. The second, and most powerful, reason is that people are afraid of damaging relationships with their friends. If you do something negative to a friend, they probably won't want to be your friend anymore. This fear of personal rejection, especially by someone you have warm relations with, is a very strong inhibitor to doing the right thing.

As a leader, your main objective must always be to do what is best for the organization. You ensure the organization reaches its goals and objectives as quickly and efficiently as possible. This is not going to happen if you give favors to friends who aren't contributing. You have to put the good of the organization above the needs of personal relationships. Don't put off doing the right thing because someone's feelings might be hurt.

 BAD IDEA #3—Fail to hold people responsible for their performance.

You create a special protected class within your organization when you don't hold some people responsible for poor performance. Your actions say, "I expect everyone to perform, except those whom I protect. They can do whatever they want; there are no consequences for them." Throughout history, many incompetents rose to important positions because of special relationships with their superiors. Those same relationships kept them in those elevated positions even after they demonstrated their lack of ability. These individuals produced some of history's greatest disasters. Your organization will experience similar disasters unless you hold everyone to the same standard.

You make things worse when you don't deal with the performance issues of everyone similarly. When someone gets special treatment, you are telling them to go ahead and try to get away with even more. They may even start bragging to others about what they can get away with because of the special treatment they receive. These people will drag down the motivation and then the performance of everyone else.

GOOD IDEA #1—Hold people accountable for what they do.

Truly enlightened individuals realize they can do what is best for them when they do what is best for the organization they belong to. The organization succeeds, and as a direct result, they succeed.

People are better team players when they see their work situation in this light. You want employees to see and treat the business's assets just like their own personal property. You need them to realize the success of the business will make them successful in turn. This realization will result in the entire organization becoming more involved in finding ways to improve and achieve even more.

You must encourage and reinforce feelings that personal rewards will come from the business's success. Individuals will not be motivated to help their group succeed unless collective success results in personal success. When those who work in a business don't get what they want by making the business successful, they are no longer motivated to help it succeed, and that is the death knell for any company.

 GOOD IDEA #2—Don't procrastinate dealing with performance issues.

When you have sufficient evidence of a problem with someone's performance, take action to correct it. The quicker you take appropriate action, the sooner improvements can start. Delay results in the problem getting worse.

Don't wait for some perfect time to deal with the situation. That time will never come. Don't wait for some artificial cycle, like the end of a review period, to take action. Waiting only prolongs the problem.

If you need to replace someone, do so as soon as you can. Once you decide that you need to replace someone, you will give up on that person, even if only subconsciously. You won't provide them with the same support you used to. Don't accept such a situation. Resolve to take prompt and timely action should it become necessary.

GOOD IDEA #3—Put the organization ahead of personal relationships.

You will suffer personally if you put the organization first. There will be a time when you have to deal with a friend's poor performance. This person probably won't want to be your friend anymore when you do this. This is the price you must pay to be a leader. If you are unable or unwilling to pay this price, you don't belong in a leadership position.

You can still be friendly with people. In fact, you should be friendly. But you cannot let personal relationships prevent you from doing what's right. Any organization must count on its leaders doing whatever they have to for the organization to be successful. True friends will understand and respect this.

CHAPTER 4

THE RUSSIAN STEAMROLLER

"Give Me Back My Legions!"

INTRODUCTION

THE Russian Army had the initiative on the Eastern Front in 1914. The Germans concentrated on France and Belgium. They left only a small group of units to fend off the Russians. The German eastern territories were vulnerable to envelopment by the Russians. The Russian Army started moving and attacked far sooner than the Germans thought possible. This surprise caused the German command to panic. The Russian execution of their invasion of Germany is a case of fact being stranger than fiction. In the telling of the story of Russian moves against the Germans, you will see the following important points:

- The most important leadership attribute
- Avoiding the negative effects of office politics
- Improving working relationships between executives
- Risk management guidelines
- Exploiting success
- Preventing predestined failures
- Avoiding regressive behavior during crisis

HISTORICAL CASE AND BUSINESS ANALOGIES

Advantages and Disadvantages

Before World War I, Russia was a great power. But it was a backward country. It had a lot of people, but compared to other powers, not much industry. The Tsar ruled the country. He was an absolute monarch whose word was law. A large aristocracy surrounded the Tsar. The vast majority of Russia's people were poor and illiterate peasants.

Russia's real strength was the hordes of soldiers it could put into battle. Its population was three times greater than any other country in Europe. It could easily raise large armies and replace the losses those armies suffered. The Russian Steamroller was the nickname other countries had for the Russian Army. It was slow and not very well armed compared to other armies, but it was big. The Russian Steamroller would push against its foes until it ran over and crushed whatever was in its way, just by the weight of its sheer numbers.

Somehow, all of this must have slipped the mind of Kaiser Wilhelm when he decided not to renew the alliance treaty between Germany and Russia in the late 1800s. As a result, Russia turned to France for an alliance. Their fear of a common enemy, the war-mongering Kaiser, bound them together, even though Russia and France had diametrically opposed political and social systems.

War with Japan

Most countries in Europe had not fought a war against a well-equipped enemy in close to fifty years. Russia had. Russia fought a major war with Japan less than a decade before World War I. In the late 1890s, Japan armed itself with modern weapons. It then looked for opportunities to expand. After grabbing some territory from China, Japan started looking at Russian occupied Korea and northern China as the next opportunity.

European countries viewed Japan with contempt during this period. They viewed Japan as a backward country whose population had little culture and no worthwhile skills. On top of that were the racial prejudices of the time. Europeans considered the Japanese an inferior people. The Russians shared this contempt of the Japanese.

In early 1904, the Japanese started the war by surprising the Russians. They sailed a bunch of torpedo boats right into the Russian Pacific Fleet's base at Port Arthur. They sank most of the Russian battleships and cruisers sitting at anchor.

The Japanese would do almost the same thing to the American Navy at Pearl Harbor almost forty years later.

Russia was both embarrassed and incensed. The Russians then sent their European fleet on an around-the-world cruise to face the Japanese Navy. This bizarre voyage had the Russian fleet sailing all the way around Africa and Asia. The Russian ships were so loaded down with coal that the crews had no quarters to sleep in. The Russian admiral in charge of the fleet died along the way. The fleet showed up in the combat zone with the dead admiral in a coffin on the bridge of his flagship. The Japanese then proceeded to sink these ships, too.

The Japanese landed a large army in Korea. Part of this army besieged the Russian harbor at Port Arthur. The rest of the Japanese Army marched into northern China. There, they fought a number of battles with the Russians. These were huge battles. Each side in these battles had hundreds of thousands of soldiers. Both sides suffered huge numbers of dead and wounded. The war ended in 1905 with Japan holding a lot of new territory but with both sides exhausted.

Both the Russians and the Japanese used the latest advances in military technology in their war. These new weapons caused the high casualty rates. Both armies used machine guns and the latest rapid-fire artillery. The Japanese used huge German-made siege guns against the Russian forts during the siege of Port Arthur. All of the weapons that surprised most of Europe at the start of World War I were used. All of the great powers had military observers there watching these weapons in action almost a decade before war started in Europe. Obviously, the Russian military did more than just observe. It got first-hand experience in the effects of these new weapons.

Failure to Adapt

Unfortunately, the Russian military did not learn anything from its defeat by the supposedly backward Japanese. The main reasons for this were the prevailing attitudes of Russian military leaders. The opinions and actions of the Russian Minister for War were the worst of the lot.

From 1909 until 1915, General Vladimir Sukhomlinov was the Russian Minister of War. He was a cavalry officer in Russia's war with Turkey in the 1870s. Sukhomlinov received Russia's highest military honors for great personal bravery against the Turks. Sukhomlinov decided that he knew everything that there was to know about warfare. He based his opinions on his personal experiences. He used his decorations, record, and position as justification for his opinions. He simply believed that he knew it all. He was extremely proud of the fact that he did nothing to expand or increase his knowledge.

Sukhomlinov thwarted any attempts at military reform after Russia's disastrous war with Japan. He saw to it that any type of commission looking into the military would be under his control. This way, he could stop the commission from doing anything. He fired people for teaching modern theories at the army's officer schools. He stopped any attempts to improve the army's equipment.

Why did Sukhomlinov stop any and all reforms? The reason is that any reform, any change in the operating principles of the Russian Army, would mean that Sukhomlinov was wrong. Reforms would mean the opinions he had from a war now thirty years in the past were invalid. He personally believed that you won wars by close combat, using the cavalry saber and the infantry bayonet. Reforms would mean that these were now methods of the past. Reforms were a threat to him and his beliefs. Most importantly of all, they could mean that his leadership was no longer needed or desired. Sukhomlinov was just not going to let that happen.

Sukhomlinov refused to accept the lessons of the reality of modern war. He totally rejected the direct experience of the Russian Army in the war with Japan. He did everything he could to move the Russian military away from reality and back into the martial myths of his youth. Under Sukhomlinov's leadership, Russia produced few modern artillery pieces for her army. Even these few had sparse ammunition. When war came, each German howitzer would typically fire a hundred shells a day in combat. Russian artillery ammunition was in such short supply that Russian troops would actually start applauding in the trenches when their own guns managed to fire a shell or two back in response. Sukhomlinov successfully forced the Russian Army to stay wedded to the practices he believed in. The Russians in 1914 had no other choice but to use the saber and the bayonet. Nothing else was available.

ANALOGY 1: THE NEED TO CONTINUALLY LEARN

Sukhomlinov was a leader who refused to change his fundamental beliefs. There are plenty of such poor leaders even today. These people will not change their beliefs even when there is direct evidence that those beliefs are wrong. They refuse to alter their thinking even after their erroneous beliefs have led to failure. These thick-headed know-it-alls are unwilling to learn or adapt to changing realities. They obstinately base all of their decisions on personal experiences, which are of a limited scope. They steadfastly cling to outmoded ideas because they are absolutely convinced that these limited experiences provide them with everything they need to know about the business. To make things even worse, these leaders brook no dissent. They do everything they can to remove people who have different opinions and new ideas. Innovation and improvements are effectively stifled.

The primary role of any leader is to be out in front, to lead in new directions. To do this, you have to be willing to change your beliefs and opinions. Above all, you must be willing to learn and have the skills to do so. Constantly seek out information on what is really going on at the front lines of your business. Stay informed about what is working or not working for your organization. This knowledge is crucial. Make sure you have it.

A wise old general with combat experience in three wars once gave a seminar on leadership after his retirement. He described what it was that made someone an outstanding success as a combat leader. He stated that the best officers were not the most physically imposing. They were not the ones that were full of bravado. Physical courage, while important, was not the most important thing. Neither was intelligence. At this point no one in his audience had a clue as to what the trait was that was so critical to successful leadership in the most stressful situation known to man.

Finally, the general made his point. The most important ability for success in leadership is the ability to learn. The best leaders in combat are the ones who go around talking to others about what had happened. They are intensely interested in other's experiences. They are always trying to find out what works and what doesn't. They are always interested in finding out which tactics are the most successful in different situations, what weapons are the most effective, what little tricks the enemy seems to fall for, and so on. They are the ones who are always trying to learn new things from any and every source they can uncover. Exceptional leaders like this are not solitary learners, they share their insights and knowledge with as many as will listen.

It is perfectly all right for you to have strong views and opinions. For a good leader, it is both necessary and expected. But you should always be willing to change those views and opinions, no matter what they are, and no matter who else out there has them. You need to change those views when evidence comes to light that they are leading the organization astray, away from optimal performance. Constantly look for information yourself that your views and opinions might be wrong. Continually look at information about what is working for the organization and what is not. Be willing to make changes in direction or operational philosophy. Be willing to make any necessary changes to improve your organization's situation.

Leaders who fail to take this course, who fail to learn, endanger the very organization they lead. They are sure to kill it if they get rid of people with differing opinions and ideas. Getting rid of non-like-minded people destroys the organization's ability to improve itself. These people are your future innovators. They are the ones who allow the organization to adopt new and different methods, practices, and strategies. If these people are jettisoned or regularly ignored, your company will be unable to cope with competitors who are improving and dealing with changes in the business environment.

The Russian Plan

Russia's plans at the onset of war in 1914 revolved around helping its allies. Russia's main allies were France and Serbia. Russia regarded Serbia as a young child needing the protection of a great power to survive. Serbians are ethnically Slavic, and Russia saw herself as the great protector of all Slavs. Anything or anyone threatening Serbia would have to deal with Russia. Russia also had commitments to France. Russia had promised the French to threaten Germany from the east should war start. Russia was grateful for France's patronage and wanted to show that she was a worthwhile ally. In the fall of 1914, Russia would make dramatic moves to help both of her allies.

To help France, Russia planned a two-pronged invasion of the German province of East Prussia. This territory of Germany stuck way out from the heart of Germany across the north of Poland, which was actually part of Russia at the time. From Russian Poland, it was possible to move into East Prussia from both the west and the south. Russia planned to move armies from each direction into this vulnerable part of Germany. These Russian armies would surround any German forces in the province, cut it off from the rest of Germany, and conquer it. The intended consequence of this plan was to force the Germans to take forces away from their invasion of France to deal with the Russian invasion of East Prussia.

Most of the Russian forces that would participate in the East Prussian invasion had to move by train to their jumping-off points along the border with Germany. The Russian rail system of the time was not very extensive, especially when compared to those in western European countries. The Russians did not have anywhere near the numbers of trains and railway cars needed to move the masses of Russian soldiers quickly to the German border. Their trains would have to make multiple trips from the country's vast interior to the border and then back again to pick up the next group. Because of these constraints, everyone believed it would take quite some time before Russia could begin any offensive operations. This is one of the German views that led them to go with an "attack France first" strategy. The German Schlieffen Plan counted on knocking off France before Russia could do anything that would pose a serious threat to eastern Germany.

France knew that she was Germany's primary military target. This is why an alliance with Russia was such a godsend for France. France pleaded with the Russians to attack Germany no later than two weeks after war started. France knew Russia would probably not be ready by this time, but she wanted Russia to move with whatever was available. Any Russian pressure on Germany would assist the French.

Russia wanted very badly to please France. Russia needed to show she was a worthy ally. She also wanted to show herself capable of quickly conducting successful military operations. Russia did not want a reputation as lumbering and incompetent. Russia also needed to recover from the bad press and humiliation due to her failures fighting Japan. All of these pressures led Russia to agree to French requests for quick operations against Germany. The Russians assembled two armies for a rapid invasion of German territory. A third army would follow them to reinforce the effort.

The Russian First and Second Armies would invade East Prussia. The First Army would advance on the German province from the west, starting from the area around Kovno. The Second Army would advance on East Prussia from the south, moving north from Warsaw. Both armies were under the command of the higher Northwest Front Headquarters.

The Russians would invade East Prussia with twice the strength the Germans had to defend it. Each of the two Russian armies was as strong as the total of defending Germans. This meant the Germans could easily hold off one of the two Russian armies. They could not hold off both of them at the same time. This is why Russian plans called for the two armies invading East Prussia to cooperate closely, coordinating their efforts as they moved forward. In order to be victorious, the Russians needed to ensure the German forces in East Prussia would have to simultaneously deal with both prongs of their advance. If the Germans massed against one of the Russian armies, the other was to move quickly against the German rear.

The Commanders

The two Russian Army Commanders were General Paul Rennenkampf and General Alexander Samsonov. Rennenkampf commanded the Russian First Army while Samsanov commanded the Second Army. The two disliked each other immensely. During the Russo-Japanese War, the two got into a fistfight at a railroad station after a heated argument. Samsanov evidently accused Rennenkampf of failing to come to the aid of his command. Samsonov felt that Rennenkampf stood idly by with his command while Samsonov's units were under heavy attack.

Neither skill nor ability led to the appointment of either Rennenkampf or Samsonov to army level command. Both reached their positions due to machinations commonly referred to as "office politics." Both men had experience in the war with Japan, yet neither had distinguished themselves in any way. Getting command of a Russian Army depended in large part on how much influence you had in the Tsar's court. You had to host parties. You had to do favors for those in the court. The Tsar needed to see you and know your name. He had to like you. His wife had to like you. The higher your standing in court, the higher the likelihood of getting the desired command.

ANALOGY 2: POLITICAL PROMOTIONS

The business world is no stranger to politically-based promotions. It has always been this way. Businesses fail when there are too many political promotions. Your company will have this problem if it fails to have good leadership selection systems. The performance of any company will decline as people are promoted for political reasons rather than for performance. Political promotions ensure that fewer people with good leadership actually get ahead in a company. Political promotions have a telling and lasting negative effect on any organization.

It is almost impossible for an organization to correct its course once it starts down the path of politically based promotions. Very quickly, masters at office politics will rise to the highest levels. They will cement in place the accession process that got them to the top. They are not going to change it. They will not admit they got to the top not due to ability, but due to courtier-like behavior. To change the system, they would have to admit that the current system, the way they got to the top, is broken, and that maybe they should not be there. This is not going to happen. Soon, all the mid-level positions are filled with those who get ahead by "sucking up," too. When you remove performance criteria from the promotion process, the performance of the entire organization will suffer.

Fortunately, there is an alternative to this system. It is the entrepreneurial system. It is the opportunity for people to go off and start their own businesses. One of the main reasons they do so is that they don't want to put up with office politics. This is how a lot of businesses lose their best and brightest.

Organizations with a strong culture of office politics will lose their best performers. Realizing that they can't get ahead, even though they are outperforming those who are moving up, the bypassed performers will leave. Either they will go to the competition, or they will start their own companies. The companies they start usually make mincemeat of their former employers.

> Organizations that want to ensure they have the best possible leaders need to take a long hard look at their succession planning and leadership selection processes. This usually entails making changes, often drastic ones, to ensure that skill and ability are indeed the criteria for promotion. This means letting go of people in senior positions without these skills. It means letting go of the people who got ahead in the old world of office politics. The alternative is to end up with a lot of Rennenkampfs and Samsonovs running things in the company. This is not a good thing.

The Russians made a critical mistake by picking two generals with more in the way of political than military skills to lead the armies invading Germany. To make matters even worse, they picked two generals who had a history of not getting along. The fight in the railroad station was a dramatic illustration of their relationship. Their inability to work together would certainly influence the outcome of any plan involving cooperation. The Russian plan called for just such an effort. The Russian First and Second Armies needed to coordinate their combined invasion of East Prussia. You would think this would have influenced leadership selection for these important commands. It did not.

The Russian First Army, based around Kovno, was much closer to the heartland of Russia than the Second Army, which would operate out of Warsaw. This shorter distance meant that the Russian rail system would complete the movement of troops and supplies to the First Army much faster than it could for the Second Army. This in turn meant Rennenkampf's command could begin operations well before Samsonov's army was ready to move forward. This was the start of the problems in coordinating efforts between the two armies.

Moving into Germany

Rennenkampf did not wait for Samsonov's army to assemble. He marched off towards East Prussia as soon as he could. Maybe he was trying to grab the rewards of conquering the Germans without assistance. Maybe he wanted to show up Samsonov. Whatever the case, he moved alone. The Germans initially only had to deal with the threat of Rennenkampf's army. Not surprisingly, the Germans met the Russian First Army shortly after it crossed the border. A heated battle took place near the village of Gumbinnen. Neither side made much headway against the other. It was a draw, but it brought the Russian First Army to a standstill. [Fig 19]

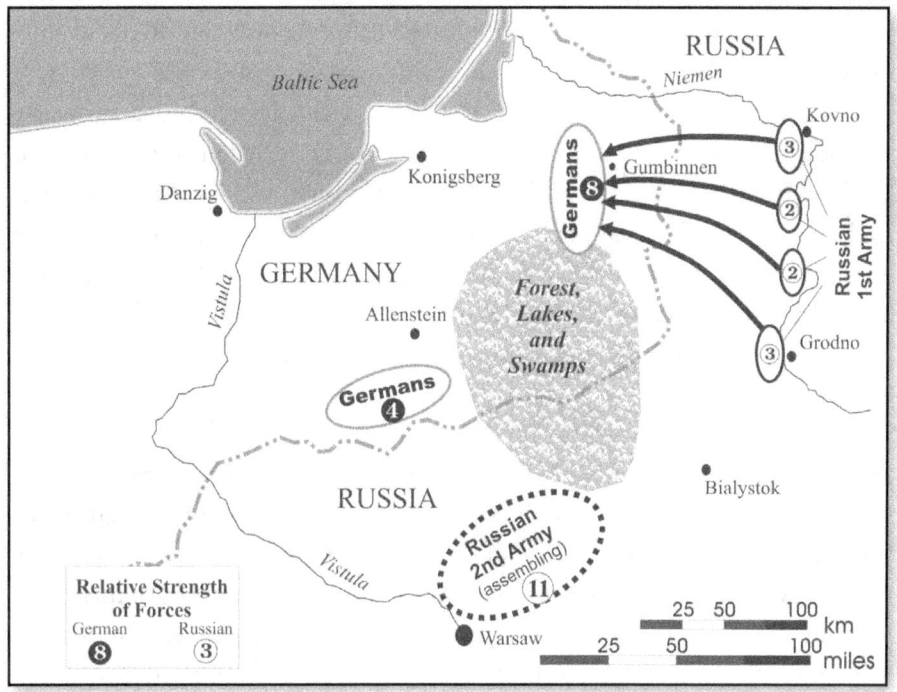

Figure 19. Situation in East Prussia 20 August 1914

Rennenkampf and Samsonov had a mutual boss, General Jilinski, commander of the Northwest Front. When Rennenkampf began his march, Samsonov began to get all kinds of pressure from Jilinski to start his army marching north from Warsaw. Samsonov had only just arrived at his headquarters. He was new to the command of the Second Army. He got the job just as the war started. He had no personal relationship with his staff. He first met them when he got off the train in Warsaw. The Second Army was in the later stages of just getting off the trains from Russia themselves. The army had not yet collected all the supplies it would need to invade Germany. The Second Army was still preparing for the march north when Samsonov started to get messages from Jilinski telling him to hurry up.

Samsonov wanted to show he could get the job done. He didn't want Rennenkampf to show him up. He wasn't going to take blame for not supporting

Rennenkampf. He was not going to allow Rennenkampf to complain about a lack of support. He also wanted the Russian plans to succeed and knew this required coordinated action between the two armies. So Samsonov started to move his Second Army two days after Rennenkampf moved out. Rennenkampf started his march with a prepared army. Samsonov's army was not.

Samsonov left Warsaw before his army had enough food, enough water, or enough ammunition. On top of this, there were inadequate arrangements for sending these things forward from Warsaw. Everyone, including the supply and support officers who could make such arrangements, left on the march for Germany. There were more problems than just the lack of basic commodities. There was a lack of codebooks and a shortage of telegraph wire. New to command, Samsonov did not have time to develop a good work relationship with his staff.

It is important to move quickly. You just cannot move too rashly. Samsonov's haste is an example of moving too quickly, before meeting the basic requirements of the endeavor. This was not a beginner's mistake. Samsonov and his staff all had long experience in the army. Most of them had combat experience in the Russo-Japanese war. They all knew how much food, water, and ammunition their army would need, given how big the army was, how far it was planning to move, and how much action it would probably see. The pre-war plans contained such estimates. The leadership knew what was needed. They just decided to move out and handle things as they went along.

Many of the people on Samsonov's staff must have realized how unprepared the Second Army was. Someone needed to point this out, even if doing so would have created a stir. In the end, it was Samsonov's decision on when to move out. Yet his staff was responsible for pointing out issues, concerns, and potential problems. They needed to inform their commander of the probable result if they left their bases before they were adequately prepared.

There is a difference between adequately prepared and fully prepared, a big difference. No army is ever fully prepared. You cannot wait until your organization is fully prepared to do something. But you do have to be adequately prepared. Samsonov's army was nowhere near adequately prepared to move, let alone face a competent foe. It did not even have the supplies it needed to sustain itself in the field, let alone fight battles. The Russian Second Army was short of water and food before it even crossed the German border.

Samsonov pushed his men and horses forward as fast as they could go. He was trying to get his army into position as quickly as possible to execute his part of the plan. Samsonov knew his army was supposed to move into East Prussia simultaneously with Rennenkampf's. Rennenkampf had moved without waiting for Samsonov. Then Samsonov moved forward without adequate provisions. The lack of coordination between the two army commanders was about to have disastrous consequences.

Rennenkampf's First Army attacked German positions inside Germany before Samsonov crossed the border. Rennenkampf was fighting all of the Germans in East Prussia because Samsonov's Second Army was not yet a threat to them. The lack of coordination between the two Russian armies had allowed the Germans to mass against a single threat.

Samsonov was trying hard to get into Germany while the German Army was dealing with Rennenkampf. He knew this would give him a chance at success. But when he crossed the border, his army was totally exhausted, unfed, short of water, and without adequate stocks of ammunition. Samsonov had taken huge risks to try to catch up with Rennenkampf. He was gambling that he could outmaneuver the enemy before his own problems would become overwhelming.

ANALOGY 3: UNACCEPTABLE RISK

You need to learn and master the art of knowing when to take risks and when not to. Risk taking is an art because there are neither formulas nor rules that will adequately forecast when you should or should not take a risk. But there are guidelines. One of these guidelines is risk return. You don't gamble a million dollars if you have a 50 percent chance of gaining a hundred thousand versus a 50 percent chance of losing everything. This gamble is not worth the risk. Samsonov was gambling the existence of his army against forcing the Germans to abandon a significant portion of East Prussia. The risk he was taking was far more significant than the potential pay out.

The German Trap

Rennenkampf's army stopped to reorganize and resupply after fighting the Germans at Gumbinnen. While the Russian First Army rested, the German forces opposing it seemed to melt away. Rennenkampf was convinced he had won a great victory, and that the Germans were running away from him as fast as their legs could carry them. In reality, the Germans had all left to redeploy to fight the Russian Second Army, and not just to stop it; they moved to encircle and annihilate Samsonov's army.

> ## ANALOGY 4: LETTING OTHERS FEND FOR THEMSELVES
>
> Do business leaders in similar situations act the same way? Of course they do. What we see here is too common. An example in a business environment might involve two department heads who dislike each other. One of these department heads sees the other in a very difficult situation. They say to themselves, "That's not my problem, he got himself into this trouble, let's see him get out of it." The department head not in trouble makes no effort to put their resources at risk to help another part of the business, one that is in deep trouble. The point is that the department head in this business example is perfectly willing to see part of the business go down the drain, just for the satisfaction of seeing someone they dislike fail. They just don't understand that when part of the business fails, there are serious negative consequences for everyone in that business.
>
> Once again, it is the case of placing personal goals (in this case, vendettas) above the needs of the organization. Rennenkampf was out to increase his personal glory. It seems he did not want his peer to succeed. Leaders who primarily seek personal laurels are the bane of the very organizations they lead. More often than not, the organization itself will fail while the leader concerns themselves with their own personal success.

The Germans could quickly redeploy against Samsonov's army because of the extensive railway system in East Prussia. While Rennenkampf's soldiers rested, the Germans opposing them were getting on trains to go and deal with Samsonov's army. The trains dropped off the Germans at assembly areas in the forest to the left and right of the Russian Second Army's line of march into East Prussia. The trap was sprung when Samsonov's army ran into a screen of Germans to their front. As the Russians reacted to the contact with the enemy

The Russian Steamroller

in front of them, the Germans massed on both sides of the Russian Army and attacked.

It seems that Rennenkampf couldn't have cared less about what happened to Samsonov and the Second Army. Rennenkampf made no efforts to come to his partner's aide, even though Samsonov's forces were less than a hundred miles away from his forward units. Almost any type of effort on Rennenkampf's part would have caused the Germans to back away from the risk they were taking in massing solely against Samsonov. Once again, there was no coordination of Russian efforts, no mutual support.

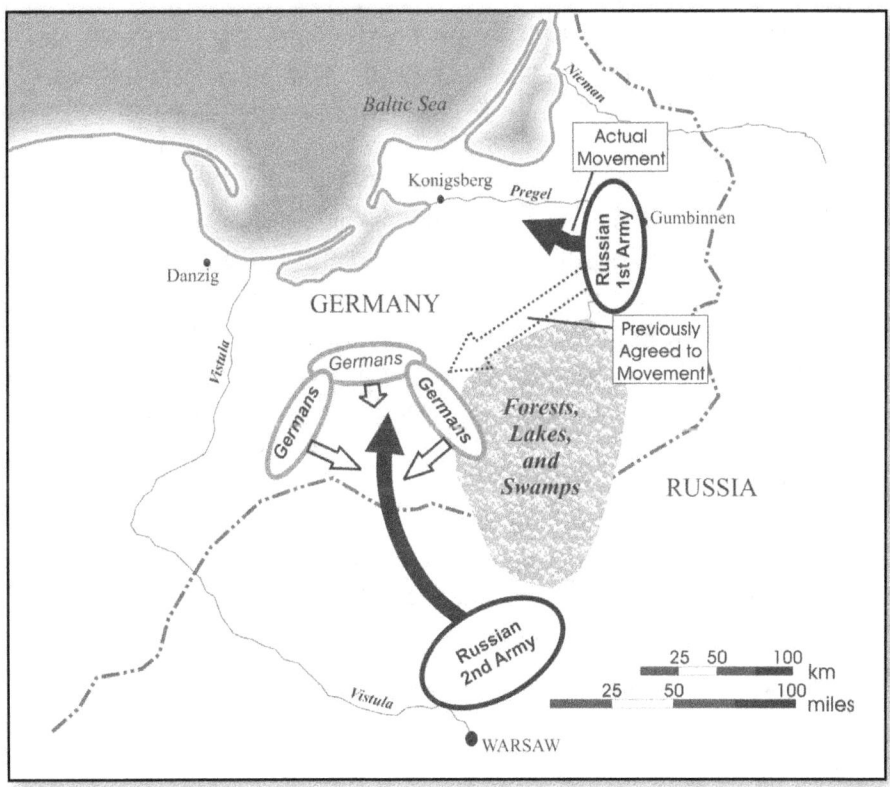

Figure 20. Tannenberg and Russian 1st Army

German movements placed Samsonov's army in mortal danger. Rennenkampf and his army did not keep pressure on the Germans, allowing them to redeploy against Samsonov. Rennenkampf felt he had already completed his part of the plan. He had advanced into Germany and, in his opinion, had beaten their army.

The original Russian plan called for him to link up with Samsonov so that the two together could move to threaten Berlin. Instead, Rennenkampf waited for a while to resupply and rest his army. Then he started to slowly move towards the historic German fortress of Konigsberg, the capital of East Prussia. This was in the opposite direction from Samsonov and his now-surrounded army. In all likelihood, Rennenkampf was going after a prize that he alone could claim. [fig 20]

ANALOGY 5: EXPLOITING SUCCESS

There is always something that is not perfect about your group's situation. There is always something else you could use. You can always use more time to prepare for the next task. Waiting for these things carries its own cost. Golden opportunities are very fleeting. When you wait until you are fully prepared, the opportunity may no longer exist. The astounding success that immediate action might have produced slips out of sight. That is precisely what happened to Rennenkampf.

Don't stop or even slow down when you are winning. Use any capacity you still have left to make further progress. Exploit success. It is the best time to be even more successful. If you hesitate after making headway, you may even lose what you just gained. Stopping to consolidate your gains gives the opposition time. They can use this time as breathing space to lick their wounds and to get ready for your next move, or they may organize their own counter move and take back what they just lost to you. You must constantly maintain pressure on the opposition, or they will come back at you somewhere that you are weak. If you don't, you will end up with little more than the momentary success Rennenkampf and his army had.

Rennenkampf's army was no help to their compatriots while the Germans destroyed Samsonov's command. In the aftermath, there were all kinds of excuses about why the First Army did little to help the Second. One excuse was they needed to rest after the battle at Gumbinnen. Another stated the First Army needed to bring up supplies and replace the ammunition it had expended. Yet another was that it needed time to reorganize the fighting units bloodied in the Gumbinnen battle. But the bottom line was that Rennenkampf risked nothing to assist Samsonov. He looked only towards the security of his own force and his own objectives, even as messages about Samsonov's predicament started pouring in. He was out to help himself, not his country, nor his fellow Russians.

The very things Rennenkampf said he needed were things his opponents, the German Army in East Prussia, were doing without. Rennenkampf may have failed to see that he was in at least as good shape as his opponents. But Rennenkampf really did think he had severely beaten his foes. As a result, he decided to wait for the additional supplies and rest his men when he thought the enemy was demoralized and in disarray. He rested on what turned out to be a temporary success. He was waiting for near optimal conditions before getting aggressive again. He failed to exploit his success by pursuing the Germans. As a result, he missed the opportunity to hit the Germans from the rear while they moved against Samsonov. This was the very thing that the Russian war plan required him to do. He lost the chance by a combination of hesitance and lack of concern for Samsonov. The Russians would rarely see such an opportunity again.

Meanwhile, at Headquarters

Rennenkampf and Samsonov were not the only ones responsible for the Russian disaster in East Prussia. Both men had the same boss, General Jilinski. Jilinski was the commander of the Northwest Front, which controlled both the Russian First and Second Armies. Jilinski was not some bureaucrat; he had command authority over both Rennenkampf and Samsonov. Both Army Commanders needed his permission to do what they did. In Samsonov's case, a lot of what he did was merely to follow Jilinski's orders.

Jilinski knew that his two subordinates did not get along. He didn't do anything about this. There were no meetings or conferences involving the three of them before the campaign started. Nor were there conferences after the war started either. The Russian Second Army had to wait for its commander to arrive, but it would not have been much of an additional delay for Jilinski to have Samsonov stop to meet with him and Rennenkampf before things got underway.

No type of long distance communication—not letters, not phone calls, not e-mails, not video-conferencing—are an adequate substitute for face-to-face meetings, especially not in the situation described here, with two large armies about to invade a competently defended foreign country. In retrospect, it is easy to see that Rennenkampf and Samsonov had fundamentally different views about the planned campaign. Jilinski made no effort to ensure alignment between his subordinates. He therefore bears a lot of responsibility for the lack of cooperation between Rennenkampf and Samsonov.

Jilinski wanted the two prongs of the coordinated invasion to enter Germany at the same time, which was the essence of the Russian plan. When Rennenkampf set out, Jilinski focused all of his efforts on getting Samsonov to hurry. He wanted Samsonov and Rennenkampf in their proper positions, with each presenting a similar and simultaneous threat to the Germans. At one point Jilinski even accused Samsonov of cowardice for not wanting to move farther and faster. Yet when Rennenkampf stopped his army after Gumbinnen, Jilinski did almost nothing. He did not put similar pressure on Rennenkampf to help Samsonov's imperiled army.

> ## ANALOGY 6: SELF-FULLFILLING PROPHECY
>
> Jilinski's lack of faith in Samsonov became a self-fulfilling prophecy. The leader had no faith in the subordinate. The leader expected him to fail. He did nothing to help out the subordinate, viewing him and his efforts as some kind of lost cause. And guess what? That is exactly what happened.
>
> Every leader encounters the situation of getting a subordinate they did not choose and in whom they initially have little faith. But you must not be like Jilinski. Find out what the capabilities of the person really are. Find out what the situation for this person really is. Determine realistic goals for the person and coach and help them to achieve those goals.

Jilinski's actions show he had little, if any, faith in Samsonov. His lack of faith may have been due to Samsonov's lack of army-level command experience. It may have been due to Samsonov just getting the command of the Second Army right as war broke out. It is highly likely that Jilinski did not approve of the choice of Samsonov as the Second Army's commander. The result certainly was that Jilinski did not think that Samsonov could do a good job. Because Jilinski had no faith in Samsonov, he gave him no support. He continually hounded Samsonov. Jilinski never asked Rennenkampf to slow down as he approached the German border. He blamed Samsonov for being late. He never looked into the difficulties Samsonov had prior to setting off. He just assumed that Samsonov was slow because he was incompetent. So Jilinski just sent him a lot of messages saying things like "Get on the ball," "Hurry it up down there; what is taking so long?" and "Why are you not on schedule while the other army is?"

Jilinski may have felt saddled with Samsonov. He could not fire Samsonov. After all, the Tsar appointed Samsonov to command the Second Army. Jilinski could not fire someone the Tsar had promoted, certainly not without a really good reason. Jilinski realized he was stuck with Samsonov. In any case, that was Jilinski's view of the situation.

> ## ANALOGY 7: ADJUSTMENT
>
> Always focus on success. Don't get mired down by trying to replace subordinates right away. Never write off a group or project just because of the involvement of a subordinate you don't like. Do whatever you can to assist that group or project to be successful. This may mean going down there and helping out. It may mean finding ways of providing them with additional resources. It might entail revising plans and schedules based on current capabilities. Remember that your involvement and help is much better than just sending off e-mails telling people to hurry up. Look at what happened to Jilinski's command. Don't repeat his mistakes. Your job is to succeed, not place blame for failure.

The Russians gave the Germans a huge edge in the campaign in East Prussia. The Germans had near-perfect intelligence. They knew exactly what the Russians were doing. The Russians themselves were the source of the German information. In their haste to move out of Warsaw, the Russian Second Army had not arranged for enough telegraph wire to connect their headquarters with subordinate units in the field. The lack of telegraph wire meant they had only two options for communication. They could either use couriers (a very slow and haphazard method), or they could use the newly fielded radios. They opted for the radios. The next problem was the Russians didn't print and distribute enough code books. Instead of coding messages, all of their radio traffic was uncoded, completely in the clear. All the Germans had to do to find out what the Russians were doing was to turn on the radio and have someone who spoke Russian listen in.

Rennenkampf's army also talked to Samsonov's in the clear over the radio. By listening in, the Germans knew that Rennenkampf had stopped after the initial fight at Gumbinnen. They knew that he intended to wait for his army to rest and resupply before moving out again. This told the Germans that they could redeploy against Samsonov while Rennenkampf's army was resting. They knew that Rennenkampf would not attack their rear while they fought Samsonov. They abandoned their positions in front of Rennenkampf's army and moved to surround Samsonov's.

The Germans moved into a semicircle around Samsonov's line of march. They waited for Samsonov's army to move into their trap. Samsonov had some inkling of the danger his army was moving into. Some of his units reported contact with German units that Russian intelligence said were opposing Rennenkampf. Yet Samsonov continued the forward movement of his army, moving them deeper into the German trap. He was trying to make up for lost time, to get the Russian Second Army he commanded back onto schedule. Samsonov received continual pressure from Jilinski to keep pressing forward and to hurry up about it. Samsonov moved his army right into the jaws of the German trap.

The Disaster Unfolds

The Germans surrounded the majority of Samsonov's army. As the magnitude of the calamity became clear, Samsonov left his headquarters. He went out to lead cavalry at the front. This left his army without leadership when it needed it most. Samsonov was a senior cavalry officer before he took command of the Second Army. He had a lot of experience with the cavalry. He was comfortable with them. Samsonov reverted to being a cavalry commander because that is what he was familiar doing. The pressure of the crisis caused him to regress to a more comfortable role. His surrounded army became leaderless as a result.

The units of Samsonov's Second Army were in dire straits within a few days of being surrounded. They were out of food and ammunition. They had no place to fall back to when the Germans continued their attacks. The surrounded units began to surrender. The Germans took the bulk of Samsonov's army prisoner. Tannenberg was the name chosen by the Germans for this crushing victory. As a footnote, Samsonov and some companions tried to sneak through German lines. During the night, Samsonov sneaked off from the group and shot himself.

The Russian Steamroller

> ## ANALOGY 8: REGRESSION IN CRISIS
>
> In a crisis where the solution is unclear, it is all too easy for a weak leader to regress into a more familiar role. Someone who is insecure in their position can very easily revert to dealing only with what they are comfortable with. These people start micromanaging the familiar details. They ignore or put off the big issues needing their attention. They become deeply involved in the minutia of the area they are comfortable in. This behavior becomes even more damaging if there is a crisis regarding ignored issues. The problems escalate while they continue to pour their energy into dealing with minor issues, things best left to subordinates.
>
> You have to learn to let go of things when you move to positions of greater responsibility. You must allow others to learn and do what you used to. You have to do this even when the person who takes on your old job is not yet as good at doing it as you were. Spend some time helping the new person out, but don't allow this activity to eclipse your focus on your new role. Give up the old responsibilities and concentrate on the new and larger ones. If you don't, it would be better for everyone if you just stayed in the old job.

With the threat of Samsonov's army totally gone, the Germans now turned their attention back to Rennenkampf. The German forces in East Prussia redeployed. Once more, they faced the Russian First Army to the east. In another large battle, the Germans pushed this Russian Army out of German territory, too. The Germans came close to surrounding the Russian First Army as well, but Rennenkampf pulled out in time to avoid that fate. The Germans did not annihilate Rennenkampf's army like Samsonov's. But they did inflict enough losses on the Russian First Army that it would not threaten them again for quite some time.

The disastrous Russian campaign into East Prussia did have some positive results. The faster-than-expected operations of the Russian armies did surprise the Germans. The invasion of East Prussia caused widespread panic in the province. This panic, in turn, put pressure on the leaders of the German Army to do something. They responded by taking considerable forces out of the fight in France to send as reinforcements to East Prussia. The German forces sent came out of the Schlieffen Plan's right wing. As a result, they were not present during the Battle of the Marne outside Paris, the battle that determined the fate of the German campaign against France. The loss of these units to the east was a significant factor in the German defeat in France. So while the Russian Second Army was lost and the Russian First Army badly mauled, their actions did contribute to saving France. But then, the Russians could have achieved these results without throwing away a couple of armies.

CONCLUSIONS

This chapter explored the bold Russian plan to conquer East Prussia at the start of World War I. The Russians moved before they were ready. A host of mistakes placed the Russians in a precarious situation. The lack of coordination between their armies allowed the Germans to defeat one Russian Army while ignoring the other. The result was catastrophe for the Russian armies. The Russian experience has numerous analogies to the world of modern business. The most important lessons include:

- **The most important leadership attribute**
  Being in charge does not mean that you know everything. It should mean that you are willing to learn everything you need to. You must be willing to question what is or is not working for the organization and change whatever is not working. You need to do this even when you need to change policies, procedures, and practices that you yourself championed in the past.
  You must constantly learn. You must learn about what is and what is not producing success. You must adopt practices that are productive and jettison those who are not. You must seek out this kind of information from all sources. Talk to people in the organization. Talk to customers and suppliers. Gather information from every angle. You have to be willing to change your mind when what you learn is contrary to what you may have believed in the past.

- **Avoiding the negative effects of office politics**
  Any organization that wants to succeed must have a valid leadership selection system. This system must promote those who have needed skills and abilities. Any organization that selects leaders through office politics is doomed. Once office politics plays a dominant role in leadership decisions, there is little hope of making a turnaround.

- **Improving working relationships between executives**
  Too often, the leaders of a company forget who the enemy is. Rather than focus on beating the competition in the marketplace, they concern themselves with intrigues against colleagues in their own company. It

is crucial that every part of the company concerns itself with what is good for the corporate whole, even if some parts must make temporary sacrifices. The common good of the business is paramount. The idea of helping each other out, no matter what personal differences may exist, must override petty notions and concerns.

- **Risk management guidelines**
  There is always a trade-off between taking action now and taking action later, when you are better prepared. You must carefully consider both the advantages and possible problems of acting now, and those associated with postponing action until better conditions exist. Yet remember to ensure at least the minimum level of preparation before taking action. Understand what the minimum requirements are before engaging in major activities.

- **Exploiting success**
  Most organizations do not enjoy the success they could. The reason they don't is that the minute they reach a level where they are comfortable, they begin to adopt very risk-averse policies and practices. They fail to exploit the breakthrough achievements they just made. They stop being as aggressive as they used to be. They stop taking as much risk. Doing this gives their competition time to catch their breath and launch their own counteroffensive.

- **Preventing predestined failures**
  When you expect someone to fail, they are going to live up to your expectations. You need to take action up front to help subordinates. You cannot leave them to their own devices or think that additional pressure from you is going to produce the results you want. All leaders must act as coaches and mentors of their underlings. If you treat someone as a failure, then that's what they'll be.

- **Avoiding regressive behavior during crisis**
  People in crisis situations tend to regress into doing things they are comfortable with. It is common for leaders to have responsibility over things they may not be fully comfortable with. The temptation is to

avoid the new and uncomfortable tasks and deal only with the familiar things managed in the past.

You must fully embrace the responsibilities of any new role. Train subordinates to take over the old tasks. Focus on the new larger picture, and learn to leave the old details to others.

ACTION FILE

HOW TO PROMOTE REAL RISK TAKING

 BAD IDEA #1—Demand strict adherence to the plan.
Many organizations say that they want people who show initiative and who are not afraid to take risks. Some of these companies then plan things out to the last detail and expect their people to follow the plan to the letter. In so doing, people are straight jacketed into acting and performing only in certain ways. This method of planning and execution is tantamount to the centralized planning of failed communist systems. Why would you want your organization to follow this model?

The answer why many do so is rather basic. The people in the organization are not trusted to make decisions or to take action on their own. For some reason, those in charge in these cases feel most are either unable or unwilling to do anything that isn't spelled out for them in excruciating detail.

Such demands for strict adherence to plans fly in the face of a fundamental truth. This truth states, "No plan survives contact with the enemy." What this means is planning cannot take into account what the competitions will do. Nor can it take into account the variables inherent in the external business environment. Plans set in concrete are usually doomed from the start.

Most people on the front lines know this fundamental truth. Yet they will follow plans to the letter if their organization demands such obedience. The vast majority of people do not want to buck the organizational culture. They are not going to do something that will get them into trouble or will put their jobs in jeopardy. They will do what they are told to do, even if this means carrying out plans they know are in the process of failing.

 BAD IDEA #2—Eliminate subordinates who disagree.
People in organizations constantly look for signals that tell them how to get ahead. They look for other signals that tell them what will prevent them from getting ahead, or worse, will get them fired. You can say

whatever you want about how you want risk taking and people showing initiative, but if this does not get you ahead, people will stop paying attention to what you say.

People who take risk and show initiative quite often have opinions that are very different from those of their bosses. Think about this characteristic for a minute. If such people did not have different opinions from their bosses, how would they be taking risk or initiative? If their views were the same as their superior's, they would just be following the bosses' wishes.

Disagreement or differences in opinion do not mean that an individual is insubordinate or trying to undermine the organization. It often means the information they have is different from what their bosses have. This could be because they are having different experiences, or because they possess better first-hand knowledge of what is really going on. In such cases, the true risk taker, the true person of initiative, is going to act on this information. That action is often going to be different from what the superior had originally wanted.

 BAD IDEA #3—Brutally punish failure.

One of the most common ways of stifling innovation, initiative, and risk taking in any organization is to brutally punish failure. Brutal punishment within most organizations includes demotion, lack of advancement, or firing. As already discussed, people are constantly looking at what gets them ahead, and what is going to get them into trouble. Few are willing to do things that could result in such serious consequences.

Let's say that someone in the organization seizes an opportunity, or takes a risk that they honestly believe is in the organization's best interest. They take that risk or initiative and it does not work out. The organization suffers a reverse.

What you do about such a case is going to determine whether your organization will have much initiative or risk taking in the future. If you brutally punish the person that took the risk, you send the signal that only successful risk taking is encouraged. Certain success is not the definition of risk. Risk taking entails a certain amount of failure. If you are not going to tolerate failure, you are not going to see anyone taking risks or showing much initiative. Why should they if there is the possibility of an extreme negative personal outcome?

GOOD IDEA #1—Allow flexibility in achieving goals.

Even though no plan survives contact with the enemy, plans are still very necessary. The most successful plans are flexible enough to allow people some latitude in how to achieve their goals. You need to view plans as a basis for change. They should spell out clear objectives. Your plans should describe desired intermediate objectives, those that show progress towards ultimate objectives. You can describe details of how to achieve these objectives while nothing unexpected happens. But when the plan encounters the unexpected, you need to rely on the initiative of those executing the plan to get past problems and obstacles. The plan needs to allow for flexibility in accomplishing the objectives.

Being flexible also means being willing to jettison a plan anywhere along the way. There are two good reasons for dropping a plan. First, if better opportunities become available than are being pursued by your current plan, why limit your options? If you insist on using your resources to finish with a plan that did not anticipate new opportunities, those opportunities may no longer exist when you are ready to take advantage of them. Second, if your plan at any point appears highly unlikely to succeed, why expend your resources on some folly? Don't just continue with a plan because it is the approved plan. Stop plans that will result in obvious failure.

GOOD IDEA #2—Reward success.

You would think it is obvious that you should reward success. It does not always happen. Think about people who have had success when they have done something their superiors did not ask them to do. Or maybe they were successful by doing something their superiors thought would fail. Such individuals usually don't receive any kind of reward. In fact, many of them end up being brutally punished instead. The reason is simply that the superiors involved did not want to admit either they did not know everything, or that they were wrong.

Those who insist they are never wrong should never lead an organization. You cannot count on such people to reward success and never punish the successful. The human ego prevents many from praising and rewarding others successful in doing something they were convinced would fail. This is no reason to thwart initiative and risk taking in the organization. You need to be able to swallow your pride and admit that someone had a better idea. Their success is indeed the proof. Give them the credit and the reward their success deserves. Actions like this will do wonders for promoting initiative and risk taking within the organization.

GOOD IDEA #3—Allow for some mistakes.

Most people are quite hesitant to take initiative or to take risks. This is because most have the basic belief they will be quickly and severely punished for failure. You have to go out of your way to prove to people that this is not the case. You need to show people that it's not necessarily bad to make mistakes while trying to do the right thing.

You do have to investigate failure. You have to find out not only what happened but why it happened. If someone has encountered a serious problem because they were doing something for the wrong reason (like trying to get ahead at someone else's expense) then you need to take corrective action. But if someone suffered a reverse because they were honestly trying to help the organization be successful, you want to help them learn from their mistakes. You want to do this so you can increase the probability of success the next time they take a risk.

All of this requires the time and effort of the leader. First, there is the time and effort involved in investigating what went wrong and why. Then there is the additional time and effort involved in helping people to learn from their mistakes. Fortunately, these expenditures yield great rewards. Those you work with in this fashion will become valuable contributors to future success. They are deeply indebted to you because you made the effort to help them instead of punish them. Their experience with you will encourage them not only to take risks again when opportunities present themselves, but they will do their utmost to ensure success.

CHAPTER 5

VICTORY IN THE EAST

"Was it that We Won, or that They Lost?"

INTRODUCTION

AT the start of World War I, the vast majority of the German forces invaded Belgium and France. The Germans had only a small army left to defend their eastern border from the Russians. This force was so small that the Germans planned to fight only a delaying action. This small German Eighth Army planned to fall back under the pressure of Russian hordes. The original commander of this army panicked as the Russians invaded. He was sacked. His replacement was a much steadier hand. The Germans stopped retreating. Instead, they aggressively attacked. They even surrounded and annihilated significant Russian forces. The account of this stunning reversal of German fortunes in the east illustrates the following important points:

- Short-term temptations
- Assessing leadership effectiveness
- Studying success
- Adapting practices as conditions change
- Resource hoarding
- Finger-pointing and the blame game

HISTORICAL CASE AND BUSINESS ANALOGIES

Plans versus Reality

In 1914, Germany faced a war on two fronts. To the west was France, with a large and well-trained army. To the east was Russia, a very large, but slower moving foe. The German war plan, the Schlieffen Plan, dealt with the two front problem by concentrating the German Army to quickly knock France out of the war. The Germans did not contemplate offensive action against Russia until after they defeated France. The small German Army along the Russian border was to delay any Russian forces that showed up while the rest of the army crushed France. After defeating France, the Germans planned to send victorious forces from the west to deal with the Russians.

The Schlieffen Plan left only a few German divisions, backed up by local militia, to face the Russians. These forces comprised the German Eighth Army. They occupied the province of East Prussia, which stuck out of the heart of Germany into the east. Russian territory was to the east and south of East Prussia. Schlieffen considered East Prussia indefensible against a determined Russian attack while the German Army was preoccupied with France. The job of the Eighth Army was to defend East Prussia as best they could, while the rest of the army attacked and defeated France.

General Max von Prittwitz commanded the Eighth Army. His appointment was due to his long friendship with the Kaiser and his wife. Just about everyone else, including Moltke, head of the German General Staff, viewed Prittwitz as a bumbling incompetent.

The German Eighth Army based its defensive plans on the geography of East Prussia. They knew that the Russians could easily invade from either the south, the east, or from both directions simultaneously. The area known as the Masurian Lakes separated the two invasion routes from each other. This area was a dense forest with many lakes and swamps. If the Russians invaded from both the south and east at the same time, this difficult terrain would separate their forces. The German plan was to deal with an attack from one direction, while leaving only a small delaying force in the other area. The Germans planned to deal with one threat, then turn and deal with the other. They intended to move back and forth between the invaders until they stopped the Russians, or until continued Russian pressure forced them out of East Prussia.

Before the war, the Germans assumed it would take the Russians quite a while to move their troops from the interior of their vast country to the border and prepare them to invade. The Germans were quite surprised when the Russians showed up much earlier than anticipated. As expected, the Russians invaded East Prussia from two directions at once. The Russian First Army came from the east while the Russian Second Army came up from the south. [Fig 21]

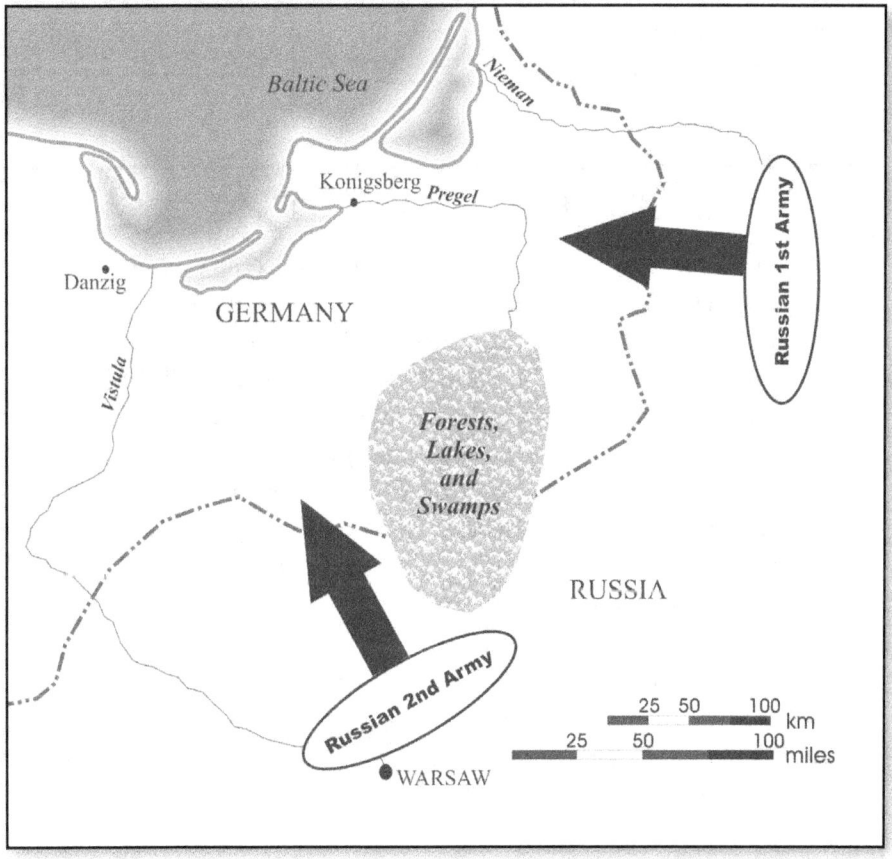

Figure 21. Anticipated Russian Invasion of East Prussia

The Russian First Army was the first to cross the border into East Prussia. According to their plan, the Germans left a small force to guard the southern approach while most of their Eighth Army dealt with the Russians invading from the east. The Germans stopped the eastern Russian advance in a pitched battle around the town of Gumbinnen. The battle was something of a draw, neither side gaining a clear upper hand.

While the Germans were still engaged around Gumbinnen, reports of other Russian movements arrived at the German Eighth Army headquarters. Word came in that the Russian Second Army was at the border on the southern approach. The news caused Prittwitz to panic. He called his boss, Moltke, and told him he was going to quickly abandon the entire province to the Russians. He said he was compelled to abandon East Prussia because his forces were woefully inadequate and that the only hope for the Eighth Army was to retreat behind the wide Vistula River to the west.

ANALOGY 1: SHORT-TERM TEMPTATIONS

Reality puts pressure on people that theoretical plans do not. Here is a typical example. A long-term strategic plan calls for a business to take a serious risk. Everyone sounds brave when they look at projections of short-term losses for the business. But when the short-term losses actually begin to happen, even though anticipated, the leadership has a change of heart. Now they are not so brave. They see real losses actually happening. They panic and make changes to deal with the short-term. They do this by crippling the long-term strategy they agreed to earlier. These actions result in the failure of the long-term strategy, one that could have produced decisive results had it been followed through to completion.

If you accept the risk inherent to a plan, you need to have the guts to hang in there when projected short-term reversals actually happen. There will be all kinds of pressure for you to interfere with the plan and fix the short-term results. The stockholders will want you to. Others in leadership positions will want you to. You cannot give in to the pressure and temptation to make short-term corrections, not if you want the long-term plan to succeed. If you waiver and make significant changes to correct the short-term situation, you will probably ruin the plan's long-term probability of success. You will also show others that you are a coward by panicking or giving in to short-term pressure. Cowards rarely have more than limited success and don't survive very long as leaders.

The Germans had always known the Russians would attack East Prussia from both the east and south at the same time. It was the logical thing for the

Russians to do. The German war plans took this into account. But when this actually happened, the German commander panicked. Instead of the theoretical combat and losses of war games, he was facing the real thing. Now he could only see the jeopardy his army was in and all of the possible negative outcomes.

The Replacements

Moltke had accepted the risk of losing East Prussia in the short-term. He just was not willing to lose it so quickly because the general on the scene panicked. The staff of the German Eighth Army was prepared to carry out the prewar plans of shifting back and forth between the two approaches into East Prussia. The staff thought Prittwitz's desire to pull out was premature. Moltke therefore decided to replace Prittwitz. He needed someone with the fortitude to stick it out in a bad situation, someone who would make the best possible use of available resources, and someone who wouldn't order a retreat across the Vistula River unless all other options had failed.

Such a man, in Moltke's estimation, was available. A senior general named Hindenburg had retired a couple of years before the war. At the start of the war, he sent a letter to Moltke, volunteering his services. Moltke knew Hindenburg personally as a solid soldier who didn't scare easily. Moltke sent Hindenburg word that he needed him.

The command structure of each of the German Armies at this time included two leadership positions. The senior leader was the Army Commander. His responsibility was the big picture. The Army Commander created the goals and operational concepts for the army. He had the final say in any decisions regarding the Army's operations. The second in command was the Chief of Staff. He aided the commander in fulfilling his responsibilities. The Chief of Staff's role was to preside over the detailed planning to achieve the commander's goals. He advised the commander on the feasibility of different courses of action. He proposed specific operations to the commander. The Chief of Staff gave the Army Commander options, and the commander made the final decisions.

Moltke replaced the Eighth Army's Chief of Staff along with its commander. Moltke thought him weak for allowing Prittwitz to panic. Moltke appointed a junior general, Ludendorff, as the Eighth Army's new Chief of Staff. Ludendorff was a good planner and someone who would ensure quick execution of operations. He had been deeply involved in the development of the Schlieffen Plan. At the start of the war, he proved his initiative by taking over command of a brigade whose general died in combat. He then proceeded to capture the center of the Belgian fortified city of Liege.

Hindenburg and Ludendorff rushed to East Prussia. Colonel Hoffmann, head of the operations staff of the Eighth Army, wrote marching orders for individual units while they were underway. Hoffmann's orders called for the Eighth Army to switch from opposing the Russian First Army in the east and redeploy against the Russian Second Army in the south. Hindenburg and Ludendorff approved Hoffmann's plans when they arrived in East Prussia. After all, the senior officers were thoroughly familiar with the strategy behind Hoffmann's planning.

Hoffmann did not initially order all of the German forces facing the Russians to the east to move to the south. He kept some forces behind to keep the Russian First Army in check should it try to help their compatriots to the south. Yet Hoffmann wanted to take the risky step of leaving almost no one behind and moving almost everyone to the south. He felt that the Russian First Army would probably stop to rest and reorganize after the battle at Gumbinnen. He made a proposal to his new superiors to move the rest of the army south. Hindenburg and Ludendorff weren't too sure about taking this much risk. After all, should the Russian First Army resume operations while the vast majority of the German Eighth Army was in the south, it could easily trap and encircle them. And with the Eighth Army surrounded, the path to Berlin would be open to the Russians.

During the debate over Hoffmann's proposal, the Russians presented the Germans with an enormous gift. The Russians were sending radio messages between their headquarters in the clear. All the Germans had to do was listen to the radio. They could hear the exact orders both Russian Army commanders were sending their subordinates and how the two Armies were coordinating operations. The radio message intercepts made it readily apparent the Russian First Army would sit where it was until its commander felt totally ready to move again. Other messages showed the Russian Second Army to the south was moving forward as fast as it could.

Ludendorff backed Hoffmann's proposal because of this windfall of information about enemy plans and intentions. The Germans practically abandoned the front against the Russian First Army. Everyone except for a few cavalrymen moved to the south to deal with the Russian Second Army. Yet Ludendorff was not totally at ease with this risky new course of action. The Russian First Army could start moving again, regardless of what it was saying on the radio. If it did so, it could trap the German units now facing the Russian Second Army. This would be a disaster for the Germans and could cause them to lose the war.

Hindenburg did not have much to say during the debate over Hoffmann's proposal. Although he was the new commander, he leaned heavily on Ludendorff and Hoffmann to make the plans and see to it that subordinate commanders carried out their orders. Once these two agreed on a course of action, Hindenburg, as the commander, gave his approval.

The key subordinate commander in the German plans against the Russian Second Army was General François. His corps of about 15,000 men moved the farthest to get into position along the southern border. Ludendorff ordered him to attack before he was ready. Ludendorff was very anxious about what the Russian First Army could do while just about all the German forces in East Prussia deployed to the south. He wanted the operations against the Russian Second Army started and completed as quickly as possible.

François refused to obey the premature attack order. He was waiting for his artillery to arrive before attacking. When Ludendorff's order came, François' guns and their crews were still getting off the trains. François knew from the previous battle at Gumbinnen that attacking without adequate artillery was a recipe for disaster. Instead, he waited for his artillery and attacked two days later when his corps was ready. It was exactly the right thing to do. While he was getting ready, the Russians moved further into the trap Hoffmann had prepared. François' artillery smashed the Russians in front of his corps. With nothing in front of him, François' corps moved behind the rest of the Russians. The Russians made no serious effort to withdraw from the trap; François' troops closed it tight. [Fig 22]

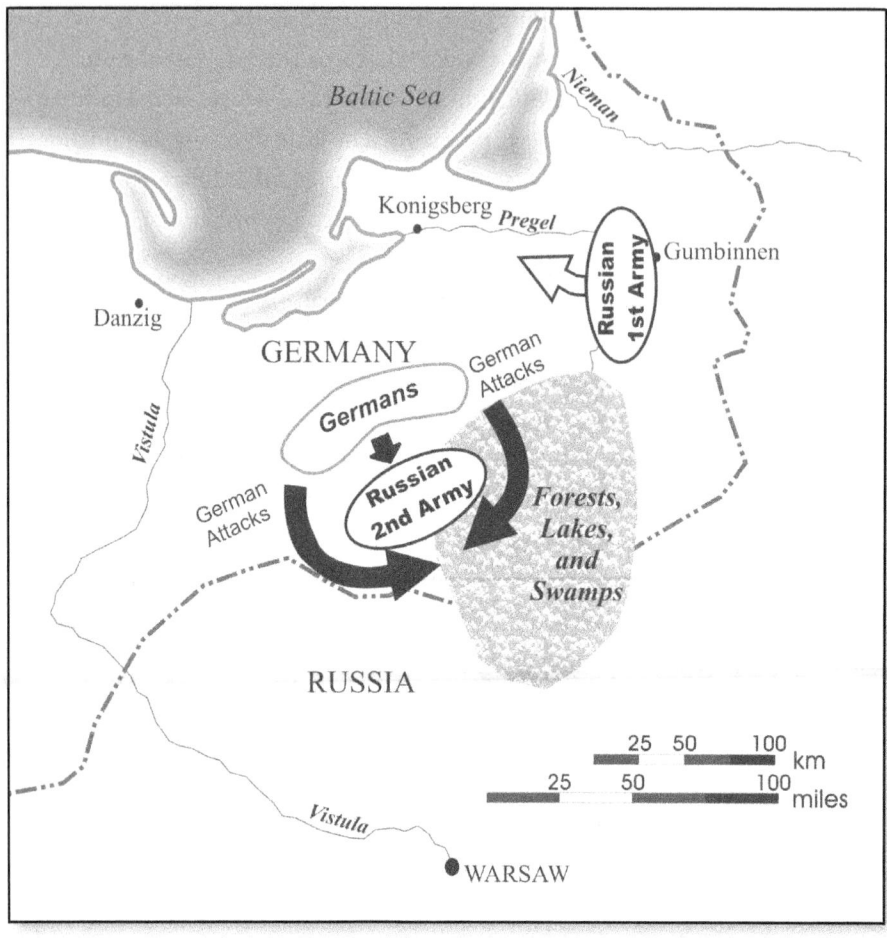

Figure 22. The Battle of Tannenberg

Out of Disaster, Victory

The bulk of the Russian Second Army was now in the worst possible situation. It was out of supplies and could not retreat. There was no assistance from the Russian First Army. With no hope of survival, the Russian Second Army surrendered en masse. The Germans had more Russian prisoners than they knew what to do with. Berlin received urgent requests for more and more trains to move the tens of thousands of prisoners into prison camps. The magnitude of the victory was beyond anything the Germans had thought possible. The small German Eighth Army had stopped one Russian Army and annihilated another.

Hindenburg named the destruction of the Russian Second Army the Battle of Tannenberg. News of the victory was broadcast everywhere in Germany with great fanfare. German church bells rang to announce the astounding news. Hindenburg was the great hero of the day. He was the mighty defender of German soil, the victor over the Russian hordes. Posters of him appeared everywhere. He was well on his way to becoming the most popular leader in the country.

Yet, when you look at the details of what happened and why, Hindenburg's role in the affair was actually rather minor. Later in the war, Hoffman would show people around the battlefield at Tannenberg, pointing out to the visitors where Hindenburg slept before the battle, where he slept after the battle, and where he slept during the battle. Hindenburg got all of the laurels because he was in charge. Everyone—the public, the Kaiser, and the military establishment—felt Hindenburg's leadership produced the victory, since he was the Army Commander.

Anyone who thought Hindenburg had help assumed it came from Ludendorff. Ludendorff was Hindenburg's Chief of Staff and was in charge of planning the details of the Eighth Army's operations. But most of the plans were prepared before either Hindenburg or Ludendorff arrived on the scene. Hindenburg was not the originator of the plans; they were already there when he showed up. Neither Hindenburg nor Ludendorff had done anything other than approve the proposals their staff had already prepared. In fact, Ludendorff's premature orders for François to attack right away would have seriously endangered the probability of German success.

The Russians were more responsible for the outcome of Tannenberg than the Germans. The commander of the Russian Second Army made an entire laundry list of mistakes (see the previous chapter on the Russian Army's operations). The major mistakes included leaving the staging area before properly provisioning the Army, not having proper communications set up with subordinate commands, and not coordinating operations with the Russian First Army. Added to this was the Russian First Army's lack of activity while its sister Army was surrounded. And then there were all the radio messages sent in the clear. It is very easy to conclude it was not the Germans who won the battle, but the Russians who lost it because of their mistakes.

No one in Germany realized this. They were too happy with the outcome to care about why they had won so big. Hindenburg and Ludendorff went to East Prussia to save the province from premature abandonment. Instead of just slowing down the enemy, they surpassed all expectations. They decisively crushed the Russians. Since it happened on their watch, everyone, including the German High Command and the Kaiser, concluded that Hindenburg and Ludendorff were the authors of the victory.

ANALOGY 2: UNDERSTANDING SUCCESS

The business corollary to the story of Hindenburg and Ludendorff at Tannenberg is very important. It is an excellent example of the great trap in leadership assessment. In business, like other endeavors, we assume the person in charge of a successful project is a successful leader. No one really delves into the specific details about how or why the project was successful. After all, the business got what it wanted from the project that this leader was in charge of, and then some. The leader gets a big plus mark on his or her record and moves on to even greater responsibilities. Most believe this leader has proven his or her abilities by their project team's success. They are therefore ready, in the eyes of the business, for even greater things.

The catch is that if the assessment of this person is not correct, the business has set itself up for disappointment and failure that will far overshadow the previous success. This is because the seemingly successful leader now has much larger responsibilities. The business can suffer a failure of a far greater magnitude than the earlier success. Only then does it find out the person does not have the abilities everyone previously thought.

You must study success with the same intensity that you would investigate a failure. It is important to find out why things went so well. Find out what actions were the most effective. Find out what you could or could not anticipate. You need to assess what helped and what hindered the project team in making the progress that it did. Do not focus entirely on the internal workings of the company in your investigation. Look at your competition's actions too. Identify what they did so that you can further exploit the mistakes they are prone to making. And, of course, you need to find out what role the project leaders played. Were they truly the architects of the success? Or were they just bystanders?

> You don't want to do all this investigative work just to assess the project leadership. You need to freely share the information on what made the project successful with other parts of the business. Leaders who keep secrets about success hinder the progress of the organizational whole. Everyone needs to learn about what works and what does not.
>
> Most importantly, you need to reward the people and promote the practices that actually led to success. The people involved in the project know what really happened. You will completely demoralize an effective work group if you allow a bystander leader to get all the credit. Worse yet is giving credit to someone who actually hindered the group. When you don't reward people for the success they create, they are not likely to produce similar results in the future. This is because they see little advantage in making the necessary sacrifices. Some may even leave the organization in disgust.

The resounding victory at Tannenberg had a profound influence on Hindenburg, Ludendorff, and the rest of the Eighth Army staff. They had annihilated the enemy and won a decisive battle. They decided the way to beat the enemy was to seek the same kind of stunning success. From this point on, these men were constantly looking for opportunities for grand maneuvers to completely destroy whole sections of the enemy's army. They had proven they could do it, so now they would try to do it again and again.

The staff and leadership of the German Eighth Army became victims of their own success. Try as they might, they could never again duplicate the stupendous success of Tannenberg. They would clamor for more and more resources for ever-larger attempts. They were convinced that since they had done it once, they could do it again. Unfortunately for them, the enemy would not cooperate again by acting as stupidly.

> ### ANALOGY 3: CONTINUOUS IMPROVEMENT
>
> Businesses can also acquire the myopia of success. When they experience an instance of undreamed-of success, they may be tempted to think the reason for it was their brilliance in planning and execution. Since they were so successful with what they did, they then try to repeat their success by doing the same thing over and over. They won't have the same magnitude of success again if they continue to use the same methods.
>
> The problem is that the competition learns from the same experience. Since they suffered the reversal, the competition has a far greater incentive to change, to do things differently in the future. After a loss, the competition will realize they will lose again if they don't make some big changes. They will recognize that repeated failure may even spell the end for them. As a result, they make changes and improvements, and it becomes more difficult to beat them the next time.
>
> Smart organizations, ones with a long-term record of success, realize this. Instead of trying the same thing the next time, they, too, look for ways to improve their attack for the next round. They will analyze why they were so successful. They accept that if their success was due to their competitor's mistakes, they might not be so lucky next time. They will learn from the success and improve on it.
>
> Companies that don't investigate success and continue to improve are often overconfident. They think they know the perfect recipe for success. Their arrogance sets them up for ultimate failure.

A Plea for Help

Germany was not alone in the war. Their major ally was Austria-Hungary. While the Germans were savoring their victory at Tannenberg, the Russians were severely beating the Austro-Hungarians. General Conrad, the supreme commander of the Austro-Hungarian Army, asked the Germans to continue to move south, from Tannenberg towards Warsaw. Conrad needed the Germans to threaten the rear of the Russians currently mauling his armies. If the Germans moved south, the Russians would have to disengage from the Austro-Hungarians and move north to protect Warsaw. Conrad felt he was fully justified in making

Victory in the East 159

such a request. After all, the Germans had asked him to attack into Russian territory in the first place. In their initial panic, the Germans asked the Austro-Hungarians to help relieve the pressure on East Prussia. They had complied to help their German allies. Now Conrad expected that since he needed help, the Germans would return the favor. [Fig 23]

Figure 23. General Situation on the Eastern Front after Tannenberg

> ## ANALOGY 4: ORGANIZATIONAL FEUDALISM
>
> Any leader is going to find something to do with the resources they get. Some will do this even when those resources could be of greater benefit to the company when allocated elsewhere. Extremely rare indeed are leaders who would voluntarily give back funds or headcount to other parts of the business. Most department heads hold on to every resource the budget gave them with every fiber of their being. Trying to get some of it back is like pulling teeth. There are all kinds of weeping and wailing over such requests. It does not seem to matter much to such poor stewards that the existence of the organization may be at stake.
>
> The leadership of any part of an organization must be willing to do whatever is required to produce the greatest benefit for the whole. It is worse than selfish to keep resources which are more urgently needed elsewhere. Such self-centered action can prevent the entire organization from being successful. No local success can compensate for a global failure.
>
> Organizational feudalism is a good name for the hoarding of resources and failing to aid other parts of the organization. People often wonder why civilization devolved from the Roman Empire into the near anarchy and almost total backwardness of the feudal system for almost a thousand years. The reality is that feudalism is the natural state of any organization. Without intervention and serious efforts to prevent it, almost all organizations end up having a semblance of local feudalism. In business, organizational feudalism is the culture where each part of the company does things only for its own benefit. Leaders in this system view their part of the business as their own little fiefdom and to hell with anybody or anything else. This system is very hard to break up. It is better to never allow it to take root. Organizational feudalism is a clear sign of an organization on the road to extinction.

Pursuing the remnants of the defeated Russian Second Army to the gates of Warsaw was not going to give Hindenburg and Ludendorff another stunning victory. Instead, such action would string out their army and bring them up against the strong Russian fortresses on the outskirts of Warsaw. Also, the Russian First Army was still operating inside German territory. Few Germans were opposing it because most were involved in the Tannenberg operation.

German moves to threaten Warsaw probably would cause the Russians to stop their offensive against Conrad's armies, but that was not Hindenburg and Ludendorff's goal. Their goal was to decisively beat the Russians in East Prussia, and that was what they were going to do. They left the Austro-Hungarians to fend for themselves.

The Germans now focused on decisively beating the Russian First Army. Rennenkampf, the commander of this Russian army, realized the full weight of the German forces in the east would now move against him. The Russian First Army moved to defend itself. The Russians built entrenchments and dug themselves in between the swamps of the Masurian Lakes and the Baltic Sea.

The Germans again quickly shifted their forces around in East Prussia. Units moved by rail from the south to face the Russians in the east. Reinforcements sent by Moltke from the Western Front also arrived. Rather than returning them to the Western Front where they were desperately needed, Hindenburg and Ludendorff found work for them to do.

Let's Try That Again

The German's plan for the next battle was very similar to the plan for Tannenberg. The idea of surrounding and then destroying the Russians worked so well at Tannenberg, the Germans thought it was sure to work again. Part of the German forces would engage the Russian First Army to its front. Meanwhile, a much stronger group would move around the edge of the Russian forces by moving through the rough terrain around the Masurian Lakes. This force would then move around the back of the Russians and surround them. Just as at Tannenberg, the German maneuvering force would be under the control of General François.

The Russians again made mistakes that improved the German's chances. The Russian commander Rennenkampf was convinced the Germans were going to attack him from the direction of Konigsberg. He therefore deployed most of his army's forces to the northwest to meet this perceived threat. He spared some forces to look after the security of his flank near the Masurian Lakes, but these were second line reserve units without much artillery. Rennenkampf held back few reserves to provide his army with the flexibility to meet unexpected German moves.

The Germans attacked the Russian First Army in the First Battle of the Masurian Lakes. The Germans started the battle by attacking Rennenkampf from the direction he expected. Rennenkampf was expecting the attack because not only is it what he thought the Germans would do, but also because he believed the false reports the Germans had planted. The Germans sent fake radio messages the Russians had picked up. They evidently were not surprised by the Germans using the same poor radio procedures they did. The initial German attacks pinned down the Russians in the middle of their line. With most of the Russian forces engaged, François attacked from the side. This time, the Russians didn't just run away. This time, they had adequate supplies. Also, the German moves did not catch all the local Russian commanders off guard. Many of them expected an attack from the side, even if Rennenkampf didn't. François had difficulty in moving as far and as fast as he did at Tannenberg. He made progress; it just wasn't anywhere near as spectacular as before. [Fig 24]

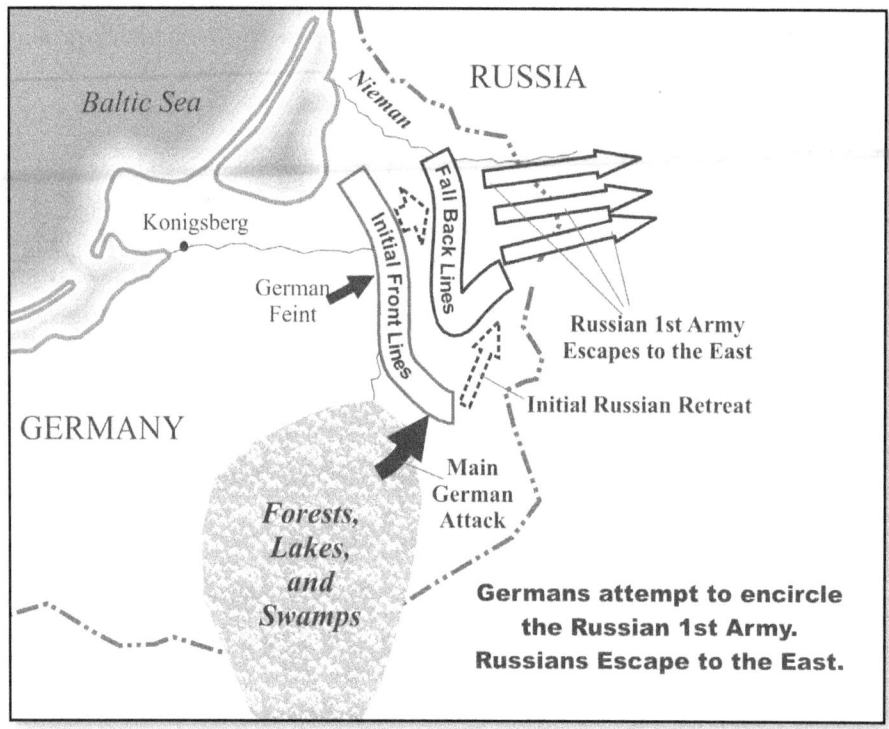

Figure 24. The Battle of the Masurian Lakes

Rennenkampf soon saw that the Germans were in a position to threaten his rear. He ordered his army to retreat. He did not repeat the Second Army's mistake of only dealing with the pressure to the front. The Russian First Army conducted an orderly retreat. The Russians even launched local counterattacks to fend off the German units presenting the gravest threats.

The Eighth Army pursued the Russians, even after they abandoned German territory. Ludendorff desperately wanted another big victory, and he didn't have one yet. The Germans continued to attack the Russian lines, even when it was clear to most there would be no decisive victory. The battle wound down as the Germans started to have their own supply problems. They had moved into Russian territory and were moving farther and farther away from the good East Prussian railways.

The German Eighth Army was somewhat successful in the First Battle of the Masurian Lakes. They captured tens of thousands of Russian prisoners. They expelled the Russians from German territory. But the Russians saved the bulk of their First Army and could invade East Prussia again in the future. Yet the Germans lost about a third of the fighting strength of their Eighth Army. They had also expended an awful lot of their dwindling ammunition supplies in their attacks.

Hindenburg and Ludendorff did not convey an accurate picture of what happened to either their superiors or to the public. The latest battle was hyped by the pair and their minions as another total victory over yet another Russian Army. They reported the destruction of the Russian First Army as an effective fighting force. They inflated the number of prisoners and quantity of captured equipment in Eighth Army reports. They did everything possible to make people believe that Hindenburg and Ludendorff had repeated the success of Tannenberg.

Privately, Ludendorff blamed François for the lack of decisive results. Ludendorff accused him of not attacking soon enough, of not taking advantage of supposed opportunities, and of not moving fast enough to catch the enemy from the rear. Hindenburg and Ludendorff were perfectly willing to take the credit for the success of their subordinates. They were also perfectly willing to lay all of the blame on underlings when things did not work out as planned.

ANALOGY 5: SUCCESS IS MINE, FAILURE IS YOURS

Too many leaders are all too willing to take the credit while they pass on the blame. When things are going great, they go all out to ensure they get credit. They play down the roles played by their subordinates. After all, the poor leader reports those subordinates were "just doing what I had asked them to do as part of my plan." Such leaders do their best to paint a picture of success that was totally dependent on them and their leadership. They want others to think that if it was not for them, the success would never have happened. This way, their power and prestige rise to new heights.

On the other hand, their finger-pointing starts when things are not going so well. "So and so didn't do what he was supposed to," and "Department XYZ didn't give us the support we needed" are common refrains as the poor leader starts shifting blame. Often, these poor leaders blame an area they have no responsibility over as they try to further reduce any taint that comes from failure. They say things like, "Our group did what it was supposed to, but the other group didn't, and that caused the failure." The purpose of this boorish behavior is to relieve themselves of personal responsibility for what happened. Their objective is to prevent any loss of personal prestige or power they have, or think they have. Notice that none of this has anything to do with the organization's best interest. The "praise hound" and "blame-game playing" leaders are totally focused on themselves.

Assigning blame can all too easily become the focus of any organization that tolerates such behavior. The organization stops trying to figure out how to do better in the future. Instead, people waste their time and energy in a combination of finger-pointing and defending themselves against accusations. Those who have fingers pointed at them put a lot of effort into proving they were not responsible for what happened. The result of all of this internal bickering is a loss of organizational focus. Failures will recur. There is no focus on improvement. The organization becomes more worried about avoiding blame for the last failure than in preparing for the next success.

Rising to New Heights

Hindenburg's and Ludendorff's prestige rose to new heights due to the turn of events on the Western Front. There, the Schlieffen Plan failed to produce the promised defeat of France. The German Army even had to retreat after the Battle of the Marne. The Kaiser cashiered Moltke, head of all German armies. Falkenhayn replaced Moltke, but he was barely able to keep the French and British from turning the German flank and forcing a retreat out of France. Up to this point, only Hindenburg and Ludendorff had decisively beaten enemy armies. They were the leaders of the only successful army at the start of what would now be a difficult two front war.

Both Hindenburg and Ludendorff were well aware of the stature they had gained in the mind of the public, the government, the military, and the Kaiser. They would do everything possible to increase their legends. They would work to propel themselves to even greater positions of authority. It had very little to do with what was best for Germany. It had everything to do with the ambitions of the two generals. It would end very badly for the country they purported to serve.

CONCLUSIONS

The Germans did better than just holding off the Russians in East Prussia as World War I began. They had some problems early on, but new leadership effectively dealt with the difficult situation. The Germans surrounded and annihilated one Russian Army and then moved to destroy another still in German territory. Russian mistakes were as much the reason for German success as any German plans. Yet success went to Hindenburg's and Ludendorff's heads. The story of the Germans in East Prussia provides a number of analogies to the business world of today. The most important of these analogies include:

- **Short-term temptations**
  People are usually very brave when plans call for them to take theoretical short-term losses to improve the chances of a long-term gain. But they lose their nerve when the short-term losses become real. Many panic under the real pressure of actual losses. They may throw away the chance for the big long-term payoff by aggressively reacting to the short-term reverses. Great leaders do not panic over negative short-term results, especially if short-term losses result from allocating resources into what will produce long-term growth. Have the courage to live through the temporary setbacks. This way, you will enjoy the long-term success.

- **Assessing leadership effectiveness**
  Don't assume that just because someone led a successful project that they are a successful leader. You cannot wait until a leader fails to find out they had little to do with the success of groups they led in the past. Find out what really made a project successful. Assess leaders on their contribution to the success.

- **Studying success**
  We frequently analyze projects that fail in depth. We rarely study successful projects in detail. You don't just need to know what results in failure. You also need to know what produces success. Share the information on the sources of success with all parts of your organization. Look for ways to exploit opportunities that are producing success. Find

out who is learning how to be successful and reward and promote those individuals for their efforts.

- **Adapting practices as conditions change**
  Future success is not guaranteed just because your organization was successful doing things a certain way in the past. Constantly look for ways to improve what you do. You need to be willing to part with techniques that no longer work. Success is always a moving target. What worked before will soon not be good enough.

- **Resource hoarding**
  Every part of an organization must be willing to give up allocated resources if they can be used more effectively elsewhere. Too often, leaders horde what their departments received through annual budgets or other allocation methods. Those who want a successful company will have no trouble sending what they can as reinforcements to other departments.
  Do not let your business devolve into practicing feudalism. Unfortunately, this is the natural state of any organization. It happens when leaders decide that their part of the business is more important than the whole. Feudalistic leaders will hold onto everything their department has, even when the company's existence is at stake.

- **Finger-pointing and the blame game**
  A poor leader is all too willing to claim the laurels of success and yet blame just about everyone else for failure. When things go wrong, such people point their fingers at just about anyone possible. The organization then degenerates into bickering between leaders and even between departments. Quickly, the overriding concern of everyone is to defend themselves against accusations. People forget about who the real competition is as they engage in internal backstabbing. The blame game is very counterproductive. All parts of an organization need to work together to produce success. They will fail if they don't.

ACTION FILE

HOW TO LEAD AN ORGANIZATION TO SUCCESS

 BAD IDEA #1—Put personal ambition first.

An organization suffers anytime someone internal decides that what they want is more important than what the organization needs. Self-serving interests damage any organization's ability to perform and adapt to changing circumstances.

People who really do the damage are those who just do not care about others or the organization. They have no loyalties outside of themselves. They will purposely damage the organization if that will get them what they want. These individuals actually need to be stopped from destroying an organization.

People who put themselves and their desires way above those of the organizational whole need to either change their ways or you need to remove them. They cannot be controlled or contained. The time and energy you must put into watching them so that they don't do too much damage is too great a price to pay. These people are among the most dangerous you will ever encounter. They *will* burn you and everyone else.

 BAD IDEA #2—Make changes to show who is in charge.

One of the silliest things you can do is to make changes quickly just to show people you are in charge. You don't need to prove you have the authority to make changes.

Now, nothing is wrong with making quick changes, as long as the changes are necessary. If the change isn't needed, don't make it. Any change requires extra effort. If you make changes that aren't needed, you've just wasted effort that could have been productive in other endeavors.

Making needless changes to show who is in charge sends a very bad message. It tells others that you care more about being the boss than about the group's performance. Such leaders rarely get the support they need from their subordinates.

BAD IDEA #3—Demonstrate negativity about the future.
Almost no one will have a positive outlook if their leadership is negative about the future. People look to the leader to form the majority of their opinions about the near- and long-term prospects of success. If the leader is negative, most will assume it is because the leader has information they do not. They assume the leader's negative outlook is due to a better understanding of the true picture of what's happening and about to happen.

Leadership demoralization is one of the first signs of defeat. Demoralization spreads quickly. Defeatism then takes hold. People are then convinced the project they are working on, or even the entire company, is on the path to certain destruction. Some may cling to a positive outlook. The odds are against these people because they have to exert so much energy to bring others around. There is little energy left to accomplish much of anything.

 BAD IDEA #4—Remove risk from your future.
A substantial portion of confidence in leadership is based on the principle of shared risk. According to this principle, leaders share the same risk in the outcome as anyone else. Soldiers view the general who never exposes himself to enemy fire as a coward. The soldiers think, "Why should I take risks the general won't?"

The risk inherent in failure for most involved in any business is obvious. If the company fails, they are out of a job. They are left without the means to support their families. But what is the risk to many senior executives today? Far too many have special severance packages. Even if they did lose their jobs, their economic situation doesn't change much. Sometimes they are even better off.

Any organization suffers when it allows senior leaders to protect their futures while leaving the vast majority at risk. The leadership is looking out for itself first. This is no secret to those they lead. The lower levels have little confidence that these leaders are looking out for the best interests of the organization. This lack of confidence saps their motivation. As a result, their productivity is not what it could be.

BAD IDEA #5—Play the Blame Game.

The Blame Game has very simple rules. When things go well, the poor leader takes all the credit. When the organization fails, the poor leader blames someone or another group as the cause. In the Blame Game, success is due to the leader while failure is not.

This hypocrisy is disgusting to all aware of it. Leaders who play this game are loathed. No one will do their best for a leader that will use them as veritable human shields should anything go wrong.

 BAD IDEA #6—Panic.

Panic is one of the worst things a leader can do, if not *the* worst. Doing nothing is preferable to panic.

Panic can take many forms. These range from outbursts of despair to flight to wild schemes. All of these hasten organizational failure. They even make the failure worse.

Outbursts of despair are emotional statements to the effect that "All is Lost!" Word of any such outburst by a senior executive will spread like wildfire. The outburst is exaggerated as it makes its way through the company rumor mill. Never allow yourself to make such an outburst. The only effect of it is to inform everyone that you have the worst possible view about the future.

Flight is pretty obvious. The members of top leadership all start leaving. People very quickly lose confidence in any organization if the leaders begin to flee. Everyone else who can also flees. This only accelerates an organization's demise.

Wild schemes include both bizarre money-making and money-saving ideas. While risk taking should be encouraged, these schemes involve unbelievably unacceptable risk. Many such schemes are unethical if not downright illegal. They are desperation moves guaranteed to do more damage than good. Just don't go into this area.

These are only three concrete manifestations of panic. It is not an all-inclusive list by any means. There are, unfortunately, many other forms of panic behavior. The common end result of leadership panic is turning a bad situation into an unmitigated disaster.

GOOD IDEA #1—Reward loyalty to the organization.

Truly enlightened individuals realize that when they do what is best for the organization, they are also doing what is best for them. The organization succeeds, and as a direct result, they are successful themselves.

People are better team players when they see their work in this light. Employees so enlightened see and treat the company's assets as they would their own property. They realize the profit and success of the company will provide for them. This understanding results in their looking for ways to improve and achieve even more.

You need to reinforce and reward such feelings. No one will be motivated to help the company succeed in the future if the company's success does not result in success of all those involved. Lack of this motivation is the end for any company's long-term survival.

 GOOD IDEA #2—Change only what doesn't work.

Successful changes have the same common basic attributes. They are based on a thorough investigation of the problem or the situation. They are designed to attack the root causes of problems, not results or symptoms. They are well communicated to the organization, and everyone understands the why and how of the change. The leadership accepts and models the change. It guides the changes through sponsorship, helping motivate others to embrace the change. Change is not just done for change's sake.

If something is not working out, investigate what is wrong. Use the results of the investigation to make the right change. Do not worry about showing up predecessors and making a big name for yourself. Worry about the organization being successful. When your area is frequently successful, people will know who you are.

 GOOD IDEA #3—Exude confidence in ultimate success.

The morale of any organization flows down from its leaders. If the organization sees and hears leaders confident in the future, they will also be confident. You need to exude this confidence even when you have your own doubts and even when you know there are serious problems.

Many in the organization will have doubts as troubles arise. But when they look to you and see and hear confidence in ultimate success, most will take courage. Your confidence goes a long way towards defeating demoralization.

Leadership optimism provides important emotional support to others. It gives people something to believe in and an attitude to support. Sometimes, it can be the only thing keeping a group going when things are really tough. Never discount the power of optimistic leadership.

GOOD IDEA #4—Inspire the demoralized.

A crucial leadership task is to raise morale. This is especially true when things may not be going so well. Success can only happen when people believe they will achieve it.

You need to sell a positive picture of the future. You have to go out and convince people there are reasons to be positive. You have to convince them that problems can be solved. You have to give them hope. You need to raise morale for a fundamental reason. People need to believe their efforts will be successful. Success can only happen in difficult situations when people rally to the cause and go the extra mile. The demoralized are just going to slow down and help bring defeat upon themselves.

GOOD IDEA #5—Make necessary changes quickly.

Indecision destroys confidence in leadership. People look to their leaders to give them a sense of purpose and direction. They want someone to set a clear course. They expect the leader to actually do something when there is a problem.

People expect their leaders to make decisions when decisions are called for. This does not mean shooting from the hip with rash decisions. Serious problems are apparent to all. People get scared when nothing gets done other than setting up committees to discuss the problem.

Being a leader involves making decisions. This is, after all, what leaders get paid for. You must step up to the plate and take the appropriate action when problems arise, when changes are necessary, when personnel changes are called for. If you don't, things will just get worse. Confidence in your leadership is undermined by hesitation and inaction. Loss of confidence results in loss of motivation and loss of productivity. The end result is failure.

CHAPTER 6

FOLLY OF THE HABSBURGS

"All the King's Horses, and All the King's Men…"

INTRODUCTION

AUSTRIA-HUNGARY is the forgotten great power of World War I. Their leadership was responsible for starting the war, a war Austria-Hungary would not survive. The country was dismembered in the aftermath. Austria-Hungary had so many problems and engaged in so much self-defeating behavior that the only wonder is how they were able to survive as long as they did. The Austro-Hungarian Army suffered huge and debilitating losses right at the outset. The quality of their army degenerated as they failed to correct serious problems and deal with critical performance issues. As the story of the failure of the Austro-Hungarian Army is recounted, the following important business issues are addressed:

- Last-minute changes
- Padding budgets and schedules
- The company dumping ground
- Cultural impact of mergers
- The increasing debt spiral
- Organizational class warfare
- Conflicts of interest
- Performance management
- Departmental feuds

HISTORICAL CASE AND BUSINESS ANALOGIES

The Habsburg Heritage

You are in serious, serious trouble if your business in any way resembles the army of this now-defunct empire. The errors made by the Austro-Hungarian Army and its leadership were real. This is neither a fictional nor an exaggerated account. The almost incomprehensible chain of events that resulted in the fall of Austria-Hungary began with the prewar situation and plans of this once mighty nation.

Austria-Hungary was one of the five great powers in Europe at the start of World War I. She had a long and glorious history as the great power of Central Europe. She was the bastion of Catholicism in the 1600s. She had saved Europe from the Mongols and from the Turks. She was a great enemy of Napoleon. Austro-Hungarian diplomats were responsible for the international diplomatic system that held sway in Europe for more than a hundred years. Her Habsburg monarchy was arguably the oldest in Europe. All of this ended with World War I, in large part because of the incompetence of her leaders.

Austria-Hungary, as even the name of the country suggests, was a polyglot empire of many different nationalities. Looking at a modern map, the area that was once Austria-Hungary is now Austria, Hungary, the Czech Republic, Slovakia, Slovenia, Croatia, Bosnia, and large portions of what today are Poland, Romania, Serbia, and Italy. Even in the times of Austria-Hungary, each of these peoples had its own culture and language. The parts were all held together by allegiance to the Habsburg Crown and by the common cultural thread of Catholicism. [Fig 25]

Figure 25. Make-Up of Austria-Hungary

Austria-Hungary had great ambitions in the Balkans. In centuries past, she was the bulwark against the expansion of the Turks and their Ottoman Empire into Europe. As Ottoman power declined, Austria-Hungary's influence in the Balkans increased. Austria-Hungary seized the opportunity to enlarge its empire by annexing the formerly Turkish province of Bosnia.

The Serbs really resented this because they had designs on Bosnia. The Serbs felt they should be the new power in the Balkans. After all, their army was actually fighting the Turks at the time, not the Austro-Hungarians. The Serbs greatly resented the diplomacy of the great powers that allowed Austria-Hungary to grab and then retain Bosnia. The ethnic Serbian population of Bosnia resented it even more.

Serbia was not alone. The Serbs had a powerful friend. They are a Slavic people, from the same ethnic group as Russians. The Russians saw themselves as tiny Serbia's protector, especially since Austria-Hungary was Russia's rival. Russia had ambitions in the Balkans too, and they saw Serbia as an important ally in realizing their own grand dreams for the future.

A Choice between Two Evils

The prewar situation for Austria-Hungary was that she, like Germany, had two fronts to worry about. Those fronts were her borders with Russia to the east and her borders with Serbia to the south. To deal with this situation, the Austro-Hungarian military developed two separate plans. Plan S allowed them to deal primarily with Serbia while some forces deployed to defend against possible Russian actions. Plan R called for most of the army to engage the Russians, while a smaller force defended the Serbian borders.

The Austro-Hungarian Army was divided into three groups. Each of the groups had orders that depended on which of the two plans was chosen. In both plans, Group A would mass along the Russian border, while Group Balkan would mass along the Serbian border. Group B provided the flexibility for either Plan S or Plan R. In Plan R, Group B would join Group A against Russia. In Plan S it would move against Serbia, joining Group Balkan. [Fig 26]

Austro-Hungarian rail resources were limited. They did not have enough trains and rail cars for all three groups of their army to move to the fronts simultaneously. In fact, Group B could only move after both Groups A and Balkan completed their mobilization and were at the borders. Only then could the trains return to pick up Group B and move them according to the chosen plan.

Count Conrad von Hotzendorf (hereafter just "Conrad") was the head of the Austro-Hungarian Army. He was responsible for the development and approval of the Plan R and Plan S options. Conrad was a real saber-rattler. His proposed solution to any diplomatic problem was always the same: declare war. Conrad was very vocal about his desire to attack either Serbia or Italy before either country could become more of a threat. The fact that Italy was actually Austria-Hungary's ally at the time did not bother Conrad.

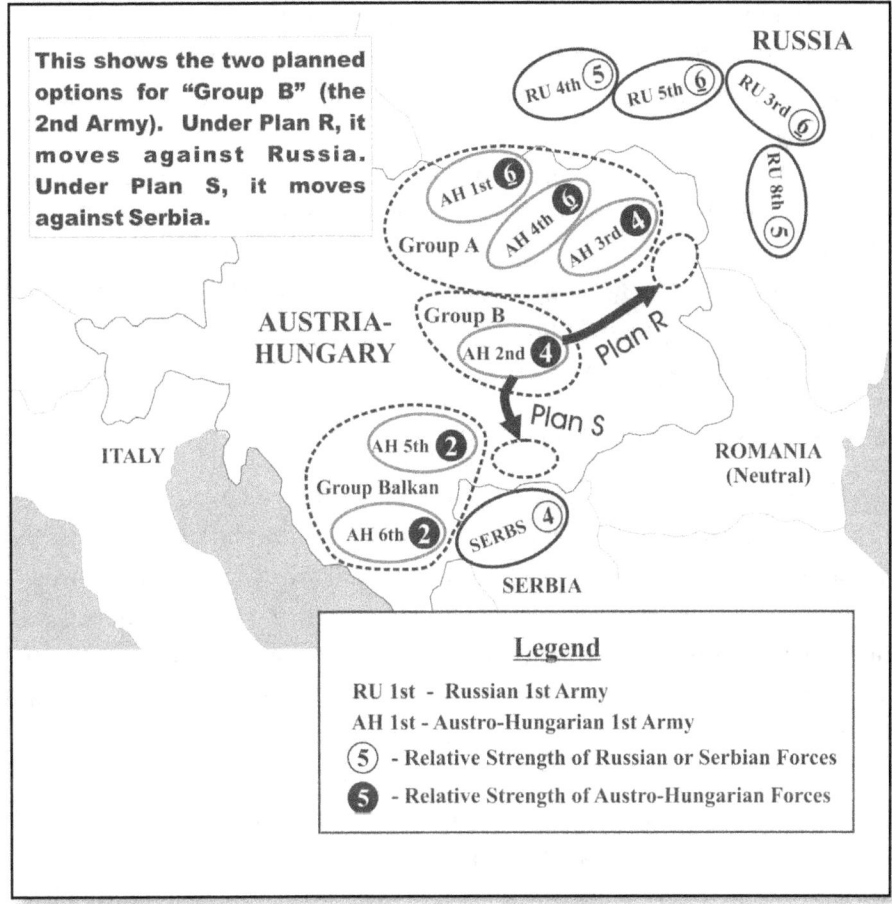

Figure 26. War Plans of Austro-Hungarian Army

The Assassination Crisis

In July 1914, Serbian nationalists in the Bosnian capitol of Sarajevo assassinated Archduke Ferdinand, heir to the Austro-Hungarian throne. This calamity provided Conrad with ample justification to clamor for war. Because of the magnitude of the deed, he was supported by the Austro-Hungarian Foreign Ministry. Kaiser Wilhelm promised Germany's unconditional support for anything Austria-Hungary wished to do. Austria-Hungary gave Serbia an ultimatum that would have resulted in the end of their country's existence. Austria-Hungary threatened to invade Serbia if it did not comply with the ultimatum's terms. Russia interjected that it would not stand idly by while Serbia was attacked.

Conrad would now have the war he so desperately wanted. Now he could put his armies into the field and prove to everyone that Austria-Hungary was still a great power. All he had to do was to tell his staff which plan to go with and everything would begin.

Plan R anticipated the scenario facing Austria-Hungary in July 1914. It was very clear that Russia would intervene in Serbia's defense. But this wasn't what Conrad wanted to do. If he went with Plan R, it would let Serbia off the hook. Plan R did not involve invading Serbia, only screening its borders. Going with Plan R would make Austria-Hungary look pretty stupid. It would be going to war to punish Serbia, and then would not even attack it.

A Change in Plans

Conrad decided to change plans, not from Plan R to the alternate Plan S, but to something new altogether. He called his transportation chief, Colonel Straub, and asked for Group B to move against Serbia while Group A mobilized against Russia. The prewar plans figured there were not enough trains and railroad cars in Austria-Hungary to have Group B moving while the other two groups were also in transit. Straub told Conrad that he could probably work something out, but that he would need a couple of days. Conrad gave him the time.

Nothing happened while Straub worked on the new plan. Nothing. No Austrian troops moved towards either front. Even though Austria-Hungary had declared war, everything was standing still. Reservists and patriotic volunteers started showing up at railroad stations. They thought they would quickly load onto trains and travel to the front. Instead, they were literally told, "Come back in a couple of days and maybe then we will have something for you to do."

There was some slack in the Austro-Hungarian rail transport system. This slack allowed Straub to find the capability to do what Conrad now wanted. Straub was able to make arrangements for Group B to arrive on the Serbian border at nearly the same time Group Balkan arrived there. Conrad could order an offensive to punish Serbia for complicity in the Archduke's assassination with these two groups. All groups were sent new orders, and they began to move according to Straub's modifications to Plan S.

Straub's changes were possible because of the slack in the system. This slack existed because of wasteful resource use in the original plans. It existed for a variety of reasons. One reason was the army bureaucracy was probably used to Conrad changing his mind a lot. The change in war plans was certainly not the first manifestation of Conrad's propensity for last-minute changes. The staff must have had experience with this before. As a result, all the departments under Conrad made sure they could deal with the last-minute changes. They did this by hiding precious resources. They tucked away trains and railroad cars. They padded their schedules with extra time so they had more flexibility than they told the boss about. When Conrad changed his mind, they had extra resources to use in their hip pockets.

ANALOGY 1: SOMETHING COMPLETELY DIFFERENT

Just about everyone has seen an example of this played out in the workplace. The big boss has the staff work out a couple of scenarios for planning purposes. Then plans are made for each of these scenarios. Everything is worked out in detail regarding what each group will do in each anticipated scenario. Plans are made for the allocation of all the resources available in each case. Many meetings are held to make sure the plans are feasible. Consensus is built while all involved vet the plans for the best possible courses of action to deal with the anticipated scenarios.

Then, when the big day comes that everyone has planned and prepared for, the big boss decides to throw all of the plans out the window and do something completely different—something that everyone had agreed earlier was too risky; something that all involved agreed they did not have adequate resources to do. Everyone now has to deal with the confusion created by this last-minute change of plans. There is no plan as people try to figure out what the big boss wants. The organization is caught off guard, and most of the people, who now are unsure as to what to do, do nothing instead. All of this costs precious time. And while this time is lost, the competition does not stand still.

> ## ANALOGY 2: SLACK IN THE SYSTEM
>
> This same mentality infects an awful lot of businesses today. No one wants to miss deadlines or fail to meet their goals. No one wants to be caught off guard by last-minute changes. One way of increasing the probability of meeting goals and deadlines, even in the face of unanticipated changes, is to include some slack in planning. This sounds like a great idea to the individual manager. But when all of the slack from all of the different managers involved is added up, it is quite significant. It turns into a lot more than what is needed to deal with unforeseen problems. These slack resources are a strain on the organization. They are a major source of inefficiency. Slack means not fully utilizing the business' available resources. Slack idles vital resources that are sequestered as protection from a crisis that may not materialize.

Word got out to others about Conrad's new plans. The German High Command was livid. Conrad had promised to hold off the Russians while the Germans attacked France. Conrad was now sending the bulk of his army against Serbia instead of dealing with the Russians. The civilian government of Austria-Hungary was panicked by the thought of Russian Cossacks moving across their inadequately defended border. Both of these groups let Conrad know what they thought of his new plan. Both groups wielded enormous clout. Conrad needed to placate them, or he would quickly be out of a job.

Conrad decided to change things again. He told Straub to move Group B to the Russian border instead of toward Serbia. Straub replied it was too late to change things again. The entire country would start to question the competency of the army's leadership. Trains were already moving.

This is why the Austro-Hungarian Army decided to send Group B to the Serbian border. There they got off the trains and waited a couple of days while things were re-organized. Group B then got back on trains and headed in the other direction, toward the Russian border.

Changing plans was not the only thing out of whack with the Austro-Hungarian mobilization. Every Austro-Hungarian train involved in the mobilization was moving at the speed of the slowest train on the slowest track. This was done to make sure there were no traffic jams in the rail system. The result was trains moving no faster than horse carts. In some cases, soldiers on the trains could have walked to the front faster.

As if they weren't moving slow enough, the trains were to stop for a total of six hours each day. This was time allotted to feed the troops. The problem was there were no kitchens or similar facilities at most of the places the trains stopped. For many soldiers this meant traveling all day without food and then stopping for two back-to-back hot meals in the middle of the night.

Interestingly, the army's field kitchens were packed on the trains with the soldiers. The planners didn't think about these, so they didn't get used. Nobody even thought about setting them up to cook on the trains while they were moving. Nobody even thought of just handing out sandwiches.

The staff section of the Austro-Hungarian Army responsible for working out rail transportation arrangements was evidently incompetent. It was only discovered when their plans were implemented. This department, so critical in wartime, was evidently the dumping ground in peacetime for people not wanted by other parts of the army. Rather than get rid of the undesirables, they sent them off to an area viewed as having little importance or prestige. Only when the army became dependent on the actual work of this group did people find out it was the weak link.

ANALOGY 3: THE DUMPING GROUND

> This practice of using a dumping ground for undesirables exists in too many businesses. It can be almost any area. Think about where such people end up in organizations you have dealt with. When any business decides to move people it does not really want into a specific department, the business must realize that these people are still there at work. Some may delude themselves into thinking these people are in an area where they can do little harm. Woe unto any company suddenly dependent on these people and their work. A lot of the business will suffer, if the company even survives.

The Austro-Hungarian Army finally got to the frontiers. As the units assembled, they moved forward to engage the enemy. In the east, the Austro-

Hungarians fought the Russians. To the south, the Austro-Hungarians invaded Serbia.

Punishing Serbia

Austria-Hungary went to war to punish Serbia for its involvement in the assassination of Archduke Ferdinand. Oskar Potiorek led the Austro-Hungarian invasion of Serbia. He had been in charge of security for the Archduke's fatal visit to Sarajevo. This said a lot about Potiorek's abilities. Potiorek wanted to attack Serbia. After all, he could use a military success to recover from the embarrassment of the Archduke's assassination while under his protection. Conrad supported Potiorek's decision to attack Serbia. Conrad had wanted to invade Serbia for years. The problem for Potiorek was that his invasion force was smaller than the Serbian army. This was not the only serious disadvantage for the Austro-Hungarian Army. Most of the Serbian border was densely forested mountains. On top of this, the Austro-Hungarian troops were inexperienced, while the Serbian army had years of combat experience fighting Turks and Bulgarians.

The invasion of Serbia was completely ill advised. The Austro-Hungarian Army only managed to push a few miles into Serbia in one small sector of the front. They were pushed out of Serbia altogether within a matter of days. Many of the Austro-Hungarian units involved suffered heavy casualties in the process.

On the Other Hand

The Austro-Hungarian Army moved against the Russians on the other side of their country. Austria-Hungary's frontier with Russia was their province of Galicia. The densely wooded steep slopes of the Carpathian Mountains separated this province from the rest of Austria-Hungary. In Galicia, things started better for the Austro-Hungarian Army than they did in Serbia, but only slightly so.

The intelligence section of the Austro-Hungarian Army had very good information on the strengths and locations of Russian forces mobilized along the Galician border. This information showed that the Russians were completing their mobilization process faster than expected. It accurately showed the Russians having greater strength than the Austro-Hungarian forces opposing them. Some kind of reasonable plan for the Austro-Hungarian Army should have come from this intelligence. Conrad didn't want to deal with this information. Accepting it would mean that the prudent course of action would be to adopt a defensive stance in Galicia. The problem was that Conrad did not want to do this. He wanted to attack. And that is precisely what he ordered the Austro-Hungarian forces in Galicia to do.

Conrad's earlier vacillations hampered the effectiveness of the Austro-Hungarian Army. Initially, Group A mobilized in Galicia under the assumption that they would be on the defensive. This was due to Conrad's change to the war plans to invade Serbia. This change sent Group B initially to the Serbian border. With a defensive mission, trains dropped off Group A far from the actual border. They debarked at areas suitable for defending Galicia against invading Russians. But then Conrad, under intense political pressure, changed plans yet again. Now Group B would joint Group A in Galicia. Group A abandoned defensive preparations and moved forward to attack.

Going on the offensive meant that Group A units now had to march almost a hundred miles in the heat of summer to the Russian border. They marched forward right along the very rail tracks trains could have carried them on. The extra marching was not the only problem. As Group A moved out of their debarkation points, their food and supplies were still dropped off at those same rear area locations. When they got to the Russian border, all of their food and extra ammunition was a couple of days' march to the rear. Some units were so bad off at this point that soldiers had to lick dew off of the grass in the morning to get water.

Conrad's decision-making rationale is not out of the ordinary. Conrad wanted to do great things. He was the leader of a large and powerful organization. Sure, there were obstacles to be overcome, but he was confident in himself and his organization. Unfortunately, for the Austro-Hungarian Army, what Conrad wanted to accomplish was nothing short of a pipe dream. He had his army attacking on every front—even when his forces were considerably weaker than the enemy's; even when everyone except Conrad thought the plans were foolhardy.

The True Condition

The Austro-Hungarian Army was in no condition to conduct the grandiose operations Conrad wanted. There were a number of reasons why. The most obvious was that the army was small and not very well equipped. Percentage wise, the Austro-Hungarian Army contained fewer military-age males than other major European armies. In fact, the army was significantly smaller than the government bureaucracy. In the early 1900s, this was extremely unusual.

The Austro-Hungarian Army just was not big enough to attack both Russia and Serbia.

> ## ANALOGY 4: REALITY CHECK
>
> Too often, poor leaders are blind to the reality of their organization's situation. They refuse to see any of their organization's limitations. They are often ill-informed of true capabilities. Poor leaders ignore the actual situation as they design grandiose schemes and plans. It doesn't seem to matter to them that they don't have the resources necessary. It is off to attack and conquer. The organization soon finds itself over committed, usually deep in debt, and worse off than ever before.

The relatively small size of the Austro-Hungarian Army was due to the budget restrictions it had lived with for years. It cost a lot of money to train and equip soldiers, and the country was continually short of funds. The annual draft of new soldiers was much smaller than for the other major powers. The country just could not afford more. It wasn't just the cost of soldiers. Money was so tight in the Austro-Hungarian Army that new field guns had brass barrels instead of steel ones. Brass was cheaper. Even with shortcuts like this, the army still could not buy enough artillery pieces. Austro-Hungarian divisions had less than half the artillery of German divisions.

> ## ANALOGY 5: MERGER PROBLEMS
>
> An awful lot of businesses have experience with large-scale mergers and acquisitions. Most have learned that if they are not careful with the merger process, they may end up with many of the problems faced by Austria-Hungary.
>
> Here is what a corporation similar to Austria-Hungary looks like. Each part of the business believes its way of doing things is better than the practices of the other parts. Each part maintains its own operational culture because of these beliefs. Some parts fight to keep as much under their own local control as possible. Operations best centralized are duplicated across the corporation within various departments instead. Each part maintains a degree of independence from centralized corporate control. Each part even has its own strategy for the future.
>
> In mergers and acquisitions, many people say things like, "We want to keep the best part of both worlds," and "Only the best practices will be used in the new organization." These are great ideals to have. Too bad they are next to impossible to attain. It is actually best to use the standards and practices of the corporation making the acquisition or to pick one side's culture to use after a merger. This way, only part of the organization is thrown into chaos when the different organizational cultures combine. This way, the new, larger organization has an anchor of accepted practices it can rely on in a stormy sea of change.
>
> Make sure you don't have redundant operations going on. Any business needs administrative processes. Duplication of administrative services is wasteful. It wastes money that should be going to operations. Administrative duplication also causes confusion, especially when different parts of the organization need to coordinate activities.

Budget limitations were not the only source of problems for the Austro-Hungarian military. There were serious organizational issues. Austria-Hungary did not have a single, unified army. It had not one army, but four. There was the national army, named the "Imperial and Royal" Army. Then there was the Austrian Reserve Army and the Hungarian Reserve Army. Lastly, there was the relatively new Croatian Reserve Army. Each army had its own administration, further draining the country's limited assets. Each separate army had its own policies, procedures, chains of command, and so on. They answered to their own local governments. They even had their own official languages. Centralized control of all four armies only occurred during wartime.

Consider this situation for just a minute. The country doesn't have enough money for its army, so it creates four of them? Why would they do this? The reason was the unique nature of Austria-Hungary. The country was not homogenous, but a polyglot collection of distinct cultures and ethnic groups. The very name of Austria-Hungary reflects this.

Before the outbreak of World War I in 1914, there were periodic crises that brought Europe close to war. In 1912, a crisis occurred over a German challenge to the French takeover of Morocco. War was a distinct possibility. At the time, the government of Austria-Hungary did not have enough money to mobilize its army. It actually had to secure loans from banks in New York for the needed funds. That's right; it had to borrow money from another country's banks so it could afford to mobilize its own army. This is how bad the financial condition of the Austro-Hungarian Army was.

ANALOGY 6: FINANCIAL FOLLY

The Austro-Hungarian Army was in serious financial trouble. Many businesses face similar trouble. Too many follow the same path as Conrad in his leadership of this ill-fated army. Like Conrad, the poor leaders do not focus on trying to rectify the problems. Instead, they are intent on some kind of expansionist policy. They put their business deeper into debt in attempts to win quick and decisive victories over competitors that are in much better shape.

What was a difficult financial situation now becomes a critical one. The company finds itself in a spiral of borrowing more and more for operations with little chance of success. Even if it does succeed, it will only be temporarily. This is because the business does not have the financial strength to hold on to what it gains. It is over-extended, over-leveraged, and in the end, bursts like a balloon to a pin prick.

On the Offensive

Even with their change of plans, the Austro-Hungarians had the initiative in Galicia. They moved across the border and attacked the Russians. Group A had three separate armies. These were the Austro-Hungarian First, Third, and Fourth Armies. Group B later reinforced these forces. Group B was the Second Army. The Second Army was the one most affected by Conrad's multiple plan changes. This army first went to the Serbian frontier. Then it got back on trains to go to Galicia.

Initially, the Russian Third, Fourth, Fifth, and Eighth Armies opposed the Austro-Hungarian Group A armies. The Russian Ninth Army arrived later on in the area as reinforcements. [Fig 27]

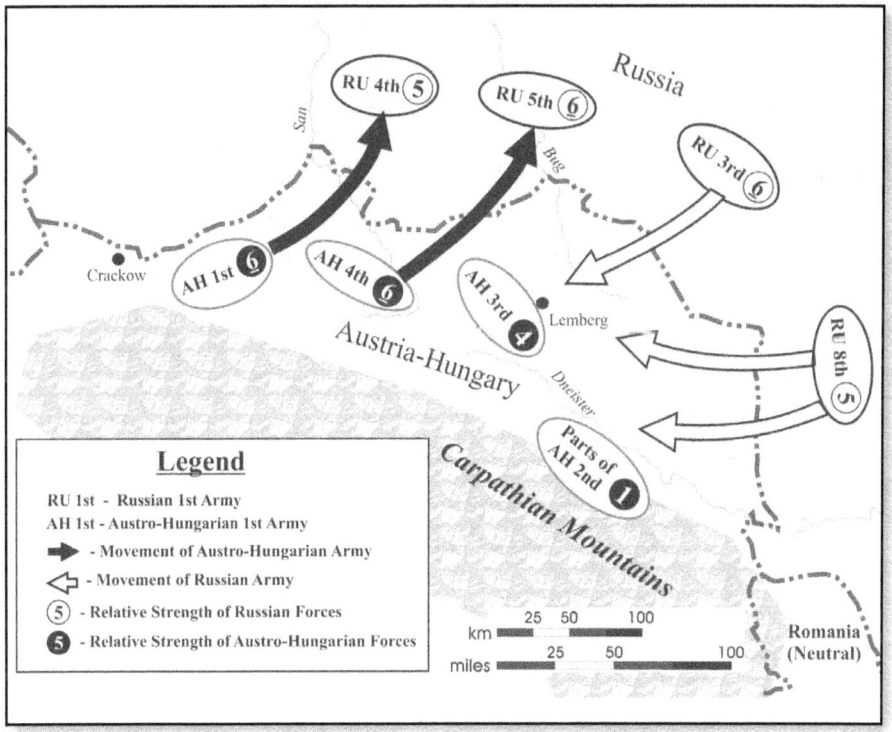

Figure 27. Initial Positions and Movements on the Galicia Front

Following Conrad's orders to attack, the Austro-Hungarian First and Fourth Armies crossed the border into Russian territory. The Austro-Hungarian Third

Army spread out to form a screen on the eastern side of Galicia. All of these armies aggressively attacked the moment they came into contact with the Russians.

The attacks of the Austro-Hungarian First and Fourth Armies were initially successful. They pushed the Russians slowly back towards their bases. As they did so, they moved farther and farther from their own supply sources. They were also losing a lot of men in the attacks against the Russians.

Things did not go as well for the Austro-Hungarian Third Army. Its attacks against the Russians moving from the east into Galicia met with disaster. In this region, the Russian forces were more than twice as strong as the Third Army. The Austro-Hungarians suffered huge losses, and the remnants streamed to the west. The Austro-Hungarian Second Army arrived from the south as what was left of the Third Army was in retreat. The Second Army was available to bolster the defenses of the depleted Third Army. Instead, the Second Army also attacked the advancing Russians. Once again the Austro-Hungarians attacked a significantly superior force. Their Second Army suffered badly as well. What was left of the Second Army joined the retreating remnants of the Third Army in a race away from the oncoming Russians.

Conrad continued to attack. Everybody was now talking about the news of the great German victory at Tannenberg. Conrad wanted victories of his own. His armies chased after the elusive laurels for him. Reality set in too late. The collapse of the Third and then Second Army in eastern Galicia put the First and Fourth Armies in a precarious position. The First and Fourth Armies were overextended and deep in Russian territory. The Russians advancing into Galicia were now south of the First and Fourth Armies. All of their hard won gains were now worthless. The Fourth and then the First Army had to turn around to avoid encirclement as the Russians moved deeper into Galicia from the east. [fig 28]

Folly of the Habsburgs

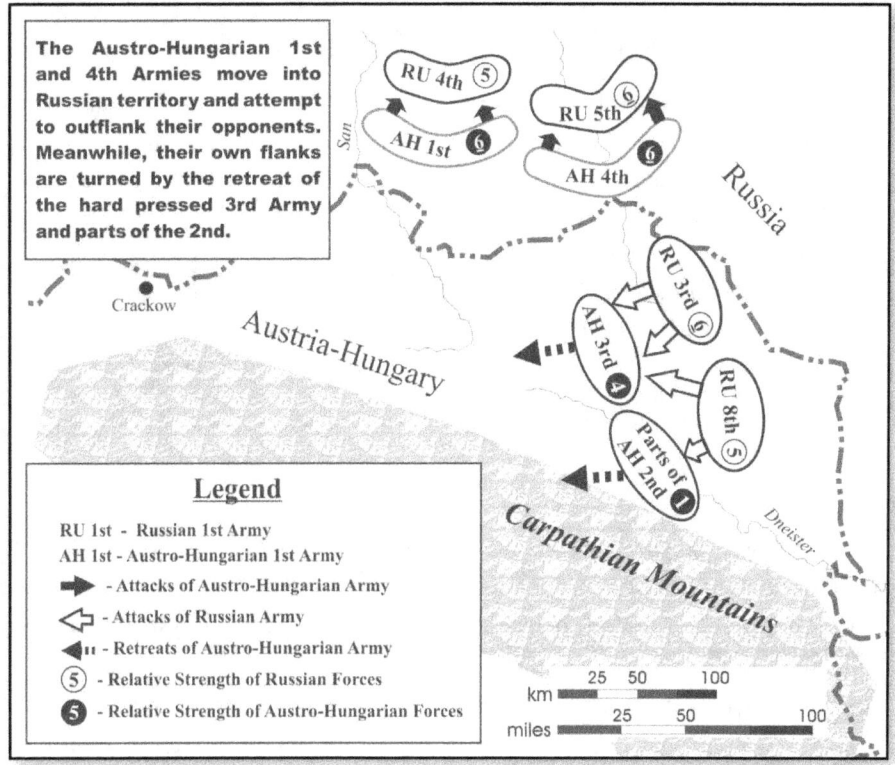

Figure 28. Galicia. The opposing armies move to encircle each other.

The Reckoning

Now the entire Austro-Hungarian Army in Galicia was in retreat. The retreat soon turned into a rout. The soldiers were not oblivious to their predicament. The Russians received a steady stream of reinforcements. There were few for the Austro-Hungarians. Conrad's ill-advised attacks had significantly weakened his armies. They abandoned almost the entire province of Galicia to the Russians. What was left of the Austro-Hungarian Army pulled back as far as the Carpathian Mountains and the outskirts of Crakow. Only the slow and cautious Russian advance saved the Austro-Hungarian Army from annihilation.

This was the predictable outcome of Conrad's decisions. He committed his army to unrealistic plans. He bled his army half to death in the pursuit of great victories over the Russians. The army that started World War I barely survived the first few months.

> ## ANALOGY 7: IMPENDING DOOM
>
> Conrad is not unlike many modern business leaders. Such poor leaders may stake their business's very existence on achieving some unrealistic and lofty goal. It soon becomes obvious to the rank and file what is happening. The boss may be delusional, but they see what the end result will be. This is demoralizing. Businesses with demoralized workers suffer from poor productivity. This in turn has an immediate negative impact on the business's performance. Many of the best people leave for greener pastures. The poor leader's unrealistic gamble results in mortally wounding the business.

Conrad's campaigns against the Russians and Serbs were disastrous for Austria-Hungary. Their armies suffered huge loses and demoralizing defeats. They lost more than half of their original fighting strength. Most of Galicia was lost. The end of the initial campaign saw the Russians positioned to invade the Austria-Hungarian heartland. The country's prestige was irreparably damaged. Her own people began to view the leadership as incompetent. The outside world, friend and foe alike, saw Austria-Hungary as a "washed up has-been." The country and its army would never recover.

The Fabric Unravels

The rest of the war is the story of the Austro-Hungarian Army's slow death. Only significant German support propped them up. The war exposed more and more of the Austro-Hungarian Army's flaws as it dragged on. Each of these flaws contributed to the ultimate demise of the army and the country it served.

The professional officers of the prewar Austro-Hungarian Army were just as good as those in any other European army. Most of these professional officers were killed or captured in the disastrous opening campaign against Russia. Due to the high losses of these well-trained and experienced officers, the Austro-Hungarian Army became more and more dependent on less competent reserve officers.

Austro-Hungarian reserve officers were less competent due to the effects of their army's budgetary problems. The army had taken a number of shortcuts because of the shortage of funds. One shortcut was to cut way back on training for reserve soldiers, especially the officers. This was a great idea so long as no one had to count on the competency of these officers in a real war. This was now the case. There was no time for remedial training. Many did not know what they were doing, and a lot of them died in the process of learning on the job.

> ### ANALOGY 8: THE TRAINING DEFICIT
>
> Whenever a company gets into financial trouble, it is often tempted to cut back on training. This seems like a great idea. After all, training is a debit on the balance sheet. Financially, it appears to cost a lot while producing nothing.
>
> Reducing training is actually one of the first major steps on the road to decline for any company. If you don't train people, they have to learn by trial and error on the job. This is even more expensive than formal training. People without proper training make big mistakes. This is bad enough at the lowest levels. The effect of inadequate training is much worse in management levels. Heaven help the company that must suddenly and unexpectedly rely on untrained and inexperienced leaders.

Lack of adequate training was not the only problem with the officer corps of the Austro-Hungarian Army by late 1914. By that time, they started to have serious problems with class distinction. The old officer corps had spent a lot of time with their soldiers on maneuvers. Most of them had learned the different languages and dialects spoken by their troops. Years of drilling together had produced a degree of camaraderie between officers and men. The best and bravest of these officers were now gone. Inexperienced rear area and reserve officers lacking these connections with their soldiers replaced the fallen leaders.

The poor relationship between officers and their soldiers was bad enough. The prevailing attitudes of these remaining officers made things worse. The vast majority saw themselves as far superior to their soldiers.

> ## ANALOGY 9: CLASS DISTINCTIONS
>
> Most companies have both salaried and hourly employees. All work together to produce goods and services for the company's customers. Yet, in too many instances, class distinctions arise between the salaried and hourly employees. Sometimes this happens when the salaried people get a lot of visible perks that the hourly workers do not. These privileges could be things like better parking spots, separate cafeterias or rest rooms, and so on. The worst case occurs when the salaried employees start to think and act as if they are better than the hourly people are.
>
> A common situation can lead to such problems taking root in your company. All too often, people come right out of college and into the business world thinking they know everything. Some of these people, unfortunately, quickly start supervising hourly workers without proper grounding. The "know-it-all" college grad treats the workers poorly, does not listen to them, and acts as some kind of petty despot. This same situation existed in the Austro-Hungarian Army. Companies that allow this to happen are heading down the same path.
>
> In some cases, this situation occurs because there is little or no management training for the new hires. In other, more malignant cases, it occurs because this thinking is part of the company's existing management culture. There are far more companies than we all care to admit where the management frequently tells jokes about how stupid its workers are. These companies always seemed to have problems with their performance and profitability. It is easy to understand why.

The Austro-Hungarian officer had many special privileges. Meanwhile, the common soldier barely got by. When the Austro-Hungarian Army abandoned Galicia, a number of units holed themselves up in the large fortress complex at Przemsyl. The Russians besieged Przemsyl for about six months before capturing it. By then, the Austro-Hungarian soldiers in the fortress had eaten all of the horses, pack mules, and anything else they could get their hands on. There was nothing left to eat, and many were starving. On the other hand, Austro-Hungarian officers in the fortress were still eating three multi-course meals a day. They had enough provisions in the officers' mess stores for another couple of months when the fortress surrendered. The officers' mail was regularly flown in to the fortress's airfield. The soldiers' families had no contact with them at all. They didn't even know if they were still alive or not.

The privileges and preferential treatment of officers over their soldiers had a terribly corrosive effect on the Austro-Hungarian Army. The soldiers obviously began to question why they should exert themselves for leaders who treated them like dirt and kept all the goodies for themselves.

The Austro-Hungarian Army had three classes. The army officers described so far were just the junior officers, equivalent to lower level supervisors and managers. Above them was yet another, even more privileged class. These were the generals, the senior executives of the Austro-Hungarian Army.

The "General" Conditions

Austro-Hungarian Army generals typically came from the country's aristocracy. Most were wealthy landowners who presided over large estates. Just like the junior officers, they too engaged in behavior destructive to their army. The vast majority of Austro-Hungarian generals were not out to win laurels on the battlefield. Their motivation was to use their position to enrich themselves and increase their social status.

Many generals used their positions of influence to get exemptions from the law. Specifically, they got exemptions from laws restricting the prices farmers could charge during wartime for their produce. This was very profitable. After all, they owned the largest farms. They also used their positions to get government contracts for their farm produce at prices small-time farmers never saw. As the war dragged on, the generals' lands and estates generated huge windfalls for them.

Small-time farmers had an even bigger handicap than government price controls. There was a serious shortage of farm workers. This was because most of them were drafted into the army. To help out farmers, the government decided to use prisoners of war to tend the crops. In addition, the army sent hundreds of thousands of soldiers back to the farms to help during harvest season. Of course, the generals controlled these labor sources. They made sure their estates had plenty of workers. Few family farms saw any of this help.

The generals were also quick to find other ways to profit from the war. An awful lot of them got appointments on bank boards. They then used their positions to get low interest loans with extremely generous repayment terms.

A lot of generals used their newly acquired funds to invest in armaments and other associated industries. They, of course, placed themselves on the boards of the companies involved. These companies were the ones that got the largest and most lucrative government contracts for army equipment and supplies.

Self enrichment was not the only destructive behavior exhibited by the Austro-Hungarian generals. They also tended to not work much at their real jobs. They preferred to go on vacation whenever possible. This meant frequent hunting trips at private forest lodges, or visits to resort spas. Their vacations kept them out of touch with the divisions and armies they supposedly led. The result was a regular leadership vacuum at many Austro-Hungarian headquarters.

There was a war going on. There were frequent crises. Too often, when the enemy launched an attack, the general was out of town. Crucial time was lost as staff groups were slow in deciding what to do in the generals' absence.

ANALOGY 10: CONFLICTS OF INTEREST

You can't open a business magazine or newspaper without reading about some kind of conflict of interest or influence peddling scandal. People with power and connections routinely get financing unavailable to the average person. Connections are more important in getting contracts than merit or value. Executives place themselves on the boards of each other's companies. Those at the highest corporate levels can arrange for special loans.

Ethical considerations aside, all of these special privileges for executives have a deep negative impact on the companies they lead. Consider: what loyalty are they inspiring in their employees? What kind of an example are they setting in terms of living values they expect their rank and file to follow? The answers are obvious. When senior executives demonstrate that they are self-serving hypocrites, the rest of the company will engage in self-serving activities themselves. The leadership has set an example, and the rest of the employees will inevitably follow. Lower-level individuals will not work to improve the company's performance. Instead, they will work to protect their own jobs and maneuver to get ahead politically. The idea of keeping the good of the business in mind has little or no meaning in such companies. Everyone is on the lookout for themselves. The company will suffer seriously in terms of productivity and profitability.

In the summer of 1916, the Russians launched a massive offensive against the Austro-Hungarian Army. The Russian General Brusilov attacked all along the Austro-Hungarian front with the armies under his command. Most of the Austro-Hungarian generals were off on vacations. The Austro-Hungarian Fourth Army, which bore the brunt of the Russian attacks, could not find their commanding general for over four days. Those left in charge were unsure of what to do. Units held in reserve to plug holes in the line were sent on uncoordinated wild goose chases. Units lost contact with each other. The Russians poured through huge gaps in the Austro-Hungarian lines. Only the combination of a lack of support for General Brusilov by the rest of the Russian Army, and the intervention of German units, saved the Austro-Hungarian Army from complete disaster.

> ### ANALOGY 11: LIMITS OF DELEGATION
>
> Any executive out of touch for days knows they are just asking for trouble. You must always remember it is impossible to fully delegate leadership responsibility to subordinates. No subordinate will ever be comfortable making "make or break the company" kinds of decisions. They know full well they will get blown out of the water if they are wrong, and there is little reward for being right. Instead of making the big decision, they will try to keep things patched up until they can find the executive and then have them make the big decisions.

The Austro-Hungarian Army also had serious problems with discipline. Contemporary German officers in close contact with the Austro-Hungarian Army frequently commented that Austro-Hungarian soldiers routinely failed to carry out assigned tasks. This should be no big surprise, given the conditions previously described. The officers treated the common soldiers poorly and derisively. The generals didn't want to deal with the discipline problem; they saw that as the junior officer's job. After all, the generals wanted to go on vacation or be off improving their personal fortunes. No one was taking care of the army's performance issues.

Performance Problems

Austro-Hungarian soldiers were notorious for not staying on sentry duty. They rarely got to their jump off points for launching attacks on time. The Austro-Hungarians did not properly man their trenches. The soldiers tended to stay in the comfort of large bunkers and dugouts. Desertion and "absent without leave" soldiers were huge problems. Shirking one's duty was not limited to the common soldiers. Officers in the Austro-Hungarian Army reported themselves sick at a rate four times that of German Army officers. The resulting effect of poor discipline was poor performance. The divisions of the Austro-Hungarian Army were increasingly unreliable. The government conducted investigations. The investigating committees referred to the Austro-Hungarian Army as nothing more than a "militia-type force." This is a nice way of saying the army had become little more than an armed mob.

ANALOGY 12: PERFORMANCE MANAGEMENT

Performance management is a job nobody really wants to take on. This is especially true in high tech industries where people are often in both technical and supervisory roles. Performance management is also problematic in other industries as organizations flatten out too far.

Performance management is very time consuming. You have to make detailed and specific goals for people to work towards. You have to make observations and take notes on people's performance throughout the rating period. It takes time to do personal coaching and discuss performance issues that arise. It is time consuming to write out accurate reviews reflecting a person's performance and accomplishments. It takes a lot of effort to do all of this. Poor leaders find other things to do. Their organizations inevitably have performance issues.

Performance management must be an important part of any leader's job. You have to insist on everyone who has a supervisory role doing it. Set a good example yourself at doing this. All too often, lower level leaders can get away with not doing it because their boss doesn't want to do it, either.

> If you don't do performance management, organizational performance remains stagnant or drops off. The good performer gets comparable ratings and the same pay raises as the shirker. Forget about keeping this kind of stuff private; people will find out. This gives the good people a bad attitude. They start to think, "Why should I go out of my way to do a good job when I don't get anything in return?" Their performance falls off. The shirkers know what their performance levels really are. They know they need to improve. But without leaders doing performance management, no one is calling them on this. So they figure they can continue at subpar levels. There are no consequences for them. Why should they work harder when no one seems to care about their performance?
>
> When you evaluate anyone in a supervisory role, you must look at their effectiveness in conducting performance management. The primary responsibility of any leader is the overall performance of the group they lead. Nothing can compensate for them not doing well at this part of their job. You need to be aware of how leaders at each level are doing. You need to provide subordinates with the skills to manage the performance of others. You need to intervene and provide coaching when necessary.
>
> Take performance management seriously. Every organization that allows "pencil whipped" performance evaluations during the last few days of the rating period suffers from reduced productivity. Any organization achieves far less than is possible when there is little or no discussion of performance between leaders and subordinates. Guaranteed.

Divisional Rivalries

The Austro-Hungarian Army didn't just have problems between the different classes of soldiers, officers, and generals. It also had serious problems between the different branches of its army. The army branches most often in conflict were the infantry and the artillery. World War I proved that close cooperation between the artillery and the infantry was crucial. The artillery needed their infantry to protect them from enemy infantry. The artillery protected the infantry from both enemy infantry attacks and enemy artillery fires. Cooperation between Austro-Hungarian infantry and artillery was sorely lacking.

The Austro-Hungarian infantry hated and despised the artillery. The artillery felt the same way about the infantry. Each believed the other branch was incompetent and only looking out for itself. These convictions became self-fulfilling prophecies. The infantry was convinced that the artillery was not going to protect them, so they frequently gave up if any enemy attack looked particularly ferocious or determined. The artillery was so convinced that the infantry would abandon them, they packed up their guns and took off the minute the infantry came under heavy attack. During the 1916 Russian Brusilov Offensive, whole divisions of the Austro-Hungarian infantry surrendered en masse. Yet every last artillery piece of many of these divisions found safety to the rear.

These self-defeating attitudes of the two most important branches of the Austro-Hungarian Army turned the army into a hollow shell, unable to withstand any serious threat from its enemies on the battlefield. Each branch abandoned its primary mission. In their infighting, they had forgotten who the actual enemy was.

ANALOGY 13: FEUDING DEPARTMENTS

The various departments of most organizations are prone to feuding. The feuding parties actually forget they are both on the same side. They forget who the real competition is. Instead, they focus on a vicious cycle of recrimination and finger-pointing about who is to blame for problems.

Here is a simple case in point. The marketing arm of a company asks customers what products they would like. They forward the customer requests to the design department. The designers design the product and send it off to the manufacturing department for production. The manufacturing department follows the design instructions, makes the product, and sends it to the customer.

This is how things are supposed to go. In real life, there are always problems in getting a new product to the customer. In this case, the manufacturing department feels the design department gave them a poor design. They feel that too many aspects of the design are difficult to produce. The design department is convinced the manufacturing people are incompetent since they cannot seem to make the product. The two groups start a feud over who is to blame for a product that now costs too much to make and has reliability problems. Each department is convinced that the problems stem from the other department's inability or unwillingness to do its job properly.

Both departments now spend a lot of time and effort trying to prove the other is at fault. They could have used their energies to work together to improve designs and manufacturing processes. Instead, they waste their time and talents on accusations and finger-pointing. The two departments now see each other as the enemy. They have forgotten that they can only be successful by working together. They have forgotten that they are on the same side and that the competition is benefiting from their conflict.

You need to actively work to defuse interdepartmental infighting the minute it arises. Internal conflicts only get worse with time. Don't allow this kind of self-inflicted wounding. All the parts of any organization need to realize they are interconnected. No one will succeed if part of the organization fails. No department can be successful individually. They need to help each other. You often need to invent processes and procedures to ensure that different departments are indeed helping each other.

Each of the Austro Hungarian army's problems contributed to its demise. In rather short order, it became a vassal of the German military. The reputation of the Austro-Hungarian Army was completely shot. Its performance consistently matched its reputation. It was only successful in campaigns where German forces played the primary role.

The demise of the Austro-Hungarian Army was also the demise of the country. The victors of World War I dismembered Austria-Hungary. Today most people don't even realize that this country ever existed. If your business emulates Austria-Hungary and its army, it will end up the exact same way.

CONCLUSIONS

This chapter explained many of the Austro-Hungarian Army's failings in World War I. Their initial operations were chaotic due to unnecessary confusion about plans. Austria-Hungary lacked the resources to achieve the goals their leaders set. In 1914, it suffered irreplaceable losses in ill-advised attacks. Additional mistakes and lack of focus then took their toll on the damaged army.

There were huge problems to overcome. Yet Austro-Hungarian leadership failed to take action. The army went into steep decline and then fell apart. Austria-Hungary had existed for over a thousand years. The failure of its army led to its destruction. The failings of the Austro-Hungarian Army provide a number of analogies to modern business. The most important lessons include:

- **Last-minute changes**

    Here is how you can throw your entire organization into chaos. Make drastic last-minute changes to a plan everyone is ready to execute. Worse yet, change to a course of action everyone already agreed is too risky and beyond your company's means to accomplish. If you don't like the plans you have, spend a little more time in planning and preparation. This is much better than issuing the marching orders and then changing them on the fly.

- **Padding budgets and schedules**

    Many ensure they can meet their goals by padding schedules and holding on to excess resources. This is wasteful. You cannot achieve maximum results when you hold back. Your business cannot accomplish everything it could if it holds too many resources in reserve, just in case problems arise. Make sure your company is not holding back. Ensure that goals are achievable, yet stretch resources to the limit.

- **The company dumping ground**

    Companies often have a department which is used as a dumping ground for poor and mediocre employees. The problem is that this keeps these people in the company. They are still working there. At some point, their work will actually impact the company's performance. It is never a good impact.

- **Cultural impact of mergers**
  Mergers and acquisitions can be difficult. Many mistakenly believe you can retain the best parts of each involved organization. Unfortunately, this belief leads to confusion about how each involved party should accomplish their goals. It is better to pick one side as an anchor. Try to reduce the chaos associated with any merger or acquisition as much as possible. Make changes and adjustments to policies and procedures after confusion has settled down.

- **The increasing debt spiral**
  Debt is often necessary. Too much is dangerous. If you take on too much debt, there are great temptations to take extreme risks to get rid of it. If you cave in to these temptations, you can easily find yourself overextended. Many of the extremely risky strategies require even more debt to finance them. When the new and riskier endeavor fails, the whole organization can collapse like a house of cards. A lot of businesses have gone down this path because they took on too much debt. Don't be another. Always carefully way the pros and cons of taking on debt beforehand.

- **Organizational class warfare**
  Many businesses have serious relationship problems between salaried and hourly employees. This often begins when new salaried employees are unprepared for responsibilities they have over hourly employees. Many salaried people operate under the mistaken belief that they are better than those whom they supervise. Either of these issues will significantly reduce worker performance. You need to work to ensure that class warfare does not start in your company. Any business with class warfare problems will have reduced profitability and employee retention problems.

- **Conflict of interests**
  Leaders need to inspire those who work for them. People are not inspired when they find out their leaders are getting special deals unavailable to them. This saps the motivation of the company's employees. It is even worse when the leader who espouses a set of values does not live up to

them. People have a hard time following hypocrites. People do not go the extra mile for leaders only looking to enrich themselves at the expense of their subordinates. In fact, most people will follow the example of their poor leaders. They will all start to do only what is in their best immediate interest. This has seriously detrimental effects on the company.

- **Performance management**

  Make performance management a significant factor in making promotion decisions. The people you promote must be good at this critical task. Unfortunately, people who are rather bad at managing other people's performance are often promoted in spite of this fact.

  Good performance management takes a lot of time and effort. You have to do a lot of observation and provide timely feedback. Reward those who are good at managing performance. Don't let people get away with not doing it.

  Poor performance management quickly results in most people getting comparable work evaluations. The second-order effect is that good performers do not see any reward for going the extra mile. Meanwhile, poor performers have little incentive to improve. All of this quickly means the organization will perform well below its potential.

- **Departmental feuds**

  Feuds between different departments of a company are all too common. This infighting becomes the focus of those involved. These feuds waste a lot of energy as people try to prove that other departments are to blame for problems. Finger-pointing wastes a lot of time. Infighting detracts from actually finding a solution to the real problems. Remember that the competition is the real enemy.

ACTION FILE

HOW TO EFFECTIVELY USE AVAILABLE RESOURCES

 BAD IDEA #1—Fail to reallocate.

Companies hold too many status meetings. These are boring meetings on metrics regarding the business. Many spend too much time asking simplistic questions about minutia during these meetings. Most people can tell the status of things by looking at charts and tables. What you need to find out is "Why is this the status?" Then you can determine what you need to do to improve the situation.

You don't improve the situation by just putting pressure on people to improve metrics. You need to actually move tools, people, money, and other resources. You need to move them from where they are not doing much good to where they can do the most good. Identify the bottlenecks in your operations. Then reallocate resources from areas that are not in such critical need.

Here is a real life example of failing to reallocate from a manufacturing operation. Studies found that the "acme" machines were the bottleneck of the entire operation. The factory's production was entirely dependent on how much material they could run through these specific machines. Additional work identified how to get more productivity out of the "acme" machines. Simply having one more operator for every four of these machines per shift would increase their output by about 10 percent.

When informed of how to increase productivity, the factory's management said, "We don't want to hire any more people." They erroneously assumed that the only way to find additional operators was to hire more staff. All they really needed to do was to take some people off of "zed" machines (the operation with the most excess capacity) and retrain those people to run "acme" machines.

The factory managers would not reassign people. They did not want to transfer anyone from one manufacturing group to another. The group controlling the "zed" machines did not want to lose headcount, especially not to the "acme" group. Management listened to this and did nothing to redeploy resources, even though it would have meant a 10 percent productivity increase. The increase in production would have translated to almost pure profit, since they could achieve it without additional overhead.

A lot of companies only reallocate budgets and resources during their annual budget cycle. Budgets or headcount changes after this cycle are difficult, if not impossible, due to organizational bureaucracy. Don't fall into these artificial traps within your business. Promptly reallocate resources to where they are most effective. If they are no longer most effective where you sent them, reallocate them again. This power is critical to effective leadership, yet it is rarely used. Don't be afraid of doing it. The most effective businesses reallocate resources in a heartbeat.

BAD IDEA #2—Focus too much on acquiring additional resources.

Poor leaders spend an awful lot of their time whining and moaning about how they don't have enough people or time or money (or whatever) to do the job. They go to extraordinary lengths to make sure their superiors, peers, and everyone else repeatedly hears this message. They are hoping to get additional headcount and budget through their use of these squeaky wheel tactics. They think that if they complain often enough and loud enough, they will get more. They spend a lot of time and energy making sure everyone knows about their complaints.

Use your resources as effectively as possible. You should only try to get more when you effectively use everything you already have. And guess what? When you are using everything at your disposal as efficiently as possible, you can easily prove your case. You can show that anything else sent your way will also be put to effective use.

Some misguided people use unethical methods in trying to get additional resources. These people are usually trying to increase the size of their personal kingdom within the organization. Their goal is to get larger budgets and higher headcount, whether they need it or not. Unethical people will try to accomplish this by using their current resources as inefficiently as possible. They hope to increase their allocations by slowing things down, by creating artificial barriers to productivity. You can uncover such schemes by looking at the productivity of what they control. Compare their group's productivity to other similar groups. Remove people employing such schemes from positions of trust.

BAD IDEA #3—Spread resources to all.
Always send your resources to where they will do the most good. Don't fall into the trap of thinking that every group should get some kind of equal share. Spreading out your resources dilutes your most important efforts. Make sure that you properly fund and staff those groups most important to your business. Make sure your money and people are where they will do the most good.

Everyone wants resources. Everyone wants more money and higher headcount. There are never enough of these to go around. You can never meet all of the demands or requests.

The problem you may have is how to figure out how much to distribute to whom with what is available. Don't think, "I have to give something to everyone." Likewise, if times are lean, don't think, "I have to take something away from everyone." Don't make the mistake of giving or taking based on some kind of percentage! It is a mistake to give everyone a 10 percent increase in budget, or to make everyone take a 5 percent reduction. This is an incredibly inefficient and cowardly way of making a quick, yet dangerous decision. Such decisions result in continued inefficient use of what you have.

Sharing resources between everyone ensures that only a small fraction goes to the most productive areas. Go through the pain of putting your resources where they are most productive for the organization as a whole. You will have to deal with the resistance of those who don't think they are getting their fair share. Remember that you are not allocating based on fair share; you are sending what you have to where it will do the most good.

BAD IDEA #4—Refuse temporary help.
Some people will refuse help when it is only temporary. Remember, there are people out there whose goal is primarily to increase their personal dominion. They don't want temporary increases in resources; they want permanent ones. In fact, they want permanent increases so badly, they

will actually refuse temporary help even when temporary changes are in everyone's best interest.

Another angle of the same problem is someone who will only agree to temporarily part with their allocations. They will only agree to reductions if they eventually get them back. You must see these individuals for what they are. Act on their unwillingness appropriately. Remind them of their responsibility to assist with maximizing the productivity of the organizational whole. If they don't act accordingly, you still need to take the action to ensure you resource your company's real needs.

 GOOD IDEA #1—Resource the "best bang for the buck."

Everyone has resource problems. Few people have enough to do everything they want or even need to do. You cannot let this stop you. Find out how to employ what you have in the most effective way. You won't be able to do everything. A lot will not be perfect. You will be better off by resourcing your priorities first. Things will improve. Waiting for everything you think you need is incapacitating. Move out and do the best you can with what you have.

Identify the best use of your resources. You may need to decrease allocations in one area to better fund and man other more critical areas. Put your people and your money where they will do the most good. This seems obvious, but most organizations don't do this. Too many allow resources to stay underutilized. Never allow allocations to stay locked in place. Move them to where they are needed most.

Always retain the flexibility to move things around. Do it frequently. Constantly analyze what is going on. Identify what is working really well, what is working, what is having problems, and what are ongoing disasters. Move your resources around to exploit opportunities and deal with disasters. Don't allow static budgets or staffing. Move things (people, money, equipment, whatever) to the areas that will use them the most productively. Never allow slack resources in your system to remain underutilized.

Encourage everyone to constantly analyze what is happening. Have them report their observations and analysis back to you. Listen to this information. Test its validity. Then take appropriate action quickly. Do not wait for the next budget cycle. Do not wait until you can hire additional headcount. Use what you can right away.

 GOOD IDEA #2—Don't cave in to complaints.

The old saying goes, "the squeaky wheel gets the grease." In most organizations, this means the manager who complains the most about not having enough resources gets more. This means resources may not go where they will be the most effective. They went to the area led by the person who complained the loudest. Don't do this just to quiet the whiner. They will just complain even more. After all, you just rewarded them for doing it.

Everyone has arguments for what they ask for. Test these arguments. Determine where the most urgent needs are. Find out if someone is over-resourced for the current situation. Be willing to take those resources and give them to other areas more in need.

The best at pitching for resources are not necessarily the most in need. Neither are those who excel at whining and complaining. The quiet types are usually doing the most they can with what they have. They are often the ones who can put additional resources to use most effectively.

 GOOD IDEA #3—Stop resourcing failure.

It is hard to walk away from something you have invested a lot of time and money in. But you need to stop resourcing unproductive activities. You need to stop resourcing failure. Resource activities that will provide you the best rate of return.

Constantly look for the evidence of your return (or expected return) from the activities you currently fund and staff. Compare the returns and expectations of different activities. Reallocate your resources accordingly. This often means reducing or eliminating the funding and staffing of specific endeavors, even ones you may have already spent a lot of time and money on.

The trap is that after resourcing something for a while, you expect results. When you don't get them, you start to think, "If I put some more into this area, maybe I can recoup what we have lost so far," or "Good times are just around the corner here; we just need to stay the course." Usually, these are delusions. It's hard to admit you may have been wrong, or that you may have lost. But that may be the truth. Always deal with reality. Stake out a loss limit before you begin any endeavor. This limit is the loss you are willing to incur before you pull out. Adhere to this limit. When you reach the limit, stop resourcing the endeavor. Just walk away. It may be painful, but just image how painful it would be to lose two or three times more.

ACTION FILE

HOW TO DEAL WITH INTERDEPARTMENTAL CONFLICT

 BAD IDEA #1—Assume teamwork will solve all problems.
You cannot assume that teamwork will solve all your problems. You may encourage and even train people in teamwork, but it may not actually occur. The higher you go in an organization, the less teamwork is usually going on. Teamwork is difficult to achieve whenever you have senior managers and directors work together on a problem. Teamwork is even more difficult to pull off at senior levels when it begins only after a crisis has begun.

Teamwork may not occur for very simple reasons. Teamwork works best in the lowest levels of an organization where those involved have already had most of their professional ambitions quashed. Such team members recognize they are not going to get ahead as individuals anyway. They want to help their company be successful so they won't be out of a job. On the other extreme, too many senior leaders think they are on the path to the top of their organizations. Their egos lead them to think they are on this path because of their individual accomplishments. They think that the way for them to pass up their peers is to have more significant accomplishments than others.

Teamwork can work at senior levels. It can be very beneficial. But for it to happen, you have to deal with the egos and dog-eat-dog mentality preventing teamwork. You must create a foundation at senior levels for teamwork to work successfully. You must spend more time with senior leaders to prepare them for teamwork than others. This preparation is critical. If you don't do it, they will still think that the best way to deal with a crisis is with their own ideas and methods. They will ignore teamwork when their goal continues to be their own personal advancement. A real crisis is the test. Most organizations quickly promote their best crisis "fire-fighters." People looking to get ahead know this, and they naturally don't want to share the glory. If you want teamwork at senior levels, you need to work to get past this mentality.

BAD IDEA #2—Ignore the lack of teamwork.

You must deal with the lack of teamwork while a team is supposedly working on an assigned problem. Don't take a hands-off approach to a team just because the team has selected its members and they have received the problem they will work on. It is not enough to just give a deadline for solving the problem and warning team members what the consequences of failure might be. You must still ensure that true teamwork occurs as the group works on the problem.

Don't assume that just because you gave people a team assignment to work on together that they will do so. You must expend the time and effort to prepare the group to work together as a team beforehand. Continue to oversee the team. Watch to make sure the team is working together in a productive manner.

It's too late to fix lack of teamwork when the team's project fails. You could punish the team members, but that doesn't fix things. The project still failed, and your company has missed important opportunities. It is too late at this point to correct the situation. Better to watch for warnings while the team is working together. Step in quickly to help them if they are having difficulty. Be proactive in helping teams in your area to accomplish their goals.

 BAD IDEA #3—Put someone in charge of their peers.

Never put someone in charge of a group of peers and then quickly turn the group over to that person. The group will spend more time undermining the designated leader than it will in solving any assigned problems.

Rarely should you put someone in charge of peers. If you do, ensure that you take the time and make the effort to prepare peers for oversight by another peer. The situation is fraught with all kinds of problems. These range from less than enthusiastic support for the new team, to ignoring the designated leader's direction, to even destructive efforts to undermine the elevated peer. Any such actions can easily destroy the effectiveness of the group. This, in turn, prevents them from achieving assigned goals.

These problems are an outgrowth of the normal human tendencies to want to get ahead of peers. Those passed over often try to prove that leadership made a mistake about who was put in charge. Realize these are default tendencies by ambitious and hardworking people. You must take proactive measures to counteract these tendencies.

GOOD IDEA #1—Provide clear lines of authority.

You need to do a couple of things before you can expect productive work from a group. First, ensure the group is ready to work together. Make sure they are grounded in how they will work together. Often this means formal teamwork training. All involved need to know what is expected of them in a teamwork situation. Do this well before forming any team. Everyone in the organization should have teamwork skills. This way, you can use these skills the moment a need arises.

Second, discuss the role of the team leader and that of the team as a whole with the newly formed team. Do this in the presence and under the direction of the people the team members report to. Make the team leader's roles and responsibilities clear. Go over what is expected from each of the team members. Spell out the benefits and potential rewards for each of the team member. Delve somewhat into the consequences and possible outcomes for the business if the team fails to function properly.

GOOD IDEA #2—Ensure teamwork by careful oversight.

Just because you prepare a team for an assignment does not mean you can forget about it and what it is doing. You must get regular feedback from the team and its members. This feedback should give you information on how the team is doing. You need to know how it is progressing in meeting goals and timelines. You also need to know how the group is functioning as a team.

This feedback allows you to help if there is a problem. If the problem is meeting some type of productivity goal, you could find ways to help the team. Maybe you could infuse the team with additional talent. Or you might provide them with additional resources to help them get back on track. Remember, the goal is for them to solve the problem or get the work done on time. If you find out after the deadline that the team has not accomplished its goals, it is too late to help them get back on schedule.

You need to act if the feedback you get informs you there are problems between team members. You often will need to step in to help them work this out. Sometimes you can get by with just talking to the individuals involved privately. Sometimes it takes more effort. You may need an outside referee to help them resolve team member conflict. The goal for everyone involved should be the success of the team and the organization. If it is not, you need to help those who do not yet see things this way.

 GOOD IDEA #3—Direct ambition into positive channels.
The main causes of poor teamwork spring from ego and ambition. If someone feels that they should be running the show, or if they feel they will get ahead by taking care of a problem on their own, they may just try and do that.

Too often, a company's practices contradict what they say they want. If you promote people based on individual effort, if teamwork and the ability to work with others is of little consequence, you are going to have serious problems with teamwork among ambitious people. This is because the company is demonstrating quite effectively that being a team player is not that important. Such companies actually get anti-teamwork. You have to show people at all levels that only by working together for the best interests of the organizational whole will they get ahead personally. Not only should there be rewards for being a good team player, there should be consequences for lack of teamwork.

CHAPTER 7

STRATEGIC CONFUSION

"Whither Should We Go?"

INTRODUCTION

WITH the failure of the Schlieffen Plan, German leadership was unclear about what to do next. Two camps with different ideas on how to win the war soon emerged. They had very different ideas, and the two camps fought vigorously over which plan to adopt. The account of the struggle over how Germany would continue to fight the war makes the following important business points:

- Good money chasing bad
- Personal success at the cost of the organization
- Flip-flopping between different strategies
- Managing earnings
- Leadership blackmail: the resignation threat
- Risk taking by executives in trouble
- Effect of restricting the leadership selection pool
- Service overriding personal ambition

HISTORICAL CASE AND BUSINESS ANALOGIES

The New Situation

Late 1914 saw the end of hope for the quick resolution of World War I. Neither Germany nor her opponents had the upper hand on either the Eastern or Western Fronts. The failure of the Schlieffen Plan put Germany in the position of fighting a protracted two-front war. Its enemies had combined resources far in excess of what Germany and her weak ally Austria-Hungary had available. [Fig 29]

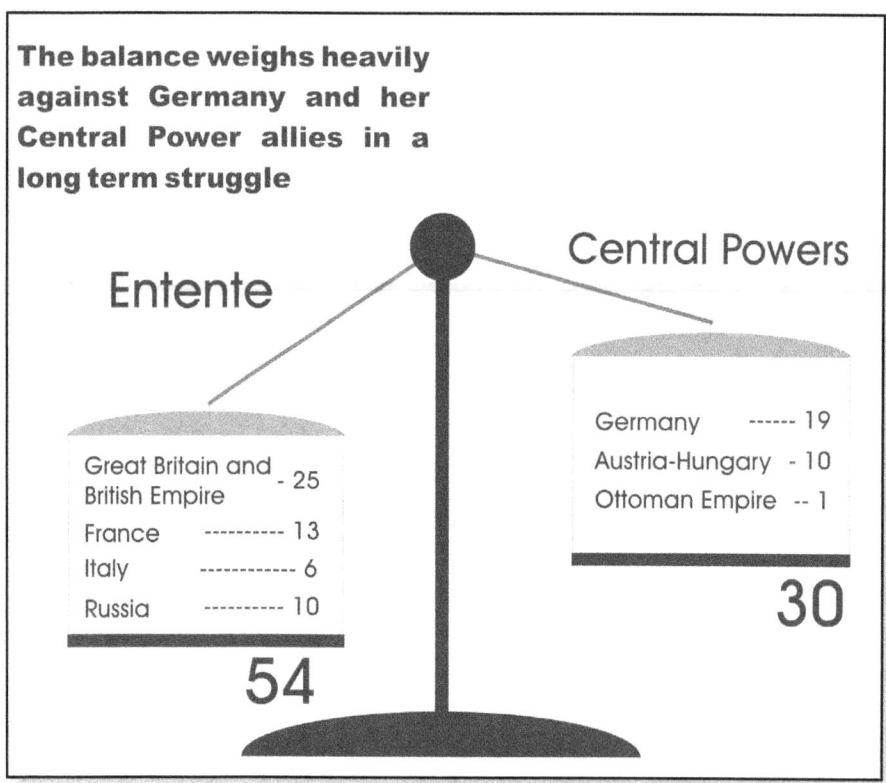

Figure 29. Relative Economic Resources of Combatants in 1915

Schlieffen had considered such a bleak situation to be hopeless. In fact, the entire Schlieffen Plan was a gamble to win the war quickly, before a long war on two fronts could overwhelm Germany. But now that Germany was actually at war, now that armies were in the field, no one in a position of leadership—not the Kaiser, not the heads of the civilian government, and certainly not the military chiefs—were willing to give up. In late 1914, they would not even consider a negotiated settlement to end the conflict.

> ## ANALOGY 1: THE ROAD TO RUIN
>
> Every business needs to know what its limits are. There comes a point where you will start to throw good money after bad, when there is no hope of recovering the initial investment made in an endeavor. Set this limit at the start, before emotion can override clear thinking. If you reach the predetermined point, pull the plug. Don't waste additional resources by putting them into something that isn't producing results. Such action may very well become an overwhelming drain on the business. It can easily lead to an outcome far worse than just the failure of a specific project.

The failure to come to grips with the lost gamble of the Schlieffen Plan would ruin Germany. Had the Kaiser, still absolute ruler in late 1914, been willing to negotiate an end to the war, he probably could have done so for as little as returning Alsace and Lorraine to France and paying damages to Belgium. By dragging the war out, the Kaiser and Germany lost everything. The end of the war saw the Kaiser deposed, the loss of considerable territory, the population bankrupt and starving, occupation by foreign troops, and anarchy, not to mention the millions killed or maimed and wounded in a war that lasted years.

The Opposing Camps

At the end of 1914, Germany had no clear plan on how to win the war. Everyone had been so confident in the Schlieffen Plan that no one really thought about what to do if it didn't work. In this vacuum of ideas, there appeared two very distinct camps in the hierarchy of the German military. One camp was lead by General Falkenhayn. He replaced Moltke at the head of the German Army after the Schlieffen Plan's failure. Hindenburg and Ludendorff, the senior officers on the Eastern Front, led the other camp. Each camp had very different views on how to win the war. Each saw the other as preventing it from being successful.

Falkenhayn tried to rectify the situation in France after Moltke's dismissal.

He had little to work with. The German Army had suffered huge losses up to and through the Battle of the Marne. Constant combat had expended most of the prewar stockpiles of ammunition. There was little left. Falkenhayn attempted to outflank the enemy's lines where they met the sea. He committed the only fresh units left in the German Army. These were the handful of new divisions raised since the war began. The attacks failed. The battle degenerated into uncontrolled chaos in muddy fields. Thousands died with no appreciable results other than more casualties on both sides.

Falkenhayn came to the realization that the war was now all about attrition. The days of sweeping maneuver were over. Belligerent nations no longer operated under the paradigm of the past, where they would surrender if their army lost a couple of big battles. Instead, they would fight on until there were no more soldiers left to draft, the civilian population starved, and their factories could not produce another shell. The objective in a war of attrition is to force your opponent into these desperate straights before you end up there yourself. This is what Falkenhayn planned to do.

Falkenhayn figured the only opponents he had a chance of defeating in a war of attrition were those on the Western Front. France's population was smaller than Germany's, so it had fewer men to draft into its army. Falkenhayn thought Russia had almost unlimited available manpower. In addition to the masses available, the Russians could also opt to retreat into the limitless expanse of their country. This would pull the Germans deep into areas where supplying their army would be difficult. The French did not have this option. They would have to stand and fight, or they would have to surrender. Falkenhayn wanted to fight the war against France and her British allies while sending only enough east to hold off the Russians. His intent in the East was just to keep the Russians away from Germany and Austria-Hungary. Falkenhayn's main objective was to grind down the French Army in battles they could not retreat from.

Hindenburg and Ludendorff had won the only decisive victory yet by Germany in the war. They led the German Army in the east that surrounded and destroyed the Russian Second Army at Tannenberg. They thought the war could be won by a series of decisive battles that would destroy large enemy armies. They believed the Eastern Front was the place to do this.

Strategic Confusion 221

> ## ANALOGY 2: WHICH WAY TO GO?
>
> The fact that each camp viewed its own theater as the most critical is nothing new. In business, executives usually point to the area they lead as the most important to their company. Since it is the most important area, they believe it deserves a greater share of the company's resources.
>
> You cannot dismiss all such talk as attempts to increase the size of the executives' dominion within the company. One of them has to be right. There is always an area critically important to the company, one that can make or break it. The problem is, who do you believe? Your company will have this difficult problem if it consistently moves people into leadership positions who worry primarily about their power and the size of their departments. Instead, you need executives more concerned with the success of the entire company. Such people are willing to point to the critical part of the business, the one most in need of the company's resources. They do this because they want the entire company to succeed.

The Eastern School led by Hindenburg and Ludendorff believed the Western Front was hopelessly bogged down. They saw the fighting in France as a stalemate neither side could break. There was no room for maneuver. Heavily defended trench lines stretched unbroken across France from the Swiss border to the English Channel. The French and British armies were competent foes. They were completely committed to defending this line. The Eastern Front was immense by comparison. There was still ample room for maneuver. Many Russian generals were incompetent. The Eastern School believed they could achieve decisive victories over Russian armies. They believed that such victories would force the Russians to give up. After that, the full might of Germany would bring decisive results on the Western Front.

The views of the two camps at the highest levels of the German military were diametrically opposed. One wanted to concentrate on winning a war of attrition on the Western Front. The other side wanted to concentrate on winning a war of decisive battles on the Eastern Front. Both sides viewed the other's opinions with contempt.

The Man in the Middle

Germany entered the war with a single plan, the Schlieffen Plan. The idea was to knock France out of the war and then turn on Russia. The plan did not produce the promised results. There was no clear plan for continuing the war. There were opposing proposals from Falkenhayn and from Hindenburg and Ludendorff. Someone had to decide which proposal to accept. Neither camp was open to debate. A compromise plan was not acceptable, especially to the Eastern School.

The only man who had the power to make a definite decision was the German Kaiser. The problem was that he had no clear idea about which path to follow. If he picked the wrong proposal, he knew he would probably lose the war. That meant he would no longer be Kaiser. Rather than pick one of the two alternatives, he decided to pick neither. He vacillated back and forth between supporting Falkenhayn and the Hindenburg and Ludendorff team.

ANALOGY 3: STRATEGIC VACILLATION

Here is the modern example. A business has reached a crossroads. Its earlier plans have not resulted in decisively beating the competition. The business must now decide what to do next. It needs a plan for a protracted competitive environment. A number of different plans are put forward concerning what the business should do next. Each of these proposals entails significant risk. The corporate leadership realizes that if it picks the wrong plan, the company could suffer severe long-term consequences.

The ultimate decision maker decides not to pick any one of the long-range proposals. Instead, the company decides to try first one proposal and then another for a relatively short time to see which produces better results. Their initial idea is to make a final decision on the long-term strategy of the company based on these short-term results. The final decision is postponed to some indefinite future date.

A business that goes down this crooked path will have the same results as in the historical case. A serious and protracted power struggle will play out at the highest levels of the company. The camps that espouse the different proposals will declare war on each other. Each will do what it can to stop the other from being successful. They will do this by tactically withholding resources or failing to provide assistance. All of the energy expended in this power struggle is at the expense of doing things geared toward beating the competition.

If that isn't bad enough, the failure to decide on a long-term strategy has other significant negative effects on the business. There is no clear picture of where the company is headed. People will wonder exactly what markets or specific business they are in. Lower-level decisions are difficult because no one is really clear on company priorities. Employee morale is sapped. Enthusiasm for the future of the business wanes. Talented people become disgusted about what is going on and start looking for work elsewhere.

Don't go down this path! Work out what your strategy will be. Build consensus on the strategy at every level. Work together to achieve success. As a great man once said, "A house divided against itself cannot stand."

The Kaiser's policy was to vacillate between the two camps. At first, Hindenburg and Ludendorff got the go ahead. They received control of the next group of newly created combat units. In 1915, they used these forces in an attempt to win a decisive victory against the Russians.

The East

In early 1915, the Germans had local successes in the East, but no decisive victories. To make themselves look better, Hindenburg and Ludendorff, with the support of their staff, engaged in activity known in the business world as "managing earnings." They inflated reports about the numbers of prisoners their forces had taken. They inflated reports on the quantity of captured equipment. They didn't inflate these figures by a mere 20 percent or so. They doubled or tripled the actual figures. To make the false picture of victory complete, they reported that Russian units retreating in good order were "out of action" and "unable to continue operations."

ANALOGY 4: EXECUTIVE DECEPTION

Lying about your operational results is not a good thing. It is not just morally wrong and reprehensible behavior. The lies will quickly lead the company astray. You can only make good decisions about the future with accurate information: critical decisions about where the company should head, what operations it should accelerate, and which it should end. False information can easily send a business down the wrong path, often irretrievably. You cannot tolerate this kind of dishonesty if you want your company to be successful, or even just survive.

Hindenburg and Ludendorff did not stop at just putting the best possible spin on their own operations. They also did things to hinder or prevent Falkenhayn from pursuing his strategy. Hindenburg's armies refused to release troops to Falkenhayn as previously agreed. They reported that these troops were in critical positions. They reported that serious consequences would result from their transfer back to the Western Front. Hindenburg and Ludendorff's staff also sent low-level emissaries back to Berlin. Their job was to initiate a whispering campaign. Low-level officers from Eastern Front army staffs were in Berlin to gain support for Hindenburg and Ludendorff's strategy and to warn of the perils of Falkenhayn's. They urged their converts to write letters to the Kaiser urging him to support the Eastern strategy.

> ## ANALOGY 5: POLITICAL INTRIGUE
>
> Political machinations and intrigues exist in every organization. You are only deluding yourself if you think they don't. They are incredibly destructive. They will eventually destroy any organization that doesn't take effective steps to stamp out as much of this behavior as possible.
>
> The best way to avoid having to take drastic action to fix this problem is to quickly deal with it whenever it appears. This behavior doesn't show up only when someone reaches some senior executive level in the company. It will show up soon after the person with such tendencies gets their first supervisory role. This is fortunate, because you can take steps to identify people that engage in such activity. Then you must stop them or eject them from the company.

Falkenhayn was the Chief of the German General Staff. He was technically Hindenburg and Ludendorff's superior. Falkenhayn also enjoyed considerable personal support from the Kaiser. How did Hindenburg and Ludendorff get away with their insubordination? Why were there no consequences to publishing inflated reports? The answer is that Hindenburg had become the golden boy of the German public. He was the only general who had won clear-cut victories over the enemy. He was a hugely popular hero. Fear of Hindenburg's enormous popularity stopped the Kaiser and Falkenhayn from taking action against the insubordination and blatant intrigues.

Hindenburg would threaten to resign whenever the Eastern School felt they were getting inadequate support, or if they were ordered to do something they did not want to do. If he actually resigned, the public would know he did not support the policies of the Kaiser and the General Staff. This could cause public support of the Kaiser and the military's policies to nose dive. The Kaiser was unwilling to deal with such a crisis of confidence and caved in to Hindenburg's demands to stop him from resigning. Hindenburg threatened to resign numerous times. Each time, the powers above him backed down and caved in to his demands. By doing so, they increasingly strengthened Hindenburg and Ludendorff's positions.

ANALOGY 6: LEADERSHIP BLACKMAIL

Here is a similar story. A business has a proclaimed "genius" in its ranks. The press proclaims this person as the one responsible for impressive recent company successes. The stockholders take great notice. The proclaimed golden boy uses his notoriety to start demanding more and more power and influence within the company. He demands the company move in the direction he wants. He threatens to resign if he does not get his way.

The head of the company is in a rather difficult position because of this resignation threat. If the golden boy resigns, there will be a lot of angry stockholders. They will not be happy with the resulting fall in the stock price. The stock will fall because the business press will make a big deal out of the resignation. The press will say that the resignation means the golden boy has lost faith in the company's leadership. They will say that he quit because he no longer believes in the direction and future of the company. All of this will call the competence and leadership of the company into question.

If the company caves in to the threat, it puts itself in a very difficult position. Giving in now shows that the company will give in to the same threat again. This greatly strengthens the power, position, and authority of the golden boy. Likewise, it greatly reduces the authority and influence of anyone opposing him or his ideas. The Kaiser failed to realize this in his dealings with Hindenburg and Ludendorff.

The resignation threat is one of the best political power plays there is. People use it not just to gain more power and prestige, but also to get more money. You must recognize that no one is indispensable. If you cave in to a resignation threat, you send a strong statement that the person truly is irreplaceable. You will greatly reduce your own ability to influence such a subordinate. You will reward someone who is blackmailing you. If someone makes this threat, it is best to just let them go. It will be difficult in the short term, but in the end, you and your company will be better off without them.

Falkenhayn tried as best he could to execute the strategy he favored. His priority was the war of attrition on the Western Front. Yet he was flexible enough to deal with issues on the Eastern Front when necessary.

In 1915, Falkenhayn personally led a large German offensive on the Eastern Front. This offensive drove the Russians out of most of the territory they had captured in Austria-Hungary and out of most of Poland. Falkenhayn conducted this operation from the Austro-Hungarian sector of the Eastern Front, outside of the areas controlled by Hindenburg and Ludendorff.

Falkenhayn's offensive broke through the Russian lines near the towns of Gorlice and Tarnow. Falkenhayn had limited objectives for this offensive. He wanted only to prop up Austria-Hungary, reducing the Russian threat to it. This would reduce the number of German troops needed to strengthen Austro-Hungarian lines in the east. This way Falkenhayn could return to concentrating on the Western Front. [Fig 30]

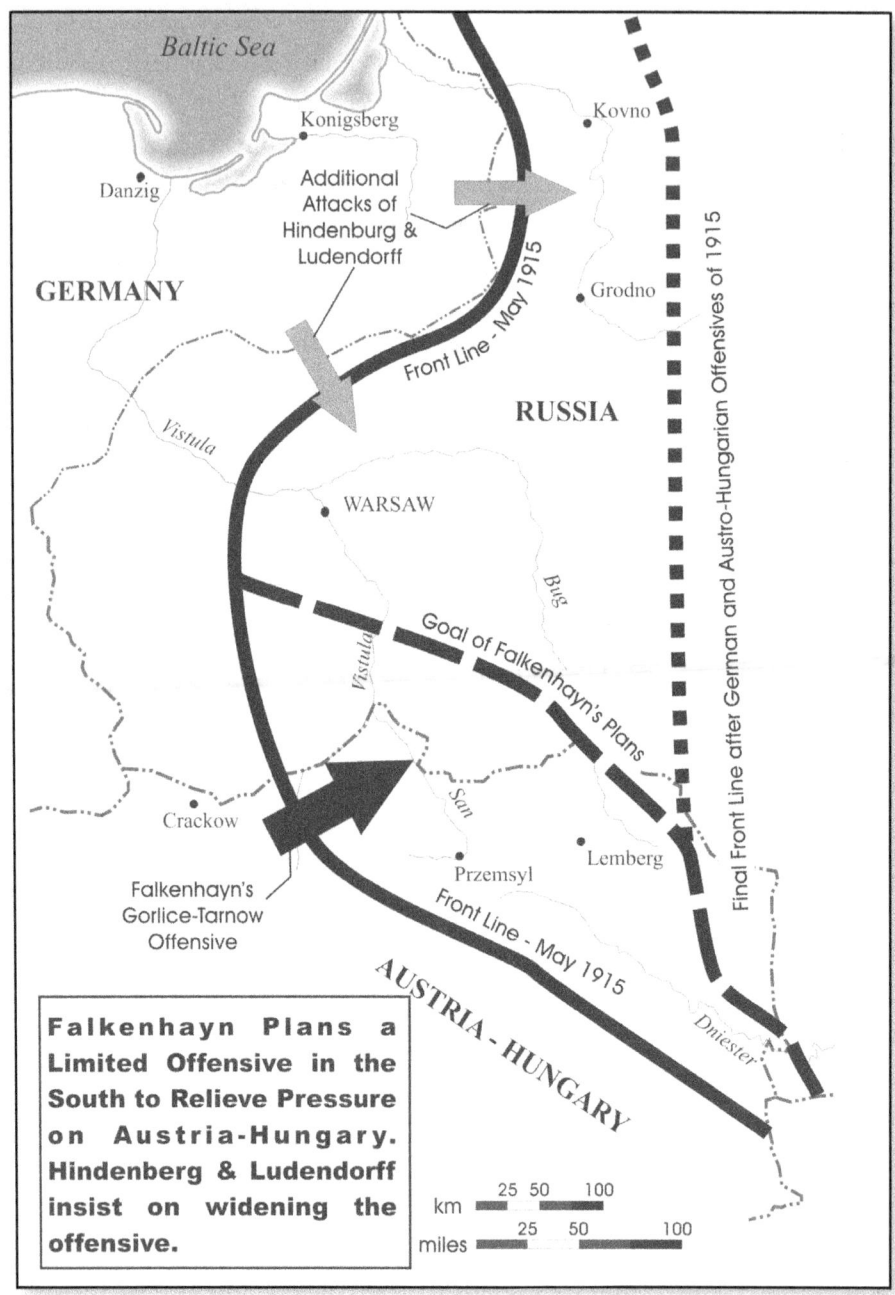

Figure 30. Eastern Front – 1915, Plans and Outcomes

Strategic Confusion

The Gorlice-Tarnow campaign met Falkenhayn's objectives. But right as he wanted to end it, Hindenburg and Ludendorff got the Kaiser's permission to widen the campaign into the areas they controlled. The Germans had further success, but only the limited success Falkenhayn predicted. The Germans pushed the Russians farther back, but the Russian armies were still intact, and they could easily replace their losses. Also, the Germans were now farther from their own sources of supply and in more difficult terrain. Of course, Hindenburg and Ludendorff proclaimed yet another round of victories.

The West

Falkenhayn could see that his position as head of all German armies was in serious jeopardy. He himself did not yet have a single clear-cut victory on the Western Front that he could point to as evidence of his strategy's validity. Hindenburg and Ludendorff expropriated a large part of his success on the Eastern Front. The logic and arguments for Falkenhayn's strategy fell increasingly on deaf ears. He saw the weight of opinion moving steadily towards adopting his rivals' views. He would have to do something drastic to maintain his position. He needed a success that no one could argue with.

Falkenhayn made plans for a great gamble to achieve this goal. He proposed a large campaign on the Western Front to force France out of the war. He picked the historically important town of Verdun as the location for months of constant combat. Verdun was the largest fortress complex in France. Falkenhayn did not intend to break through the French lines, but to bleed the French Army dry. He planned the Verdun campaign as a protracted battle of attrition over an objective the French would not abandon. It was an extremely risky plan. The German Army would itself take irreplaceable losses while it tried to break the French. Falkenhayn's desperation was behind the gamble.

Verdun

Falkenhayn correctly guessed that the French would not abandon Verdun. They fed division after division into the battle. The maelstrom also ate up entire divisions of German troops. Verdun didn't just bleed the French Army white; it had the same effect on the German Army. With each passing day and week, the German Army expended more of its reserves to keep the bloodbath going. French morale faltered, but it did not break. They still had the will to fight on.

The German Army weakened itself with repeated fruitless attacks at Verdun.

The use of their reserves made them vulnerable. The German Army did not have enough reserves left to deal with subsequent enemy attacks. This is exactly what happened next. First the Russians and then the British launched massive offensives.

Brusilov, the most competent Russian general, led the Russian offensive. He aimed his attacks primarily at the Austro-Hungarian Army. The Russians broke through the Austro-Hungarian lines and routed large portions of their army. The Germans had to send units to plug the holes, restore the front line, and minimize damage.

Then the British attacked along the Somme River on the Western Front. The British attacks were very costly, but the Germans also had to send reserves to stop the British from breaking through their lines. [Fig 31]

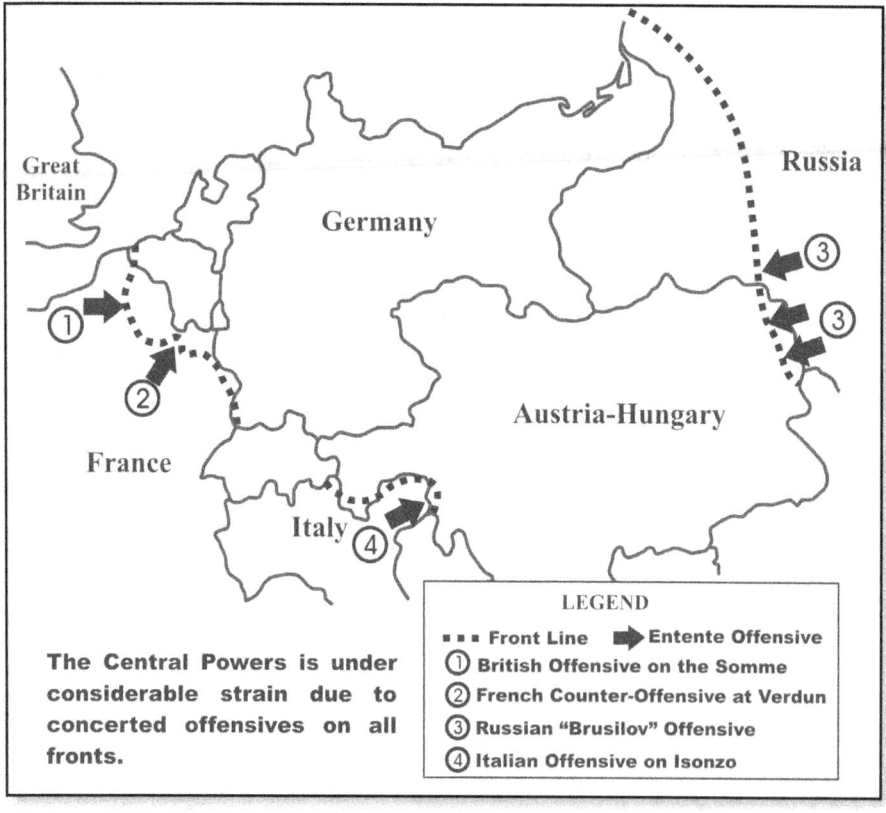

Figure 31. *Pressure on Germany and Austria-Hungary in mid-1916*

The combined weight of the enemy offensives stretched German resources to the breaking point. The Russian and British attacks came close to causing a German and Austro-Hungarian collapse. The reason the Germans came so close to losing was that Falkenhayn had used up the resources needed to deal with these new situations. Falkenhayn placed Germany in dire straits by expending irreplaceable reserves in an attempt to gain the upper hand in his power struggle with Hindenburg and Ludendorff.

ANALOGY 7: SELF-PRESERVATION GAMBLE

People are apt to take abnormally high risks if they believe their position is in jeopardy. Options previously considered too risky start looking good. Someone who thinks they may be on the way out becomes willing to take risks not in the company's best interest. They are no longer thinking about the company. They are thinking of themselves. Their motivation is personal preservation.

The executive in danger becomes willing to gamble more than normal. It is an attempt to gain the upper hand in the politics of the business. The idea is that by scoring a big win, they will maintain their position, power, and prestige in the company. Unfortunately, such gambles usually make the business vulnerable. This is because the business is expending its finite resources on a very risky course of action. Also, the first gamble is often not the last. When the first gamble doesn't pay off, the increasingly desperate executive will grasp for even more risky endeavors. This spiral will continue until the company is completely drained.

You need to frequently ask yourself, "Who's best interest is this in?" Ask this especially about extremely risky endeavors. If it's not in the business' best interest, then don't pursue it.

Falkenhayn's gamble at Verdun failed to pay off. In fact, it made things worse for the Germans. The situation for Germany became increasingly precarious. There were the heavy losses at Verdun and on the Somme. Brusilov's attacks had come very close to knocking Austria-Hungary out of the war. As if these situations were not bad enough, yet another country decided to declare war against Germany and Austria-Hungary. This was one disaster too many for the Kaiser. When Romania joined the list of German enemies, Hindenburg and Ludendorff instigated the Kaiser's removal of Falkenhayn. Hindenburg was elevated to lead all of Germany's armies. He brought along Ludendorff as his right hand man.

Under New Management

So Hindenburg replaced Falkenhayn. Hindenburg and Ludendorff's underhanded political maneuvering finally brought them to the top. The Kaiser knew about most of their actions. But he thought that these two would win the war for him. He based his decision on the fallacy that "one side was wrong, so the other side must be right." He did not consider that both camps could be wrong. The Kaiser did not consider anyone else for the top job. He believed Hindenburg and Ludendorff were the only ones competent enough to lead the German military effort.

ANALOGY 8: MYTH OF THE SPECIAL FEW

Many in the business world today are of the opinion that there is only a handful of people competent enough to lead a corporation. Extensive manhunts ensue whenever a major corporation decides it needs a new leader. These manhunts start by identifying the few worthy candidates. The business then waves huge sums of money in these people's faces. The business wants one of them to take on the responsibility of leading them through what is usually a very difficult time.

You don't need to limit your options. There are plenty of people around competent enough to run the business. Many of them are already in the company. They can probably do a better job than the last guy did. After all, they will have learned from his mistakes. They are ready to make changes and do things differently.

Now, these people may not have held the lofty positions often seen as prerequisites to such responsibility. Many of these prerequisite jobs are good for gaining experience. But they are not mandatory. Experience and ability are not the same thing. Remember that when you consider people for increased responsibility.

Military history is full of stories of people who suddenly found themselves two or three levels above where they had been working, and they excelled at their new jobs. Of course, these people had shown talent and skill. Most importantly, they had shown the capacity to learn and quickly deal with new challenges. Here are some examples to consider. What kind of experience did George Washington have before he led the Revolutionary War army in America? He had only been the deputy commander of a small failed expedition in a war almost twenty years in the past. What was Ulysses S. Grant doing before shortly before his campaigns won the American Civil War? He was a failed farmer working in a leather store for his brother. Then there is Eisenhower in World War II. He had never had a command, had never been in combat, and was not even a general when the war started. There are many other examples. The point is that these people were highly capable. But they were not very experienced. The lesson is to *not* restrict your options to only the experienced when thinking about who should take on leadership roles.

Romania's entry into the war created near panic in German leadership. The Kaiser was seriously worried that the war was now lost. The Germans scraped together whatever they could to deal with this new development. Falkenhayn himself was sent to the area as the new commander of this front. This was the mechanism used to ease him out of his old position. He did a fine job. Soon the Germans and their allies overran almost all of Romania. [Fig 32]

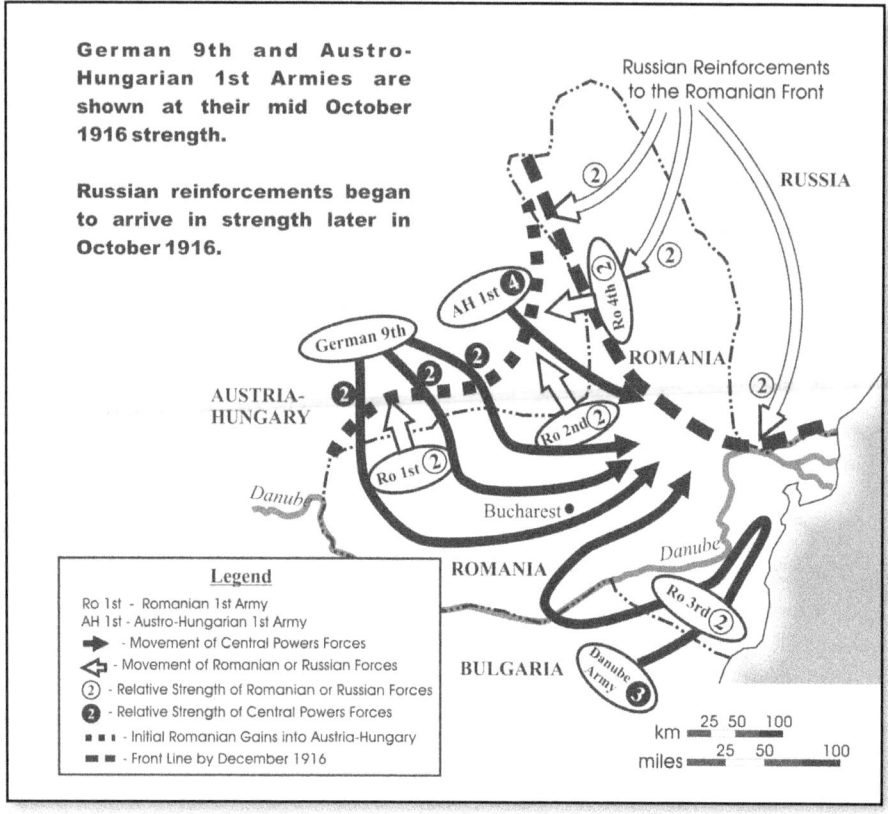

Figure 32. The Romanian Campaign, Late Aug - Dec 1916

Hindenburg and Ludendorff now took over at the German High Command. They became deeply involved in dealing with French and British offensives on the Western Front. Their views and opinions started to change. They did not drastically reduce forces on the Western Front to enable larger operations on the Eastern Front, even though this is what they had previously demanded.

They quietly began to accept many of the theories Falkenhayn had expounded. Western Front operations quickly absorbed most of their attention.

> ## ANALOGY 9: CONTROL OF THE SELFISH
>
> You cannot place control of your organization into the hands of people who have no real goal outside of satisfying their own ambitions. The problem is that the ambition of such people is never satisfied. They continually want more power and more control. They are not serving in the best interest of the business. The welfare of the company is not the most important thing to such poor self-absorbed managers. All they want is to be in charge and to be in charge of more and more. They will actually damage the business itself if that is what it takes to accomplish their selfish goals.
>
> You must consider the background and tendencies of people you are thinking of placing in senior positions. Fortunately, the tendencies of these people are usually quite well known. Many others will have had experience dealing with them while working on different projects. Tap into this information to find out what people are like.
>
> Don't make the big mistake of ignoring self-serving behavior. Never think, "We know he cares for nothing but himself, but he produces results, and we can control him." Such people are incredibly dangerous to any group they might lead. Their goal is not the long-term welfare of the organization. Neither is the organization's performance. What they usually have done is to improve short-term results, often by damaging long-term prospects. These people cannot be controlled. The minute their goals and the goals of the company diverge, they stop considering what is best for the business. Heaven help you if they control critical assets or functions, because they won't.

Elevation to the highest posts in the German military did not satisfy Hindenburg and Ludendorff's ambitions. Soon, they engaged in political intrigues to replace the Chancellor, the head of the civilian government. The Kaiser caved in to these demands, just as he had given in to their demands for Falkenhayn's dismissal. The Kaiser himself was soon no more than a figurehead. Hindenburg and Ludendorff ran everything, even things not normally under military control. Important areas like foreign policy, the economy, and even the criminal justice system were either completely under their control, or solidly within their sphere of influence. As long as the war continued, they, not the Kaiser, were the dictators of Germany.

In the end, Hindenburg and Ludendorff destroyed the organization, institutions, and very nation they purported to serve. They attempted increasingly high risk military operations in attempts to achieve their personal goals. There was an unsustainable escalation in the cost of continuing the war. Many wanted to negotiate an end to it. The pair quashed every such attempt. They continued their gamble of winning everything or losing all. The final result found Germany militarily bankrupt, economically ravaged, and politically destroyed.

Who was to blame? In their own opinions, certainly not Hindenburg and Ludendorff. Their post war memoirs were the origin of the Stab in the Back theory. They blamed the people at home for not adequately supporting the military. They pointed their fingers in every direction except at themselves and their own methods. These views had serious repercussions for the world. They are the origin of thoughts that a certain element of German society had betrayed the army and the country. These accusations were directed at the Jews.

After the war, Ludendorff became actively involved in trying to overthrow the new German government. As someone who had wielded dictatorial powers, he had little love of democracy. He was a key participant in the Beer Hall Putsch, the failed attempt by a young Adolf Hitler and his Nazi party to take over the country.

Hindenburg became involved in politics as well. He remained immensely popular after the war. People saw him as the man who could stabilize the country after the anarchy that followed the collapse of the monarchy. He became president of Germany. One of his last acts was to appoint Adolf Hitler as Chancellor. One of the arguments Hindenburg made in appointing Hitler as German Chancellor was, "We can control him."

CONCLUSIONS

This is how the struggle within the German High Command about how to win World War I played out. Two camps emerged with very different ideas on how to go about winning the war. One side did everything it could to undermine the other. This group successfully consolidated power. Hindenburg and Ludendorff came to control every aspect of Germany's war effort. The result was disastrous for Germany. In exploring how this happened, there are a number of important lessons for the business world. These include:

- **Good money chasing bad**
  Set limits for the amount of resources you will put into any new project or endeavor. Pull the plug if and when you reach this limit. If you don't do this, there is a very high likelihood the project will drain resources away from successful activities or other more promising opportunities. Don't throw good money after bad. End projects that have failed.

- **Personal success at the cost of the organization**
  The most dangerous leaders place personal gain ahead of the organization's success. They will engage in selfish behavior to enrich and elevate themselves. They will do this even if it means ruining the very organization they supposedly serve.
  You never first see selfish leadership behavior only when someone reaches a position of great power. You can find such behavior throughout the person's career. Elevating people with these tendencies just gives them a greater opportunity to do harm. Avoid putting them in charge of very much. They need to undergo significant change before you can entrust them with significant responsibilities.

- **Flip-flopping between different strategies**
  Making momentous decisions can be scary. Setting out the long-term plan for a company is such a decision. Don't be scared into not making a definitive decision. Weak leaders have a tendency to do this. They flip-flop between different short-term strategies while they vacillate about what to do.
  If you don't make a clear decision about how to proceed, there can be

serious immediate consequences. Your business may find itself embroiled in internal infighting over which strategy it should follow. The company's decision making processes at lower levels will become lethargic. This is due to people being unsure about where the organization is going and what the priorities are.

- **Managing earnings**
  The phrase "managing earnings" is just a polite way to say "lying about results." You must make decisions about what practices and methods to employ to make your business successful. You need to base such decisions on accurate information. If you make decisions based on inaccurate data, your business will quickly find itself headed down the wrong road. You will adopt methods that do not work. You cannot tolerate lying about results if you want your business to succeed.

- **Leadership blackmail: the resignation threat**
  You greatly curb your own power and authority when you give in to the blackmail of a resignation threat. You greatly enhance the power and influence of the person you caved in to. You have significantly curtailed your own ability to oversee and influence such an individual. Let people who use the resignation threat leave. If you give in, they will repeatedly use the threat as leverage to get their own way.

- **Risk taking by executives in trouble**
  Executives who think they may get sacked will be tempted to accept a great deal of risk. They think that they can save themselves by hitting the proverbial home run. The problem is that they may accept risk far beyond what is normally acceptable. In fact, they may take the whole company down the drain with them if their gamble does not pay off. You need checks and balances in place to stop people from gambling with way too much.

- **Effect of restricting the leadership selection pool**
  It is a myth that there are only a very few people capable of assuming high level leadership positions. There are many people capable of good leadership and decision making. You only limit your options when you

accept the myth as fact. Don't restrict the pool of candidates you consider for senior positions. Do not forget to look at capable people from lower levels who have shown great abilities. Do not pass people over just because they have not held certain prerequisite positions. Remember that experience does not always equal capability.

- **Service overriding personal ambition**
  Truly great leaders will sacrifice their own personal ambitions for the good of the organizations they lead. Poor leaders will put their personal ambition ahead of the good of the organization. They will look out for themselves first and the organization later. They will do what is good for the organization only when it benefits them. You cannot control people like this and prevent them from doing damage. And they will do a lot of damage if you keep them around. Let them find ways outside of your business to make themselves successful.

ACTION FILE

HOW TO ASSESS AND SELECT LEADERS

 BAD IDEA #1—Base decisions on elitism.
Many people tend to think that their own personal life experiences are the best. They fail to understand that others with very different experiences may be just as capable at they are. Unfortunately, this limited thinking often influences their consideration of others. People think things like, "No school is better than *my* alma mater" or, "Since I am an accountant, the best qualified person is probably also an accountant." The errors about what might make someone a good leader apply to other backgrounds as well. Those making leadership choices might consider a host of irrelevant background issues. They might place value on unimportant things like where someone is from, what sports they play, their religion, and so on.

This narrow-minded thinking spawns elitism. Under elitism, people with the preferred background get ahead. Those without it, regardless of their talents and abilities, languish. It does not seem to matter who is the most productive, or who is most likely to be successful with additional responsibility. Elitism moves the focus of the leadership selection process away from skill and ability. Instead, the focus is on other, often meaningless, criteria.

Elitism results in less than optimal leadership choices. The organization ignores better choices because they don't have the desired background or experience. The best people are not in charge. Instead, the company has leaders who may very well feel they are entitled to their positions because of their background. They will not focus on maximizing organizational performance with the same zeal. This is because they realize their promotion was not due to their performance, but because of a special background. They may believe that they are entitled to their position because they have the right punches on their ticket.

There are criteria used for leadership selection that are even worse than some special background. These come in to play when leadership decisions are made based on a person's appearance. This appearance factor is not about how someone dresses. It solely means what they look like. This is not just about nationality or ethnic background. This is obviously wrong, yet it is a major factor way too often.

We mistakenly assume that attractive people have all kinds of positive attributes. The fact is that their appearance shows only one: they are attractive. Remember that the only thing you can really tell about someone based on their appearance is what they look like. Don't make leadership decisions based on appearance. It is a juvenile thing to do. Base your decision on the appropriate criteria—things like what they do, what their accomplishments are, and how they deal with stress. Falling into the trap of using physical attractiveness as part of the leadership selection processes can easily lead you to make a very bad decision.

BAD IDEA #2—Be influenced by resignation threats.

Sometimes someone gets too big for their britches. People with very high opinions of themselves often threaten to quit if they don't get an available promotion. This is little more than blackmail. Yet too often, decision makers cave in to the threat. Don't let it be you.

No one is irreplaceable. If you think they are, and succumb to the resignation threat, they will do it again and again. You might as well hand the keys over to them right now. They will soon be at or near the top of your organization.

Why do you think they make the threat? It is because they are worried that their merits and accomplishments won't get them the job. You are actually picking a less desirable alternative when you fall for resignation blackmail.

Assist in the departure of anyone who threatens to quit if you don't give them what they want. If you don't, you will wish you did. The price you will end up paying will just get higher and higher.

BAD IDEA #3—Select people who put themselves first.

You want people in charge who put the organization first. The exact opposite are the people who put their wants and desires ahead of what is good and proper for the business. They constantly look for ways to get what they want from the company, using their position to do so. It does not matter to them if doing so is detrimental. They don't really care about the business. They care about what the business is doing for them. These self servers seek perks and other tangible benefits for themselves. They spend a lot of their time doing this. It is their primary motivation. They won't make sacrifices unless forced to do so. They will never offer to do things that don't benefit themselves. They are selfish and self centered.

They ask for more resources than they need and hoard what they already have. Their primary concern is for their personal success. They will march down their own path even if it means others will fail as a result; even if it means the business might fail. This is the result of their greed. Avoid putting people like this into leadership positions. If they are already there, let them know that continuing self-serving actions will have serious negative consequences.

 GOOD IDEA #1—Assess success.

Just because someone was in charge of something that succeeded, does not mean that person was the reason for the success. Often times, projects succeed in spite of the person in charge. Sometimes the leader actually hindered the project. People are more than happy to accept responsibility for successes. You need to understand *why* a particular project was successful. If you don't understand this, you could make a big mistake. You might promote someone whose project was successful in spite of the leadership. By doing so, you set up your business for all kinds of catastrophes.

Understanding why a project was successful will put you at ease. You should feel good about giving greater responsibility to a person whose leadership significantly contributed to success. You should also feel good about removing someone from a leadership role if you find out they hindered an important project. This will reduce the chance of future projects failing. Putting the right person in charge increases the probability of success.

Be careful in assessing success. Be wary of getting all of your information from a single source. This can happen without you realizing it. It goes like this: you get information on Paul from Bob. But you also get information on Paul from Nancy. It just turns out that Nancy's only source is

Bob. You also get information from John. But John's only sources were Nancy and Bob. The reality is that Bob is your only source of information on Paul. Information is always tainted by the opinions, likes, and dislikes of the source. Be aware of this. Always look for multiple sources of information.

GOOD IDEA #2—Match position to skills.

You hear these stories a lot: someone was a great nurse, but ineffective as a nursing supervisor. Someone was great as a pilot, but failed as a squadron leader. Someone was a fantastic teacher, but had serious problems while school principal. The reason for these problems is quite simple. In each of these stories, the performance in the first position was due to very different skills than they would need to succeed in the new position.

You must look at the position you are filling, *not* the position someone is in right now. First, look at the skills needed in an open position. Then look for people with *those* skills. Success in one job doesn't ensure success in a different job that requires different skills.

The need for good interpersonal skills, so-called people skills, increases exponentially as you move higher in any organization. The need for specific technical skills decreases. Yet people are often promoted to management positions just because they excel at highly technical jobs. They then often fail because they lack good people skills. Be careful not to try to put round pegs into square holes.

GOOD IDEA #3—Consider wider possibilities.

Severely limiting who you consider for a leadership position increases the chance of making a poor choice. You do this when you only look at individuals with some specific prerequisite experience.

This myopic view is rather limiting. It says that someone can't be successful leading a hundred people unless they already have experience leading fifty. As a result, you don't consider people who have only led ten or twenty. You can take your best candidate out of consideration by doing this. You have certainly reduced the pool of available candidates, but that's not your objective. You want to make the best choice. What if you only consider four people, and all of them are mediocre? Will you actually pick one of them? Don't do this.

Look for the skills and abilities needed, not necessarily for past experience. Consider many more people. Consider people from other areas. Do not put prerequisite experience on such a high pedestal. Match the person to the skills required. Allow yourself some faith that good people will rise to the challenge.

CHAPTER 8

VERDUN

"They Shall Not Pass!"

INTRODUCTION

THE French and Germans fought one of the greatest battles in all of history at Verdun. The French fortress system at Verdun was arguably the best in the world. Yet by the start of the battle, it was in a sorry state. The French had relocated most of its guns and garrison troops to more active areas of the Western Front. The German general Falkenhayn chose Verdun as the site for the campaign in which he intended to bleed France's army dry. Here the Germans intended to win the war by attrition. Falkenhayn's plan was not to capture the town and fortress system, yet that is almost what happened. A series of French mistakes put Verdun in a precarious position. The story of Verdun correlates well to the following important points:

- The "That's not my job" syndrome
- Dangers of refusing temporary help
- Teamwork versus individual ego
- Common communication failures
- Taking credit for other's work

HISTORICAL CASE AND BUSINESS ANALOGIES

The Fortress Salient

Verdun was an important historic site to France. Its forts had withstood sieges in almost every major war France had fought. Verdun remained France's most impressive and prestigious fortress system. In the campaign of 1914, the site withstood German efforts to take it as they advanced through the French countryside. As the French armies fell back towards the Marne River, Verdun was the pivot point of their line. The front lines solidified after the French stopped the Germans in the Battle of the Marne. Along these lines, Verdun stuck out like a finger pointing back to toward Germany. [Fig 33]

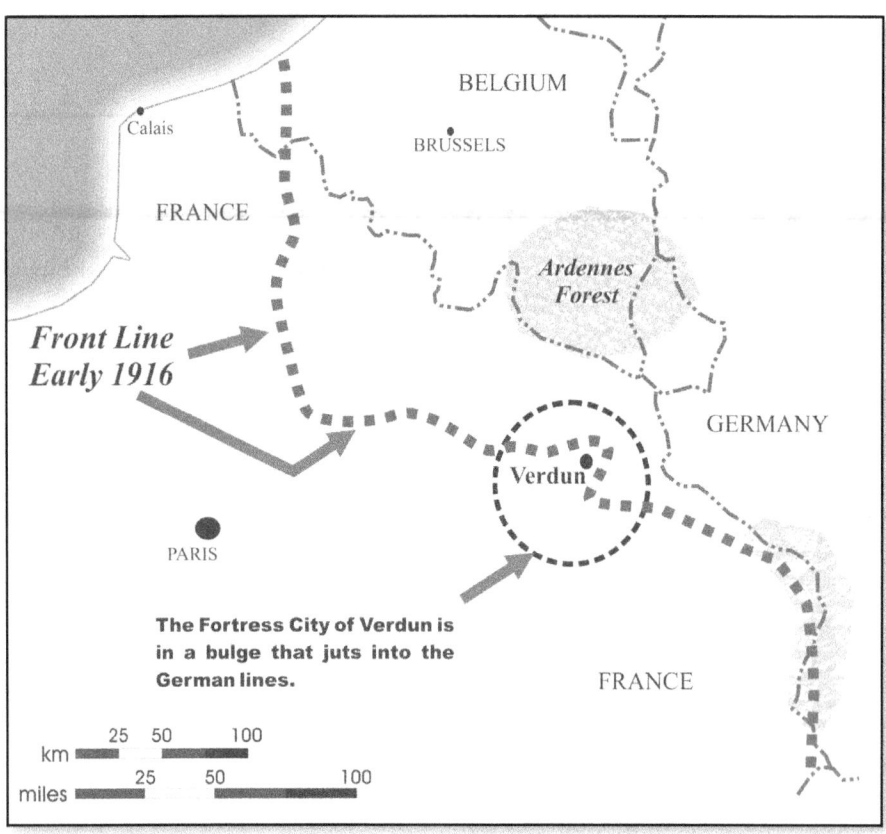

Figure 33. The Verdun Salient

During the first year of the war, the French Army had a serious shortage of artillery pieces. To make up part of the shortfall, the French Army had most of Verdun's fortress guns removed and sent to units in other front line sectors. They removed anything not permanently fixed in place from the forts. Many of the troops garrisoning the forts went with the guns.

The fact that Verdun was right on the front line did not dissuade the French High Command from cannibalizing its assets. The Germans had shown they could quickly destroy fortresses with their huge Big Bertha guns. These massive howitzers fired shells weighing more than a ton. They made quick work of the Belgian fortresses in 1914. The French believed the Verdun forts were just as vulnerable and therefore had little remaining military value.

The German High Command selected Verdun as the focus of their major offensive for 1916. Verdun was important to French prestige. The Germans were looking for a target the French would defend at all costs, one they would not abandon to the enemy. Verdun fit the bill. The Germans intended to draw the French into a great battle of attrition at Verdun.

The initial German attacks came very close to actually taking the place. Had it not been for a sudden blizzard the day the Germans had originally planned to attack, they probably would have overrun the entire fortress complex. The delay was enough to warn the French of the German preparations. The storm gave the French a couple more days to get ready for an onslaught.

The Germans still came very close to overrunning Verdun outright in the first few days. The French avoided a total disaster, but they still suffered huge reverses. They lost the most famous of the forts in the first few days.

Fort Douaumont

The most important of all of the forts in the Verdun system was Fort Douaumont. It was the largest fort in the system. Its particular hilltop position provided the best vantage point over the entire battlefield. And as far as prestige was concerned, the average Frenchman knew the place by name.

Fort Douaumont was extremely well built. Earlier German success with their Big Bertha guns had been against fortresses made of solid concrete. Fort Douaumont was different. Instead of solid concrete, it had two layers of concrete separated by an insulating layer of sand. The sand absorbed most of the force of a large shell hit. This sand layer made the fort relatively impervious to the Big Berthas.

Only a direct assault by German infantry could take Fort Douaumont. The

Germans had launched such attacks against the Belgian fortresses before bringing up their Big Berthas. The Belgians had easily repulsed attacks by thousands of German infantrymen against their forts. Both sides expected that similar attacks against Fort Douaumont would be even more costly and have little chance of success.

What actually happened was a complete shock to everyone. The Germans quickly captured Fort Douaumont. Even more stunning was how few German soldiers were involved in the capture. Less than ten Germans got inside the fortress and took the whole thing over, going from room to room, capturing the French occupants and locking them in their rooms after disarming them. The Germans heralded their capture of Fort Douaumont as a great victory. Its loss was a huge embarrassment to France. The French would lose over a hundred thousand men in attempts to get it back.

Tragedy of Errors

Anyone who has worked in a large organization will recognize the familiar sequence of events that led to the stunning capture of Fort Douaumont. It took more than a single mistake to cause the catastrophe. The loss of the great fortress was the result of a combination of mistakes, assumptions, carelessness, and poor communication.

Fort Douaumont should have had a strong infantry garrison protecting it from direct assault. It turns out that the removable guns were not the only things taken from the Verdun forts by earlier orders. The French Army also removed the infantry garrisons guarding each of the forts. They needed additional troops everywhere. They assumed the fort garrisons were sitting idle while there was intense fighting in other sectors. The French Army decided to use the garrisons as replacements for units taking heavy losses elsewhere.

Two different commands controlled military assets at Verdun. One was the fortress system command. The forts and soldiers in them were under Verdun's military governor. The soldiers manning the trenches on the front lines around Verdun had different chains of command. The troops in the trench lines were commanded by the Regular Army. Verdun's military governor did not report to the Regular Army command, nor did the regular army commands in the area report to him. The division between the two commands is best illustrated by the fact that when the local corps commander, a regular army general, tried to inspect Fort Douaumont's defenses, he was not allowed into the fort. The sentry told him he could not enter unless he had an order signed by the military governor granting him access.

Immediately prior to the German attack, the military governor finally asked the corps commander to occupy and defend Fort Douaumont. The corps commander ordered a message sent to the division commander in the area to do this. Unfortunately, the message was never sent. The corps commander did not check up on the situation. The message only had to travel from the corps staff to the subordinate division's staff. These two staffs were actually located in the same building, with only a partition separating them.

ANALOGY 1: "THAT'S NOT MY JOB"

Here is a very good example of the "That's not my job" problem that plagues organizations. It's a great example because it involved multiple layers of management. At each level, multiple people adopted the "That's not my job" mentality. They were all too happy to assume that someone else had the responsibility to take care of the fort. They didn't want to do it. Had anyone in the chain of command broken out of this pattern of destructive behavior, they could have saved the fort.

Companies have similar problems with the "That's not my job" mentality. Too many take the stance that unless something is very clearly specified as their responsibility, it's "not my job." This is usually the case with difficult tasks. No one wants to do them, and "That's not my job" is an easy way to avoid doing them. The problem for the company is that they are often critical tasks.

Businesses fail over the "That's not my job" problem. Any company will fail if people only do what is in their job descriptions. Everybody needs to know this. There must be serious consequences for people with this attitude. You need everyone to focus on ensuring the accomplishment of all critical tasks. Stamp out "That's not my job" from your organizational culture.

The army division stationed around Fort Douaumont had two subordinate brigades. The two brigade commanders positioned their brigades to each side of the fort. One brigade was to the left of the fort, the other on the right. Each assumed the other was responsible for defending the fortress. Neither wanted the responsibility. The place was drawing all kinds of German artillery fire. Neither wanted to have his troops suffer under the intense bombardment. Neither brigade commander checked on the fort's situation as they busied themselves with their trench line's defense.

Verdun's military governor, supported by others in his organization, did not want others involved in their business. This is why the corps commander couldn't get into the fort. The governor knew full well that the forts were inadequately defended. He had been complaining to the army's high command about it for quite some time. What he wanted was for additional resources to be assigned to his department. He was not really looking for help from someone he did not control. He only sought outside help when an enemy attack appeared imminent.

ANALOGY 2: REFUSAL OF HELP

The same thing happens in the business world. The head of an understaffed department needs help. The group is straining to complete its work. It lacks the needed resources to accomplish its assigned tasks. But the department head doesn't want temporary help. He or she wants permanent help. He or she wants a permanent increase in their department's headcount or budget. Accomplishing the tasks at hand is not the focus. Increasing the size or budget of the department is.

To get a permanent increase in available resources, poor leaders will shun temporary assistance. This is because they fear their bosses will see the temporary measures as adequate. They fear that they won't get permanent resource increases as a result. Of course, without the temporary help, the strained department still cannot achieve its goals. Refusing help from others to accentuate continuing problems is taking a dangerous gamble. You don't want someone prone to such gambles in a position of responsibility. Their refusal of temporary help can result in failure that can soon negatively impact the performance of the entire company.

The corps commander, for his part, did not insist on inspecting the fort after being turned away at the gate. To have gone to the governor to ask for permission to enter the fort would have meant placing himself in a subservient position. He probably assumed that everything was in order at the fort anyway.

ANALOGY 3: SWALLOWING ONE'S PRIDE

In business we all face dilemmas similar to the French corps commander. On the one hand, he wanted to find out information about how effectively another part of the organization could be expected to perform. He went out to get this information but he couldn't readily get it. He had three options. First, he could have made a big stink about the whole thing and demanded to inspect the forts in his area. Second, he could have gone to the governor and requested entrance. Third, he could just assume that things were fine and not trouble himself anymore to find out about something that wasn't his responsibility anyway.

The first of these options, making a big stink, would probably have ruined any kind of working relationship with the governor that might have been worked out over time. Also, he would probably have gotten a "dog and pony show" tour of the fort. This would have given him a false impression about the true state of the fort's defenses. On top of this, the governor would view him as someone trying to increase his area of influence at the governor's expense. The possibility is rather high that following this option would cause some kind of feud between the two commands, even when one group could, in fact, use the other's assistance.

The second option would have required the corps commander to swallow his pride and go to the governor to get permission to enter the fort. He just didn't want to do this. After all, he was a general of as high or higher rank than the governor. Maybe he thought that if anyone should go out of their way, it should be the governor coming to see him. And so the corps commander didn't try further to get into the fort. He went with the third option. The disastrous fall of Fort Douaumont was the result.

This bit about "He should come to me; I shouldn't have to go to him" happens all the time in business. The results usually aren't as drastic, but they are just as undesirable. Everyone in a company, not just the workers at the lowest levels, needs to be committed to the concept of teamwork. People need to view the company's needs as the highest priority. Unfortunately, the need of the individual ego is too often a person's top priority. And this is always detrimental to achieving the business's goals.

Added to this view of "He should come to me" was the additional weight of the "That's not my job" syndrome. The corps commander was not responsible for the defense of the forts. He could rightly say, "It wasn't my job to make sure the forts were defended." But then, the lack of adequate forces at the fort would make his job, the defense of the front lines, extremely difficult to carry out.

We all hope that our results are only dependent on our own labors. The reality is that we are all dependent, to varying degrees, on the work of others. Just because some critical component to our success does not lie directly within our own sphere of influence doesn't mean that we shouldn't be concerned about it. We should be willing to assist with anything that helps our company, whether it is something we directly control or not. Don't give up too easily if you are rebuffed when you offer assistance. Don't cave in to this aspect of the "It's not my job" syndrome. If you do, you may be contributing to the failure of your company to achieve its goals. Your company's very survival may be at stake if you give up trying to help others.

It is important to note that the man used as the example here was actually a very good corps commander. His corps performed well during the battle. His corps had a reputation as one of the best in the French Army. The point is that the mistakes he made can happen in any organization and to any leader.

The failure to find out about Fort Douaumont's lack of protection was not the only mistake made by the corps commander. When the governor finally asked for his assistance in sending troops into the fort, the corps commander issued orders to do this. But he never checked up on the execution of these orders. What probably happened is that some clerk lost the piece of paper the order was written on. The order never made it to the troops in the field.

ANALOGY 4: TASK FEEDBACK

One of the simplest leadership mistakes is assuming that something will happen because you issued the instructions. The message might get lost. Or it could go to the wrong people. Maybe those who get the message don't understand it correctly.

You can fix each of these problems to a large extent by feedback loops in your communication processes. You need to get feedback that your people have received your instructions, understand them, and are following them. You also need to make sure that you can confirm the result of your instructions. This does not mean that you have to personally check up on everything. What it does mean is that you need to have mechanisms set up to get back accurate reports. You need confirmation that the intended recipients got your message and understand it. Then you need to know what actually happened after that. You leave yourself open to all sorts of bad surprises when you don't have good feedback loops in place.

The next communication failure should seem very familiar to business organizations today. The problem was with the two staffs in the same room who failed to talk with each other. The corps commander's order was never transmitted to the division staff in the next partition over. The corps staff and the division staff were in the same room, separated only by a sheet hung from the ceiling. The corps commander told his staff to direct the division to occupy the fort. The division staff never got the message. No one went over to the other side of the room to talk. Instead, the corps bureaucracy relied on the standard procedures it had. They transmitted the message by written communiqué.

People fail to talk to each other even more today. Technology provides us with all kinds of alternatives to face-to-face discussion. People will actually e-mail messages to someone sitting in the next cubicle over. Or they might even call and leave a voice mail. Face-to-face communication is best, and other methods are substitutes that should only be used when face-to-face discussion cannot take place. The best example of the reduced effectiveness of these alternatives is e-mail. How can you expect to ensure your most important messages get through to your people by e-mail when they get hundreds of e-mails a day? It is too easy for crucial communication to get lost in the crowd of noise. It is not that new methods of communication are bad. They are an immense help. But they are just that, helps. You cannot rely on these methods as the primary means of transmitting important messages and instructions.

The next mistake in the litany of French failures at Fort Douaumont was the inaction of the brigade commanders on the front line to each side of the fortress. Each incorrectly assumed that the other was responsible for defending the fort against enemy infantry. And then each of them had their soldiers stay away from the place since it was such a prominent artillery target.

> ### ANALOGY 5: "THAT'S NOT MY JOB" PART 2
>
> Here is a manifestation of another aspect of the "It's not my job" syndrome. Neither brigade commander wanted the job of protecting the fort. This helped them to assume that the other guy was taking care of it. Of course, neither of them asked the other if he was taking care of it. They probably didn't do this because if they asked about it, their peer may have asked for help. The idea here is that if you don't want a job in the first place, you probably don't want to help out with doing it either. Neither of these leaders wanted to take on the additional job. It turns out that the commands they were responsible for were seriously endangered because the fort was left unprotected.

One Lucky Man

The true story of the German conquest of Fort Douaumont is almost unbelievable. It is one of those stories where fact transcends any possible fiction that might have been concocted. A single German sergeant, named Kunze, was leading a section of about ten men. They were clearing paths through the French barbed wire for other advancing infantry near the fort. Because his section was close the fort, the sergeant decided to check it out by cautiously moving towards it. Nothing other than the fort's turret guns (which even Joffre's orders could not remove) were firing, and these were firing off at some unseen point in the distance. Kunze and his section made it to the moat surrounding the fort. This dry moat was an obstacle to keep people from getting on top of the fort. It was about 20 feet deep, and, had the fort been properly garrisoned, it would have been swept by machine guns firing from slits on both ends. With no one covering the moat, Kunze and his section got into it. To get into the fort itself, this group actually formed a human pyramid, the kind that cheerleaders make. Kunze climbed up to get through a gun port that was about twelve feet above the moat floor. Once inside, he started going from room to room capturing people.

Kunze's section thought he was nuts. Once he got inside, most of the rest of them took off. After all, if just a single Frenchman manned a machine gun at the end of the moat, they would have been perfect targets in a walled shooting gallery. Luckily for Kunze and the two others brave enough to follow him inside, another group of Germans made it to another point along the moat. A Lieutenant Radtke led this group. Radtke's group built steps down into the moat and up to the top of the fort with debris that was lying around. As Radtke and his group were working through the fort (separately from Kunze), another larger group of Germans under a Captain Haupt got there. Less than an hour after Kunze dropped into the moat, the fort was securely in German hands.

While these German soldiers were capturing the fort, a Lieutenant Brandis saw some activity there from a slight distance away. He also decided to head over to check out what was going on. He got to the fort after its capture. He reported to Captain Haupt, who was the senior officer on the scene. Haupt sent Brandis back to Battalion headquarters to get reinforcements to secure the position. He went back and told the battalion commander of the fort's capture. Brandis then asked for permission to go to the regimental headquarters to tell them what happened. The major at battalion headquarters was already busy directing additional troops to the captured fort, so he told Brandis to go ahead. Brandis had nothing to do with the achievement of taking the fort, but guess what he was doing. He managed to claim the lion's share of the credit for the fort's capture. He and Captain Haupt received Germany's highest military decorations personally from the German Crown Prince.

The battalion commander, to his credit, tried to correct the mistake about who was getting credit once he found out what was happening. But no one listened. Kunze was assumed to be some kind of peasant peon who could not possibly have done what he did. Radtke was a smallish man with glasses who looked like he got bullied a lot as a child. Brandis, on the other hand, was a fine looking, strapping young Prussian officer who looked like everyone's picture of a hero. No one above the major was willing to admit their mistake, a mistake in which appearances became the basis of making judgments about who was responsible for a stunning achievement.

Captain Haupt was a quiet and unassuming character who returned to anonymity. Brandis, on the other hand, used the capture of the fort as a springboard to fame and fortune. He wrote a best seller detailing how he captured the fort. He went on wildly popular lecture tours after the war in which he regaled audiences with stories of his bravery, daring, and achievements.

Any kind of serious inquiry into what had happened would have revealed Brandis as an imposter. But a very senior leader wanted to hand out a quick reward to someone who looked like a hero. The Crown Prince wanted someone like Brandis to be the hero. He didn't want someone like Kunze or Radtke. And he most certainly was not going to admit a mistake in giving the award to Brandis, who, by now, was his protégé.

ANALOGY 6: STEALING OTHER'S LAURELS

Brandis' behavior, taking credit for someone else's accomplishments, is utterly despicable. It is, unfortunately, rather common behavior. Even worse is leadership that promotes the imposter or even just allows him to retain the laurels when the truth of what really happened comes out. Of course, shame on any leader who allows it to go that far in the first place.

You can barely begin to describe the damage done to an organization by the deceitful behavior characterized by Brandis in falsely claiming credit for something he did not do. A leader greatly intensifies the damage by rewarding the behavior and elevating the imposter. Even worse is sticking to this *after* discovering the deceit.

The members of any organization where any of this happens will stop exerting themselves to attain results. They will stop going the extra mile to get things done. They will just do what is required to stay out of trouble. They will do nothing more. And why should they? After all, they already know that someone else, some pretty boy protégé, will get the credit for their hard work. Have you ever seen the results of any organization where people are just doing the bare minimum? It is always a disaster. No company or business can withstand the effects of its employees not doing things that are not in the job description, things that call for extra effort. Companies that are only getting the minimal effort from their employees do not last very long.

CONCLUSIONS

This chapter was an exploration of a few of the mistakes made by both the German and French armies during the initial stages of the Battle of Verdun. Flawed thinking and poor execution led to the mistakes. The Germans were able to exploit many of the French mistakes, especially at Fort Douaumont. The French paid dearly for the loss of this fort. The stories of Verdun and the accompanying business world analogies provide insight into a number of important points:

- **The "That's not my job" syndrome**
  One of the worst things that can happen to your business is to have people with an attitude of "That's not my job." Your company must depend on its people doing things that are beyond their specific job descriptions. If your people adopt this attitude, your business would be unable to keep its customers happy, and would fail. You need people at every level to constantly look for ways they can help the organization to be successful, whether it is specifically "their job" or not.

- **Dangers of refusing temporary help**
  You may often find yourself in situations where you do not have adequate resources to accomplish your assigned tasks. Some people in this situation are very hesitant to accept temporary help. They may feel that they cannot make as strong a case for long-term resource increases if they do. But the result is that if they don't accept temporary help, their organization has a greater likelihood of failing to meet its goals. It's always best to accept help and yet continue to look for longer-term solutions.

- **Teamwork versus individual ego**
  We hinder good communication when we allow our egos to dictate that others should take the initiative to keep us informed. Everyone needs to be concerned about how things are going, what is working, and what is not. This often means getting off your own perch and going out to talk to others. You need to talk to them about what may or may not be happening. You need to discuss possible solutions to potential problems. You cannot wait until someone decides to come to you with a problem

and asks for your help. You must proactively look for ways that you can help. *You* need to take the initiative. Don't wait for someone else to.

- **Common communication failures**
  Never assume that your people received your instructions and that they are following those directions. You must have a feedback loop in place that informs you of what happens with your instructions. You need confirmation that the proper recipients actually received the instructions. Next, you need confirmation that the recipients correctly understand and are following those instructions. If you don't have these feedback loops in place, your instructions will have a high probability of vanishing into thin air, and you won't know about this until some disaster occurs.

- **Taking credit for other's work**
  One of the most despicable acts is someone taking credit for the accomplishments of another. You cannot tolerate this kind of behavior if you ever want to motivate your people. If people think that someone can steal credit for their efforts, they will think there is little point in making any kind of extra effort. You certainly wouldn't want to work for someone who would do this. Neither does anybody else.

ACTION FILE

HOW TO FOSTER COMMUNICATION

 BAD IDEA #1—Let conflict hinder communication.

People who don't like each other don't like to talk to each other. This is a major cause of communication breakdowns in any organization. People don't want to deal with people who they don't like. This leads to even bigger problems.

One of the most overlooked leadership roles is the urgent need to deal with interpersonal conflicts between subordinates. You cannot stand idly by. You cannot just hope they will work things out. If you don't do anything about it, it will usually get worse. You can quickly end up with an organization where half the people don't talk to the other half.

Serious interpersonal conflicts require mediation with the individuals involved. You may not be able to solve the cause of the conflict, but you can usually work out some kind of arrangement that helps the individuals involved work together better. Sometimes you can even solve the problem completely.

If the situation does not get better after mediation or other intervention attempts, you still need to do something about it. You may need to reposition people so that the conflict does not interfere with necessary communication in your business. This may mean repositioning one or even several involved individuals. This sends a message to the rest of the organization that they do indeed need to work well together. Doing nothing about a conflict ensures that you will have communication problems. Conflicts usually get worse. You can easily end up with a very adversarial workplace, one that is inefficient and ineffective. Do something about it before it gets even worse.

 BAD IDEA #2—Assume people are following instructions.

People in charge often assume that their position means they can tell people what to do. This is true. What many do not realize is that just because you tell subordinates to do something does not mean they will do it. Any parent knows this about their children. Unfortunately, the same thing goes for many adults, too.

You need to find ways to ensure your group carries out your instructions. This does not mean watching everything. Nor does it mean becoming punitive. The solution to getting people to follow your directions is actually much more involved.

First, you need to ensure that you have given proper and beneficial instructions. People have a hard time following instructions that they know will create problems. This is a good thing. Learn to give good guidance to your group. Be willing to listen yourself. Also, listen to inputs and opinions from others about what to do and how to do it. Be willing to make changes if there are problems with your instructions.

Next, sell people on your instructions. You need to convince them of the need and wisdom in carrying them out. People are much more motivated to do something when they know the reasons why. This does take more time initially. The result will be less need for supervision, so the sales job will pay off for you in the end.

Last, have ways of getting feedback. You need to know that your people have completed your instructions. Part of your solution needs to be personal observation. But you can't watch everything, nor should you want to. Look for the evidence of results. Have people come back to you to report on what they have done and how well it has gone. Again, be willing to listen. Change or adjust your directions whenever necessary.

 BAD IDEA #3—Stay in your office or at headquarters.

The old saying goes, "The best leaders lead from the front." This means going out and seeing for yourself what is happening on the front lines. Observe what is actually going on. Don't stay in your office. Get out of headquarters. Go to wherever the front line is for your business and see what is really occurring.

There is a simple reason why this is so necessary. All communication is filtered by the opinions of those who report back to you on what they see, by opinions about what they think you want to hear, and by opinions about what will get them ahead. All second-hand information is tainted in some way. Always keep this in mind. Don't rely primarily on second-hand information. Go and get first-hand information yourself.

The best picture you can get comes from going and seeing for yourself. Talk to people involved on the scene. Ask for opinions and ideas. Make contacts and build relationships. Do more listening than talking. Soak in information rather than spewing out your own opinions. Get to where things are going on and get your own feel for what is working and what is not. Use the gained personal experience as a check on the second-hand information you will still get.

GOOD IDEA #1—Promote idea sharing.

Communication is the sharing of information. Broaden that definition within your work area so that communication is not just the sharing of information, but also the sharing of thoughts and ideas on the implications of that information. It's nice to know things. It's even better to have good ideas on what to do next because you know those things.

Discussion and debate should be part of your organization's culture. If they are not, make them part of the culture. Your meetings shouldn't be boring lectures on facts, figures, and directives. They should include healthy debate and intellectual interaction. Discuss what is going on and what should be going on. Take care that you don't allow the discussion to degeneration into bitch sessions about how bad things are, but constructively discuss what you can do to make things better.

Promote idea sharing. Share your lessons learned. Send experienced people around to share information on what works and what creates problems. Encourage others with success stories. Encourage everyone to investigate their results and share that information with others.

GOOD IDEA #2—Fight the "That's not my job" syndrome.

Every business must fight the tendency for people to fall into the "That's not my job" syndrome. This is where people refuse to do something or to help someone because "It's not my job to do that." Any organization with a "That's not my job" culture is doomed. You need to move people past this. Stop this destructive mindset from ever taking root.

To stop the "That's not my job" mindset from taking hold, you must ensure people know your organization's goals and objectives. But this is just the initial step. Everyone needs to know how they, personally, can be a part of making those things happen. They need to know how they fit into the big picture and how what they do contributes to meeting those goals and objectives. You need to communicate these things.

Not all communication should be directives flowing from the top down. Nor should it be primarily information moving from the bottom up to the top. Communication needs to be moving in both directions simultaneously. Everyone needs to gather pertinent information and share it. Share it with peers, with superiors, with subordinates. Everyone needs to be in the know. Most people will do more than just what is in their job descriptions when they know they can make a positive impact. They want to be more involved in making the organization successful and in helping it meet its goals. And by doing so, they ensure the goals are met. People just need the information and encouragement. With it, they will step outside of their accustomed patterns. They will do more for you than just get by.

GOOD IDEA #3—Promote interaction.

Good things happen when people leverage the contacts and relationships they have with others. Bad things happen when people do not know where to turn. The more contacts someone has in your business, the greater the likelihood they will be successful. Their connections help them immensely when dealing with complex issues.

Find ways to increase interaction between people from different backgrounds, groups, and departments. Encourage personal relationships between people. People have a tendency to only interact with others similar to themselves. Find ways to break down social barriers. Use social events where you encourage people to interact with people outside of their normal daily work groups. Have people from varied areas take classes together. Have some kind of personnel exchange program between different departments. Constantly find ways to mix people up to get them to make contacts with others they would not regularly work with.

Informal personal relationships are crucial to your company's success. People need to feel comfortable going to someone else to get help. They will be much more likely to ask for help when they actually know someone they think might be able to assist them. So help them to feel comfortable. Give them opportunities to create new relationships with those who would otherwise be strangers.

CHAPTER 9

PETAIN AND NIVELLE

"What Will Get Us Farther, a Carrot or a Stick?"

INTRODUCTION

THE cataclysmic battle of Verdun caused a number of important leadership changes in the French Army. This chapter is about two famous French generals who rose to prominence due to their efforts at Verdun, Generals Petain and Nivelle. They had very different styles and very different effects on the French Army. Both found themselves in a position to either save their country or place it in the utmost peril. One succeeded. The other failed. The stories of Petain and Nivelle illustrate the following important points:

- Failing to continuously innovate
- Volatile policies and practices
- The management-employee relationship
- Inspirational leadership

HISTORICAL CASE AND BUSINESS ANALOGIES

Out of Obscurity

Generals Henri-Philippe Petain and Robert Nivelle became prominent French leaders during the course of the war. Both were merely regimental commanders when war broke out. To put their initial positions into perspective, there were approximately four hundred different regiments in the French Army when the war started in 1914. Yet, in very quick order, both of these initially obscure individuals rose to the very top. Their contrasting motivations and vastly different leadership styles had very different effects on the armies that each came to command.

Both Petain and Nivelle owed their meteoric rise to Joffre's leadership system. Joffre, head of the French Army at the start of the war, quickly sacked incompetent and unproductive generals. Even though he was the head of the army, Joffre could not kick other generals out of the service. Most of them had connections and some political clout. Outright firings would cause Joffre all kinds of problems. Instead of firing them, Joffre transferred them to meaningless commands in the remote French city of Limoge. Joffre didn't just replace ineffective or deficient generals. He also elevated people who produced results, especially those who showed initiative in overcoming difficult situations.

Both Petain and Nivelle commanded units with exceptional performance. Each produced local successes during the French Army's retreat to the Marne River. Nivelle led his artillery regiment forward to the front lines to shoot point-blank into attacking Germans while the infantry of his division fled. Petain's infantry regiment had shown repeatedly that it could fend off attacks by much stronger German forces. Petain's regiment displayed exceptional coordination in holding back the enemy. Joffre's system quickly promoted both men to positions of increasingly greater responsibility.

Savior of Verdun

Petain was the first of the two promoted to a nationally prominent command. Joffre selected him to command the French forces defending Verdun. The Germans had just launched a massive attack against the fortress town, and things looked very grim. Joffre saw Petain as the man who could hold onto the town. He based his decision on Petain's demonstrated prowess at handling defensive situations.

The great success of the initial German attacks at Verdun greatly disturbed all of France. Joffre had previously stated he was willing to abandon the place if necessary. Public despair made him see the importance of holding Verdun. Yet things looked bleak. The units defending Verdun were badly mauled. Fort Douaumont was lost. A sense of defeat and even panic pervaded French troops in the area. They continued to fall back under the pressure of determined German attacks. Joffre needed someone to direct Verdun's defenses who could reverse the situation. He needed someone with a reputation for holding ground. And he needed someone who could put demoralized units back into fighting shape. He believed Petain was the man for the job.

Petain had been a mere colonel at the start of the war. He was very close to retirement age, so close that he had already bought a small farming estate to relax on during his remaining years. He had advanced slowly during his undistinguished career. If the war had not started, his career would have come to unsung end.

Petain's career was stifled because he, almost alone, did not agree with the French Army's prevailing theories on warfare. He adamantly opposed the beliefs in attack and *élan* so cherished by the army. His own studies and investigations of events in current military affairs led to very different opinions compared to those of his peers and superiors. He closely studied the details of reports from the Russo-Japanese and Boer wars. He drew his own very different conclusions. He believed that firepower was the deciding factor in tactics, not *élan*.

There was a further brake on Petain's career. He was just awful at politics, both within the army and in dealing with government officials. Once, a prominent politician was assigned to a unit Petain commanded. Rather than delicately deal with the politician's substandard performance, Petain made an example out of him. There were career implications for doing this. This does not seem to have dawned on Petain.

When the war started, Petain was able to demonstrate his abilities and the soundness of his beliefs. The units he commanded were successful. He was rewarded and promoted. He quickly rose to higher and higher positions. Petain continued to shine as he commanded larger and larger formations. He was remarkably successful in defeating German attacks. He applied his theories and beliefs to the offense as well. In attacking, Petain was successful by going after specific and limited objectives, using massive and concentrated firepower.

An Unusual Style

Petain's leadership style was very different from his contemporaries. He had a distinctive way of dealing with the individual soldiers under his command. Most generals conducted their operations solely from the confines of their headquarters. Petain was one of the very few ranking French generals who frequently visited the front line. He talked on a regular basis with the rank and file of the units he commanded. He did not pal around with the soldiers but listened intently to their stories. They told him about what was really going on, what worked, and what didn't. He could explain to the soldiers the purpose and meaning of their operations. The soldiers came to believe that if Petain ordered something done, it had a purpose and a good chance for success.

Because Joffre believed Petain was France's best hope for saving Verdun, he gave him command of the Verdun sector. But there were limits to what Petain could do. Joffre gave him some very specific orders. Above all, he was to hold on to Verdun, no matter what the cost.

When Petain arrived at Verdun, the defenders were in a state of panic. Troops supposed to be occupying front line trenches were streaming to the rear. Confusion reigned everywhere because accurate reports from the front lines had ceased. The absence of accurate information led to inflated rumors about what was really going on. Gossip had the Germans advancing here, there, and almost everywhere. Most senior commanders believed the fall of the city was imminent.

The fortress complex at Verdun sat astride the Meuse River. The part on the right bank of the Meuse was in a decidedly difficult position. Here, the Germans enveloped the French on three sides. The French could only get into the area by crossing one of the few bridges over the river inside the town. The area was even less defensible due to the recent loss of Fort Douaumont. Abandoning the right bank would have made it easier to defend Verdun. This is what Petain wanted to do initially, but Joffre's orders prevented him from taking this course of action. The French felt that politically, they could not afford to lose any more of the Verdun complex. The situation was desperate, but Petain did not give up. He set out to do the best that he could. [Fig 34]

Petain and Nivelle

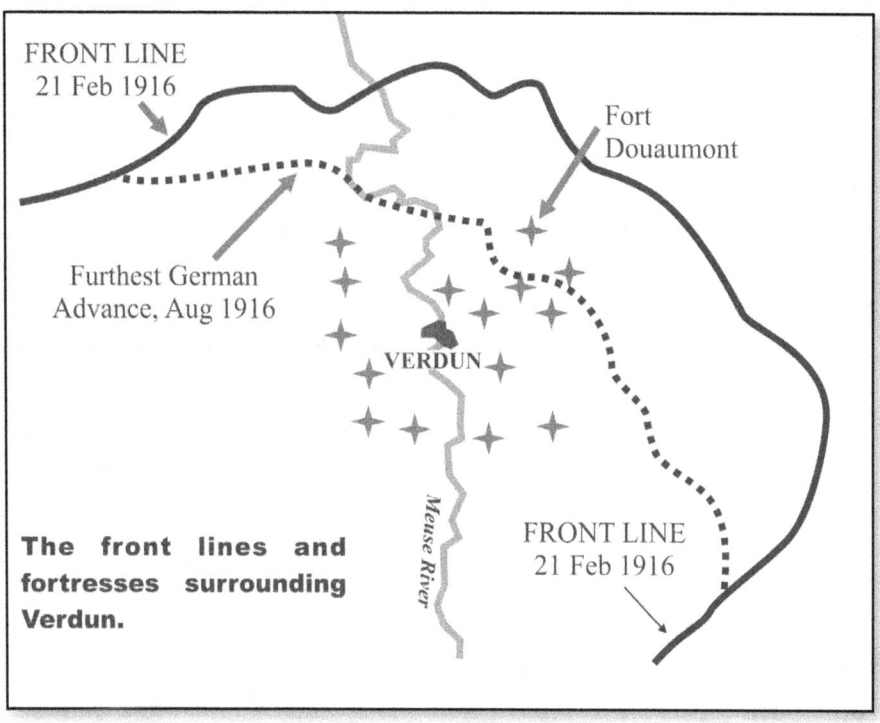

Figure 34. The Battle of Verdun

Petain calmly issued orders to put the defense of Verdun right. He put all of the artillery from all of the units in and around Verdun under a centralized command. This removed the artillery from the direction of local commanders. The centralization allowed the French to mass all of their artillery to dramatic effect against the Germans. Petain also found a way to ensure the delivery of the needed quantities of supplies and ammunition to the sector. There was only a single, small gauge rail line into Verdun. Alone, it could not bring in enough supplies for the defenders. Petain became an innovator of truck convoys, and they brought in the supplies the rail line could not.

Petain's efforts slowed the enemy. The Germans found it increasingly difficult to make forward progress. The battle bogged down into attrition. Countless numbers would die on a dead and barren landscape as the front lines solidified.

Petain went to his superiors to get more men for the massive struggle. At his urging, the French Army worked out a system of rotating units in and out of the maelstrom. Petain realized that soldiers could not stand the strain of the battle very long. Rotation would mean the Germans would constantly face relatively fresh French troops.

Petain insisted on ceasing unnecessary attacks. The French Army had lost a good bit of ground to the Germans at Verdun, including the famous Fort Douaumont. Petain did not want to attack to get this ground back. He saw no point to it. Joffre was of a completely different opinion. He urged Petain repeatedly to attack, to retake the lost ground, to recover some of France's lost honor. Petain would not do it.

Joffre started having other disagreements with Petain. Once Petain had stabilized the situation at Verdun, Joffre moved on to other priorities. Joffre began working with the British in planning attacks along the Somme River. But the French role could not be what Joffre wanted it to be. This was because Petain was using up all of the fresh French troops at Verdun with his rotation system. This limited the number of troops Joffre had available for the upcoming Somme offensive.

After a while, Joffre wanted to sack Petain for ignoring orders to attack at Verdun and for using up too many troops. But now Joffre had a problem. Petain had become a national hero. He had turned around what had seemed like a hopeless situation at Verdun. People thought Joffre was at least partly to blame for the mistakes leading to the loss of Fort Douaumont. It was just no longer politically possible for Joffre to fire the person that had saved the day at Verdun.

An Aggressive Commander

Joffre could not fire Petain, and he could not send him off to Limoge. Instead, Joffre bypassed him. Joffre started going directly to Petain's subordinates, the ones he felt would do what he wanted. Later, he promoted Petain out of the way. He put Petain in charge of the army group. This allowed Joffre to install his new favorite, the one who followed his wishes, in charge of the army at Verdun. The man who did what Joffre wanted was Nivelle.

Nivelle was very willing to launch the attacks that Joffre wanted. Nivelle did not care about the length of casualty lists. All that mattered to him were results. For Nivelle, the way to get results was to attack. Nivelle had not lost his faith in the prewar French doctrines of attack and *élan*. Nivelle repeatedly launched attacks towards Fort Douaumont in attempts to retake it from the Germans.

The Battle of Verdun started in February 1916. The French recaptured Fort Douaumont that November. By then, the British had been attacking the

Germans in the Somme Valley for more than four months. The Germans were sending their reserves there instead of reinforcing units around Verdun. Verdun was no longer the German's priority. The attritional battle at Verdun had also severely affected the Germans. They cut way back on reinforcements to the units committed there. The Germans went on the defensive around Verdun. By the time the French retook Douaumont, the defending German units were weak and depleted.

Nivelle did develop some innovative practices for use in his attacks at Verdun. He pioneered the use of the saturation bombardments. This focused large numbers of guns on devastating a specific area shortly before attacking it. Then, as the infantry rose out of their trenches, a creeping artillery barrage moved in front of them like a curtain of steel. This kept the Germans in their dugouts until the French were almost on top of them, giving little time for their machine guns to beat off the attackers.

The recapture of Fort Douaumont convinced Nivelle his beliefs on conducting warfare were correct. He was sure his innovations would produce victory after victory. He believed his successful attacks were proof he had found the recipe for success against the Germans. France would give him the chance to apply his recipe on a far grander scale.

Rising to the Very Top

By late 1916, Joffre fell out of favor with the French government. In 1914, he saved France from the initial German onslaught. Since then he had achieved little. The French 1915 attacks against German positions were costly and ineffective. Joffre's headquarters had stripped Verdun of its garrisons and fortress guns before the Germans had attacked there. In mid-1916, Joffre approved the unproductive attacks made in cooperation with the British on the Somme. The government promoted Joffre to Marshal of France. Then they asked him to relinquish his command. On his way out the door, they asked Joffre to nominate his own replacement.

Joffre did not want to go. He wanted, at a minimum, to retain his influence in the French High Command. He nominated someone seriously lacking in high command experience. Joffre was probably hoping the nominee would rely on his advice about what to do. Nivelle was Joffre's nominee to lead the French Army.

The politicians were happy to oblige Joffre by promoting his candidate. Nivelle certainly had a way with politicians. He radiated confidence in himself and his plans. He could easily explain complicated operations to the uninitiated. He was a charmer and a persuader. He excelled at coming up with great catch phrases. He was the author of "They shall not pass." This sound bite came to represent the French spirit of resistance in the war. It was easy for Nivelle to cast others under his spell. He had recaptured Fort Douaumont. He was the hero of the hour.

In promoting Nivelle, the government bypassed the savior of Verdun, Petain. It did not help Petain that he was a rather unassuming character. Many of his peers considered him a rather cold and icy character. It didn't help that Petain loathed politicians. At one point, he actually told the President of France "No one is better placed than the President himself to know that France is neither led nor governed." The President had not forgotten the insult.

Another Great Plan

Now the supreme commander of all of France's armies, Nivelle set out to design a grand offensive to win the war. He cast aside Joffre and his ideas. Nivelle was convinced his recipe would produce victory. He would validate the theories of attack and *élan*. Nivelle's grand plan called for a major attack against a bulge in the German lines from the south while the British attacked from the north. The attackers would cut off and surround the German forces in the bulge. This would then open up a gap in the German lines. The French and British armies would advance through this opening and on toward Germany. [Fig 35]

The attack's initial objective for the French was the Chemin des Dames, a high, long ridge dominating the Aisne River. It was one of the most heavily defended points of the entire German line. It looked like a very tough nut to crack. Both politicians and other generals were rather skeptical of Nivelle's plan. Nivelle used his great charm to swing them around to his thinking. They all wanted to believe that success was right around the corner. Nivelle promised such a miracle. He tirelessly promoted his plan to governments and soldiers alike. Nivelle's force of character and optimism even swayed the opinions of British government leaders. The British were extremely hesitant to launch new attacks after the recent bloodbaths they had experienced on the Somme. Nivelle promised his attack would pierce the German lines in less than twenty-four hours. To settle the fears of those still worried, he promised to call off his offensive without delay if it appeared to be unsuccessful.

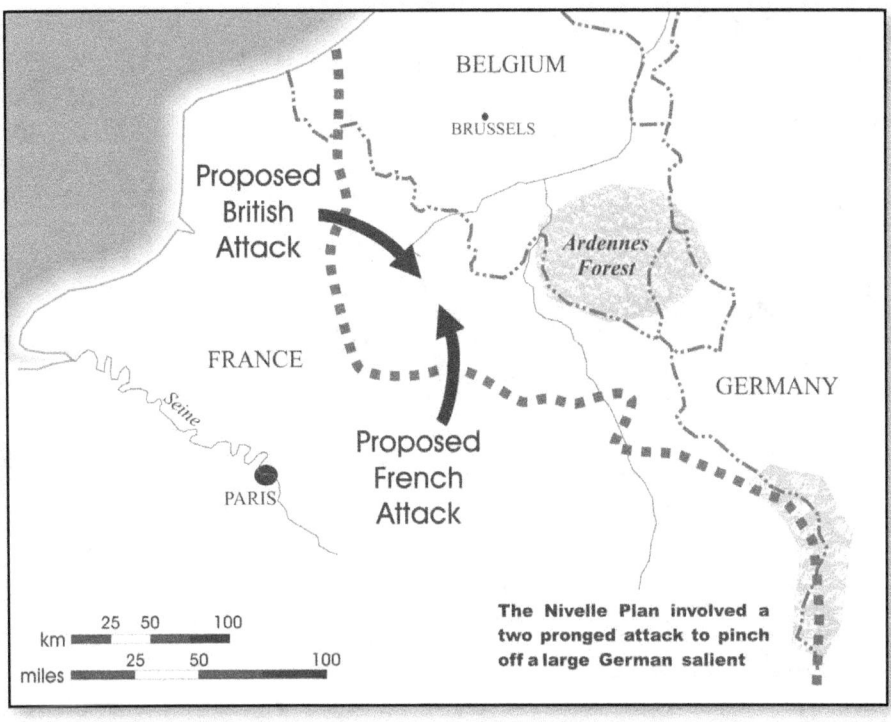

Figure 35. The Nivelle Plan

The Germans did not cooperate with Nivelle's plans. They too could look at a map. They knew that the salient between the Somme and Aisne rivers was a precarious position. Because they foresaw that an offensive similar to Nivelle's proposal could possibly envelop this salient, they decided to withdraw from this difficult position and retreated to more defensible positions. In doing so, they also shortened their line, freeing up more troops for their defenses in France. [Fig 36]

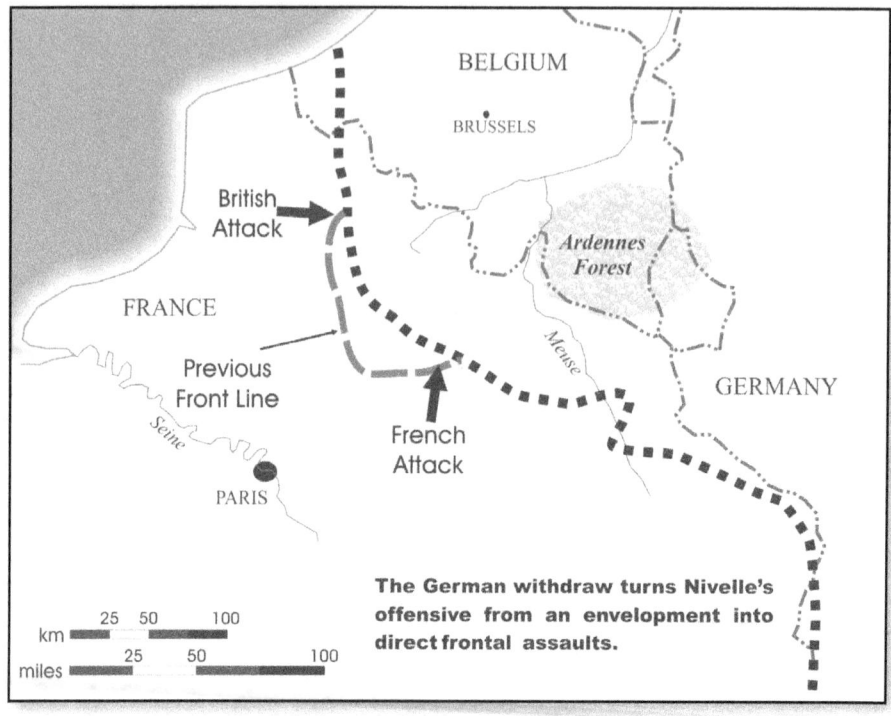

Figure 36. The Nivelle Offensive

The Germans did even more to thwart Nivelle's grand scheme. They also had gained experience with Nivelle's recipe at Verdun. They, too, learned lessons from these experiences. They made changes to their defensive practices to minimize the danger from Nivelle's tactics. Before, the Germans had posted most of their troops on the actual front line. They now changed to a system of defense in depth. This new German tactical doctrine placed only a skeleton crew in the most forward trenches. Their main job was to just fire off flares when they saw the enemy troops coming. The Germans moved most of their troops back into a second line of trenches. This second line was further to the rear. It was also out of the sight of enemy artillery. The Germans even constructed a third line, to protect reserves they would use to counterattack any enemy penetrations.

> ## ANALOGY 1: THE MOVING TARGET
>
> You will have difficulty with planning and strategizing for the same reason Nivelle did. The reason is that your competition does not stand still. They are not going to just sit there and repeatedly lose to the same techniques. At some point, they are going to make changes that will drastically reduce the effectiveness of your techniques. At some point, your techniques will fail because of the changes the competition makes. You must continue to innovate, to find new ways of beating the competition. If you don't, you will find yourself relying on outdated and ineffective methods and strategies. If you continue to try things that are no longer working, you will sap your own company's strength. You will then find yourself unable to parry the competition's next thrust.

Nivelle did not know about the changes in German tactics. On the other hand, he did know about the change in German strategy. The Germans vacated the salient. Nivelle at first refused to believe it. Then he failed to deal with the changed situation. His offensive was no longer attacking into the flank of the exposed enemy position. Nivelle's planned attacks would now attack the enemy frontally. The Germans were in a much stronger position. Due to the withdrawal, they now had even more troops to defend their lines.

Nivelle refused to change his plan. He refused to deal with the new situation. Instead, he went off into greater flights of fancy about what his coming offensive would achieve. He had the red lines and arrows showing projections on planning maps extended farther and farther into the enemy's rear. He made more and grander promises to politicians and the army on the magnitude of the success he told them was sure to come.

> ## ANALOGY 2: FLEETING OPPORTUNITY
>
> You must be quick to exploit the competition's weaknesses. What is a weakness right now may not be a weakness for very long. Like the Germans, the competition can look at a map of the current situation. They can determine where they are weak and take steps to correct the situation. If your business is slow and plodding and does not quickly move against the competition's weak spots, they may get wind of what is in the works. They will make changes to fortify themselves against your coming blow.

Nivelle did not have the option of moving faster. 1916's fighting at Verdun and on the Somme expended most of the French and British Armies' resources. Both armies had expended their stockpiled reserves of ammunition in these two great battles. They would not be ready for renewed efforts until the following spring. By this time, the Germans were more than ready for what Nivelle had in store for them. Nivelle had bragged too much and too loudly. His plans were not a secret to the Germans for very long.

Nivelle was ready to go by April 1917. He gave grand new names to the armies assembled for his attacks like "Groupe d'Armée de Rupture." He promised the troops that this time they would cut through the German lines like a knife. He told them that this battle would win the war outright. Masses of French artillery, numbering thousands of guns and howitzers, fired off the Nivelle-style bombardment of the German trenches. The soldiers climbed over the top of their trenches at the appointed hour.

The Mutiny

They didn't get very far. This time Nivelle's recipe for success didn't taste very good. Solid gains were either nonexistent or measured in just a few yards. Any real gains were quickly lost to German counterattacks. German reserve forces, untouched by the French bombardment, moved forward and eliminated French penetrations. Reports on the failure of the initial attacks streamed back to Nivelle and his staff.

Nivelle had promised that he would quickly call off the attacks if his offensive was not successful at the outset. But when these reports came in, Nivelle didn't cease any operations. The French Army continued to attack for the next ten days. There were plans to continue the attacks even longer. But by then the French Army had taken matters into its own hands. There was a serious breakdown of military discipline. The soldiers themselves refused to continue the attacks. Widespread mutiny and revolt broke out in the French Army.

On the front line, men refused to go over the top. They would not leave their own positions and step into the deadly no-man's land that separated their trenches from the German lines. It wasn't just a problem on the front line. Units supposed to reinforce the front lines for further attacks refused to leave their assembly areas. Men stopped listening to their officer's orders. Some went as far as starting to march on Paris to confront the government. Some units attempted to get to important French armament and munitions factories so that they could blow them up and thereby stop the war.

The most mutinous units had previous experience with Nivelle. These units had been directly under either Nivelle or his henchman Mangin (nicknamed "The Butcher") at Verdun. These units knew what had happened to them at Verdun. They felt they knew what was going to happen to them again in an operation directed by Nivelle. The soldiers in these units already knew that neither of these leaders cared anything about their lives or their conditions. They did not want to go through an experience like the one at Verdun again.

A couple of points illustrate the magnitude of Nivelle's uncaring attitude toward his men. Troops were actually marched past stacks of coffins on their way to the front lines prior to the offensive. Soldiers found that Nivelle had made few provisions for medical supplies and treatment for the wounded. The common soldier began to feel, with justification, that his leaders did not care about him. The French soldiers resented their treatment as some kind of disposable resource.

Within days, less than half of the French Army could be considered reliable. It was no longer a question of whether or not the army could press on with the attacks. It was now a question of whether or not France would even continue to have an army. The French generals were worried their soldiers might not even defend their own lines. Many quickly understood that the situation could suddenly spread into an outright revolution. Only drastic and effective action could remedy the situation.

Please Save Us! Again!

The government promptly fired Nivelle. The politicians now feared for their own personal safety, let alone their political survival. France again called upon Petain to save the nation from disaster. He was promoted to head of all of France's armies. The government gave Petain broad powers to quell the mutiny.

Petain got plenty of advice about what he should do. Many felt the only way to stop the rebellion in the ranks was through extreme measures. If he wanted to, the government was perfectly willing to let Petain hang or shoot thousands. He certainly had approval to flog soldiers or even to use more medieval tactics, like tying mutineers in spread eagle positions to cannon wheels.

Petain had other ideas in mind. He thought the mutiny happened because the soldiers had lost faith in their leadership. He recognized that the soldiers had concluded that their generals did not know how to make them successful. They thought that their lives were being wasted in efforts that had little, if any, chance. Further, they felt their leaders did not care about them as individuals. No one in authority seemed to care about meeting their basic needs. No one was dealing with the abysmal conditions in the trenches. Soldiers actually bleated like sheep to the slaughter as they marched to the front lines.

Petain went out to visit the troops in every division of the French Army. There were roughly 150 divisions. He talked to soldiers and listened to what they had to say. He heard their stories and their complaints. He also heard about what was working and what was not. He gained insight from the perspective of the soldiers' experience. Petain shared his ideas with them on future operations. He told them he would not sacrifice them in large-scale attacks unless there was both a reasonable purpose and a good chance of success.

Based on what he learned, Petain made some changes that immediately improved the lot of the common French soldier. One of the first things he fixed was the food. Unbelievable as it may seem, the French Army was randomly assigning people as cooks. The army didn't train people to cook if they didn't already know how. This was a serious complaint in the French Army. After nearly three years of war, Petain was the first to actually do something about this. He sent the cooks to cooking school. He instituted a program to improve the quality of the soldier's food. Morale in the army went up.

Petain also fixed problems with soldier's leave. Up to this point, the French Army did not have a system for getting soldiers on leave back home to visit their families. A soldier's immediate superior determined how often he could go on leave. Some let their soldiers have time off, others kept them from ever leaving the front.

> ## ANALOGY 3: COMMON COMPLAINTS
>
> All around the world, when you talk to people about how they feel about their company and their bosses, a couple of things always seem to come up. If anything is wrong with either the food or the vacation system, employees will fixate on these problems as evidence that their company doesn't care about them.
>
> Have good food available for your employees to eat at lunchtime. If it isn't available on site, allow your people the opportunity to get good food. You may think this is their responsibility. They think it's yours. This is one of the most complained-about situations. It affects the morale and productivity of people who work for your company. Making sure that this is not a problem goes a long way to show people that you care about them and their welfare. If this is a problem, you are sending the message that you couldn't care less about them as human beings. If you send this message, even unintentionally, you will get the same kind of message back. People will show you that they don't care about your company in terms of poor work quality and reduced productivity.
>
> You create a volatile situation if you start making what your employees perceive as arbitrary changes to the vacation system. People feel that they own their vacation time. It is one thing to tell people the limitations regarding taking vacation when they join the company. It is very different when you make changes with little notice.
>
> It has become a recurring management practice to force people to take vacation. This looks great on the financial reports as you take vacation liability off the books. The problem is surprising people with this. Companies often come right out and say, "Next month everyone must take a week of vacation time. If you don't have enough time, you will borrow against your future vacation allowance." People view this as a real kick in the teeth by their company. They will view the employer that does this as the enemy. Worker morale and productivity will fall off. Reducing the vacation time on your books is a short-term reaction to a temporary problem. You will have much worse long-term problems if you do things like this to the people your business depends on.

This wasn't the only problem with leave in the French Army. There were no arrangements for troops to get home once they were on leave. The army had scheduled trains to get ammunition and supplies to the front lines, but they had no arrangements for getting a soldier on leave back to his home town. Soldiers on leave spent most of their leave time at train depots trying to hitch rides on trains that might be going in the direction they wanted to go. The majority never made it home.

Petain saw to it that all soldiers received a regular allotment of leave time. Leave was no longer only at the discretion of low-level officers. He also diverted some of the trains the army was using. He saw to it that soldiers could get from the front to their homes and then back again. This way, soldiers could spend their time off with their families, not lying around train stations.

Petain did use extreme disciplinary measures when he felt that they were called for. If the particular case was bad enough, Petain did sanction firing squads. Yet such cases were very rare. Hundreds of thousands of troops were in revolt, engaged in behavior that warranted the death penalty by the laws of the day. Yet Petain had less than fifty shot. What he liked to do was to transfer people out of units without notice. This way, the others would not know what happened. Many just assumed the missing troublemakers had been taken off to a firing squad. To his dying day, Petain regarded the small numbers of executions as his greatest achievement.

The French Army responded to Petain's treatment. The mutiny ended. The French Army continued to defend their country. Petain postponed offensive action until after the tide of war changed.

ANALOGY 4: FOUNDATION FOR A GOOD RELATIONSHIP

Petain and Nivelle are great examples of contrasting leadership styles and their corresponding effects. On one hand, Petain understood how to build positive and meaningful relationships with his organization. On the other hand, Nivelle created an extremely adversarial relationship with his work force. He did not intend to do this. The relationship is certainly not one that he wanted. Yet Nivelle's methods and practices produced it.

If you want to build a good relationship between your company's leadership and the rank and file, you can't do much better than following Petain's World War I example. Here is the foundation of his style: go out and have meaningful dialog. Talk with people from all levels of your business. Talk to them about what is going on, what is working, and what the problems are. Don't stop at just getting the information. You must take meaningful steps to quickly resolve situations causing problems. Use the information to make improvements. If you do these things, your business will have better morale and higher productivity.

A lot of business leaders are not comfortable going out and talking with their people. This is not uncommon, and it is quite natural to feel this way. We are all human beings with feelings. Business executives are no different. We all want to avoid uncomfortable situations. Many are afraid it could be very awkward to go out and talk with their people.

You will encounter difficult situations if you go out to talk. Some people may not like you. They might see you as the source of their problems, and they could let you know that in very direct and even insulting terms. This is an uncomfortable situation for anyone. It is not surprising that many leaders avoid any situation that could produce this kind of exchange. You cannot—you must not—let these kinds of difficult situations stop you from having an ongoing dialog with your people. Anyway, most of these bad experiences can be avoided by setting ground rules regarding respecting others before the dialog begins.

You do not have to pretend to be somebody that you are not when you go out to talk. The point here is that you are going out to get important information for your business. Don't mistakenly think that you have to pretend to buddy around with people you may not know very well. Certainly, no one wants to come across as a fake. The unfortunate thing is that this misplaced concern results in too many having little or no interaction with their people outside of meetings and formal presentations.

Here is the great secret to Petain's story. He did not pal around with soldiers. He didn't make them come to his office with formal presentations, either. He went out to the front. He talked to people in their camps and in the trenches. He was there to find out what he as the leader needed to know about the issues and problems of his organization. He did not put on an act or try to sell his soldiers on what a good job he and they were doing. Instead, he went out as himself. He asked people what was going on so he could make improvements. More than anything else, he came across to others as someone who was asking these questions because he was genuinely concerned. He was concerned about the organization as a whole and how it was doing at achieving its goals. Yet he was also concerned about the people in the organization as individuals. He himself was not an overly friendly guy by any means. Most accounts paint him as a rather reserved person. But this didn't matter! His organization saw him as an honest man who wanted to make things better. That's what mattered to everyone. They responded quickly to him. They didn't care about his personality. What they cared about was having a leader who would make the effort to find out what was wrong and then fix it.

This leads to the next important point. Petain was not out there listening to people just to get them feeling better by giving them an opportunity to vent. If you go out to get information about what is really going on and then don't do anything with that insight, you will have some big problems. People will view you as a phony who is trying to manipulate them to feel better without making any improvements. If you do this, you will end up being even more disliked, and less effective, than someone who locks themselves in their office all day. If you go out to get information on your business, *use it*. Otherwise, your dialog is a waste of everyone's time.

Petain made significant changes for his soldiers. He did *not* set up commissions or teams to look into leave policies or food quality. He did not chair year-long meetings investigating minor changes to the French Army so people would feel better about it. Instead, when he saw problems he took direct, quick, and decisive action to make things better. People could see the positive effects of these changes within weeks. He turned the morale of his organization around. The soldiers responded by improving their performance.

Now for the contrasting example. Nivelle did not go about his job with the attitude "So, what can I do to ruin the French Army?" But this is what he very nearly did. This result was the predictable outcome of his leadership practices. It is unfortunate that so many actually follow Nivelle's example. His practices are far too common. If you use the same practices today, you will experience similar results.

If you view the people in your business as existing just to serve you and your ambitions, you will experience Nivelle-type outcomes. You might be successful for a while, but eventually you will run into a situation where people will actually rebel against your methods. This rebellion can take many forms. Key people might flee to find work elsewhere. There might be a passive slowdown in work production. Your company might have other problems that cause productivity to fall to unprofitable levels. You could encounter any of a host of labor relation woes. But in each case, the ultimate result is the demise of your business.

> Don't follow Nivelle's example. Take the stance that you are there to help the organization to meet its goals, to be productive, to look out for the common good. Position yourself as the servant of the organization. Do *not* adopt the attitude that others are there to serve you and your ambitions. You will see results. Dynamic and positive things will happen in your company. You will find a bond between you and your people, one that transcends the meaning of the word loyalty. Others will feel indebted to your efforts on their behalf. Your people will want to pay you back for your efforts. They will improve their job performance to do so. You will see output and productivity increases. Your people will find solutions to seemingly insurmountable problems. You will engage your organization at levels which are impossible to demand.

CONCLUSIONS

The leadership styles of generals Petain and Nivelle are an insightful study of contrasts. One believed he had all of the answers. Nivelle moved forward with plans based on his beliefs. The plans ended in the near-collapse of the French Army. Petain had very different ideas and motivations. He constantly sought information from soldiers on the front lines. He learned about what was effective on the battlefield and what was not. Petain also had to fix the desperate situation Nivelle created. The story of the two French generals illustrates the following important points:

- **Failure to continuously innovate**

  There is no such thing as a permanent recipe for success. What worked in the past may yet work again. But each time you use the same methods, you have a reduced probability of success. The competition is not going to stand still. It will learn from its defeats. It will make changes to make it more difficult for you to beat them again with the same techniques. You must constantly innovate, finding new ways to be successful. You cannot wait until you have a failure to start looking for ways to improve how you do business.

- **Volatile policies and practices**

There is always an unwritten contract between a business and its employees. The contract states in general terms, "I will take care of you if you take care of me." You will greatly harm your business when you do things that violate this unwritten contract. People need to feel that the company they work for will take care of them. If they feel this is happening, they will go the extra mile to ensure the continued success of that business. On the other hand, if the company somehow signals a decreasing concern for their employee's welfare, there is a price to pay. Employee performance will fall off. The business will have problems achieving its goals. It will also have problems due to significant turnover.

- **The management-employee relationship**
  To maximize productivity, you need to work at building and maintaining a positive management-employee relationship. This will reinforce your message that you value your employees. You cannot do this by staying in the office at headquarters. People need to know who their leaders are. People need their leaders to motivate them and share their ideas about the future with them.

  You must engage in meaningful dialog with those you lead. This dialog will provide you with valuable insight into what is working in the business and what is not. Put in place quick and effective changes based on what you learn. People become very motivated when they see that what they have told you results in significant positive changes. This will motivate them even more to help you and your business achieve its goals.

- **Inspirational leadership**
  Poor leaders see their organization as existing to serve their ambitions and provide for their personal needs. Such selfish leaders motivate no one. They are a hindrance to their organization. You can only inspire people by being willing to make sacrifices, by putting the organization's needs in front of your own personal needs and desires. By doing these things, you motivate others to follow your example. The end result will be achieving the seemingly impossible.

ACTION FILE

HOW TO PROMOTE GOODWILL THAT PRODUCES SUCCESS

 BAD IDEA #1—Allow class culture.

In the dark ages, there were two classes of people, the nobility and the peasants. The nobility looked down on the peasants as inferior riff-raff, while the peasants hated the nobility. The nobility lived in castles and got all the rewards. The peasants lived in squalor and did all the hard work. Each group treated the other with contempt. The nobility took most of what the peasants produced. The peasants, understandably, often revolted and killed the nobility. Such class distinction, and the accompanying animosity between the classes, will exist in any group that allows it. People have an unfortunate natural desire to try to show they are better than others. You must work hard to prevent such divisions from becoming a part of your company's culture.

Many businesses enable class division by how they place many of their new hires. Many companies immediately place new college graduates in positions of responsibility over blue collar workers, most with years of experience. When anyone is put in charge of other people, there is a natural psychological tendency for them to believe that they are in charge because they are better than those they supervise. This leads to serious problems.

The other side is not totally innocent either. They may think, "Why is this person in charge when I'm the one with all the knowledge and experience?" Because of this opinion, they don't support the person in charge. They withhold their best efforts, or otherwise try to undermine the person they see as an underqualified boss.

The formation of classes is not just a problem between new college grads and blue collar workers. Humans will use any easily identifiable difference to create a class structure. It could be anything in someone's background. It could be any talent or lack thereof. It could even be nationality or ethnicity. In all of these cases, creation of any kind of class structure within the organization is a disaster. Classes foster class warfare. People are hurt and demeaned. People lose focus on the business competition. Productivity in any class-distinguished society is far below what it could be. In the end, class warfare will destroy the business. Don't let this be the case in your business.

Frequently remind people that while they have different job functions and responsibilities, they are not better than anyone they work with—not their peers, not their superiors, and not their subordinates. You need to start this discussion during the training and assimilation of new people into your organization. We all have different talents, knowledge, skills, and abilities than others. But none of us are better than anybody else. We need to treat everyone with respect, civility, and kindness. In this kind of environment, people are much more productive, because they feel appreciated and respected.

BAD IDEA #2—Use adverse policies only for lower levels.

You will create a class culture in your company if you make policies that only adversely affect certain categories of workers. It could be any kind of policy: compensation, vacation, health care, working conditions, parking privileges, security—anything, really. The litmus test is: "Does it apply only to a certain group of people?" If the answer is yes, then you probably have a big problem.

Such selective policies loudly proclaim, "The rest of us are better than you" to those affected. Policies that only apply to certain groups generate a huge amount of ill will. They will certainly view the policies as a concrete example of unfairness by management. Now we all know that life is inherently unfair. Just don't go out of your way to make it even more so. If you do, the impacted lower classes will find a way to make a corresponding impact on the upper classes. They may even do this unconsciously.

Successful businesses rely on the combined productivity of all involved to meet customer expectations. But if part of the company wants retribution against another part, people are not thinking about making the organization as a whole successful. Instead of focusing on beating the competition, your people focus instead on getting even with their tormentors. This is obviously counterproductive.

Avoid all of this by making sure that all policies affect everyone equally.

There should be no exceptions. The policy should not just be for some people. It should apply to everyone. If not, elitism will rear its ugly head. Elitism always has a negative impact on organizational productivity.

Often times, management publishes poor policies while they try to solve some problem. Their intentions may have been good. They just did not understand all the implications of their new policy. Always review and carefully consider any policy before signing off on it. Stop bad policies before they become self-destructive practices.

 BAD IDEA #3—Create a mercenary work force.

For thousands of years, most soldiers did not come from the country they were fighting for. They were mercenaries. Mercenaries are professional soldiers whose allegiance belongs to whoever paid them last. When the treasury ran out of money, mercenaries became very dangerous. They could turn to the other side. They might plunder the country they had just been fighting for. Mercenaries did not care who won or lost in a war. They were out to make the most money for themselves.

When you show no allegiance to your people outside of paying them, they will show no allegiance to you or your company. They will become mercenaries. They will focus primarily on maximizing their own gain. Their primary motivation will be to get what they can and then move on. Often they move on to the competition. This does not bode well for a company with a mercenary work force.

Mercenary workers will quit whenever it is best for them. They won't care that you have some important project you need them to finish. They may even plunder your company when they leave. This plunder is the knowledge of how you do things better than your competition. They will sell this knowledge. You may think, "Well, I would just sue whoever did something like that." The problem is that this is almost impossible to prove in court. And when you have hundreds or thousands of such mercenaries, you cannot stop this kind of activity.

It is far better to foster allegiance between your business and your work force. You want people to be loyal. They want you to be loyal to them. Money isn't the only source of allegiance. You generate the strongest ties by treating people well.

GOOD IDEA #1—Treat employees as yourself.
You generate vast amounts of goodwill between your company and your employees when you treat the employees well. This does not mean showering your people with all kinds of expensive things. It means that you should treat them as you would want to be treated yourself. This is called the Golden Rule for a reason. The results you get from this rule are indeed golden. Following the Golden Rule will ensure your workforce is loyal to your company. And this loyalty will produce results when your people go out of their way to show their allegiance to you, your business, and your business's goals.

You need to ensure that everyone, especially senior leadership, is equally affected by cutbacks. In fact, leadership should suffer more negative effects than those who make less. Make sure that the entire organization knows that this is the case. If you don't, people will just assume that the bosses are not affected, and this will lower morale.

When people experience tragedies or other sudden difficulties in their personal lives, do what you can to show compassion and provide help. When people do something extraordinary, show them you appreciate it, both by word and by action. Your people will return the kindness you show in the form of higher productivity.

 GOOD IDEA #2—Use open-book management.
In all organizations, the real power involves the budget, the power to spend money. Those with this power usually guard it closely. Few people with real power want to give any of it up. Most organizations even have layers of secrecy to protect this power. As a result, only a few know what is really being spent, and on what. Consequently, only the most senior executives even have access to critical financial information.

You should widely disseminate your financial information. Everyone should have access to it. Everyone should know the financial implications of their jobs. Everyone needs to understand how what they do impacts both revenue and spending. They need to gear their activities to maximize revenue while keeping a lid on spending. It is astounding that so few people understand the financial impact of what they do on the job.

It will take time and some initial expense to spread out financial information and train people how to interpret and make it pertinent to their activities. The effort will do much more than pay for itself. It will significantly increase your company's profitability. The gains this type of program will provide cannot come from top down initiatives.

There is a catch. To get the maximum possible gain, you must share the results of your gains with those who produced them. If someone goes out of their way to make a dollar for you, you should at least give them some of it. If you don't, the ideas and efforts you need will stop. People do not want to just enrich someone else. They need a just reward for their efforts.

GOOD IDEA #3—Use employee feedback.

The information your business needs to make dramatic improvements almost always exists within the organization itself. The insight, ideas for change, well thought out implementation strategies for those changes—all of these things are there. It just takes effort to uncover them. Unfortunately, few companies make the effort. The information stays hidden because either those with it do not have a trusted mechanism to bring the information forward, or your organizational hierarchy actually suppresses it.

What you need is a process by which any employee, regardless of their status or position, can bring information and ideas to the people with authority to make changes. You need to prove to your people that you are willing to listen to their concerns and their suggestions. You give them proof by actually making changes, not just by discussing what you might do.

You need an open and continuous dialog between those on the front lines and those making decisions about what to do and how to do it. This way you can identify information crucial to better performance. You then have the opportunity to design and implement dramatic improvements. The power of the idea must be your main consideration, *not* the status of the person who came up with it. Senior executives intimidate many of their people just by their presence. Many are afraid to talk to someone who they know has the authority to significantly impact their life and career. They are very uncomfortable talking with them, or telling them what they think. When you first start to crack this barrier, you often get a litany of grumblings and complaints. It will take you a while to build a relationship of mutual trust and have nothing but constructive dialog. Both sides will need to do some bending to get to this point. But if you make this effort, the results are significant, dramatic, powerful, and profitable.

CHAPTER 10

PASSCHENDAELE

"We Sent Men to Fight in This?"

INTRODUCTION

BRITISH offensives on the Western Front in the middle of World War I were all very similar. In each of these battles, the intent was to breach the enemy's lines so the cavalry could pass through the opening and into the enemy's rear areas. The battles started with days or even weeks of preliminary artillery bombardments. When the shelling stopped, the attacking infantry would climb out of their trenches and head toward the enemy, taking horrendous losses from enemy machine guns and artillery fire as they crossed no man's land.

This is the story of one such battle, Passchendaele. It was a fiasco fought under abysmal conditions. The story of this tragic battle illustrates the following important topics:

- Plans with little chance
- Fantasy-based strategies
- Common background limitations
- The leadership assessment matrix
- Leadership prerequisites
- Pitfalls in judging others' abilities
- The need to "lead from the front"

HISTORICAL CASE AND BUSINESS ANALOGIES

The Rationale

Each battle in World War I had its own particular character. Each battle had its own objectives. Some had goals outside of just breaching the enemy's lines. Many of the plans were based on mistaken assumptions. Of all the battles, Passchendaele (pronounced "Passion-Dale") probably comprises the largest set of blatant blunders. [Fig 37]

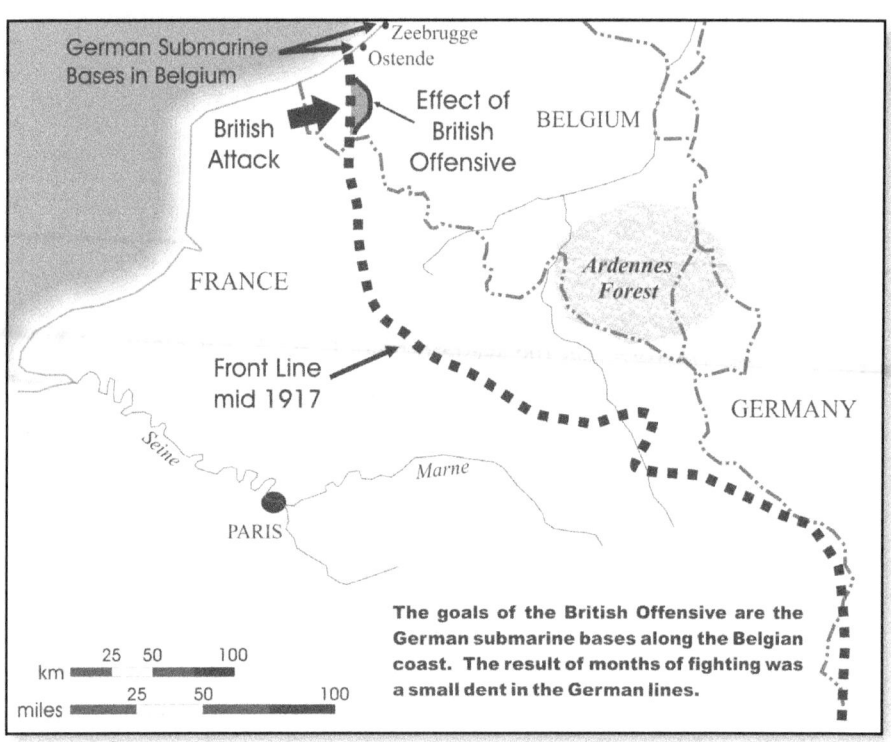

Figure 37. The Passchendaele Offensive

Passchendaele's alternate name is The Third Battle of Ypres. It was the third major battle fought just outside of this small city in northwestern Belgium. This particular battle lasted for about four months in the summer and fall of 1917. It was yet another attempt by the British Army to smash through German defenses. Since late 1914, the lines on the Western Front had remained relatively static. For the past three years, the British and Germans faced each other over these same trench lines. The British intended to change that at Passchendaele. To say that British plans did not work out that way would be a gross understatement. The battle cost hundreds of thousands of lives for negligible results.

The British Army had multiple reasons for starting this particular battle. The French Army, drained by Verdun and demoralized by the recent failure of Nivelle's offensive, had actually mutinied. French troops refused to attack, some even abandoned their trenches, and many units had outright revolts. If the Germans figured out what was going on in the French Army, they could win the war. As a result, the British Army decided to attack, to focus the German's attention on them. If they were busy with the British, they couldn't put pressure on the French. This would give the French leadership time to calm things down and reestablish discipline.

The most pressing reason for attacking at Passchendaele lay in Great Britain's strategic situation in 1917. In early 1917, Germany launched a crippling submarine campaign against British shipping. The Germans were well on their way to sinking enough ships to starve Great Britain into submission. In 1917, the German submarines, the U-boats, got much closer to this goal than their World War II descendants. German U-boats were sinking about 2.1 million tons of British shipping per quarter in 1917. Compare this statistic with the 1.7 million tons per quarter sunk in 1942, the German's best efforts in World War II. The comparison shows just how bad things were for the British in 1917. It wasn't just the higher losses; shipping was much harder to replace in 1917. Building a merchant ship in World War I took much longer than it did during World War II.

The 1917 U-boat campaign was a major cause in bringing the United States into the war. But it would take a while for the United States to be a factor. The American army was almost nonexistent. It would take the Americans some time to build and train an army. It would take them even longer to get it into action on the Western Front. The Royal Navy was convinced that unless something was done about the German U-boats, and quickly, Great Britain would be forced out of the war before the Americans could play a decisive role.

The British navy put pressure on their army to eliminate the German U-boat bases on the Belgian coast. These bases were located in the Belgian ports of Zeebrugge and Ostend, captured by the Germans in 1914. These bases were about thirty miles behind the German lines. The British Army High Command decided on these ports as the objective for the upcoming battle. The fact that no army on the Western Front had gained more than a few miles in previous offensives did not deter the British from believing that they could reach these objectives.

Unfortunately, the Royal Navy was ill-informed over the role of the Belgian ports in the U-boat campaign. The Germans were only operating small, short-range U-boats from the Belgian ports. These played only a minor role in the overall submarine campaign. The U-boats doing most of the damage to British shipping were sailing from ports in Germany. Capturing the German U-boat bases in Belgium was not going to fix the Royal Navy's problems.

What was defeating the U-boat problem was the practice of merchant shipping sailing together in convoys. Bunching ships into convoys drastically reduced the ability of U-boats to find and sink ships. In April 1917, when the British navy was screaming for help, German U-boats were sinking 860,000 tons of shipping a month. By the end of fighting at Passchendaele, the use of convoys lowered the losses to 302,000 tons per month. Monthly shipping losses would continue to drop for the rest of the war, thanks to convoys.

The British attack at Passchendaele had two main goals. One was to distract the Germans while the French Army recovered from mutiny. The British could have achieved this goal by an attack anywhere. They selected Passchendaele as the attack location due to the navy's desperate pleas for help. This was unfortunate, because even the complete success of the army's plan would have done little to help the navy, which was already well on its way to fixing its problems on its own.

Nothing Can Stop It Now

Once the decision was made to attack at Passchendaele, the battle took on an impetus all its own. The momentum built as planning and then preparations progressed. The British launched the initial attacks at the end of July 1917. The battle went on and on. Even when it became clear that the British Army was not going to get anywhere near the Belgian ports, even when the navy's convoys reduced the U-boat danger, even when the crisis in the French Army was over. The British Army continued to attack until it exhausted itself.

> ## ANALOGY I: WHEN TO PULL THE PLUG
>
> Businesses often repeat the British example at Passchendaele. It all starts with a hasty decision, made under pressure, to undertake some large new project. When the business conceives the project, the reasons for it seem valid enough. Yet, as time passes, the reasoning appears increasingly flawed. But by now, there is more than just a project manager and a proposed budget. The project has actually started. A complete project staff is already working away. This staff believes they are doing good work. They take pride in what they are doing and intend to make the project successful. They defend their project and its continued need for funding and head count with passion and conviction. They don't want their efforts cast aside as worthless. This is how they view any discussion of stopping the project. People just do not like this happening to them. They want to carry on with the project until it is completed. Once you start a project, it is difficult to stop it, just like it was difficult to stop the battle of Passchendaele.
>
> You need to see past what you hear from individual project teams and their leaders. Be willing to question the validity of the opinions you may have had even just a short time ago when the project started. Don't lock your company into taking a particular path unless you are sure it will lead to success.
>
> Here is a real illustration of a project with a life of its own. Hundreds of engineers in a company worked to design a new product. They were all highly committed to the project's success, as was the project's management team. Thousands of man-years of time and effort, not to mention huge amounts of cash, went into the project. New corporate leadership began to rethink the wisdom of continuing the project. They determined the product had a very low probability of success. They closed down the project, writing off huge losses for it. The company reassigned the project's engineers to other programs with potential for greater returns. The entire project staff screamed bloody murder when this happened, and many went kicking and screaming to their new assignments. However, their efforts accelerated completion of the newer projects. The company jumped way ahead of its competitors in multiple product fields as a result. All involved later readily admitted that the company would have incurred hundreds of millions in losses had the old project continued.

> This correction was possible because of new leadership at the company. The old leadership probably would not have changed course. They would have had to question their own previous decisions to do so. Very few people are willing to do this. Few will swallow their pride, admit they made a mistake, and redirect resources into more promising directions. But if you don't do it, you, and your company, may ultimately fail.

There was a big problem for the British with the location they selected for the Passchendaele offensive. The entire battlefield area contained a very fragile drainage system. The area was originally a giant swamp. The local populace converted the swamp into usable farmland over hundreds of years, using this drainage system. Significant damage to the system, coupled with any appreciable rainfall, would return the area to its original state. An attack by hundreds of thousands of soldiers supported by thousands of artillery pieces would certainly destroy the system. A large battle would turn the area around Passchendaele into a swamp.

No Doubts at the Top

Sir Douglas Haig led the British Army. He was one of the two original corps commanders in the BEF (British Expeditionary Force) Sir John French had brought to France in 1914. Haig replaced Sir John in late 1915. Haig oversaw the massive British offensives on the Somme in 1916. He had heard the desperate pleas of the French Army and of his own navy. Haig made the decision choosing Passchendaele as the site of the next great battle.

Haig had received reports from multiple sources about problems with the Passchendaele location. The army's engineers were responsible for making any battlefield passable to friendly troops and equipment. The engineer officers warned army headquarters about the fragility of the Passchendaele drainage system. The meteorologists, the army weathermen, warned that the army could only expect two or three weeks of good weather at the start of the battle. They predicted it would rain, often heavily, after that. The technicians of the fledgling tank corps warned that the terrain either was, or soon would be, impassable to their vehicles. This would take the new weapons completely out of the fight.

Haig dismissed all of the nay-saying. He accepted opposing views concerning each and every warning about Passchendaele. The British Army leadership wanted the attack to be successful. They expected their subordinates to greet their plans with enthusiasm and optimism.

Not all of the engineers raised alarms about the Passchendaele drainage system. Some were supportive of the battle plans. Engineers had solved problems with drainage elsewhere on the front. They used sandbags to create channels for the water. They were ready to do this again at Passchendaele. The engineers had also accumulated all sorts of building materials for the construction of roads across any difficult terrain. The army leadership viewed the alarmist engineers as lacking in initiative and problem-solving ability.

The next group with a credibility problem was the weathermen. The meteorologists were not real soldiers. Their opinions were widely discounted. After all, their profession is often wrong. The fact that they were basing their predictions on eighty years of the region's weather data did not increase the force of their arguments. And what if it did rain? The enemy would have to fight in the same conditions. Of course, this last opinion did not consider that the attacker would be moving across a blasted landscape, while the Germans would be backing up into previously prepared positions.

The generals also discounted the opinions of their own tank corps. The tank corps had barely existed for a single year. Their equipment had all kinds of mechanical troubles. The army establishment viewed the men going into this new branch of the army as technicians, not as warriors. The generals thought, "Of course they want perfect conditions for their equipment. Who wouldn't?" Many thought that if the tanks had difficulty with swampy terrain, that they could move into the woods instead. The problem was that woods in a World War I battlefield were nothing but tree stumps and blown-over tree trunks. The woods were even more impassable to tanks than the swamps.

Actual events validated every warning about the difficulties with attacking at Passchendaele. The ten-day-long pre-attack bombardment by three thousand guns firing millions of shells destroyed the drainage system. The attack started in a pouring rain that never really ended throughout the four-month-long battle. Not just tanks, but guns, horses, and men sank in the quagmire the battlefield became. Attempts by the engineers to restore mobility to the battlefield were woefully inadequate. The enemy could easily spot and target parties of men working on roads. Repairs to the drainage system could not deal with the ongoing damage. Thousands of artillery shells fell in the area daily. The shelling destroyed any repair efforts.

Convincing the Politicians

Others had serious reservations about the battle before it ever started. The British government, led by Prime Minister Lloyd George, was very skeptical of the Passchendaele plan. Haig personally met with the Prime Minister and the cabinet. He brought them around to his way of thinking. Haig presented the government with all kinds of estimates about conditions in the German Army. He told the government that the Germans were near collapse due to the losses they had suffered so far in the war. He explained the Germans needed to shore up their ally, Austria-Hungary, which was in desperate shape. Haig believed the Germans were out of reserves and would not be able to prevent a breakthrough on the Western Front. The British navy bolstered Haig's arguments by their pleas to knock out the German submarine bases in Belgium.

The government did not seriously question Haig's estimates. If they had, they might have discovered that the Germans were not out of reserves. Haig based his estimates on available German strength on continued Russian participation in the war. This was not going to be the case. The British government had a good picture of conditions in Russia in 1917. The Russian Army was in the throes of a revolution, desertion was rampant, and the population was clamoring for an end to the war. The Germans greatly reduced their forces facing the Russians. They redeployed the eastern armies to face other, more dangerous threats.

German losses had not brought them close to collapse. All of the war's participants had suffered huge and debilitating losses. They were all in the same boat. In fact, the British were in a more precarious position due to the mutiny of the French Army.

Haig based his reasoning for the Battle of Passchendaele on extreme optimism. He thought that everything would turn out just the way he wanted it to. He believed everything positive about his army's chances. He viewed the German situation with corresponding pessimism. He thought the German Army would have all kinds of problems dealing with his attack.

> ## ANALOGY 2: TOO GOOD TO BE TRUE
>
> Haig's attitudes prior to Passchendaele are similar to the root cause of many problems with strategic planning in the business world. Leaders believe rosy estimates of their own company's abilities and prospects. Similarly, they often only believe the worst possible estimates about the situation on the other side of the hill. There are constantly way too many pie in the sky projections in business plans. Too many base their plans on the competition just sitting idly by while they pummel them in the marketplace. It usually doesn't happen that way. The competition will put up a tough fight. Be prepared for it.

Why were Haig and his staff so intent on launching the attacks at Passchendaele? Why did they not listen to any of the arguments about why it was not a good idea? Why did they put such faith in optimistic projections on the outcome of the struggle? The misguided thinking resulted from the background and personalities of Haig and his staff.

The "In" Crowd

At the start of the war, most of the British Army's leaders were cavalry officers. The only notable exception was General Smith-Dorien, an infantry officer. In 1915, the head of the BEF, Sir John French, replaced Smith-Dorien after a long and protracted campaign to get rid of him. Smith-Dorien's replacement was yet another cavalry general.

Cavalry officers firmly believed the army's object in any battle was to pierce the enemy's front lines. This would enable men on horseback to ride through the breach and into the enemy's rear. Only a large-scale infantry assault could create the breach, and only after finding a weak spot in the enemy lines. The cavalry generals believed that a series of large-scale infantry attacks would eventually find a weak point in the enemy's lines. The attack against this weak point would result in the breach the cavalry could finally exploit. The long list of British offensives in 1915, 1916, and now 1917 were all attempts to breach the German's vulnerable spot. When each of these attacks failed, the cavalrymen would say, "Well, that wasn't the weak spot. But we've stretched their resources pretty much to the breaking point. The next attack has a much greater chance of success." Then they would begin planning the location and timing of the next massive assault.

The leadership of the British Army at this time reached their high rank and positions by being good cavalry officers. No one got ahead in the cavalry by saying things like "The cavalry's day is over," or "The cavalry should only play a minor supporting role to the rest of the army." Those who rose to the top of the cavalry really did believe their branch of the army was the "Arm of Decision." They truly believed that once the cavalry got through the enemy trench lines that they would win the war.

ANALOGY 3: SIMILAR BACKGROUND MYOPIA

The British Army cavalry leaders had very narrow views about how to be successful. The same thing happens to any business when the vast majority of its decision makers have the same background. They will focus on using the exact same techniques that got them to the top of the company. They will espouse the philosophies their backgrounds have taught them to accept. They will do this even when the techniques and philosophies they believe in are no longer valid. Examples abound of marketing heavy staffs determined that increased market share is the only path to success. There are plenty of examples of accounting-heavy staffs convinced that cost cutting is the way to improve their company's performance. Then there are the technology-heavy staffs that are totally committed to success through a particular type of product they all have experience with. Each of these homogenous groups has stopped thinking about other options. They are locked in to pursuing a strategy typical of their background. They don't consider other options until disaster is staring their business in the face.

Haig fully embraced the cavalry's cherished beliefs. He wrote about the virtues of the quick cavalry thrust before the war. He honestly believed that recent technological advances even increased the cavalry's value. Haig actually wrote that the machine gun was less dangerous to the horse and rider than it was to the infantry soldier. He reasoned that the horse's faster speed reduced the time it was a target. He also put down in writing his opinion that the smaller bullets introduced in the early 1900's did not have sufficient power to stop the charging horse. It is even more amazing that he wrote these opinions after his own experience in the Boer War that showed the cavalry could not deal with entrenched infantry. This had been the case in every engagement with modern armed opponents since the American Civil War. No one in the cavalry bought into these lessons because it would mean their own obsolescence and a significant reduction in their social status.

The cavalry was not the only area that had a lot of invalid beliefs. The preliminary bombardments so typical of World War I battles were the result of erroneous thinking by the artillery. The artillery believed that it could single-handedly neutralize or destroy the enemy's defenses. The gunners believed that if they fired enough shells, they would cut up all of the barbed wire in no-man's land. They thought the shelling would also destroy the enemy's machine guns. The artillery officers told the generals that the shelling would either kill the enemy infantry or leave them paralyzed in a state of shock. This is why British attacks started with days of bombardment of the German lines by millions of shells.

In reality, the artillery bombardment had little effect on mobility across no-man's land. The barbed wire was not destroyed, it was just rearranged. The long bombardment made it obvious to the enemy just where the next big attack was going to take place. The Germans then positioned reserves just outside of the artillery range in the sector under fire. They waited out the bombardment in reinforced concrete shelters dug well beneath the trenches. After each battle, the artillery blamed their failure to achieve promised results on either not having enough shells, or on not having enough guns to fire them with fast enough.

The Leadership Matrix

There was a very important reason why Haig never questioned the cavalry's and artillery's beliefs, even when there were all kinds of evidence to the contrary. Haig had a serious handicap, one that was not readily apparent. To see this source of this problem, it is necessary to look at Haig's early academic life. Haig came from a very well off Scottish family. His father, a prominent banker, sent him to a boarding school founded by a famous educator. Haig failed to distinguish himself in any way while there. He got into Oxford, but only into a college that allowed entry without an entrance examination, and this only because of his boarding school master's connections. He got a degree from Oxford that in the

British education system is called reading for a pass. You get this type of degree by just showing up for lectures. Haig then went on to the military academy at Sandhurst. He got in to Sandhurst without taking any exams only because he had gone to Oxford. Once in the army, he failed the entrance exams to the army staff college, a prerequisite for high rank. Fortunately for him, he got an exemption by the head of the army to go anyway. The point here is that Haig was just not very bright.

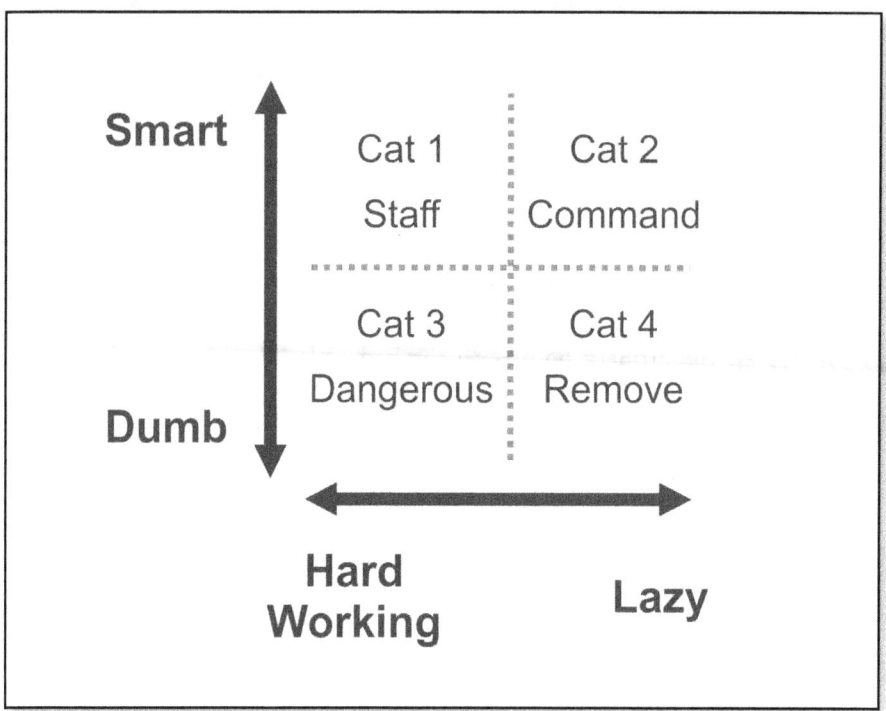

Figure 38. German Officer Assessment Matrix

ANALOGY 4: THE MATRIX

The German Army published a book about their officer development methods a decade prior to the First World War. Their armies in the World Wars consistently produced better mid level leaders than any of their foes, so there is a lot of value in looking at their leadership development process. The book contained some of the greatest truths ever written on leadership selection and development.

The book contained a simple two-by-two matrix. The labels on one axis were the extremes "fleisig" and "faul," German for "hard working" and "lazy." The other axis had its extremes labeled "klug" and "dumm," German for "smart" and "dumb." The resulting four categories on the matrix were labeled I (smart and hard working), II (smart and lazy), III (dumb and hard working), and IV (dumb and lazy). Accompanying the matrix was first a detailed explanation of the attributes of each of the four categories. Then the best uses for individuals identified from each category was explained. [Fig 38]

The category I officers, the smart and hard working ones, were identified as best suited to be staff officers. They were the best at dealing with the intricate details so necessary to ensure successful planning and execution of operations. They would see to it that every *t* was crossed and every *i* dotted. Their hard work and attention to every detail would ensure all of the needed arrangements for any endeavor. But these people were not the best candidates for senior leadership positions. The German Army's experience with them was that they would look at too many details and, by doing so, lose the large picture. They tended to try to do too much by themselves. They also had a tendency to unravel emotionally when they saw little things start to go wrong, or when they found some overlooked detail. These attributes could cause them to focus on unimportant issues at higher levels.

The category II officers, the smart and lazy ones, were the most desirable for leadership positions. These people knew the best way to get work done was to get others to do it. They excelled at training others to take over the mundane parts of their jobs. They excelled at delegation. They could get the organizations they led to do the assigned work and they wouldn't try to do it all themselves. They were also much less likely to panic, compared to the category I officers, if things started to go wrong. They were good at finding ways to accomplish their assigned objectives, even when plans ran into trouble. These officers were very good at improvising.

> The book bluntly stated that the army should quickly jettison the category IV officers, the dumb and lazy ones. The really biting commentary was reserved for category III, the dumb and hard working officers. These were labeled "highly dangerous" individuals who would inflict untold damage on any organization they are involved with. The higher this type of people goes, the more damage they will do. These people come up with the most dubious of plans, the most ridiculous of ideas, and the most bone-headed of strategies; and then would work extremely hard at making sure their organization expends itself and its resources on these bad ideas. Unfortunately for the British, Haig and his staff were mostly category III leaders.
>
> The same kind of people, put in similar leadership positions, will do the same kind of damage today. Don't let your business fall prey to the hard working yet not too bright. Promote those who produce results. Never confuse "hard work" with results.

The "Ticket Puncher"

Haig got to the top of his profession due to a combination of factors. He was in the right place at the right time quite often in his career. He had an influential family's help to get started. He was a handsome man who looked the picture of what everyone thought a gallant commanding officer should look like. He was a hard worker. He excelled at what we today call office politics. And, as already mentioned, he was in the cavalry.

After he got out of the army staff college, Haig went from one choice assignment to the next. He was with General Kitchener during his expedition to the Sudan. He was Chief of Staff to Sir John French, the commander of British cavalry in the Boer War. He was even Aide de Camp to King Edward VII. Haig moved ahead in his career because he punched his ticket so well. He had a resume full of increasingly important and influential positions.

ANALOGY 5: "PREREQUISITE DISASTER"

"Golden Paths" to senior positions exist in the business world. You need to evaluate what your business is using as advancement criteria. Are you promoting people based primarily on previous positions they have held? If so, why? Experience in a particular position does not necessarily ensure that someone has the skills and abilities your company needs. A better process is to identify who is good at leading and send them to gain the experience they need.

Far too often, people move ahead by just being in the right place. Here is a real example. An engineer at a very high tech company reached the highest levels of the business. This engineer came from an area that other engineers considered obsolete for quite some time. All of the peers he had had at the start of his career left to go on to some newer technology, to some other area that looked like it was going to be the cutting edge. All this particular engineer did was to stay. As the others left, he was the only remaining engineer with more than a few months experience. The technology of the group continued to hang on as customers found other applications for it. This engineer found his way to the top of the area because he had stayed in the group so long. As the others left, his bosses rotated him through a number of positions. Senior corporate management then selected him to lead this area because he was the only candidate with the prerequisite experience. From there he found himself on a number of committees. Membership on these committees was the determined prerequisite for positions of higher responsibility. He was not a bad person. He was just average. Is this what you want leading important parts of your company? Is this how you want people to move to critical senior positions in your company? If not, you must have more important advancement criteria than just prerequisite experience.

ANALOGY 6: JUDGING BY APPEARANCES

Haig had a distinct career advantage. He looked the part. Tall, handsome, and fit, he just looked like the kind of person that should be a general. The fact that this helped him to get ahead is proof of one of the greatest failings of humans. We are all horribly bad judges of each other. The reason is that our judgments about other humans are based, for the most part, on appearance. We automatically assume that people who look a certain way have certain strengths or flaws. We mistakenly assume that attractive people have a whole range of positive attributes while we wrongly assume that unattractive people have all kinds of flaws.

Too often, we hear people make comments about why someone was passed over for promotion, even when that person had a proven track record of solid performance. Phrases like "He just doesn't look like a director," or "She just wouldn't fit into the picture that we have of a VP" are more commonly used than any of us think. It is a good thing that Bill Gates went off and started his own company because he probably wouldn't have gotten too far in somebody else's. He just does not fit the image that most people have of an extremely successful executive.

If you want to find a business that is in or about to be in serious trouble, look for one with nothing but good looking senior executives. This is an indication of the primary basis for leadership selection within that company. The odds that all of the top performers are also all physically attractive are miniscule. Less attractive people, those with the skills, abilities, and vision to move the company ahead, figure out they are only going so far in such companies. They go elsewhere to find the career opportunities that value their abilities.

All of the things that combined to propel Haig to the head of the British Army in World War I are still around. It is dangerous to use any of these factors (appearance, family connections, office politics, elitism), because none of them have anything to do with delivering results. When a combination of these factors plays major roles in leadership decisions, disaster is usually right around the bend.

Surprising Reality

Haig's story is not the only one from which we can learn important lessons from the Battle of Passchendaele. His chief of staff, General Kiggell, illustrated another very important point. At the end of the battle, Kiggell decided to take a tour of the battlefield. He got a car and driver and set out toward the front. As they approached the now relatively quiet trench lines, Kiggell became more and more uncomfortable. His driver commented to him that the terrain would be noticeably more difficult as they continued ahead. The car stopped and Kiggell got out. Looking at the countryside, he started to cry. He sobbed, "Good God, did we really send men off to fight in this?" The point is that this was the first time Kiggell, or for that matter anyone from Haig's staff, had actually gone out to inspect conditions on the front line.

People operating solely within the confines of a headquarters developed a plan involving huge amounts of resources, not to mention the lives of hundreds of thousands. No one making the plan had gone out to look at the actual battlefield conditions. No one on the planning staff had gone out during the battle to look at what was going on and why, and how conditions impacted the ability of the army to reach its objectives. Instead, they stayed back in the relative comfort of their headquarters, looking at maps and moving pins around to show reported progress.

ANALOGY 7: KNOW THE BATTLEFIELD

There was no substitute for personal acquaintance with the battlefield then. There is no substitute for similar knowledge about your business environment today. You need to go out and talk with the people you are counting on to execute your plans. Find out what the probable obstacles are. Help them find ways around those obstacles. Find out what the real conditions are out there in your company's trenches. See what is happening in the marketplace with your customers. There is no substitute for this type of knowledge. No report will give you the information you need. You cannot gain this knowledge by tasking some subordinate to find out, come back, and tell you. If you really truly care about your business's success, you will make time to get out there on the front lines with your people. Otherwise, you are not much different from Haig, Kiggell, and their imitators.

The Battle of Passchendaele was only a slight variation of an oft-repeated script. The preliminary bombardment churned up everything in no-man's land. The area was devastated already to begin with. The pre-Passchendaele bombardment finished the job. The landscape of the battlefield was a complete wasteland. The shelling completely wrecked the drainage system. Heavy rain turned the area into a muddy quagmire. The infantry climbed out of their trenches and slogged towards the enemy. The survivors of machine gun and shellfire reached the first line of German trenches. The Germans counterattacked the exhausted survivors. Gains were miniscule.

After a period of intense fighting, a kind of lull would occur for a couple of days or even weeks. Soldiers dug new trenches across no-man's land to connect the newly won ground with the trench systems now to the rear. Reinforcements moved up to the new front line so that the attack could continue. The artillery had to reposition farther forward so that they could reach the enemy's rear. All of this movement required roads, which were obliterated by the bombardments. So the army had to construct replacement roads. Teams strung telephone wire to connect the new front lines with headquarters. They had to bury all of the wires to protect them from enemy artillery fire. Once all of this work was done, the attack could continue again, repeating the cycle. In the end, the front line moved forward a couple of miles or so, but each side of that front line was still very much intact.

CONCLUSIONS

This was the background of the British Army's decision to launch the Battle of Passchendaele. The British set their sights on lofty goals that, even if miraculously attained, would not have solved their problems. Many involved voiced opinions before the battle that the location was unsuitable. Senior leadership dismissed each of these warnings for various reasons. The British Army's High Command was overly optimistic. They thought that this time they would crush the Germans, even though they had failed miserably in recent battles using the same techniques they planned to use yet again. The story of the origin of Passchendaele illustrates a number of important lessons, including:

- **Plans with little chance**

    It is very hard to stop a project once it starts. Any project will take on a life of its own once people are assigned to execute it, when leaders are given responsibility for it, and especially when it is funded. Later, even if the project has little chance of being successful, it is still very difficult to cancel it. The project team will be committed to completing the project, come hell or high water.

    You must stop any project when it becomes apparent there is little, if any, hope for its success. Constantly evaluate the progress of your company's projects. End those that no longer serve a useful purpose. This may mean changing decisions you've made in the past. Don't lock yourself into a particular course of action just because you don't want to end a project that will no longer pay off. If the conditions have changed or if the original decision to start the project was based on erroneous information, then you need to make changes. To continue with a bad project can cause catastrophic failures.

- **Fantasy-based strategies**

    Don't be overly optimistic about what your company can do while negatively viewing the competition's abilities. Don't assume the competition will do nothing while you attack them. You cannot assume that your company will flawlessly execute all of its plans. Any plan dependent on both of these things happening simultaneously will fail. You must recognize that some parts of your plan will not come off properly and that your competitors will do their best to defeat your efforts. Discuss these issues while you are still planning.

- **Common-background limitations**

    If everyone involved in making a particular decision has the same background, they will look at issues the same way. They will probably choose a solution very similar to what they have done in the past. You need insightful input from many different functional areas to assist you in making important decisions. You must consider the input from each area as equally valid. You will only get the diversity in options you need from a diversity of backgrounds. The more options, the more dissection of those options from every possible angle, the better. You have blinders on if you only use the views and opinions of one functional area in making critical decisions.

- **Using the leadership assessment matrix**

    The leadership assessment matrix has four general categories; I—smart and hard working, II—smart and lazy, III—dumb and hard working, IV—dumb and lazy. Category I excels at staff work. They will take care of all of the details necessary for a project's success. Category II excels at leading projects. They know how to use all of the people involved to get the work done, and are not prone to panic if problems appear. Remove Category IV people as dead weight. Category III types are truly dangerous. There is little hope for any organization that promotes people from this category into leadership or decision-making roles.

- **Leadership prerequisites**

    Most organizations only consider people with certain prerequisite positions for greater responsibility. Unfortunately, those who have occupied these positions may have ended up being there by little more than chance. If you want your organization to have good leadership, you need to be looking for people that have the skills, abilities, and attributes that you want. Ensure that your organization has a plan to get these desirable individuals the experience they will need for greater responsibility. You are taking a real chance that the wrong person will rise to the top without such a leadership development system.

- **Pitfalls in judging others' abilities**
  Humans are poor judges of each other. We base too many of our judgments of others on their appearance. Appearance is a very poor criteria for making leadership selection decisions. You must look past appearance—at skills, abilities, and, above all, proven results. If you don't, all that you will have are a bunch of physically attractive leaders. There isn't a business out there that will succeed because their executives are better looking than the competition's.

- **The need to lead from the front**
  There is no substitute for personal knowledge about what is going on out on the front lines. No report will give you this kind of insight. You cannot get this insight by sitting in the office. You can't send a subordinate to get this information for you. You have to go out and talk to the people who are doing the real work, the ones you are depending on to make the company successful. You need to see what things are like for yourself. Base your plans and decisions on that information. If not, you are operating in the same vacuum most generals in World War I did, and you will have similar results.

ACTION FILE

HOW TO KNOW WHAT'S REALLY GOING ON

 BAD IDEA #1—Stay in your office.

Throughout history, the worst commanders were those who stayed at their headquarters, never venturing out to see first hand what was happening. The worst business leaders are those who stay in their office and rarely venture out to see what is really going on. Both types are operating in a world of fantasy more often than reality.

No amount of e-mail, telephone calls, video conferences, reports or presentations will give you the accurate feel for what is actually going on that you need. You have to get out and get around. There is no substitute whatsoever for first-hand observation and experience. Other sources of information are important, too. It is just that they can't give you the insight that personal observation does.

You are extremely vulnerable to lies, deception, and ignorance if you make it a habit to stay in your office and depend on others to tell you what is going on. This kind of situation is a precursor to real disaster. And if you don't venture outside the palace grounds, you won't know about the impending doom until it's too late.

 BAD IDEA #2—Trust the accuracy of reports.

Second-hand information like e-mail and reports are dangerous because they are often inaccurate, and sometimes dead wrong. A big reason for this is that the people presenting the information want you to see them in the best light. They want you to think they are doing a great job, no matter what is really going on. And if the people preparing reports know that little or no double-checking is going on, the information you get will become increasingly optimistic. Any decision you make based on false or misleading information is ill advised. Such decisions can easily lead to ruin.

BAD IDEA #3—Believe your instructions are instantly obeyed.

You do not have a clear picture of what is really going on if you believe that people instantly follow your instructions. You just cannot assume that people will follow your instructions just because you are now in charge.

Resistance to change, any change, is deep-seated. This resistance is especially difficult to overcome if you tell people to do something that they don't want to do. People will not embrace change just because you issued new instructions. People will actively and passively resist. You can't deal with this if you don't know that it is going on. And you certainly won't know about it if you don't go and check to make sure the changes you want are actually happening.

Going out and checking only once is not much better than not checking at all. If this is your habit, people will quickly know it and react with their own habit of returning to the old way of doing things once the check is over.

 GOOD IDEA #1—Have frequent multi-level contact.

A good way to know a lot about what is really going on in your business is to have frequent discussions with people from all the various levels of your company. Don't treat any department or site like Siberia. Visit as many as you can. Contact with people at every level, and at every possible site, is the only way to get the information you need to make proper and timely decisions.

Visit with people. Talk to them about what is going on, what makes them successful on the job, and what is causing them problems. People want to tell you the truth about what is really going on. The only reasons they might not are that either they don't have the opportunity, or they feel that they will be ignored or punished for telling it like it is. You have to allay these fears and show them that you will use their insight to make things better.

Sometimes you will have to deal with people who are not very friendly. They might view you as someone responsible for making their work life miserable. You might have to sometimes deal with resentment. Do not let the fear of maybe having to deal with this stop you from getting out there and talking to people. Deal with uncomfortable situations by telling people that you are there to find out what is really going on, that you are there to make things better with this information, and that constructive discussions are the way to do this. Most, if not all, resentment will go away as people see that you are earnestly trying your best to make things better.

In time, you will gain more and even better information. As people see you and recognize your efforts in making changes, they will decide that their insight and opinions do matter. They will want to be part of making things better, and they will share more of the information they have. Your business will become quite formidable with this kind of communication. You will find that the information you get will enable your company to react quickly and effectively to any problem or obstacle it encounters.

 GOOD IDEA #2—Know the situation on the front line.
There is not a single example of a successful general without personal first-hand knowledge of the situation on the front lines. None. You must run your business with similar first-hand knowledge. There is no substitute for personal familiarity with your battlefield.

Go into the factories. Visit the customer service centers. Call on customers or leads with your sales people. Visit the work sites to see how things are going. This is how you get the front line experience you need. It is also a good way to maintain personal contacts with your people. They will be happy to see you. The more they see you, the more information they will share with you.

Just because you have done this in the past does not mean you don't need to do it any more. Do not rely on experiences you had years ago, or even months ago. Things change. Your company is constantly encountering new problems and challenges. You need to keep your knowledge of the front line up to date.

Be wary of "dog and pony" shows. Worried subordinates who want to show you only a rosy picture of what is going on come up with these canned presentations. These "dog and pony" shows are meant to deceive you. Your best front line observations come when it is a surprise to those you visit and their supervisors. Visits planned too far in advance give too much time to people who don't want you to know what is really going on. They will try to hide problems and the true state of affairs that you need to see.

 GOOD IDEA #3—Question information and demand proof.

You have to probe what you hear and what you read. You need to do this to determine what is true and what are exaggerations or otherwise misleading information. You need to ask for proof of the facts. You have to find out what the people providing information are basing their assumptions on. You will have to figure out if these assumptions are valid or not. You have to find out where the information came from, or how it was derived.

You need to most seriously question information concerning projections for the future. Find out what models were used in calculating the projections. Determine whether those models are valid or not. Find out if similar results came from similar inputs in similar environments. Too often, projections based on guesses and wishful thinking influence major strategic decisions. Erroneous projections result in very bad decisions.

Your hair should stand on end when your questions are not answered. People will fail to get back to you. Others may become indignant that you have asked for proof. In any case, you must insist on answers to your questions. This way you greatly increase the amount of accurate and thoroughly researched information you will get.

CHAPTER 11

TECHNOLOGY

Invention and Application

INTRODUCTION

WORLD War I saw the introduction of most modern weapons. Tanks, airplanes, machine guns, rapid fire artillery, and poison gas were all used by European armies for the first time in this Great War. These new technologies created an environment of rapid change. Yet the armies using the new weapons were slow to change their methods, practices, and operational philosophies. They stayed very wedded to the past. Each of the armies made common mistakes in developing and fielding new technology. Businesses still make similar mistakes today. The discussion of technology in World War I will make the following important points:

- Failing to embrace new technology
- Why innovation is often dismissed
- Failing to exploit technological advances
- Training to effectively use new technology

HISTORICAL CASE AND BUSINESS ANALOGIES

New Weapons

World War I was not a static environment. The war took place in an environment of almost constant change. The First World War was the greatest explosion of new and improved military technology that has ever occurred. Most weapon systems in use today originated in World War I. The military leaders in the war had to deal with constant change due to technological innovation. Their successes and failures in dealing with technology had a great influence on the outcome of the war.

The failure to embrace new technology is one of the easiest lessons to illustrate by looking at the history of World War I. Many assume Germany lost the war because they did not have tanks while the Western democracies did. This is an oversimplification of what happened, but it does point to the truth. The Germans were not technophobes; they did not distrust technology, nor did they fear it. Here is a short list of the weapons first used on a widespread scale during the war: the fighter, the bomber, the tank, the machine gun, rapid fire artillery, poison gas and gas masks, the flame thrower, and the submarine. Of all of these innovations, the only one that the Germans were late in developing was the tank. Contrary to popular belief, the Germans actually produced and used their own tanks by the last year of the war. The German tanks were just not very good, nor did they have many of them.

The Germans either invented or quickly adopted all of the other technological advances in weaponry during the war. They certainly embraced the fighter, bomber, machine gun, quick firing artillery, and the submarine. The flame-thrower and poison gas were German innovations. The Germans were indeed looking for technical solutions to the problems of trench warfare. They just were late in adopting a single technological advance. In the development and production of tanks, they were eighteen to twenty-four months behind their competitors.

Tank Development

Both the British and the French had independently started to work on tank development in 1915. Even then, it was apparent to many that the defender on the battlefield had overwhelming advantages because of the trenches protected by barbed wire. The only solution was to find a way to get through the barbed wire and across the enemy trenches. Having soldiers walk unprotected across no-man's land towards the enemy's trenches was increasingly suicidal.

The British and French tried a number of ideas before settling on the tank as the most promising potential solution to the trench problem. The British toyed with the idea of using a giant armored wheel big enough to roll over a trench. The French tried a small contraption that a soldier crawled into and then pushed across the battlefield on his hands and knees. It was made of armored plate, had large wheels, and had a place for the soldier to stick his rifle out of its front end. The soldier's rear end was unprotected, and pushing anything across the mud and obstacles of no-man's land was highly impractical.

Both British and French innovators decided on using forms of the American caterpillar tractor as the best way of getting across the fractured terrain of no-man's land. The caterpillar tracks of such a vehicle could also span an enemy trench. The prototype tanks were tractors armored enough to protect the crews from bullets and shell fragments, the great battlefield killers. Each tank was armed with machine guns or small artillery pieces.

Tank Problems

The first tanks, like almost all new technology, did not work very well. The first French tanks were very top-heavy boxes. They tended to tip over. They were also very vulnerable. Their guns could only be moved a few degrees left or right from their fixed positions. The enemy could approach them from the side because the tank's gun couldn't turn enough to shoot back. The first British tanks were better, but both they and the initial French models were mechanically unreliable. Most broke down on the way to their own front lines. Those that made it to the front broke down quickly thereafter.

The tank also had another major problem. A tank is basically a big mobile steel box. All that the crew could see out of were tiny slits cut into the box. They could hardly see anything. Forget about hearing anything because the noise of the engine was deafening. The people inside the tank were deaf and almost blind. They could not detect enemy soldiers sneaking up close to blast them with flame-throwers or grenade bundles. Nor could they effectively deal with small field guns that the Germans moved up to the front lines to shoot at them like so many mechanical ducks in a shooting gallery. The tanks could only overcome these problems through close cooperation with their own infantry, who had extremely good eyes and ears. Yet, their infantry was staying far away. When tanks appeared, every German in the vicinity would start shooting at them. This led British and French infantry to initially form the opinion that being close to a tank was life-threatening. Naturally, they avoided them. Some generals even went so far as to order their troops to stay at least a couple of hundred feet away from any tank. So the first tanks moved into no-man's land alone. And as long as the friendly infantry stayed away, the tanks were ineffective.

The tank needed better mechanical reliability. Just as important, policies, procedures, and practices would need to change to overcome the tank's sensory problems. Without both of these improvements, the tank would be a waste to the countries producing them.

This is exactly what the Germans thought when tanks first appeared in battle. They thought that building tanks would be a waste of their efforts and industrial capacity. They convinced themselves that the tanks were some kind of novelty toy and that they weren't going to waste their limited resources fiddling with it. After all, they had effectively dealt with tanks so far.

ANALOGY 1: SEEING POTENTIAL OVER PROBLEMS

The tank's introduction is remarkably similar to the introduction of any new technology, even today. At first, the new devices are rather unreliable. They break a lot. Few people know how to fix them. A lot of people form very negative opinions about the new technology. They say things like, "That thing will never work," "Why waste your time with that?" or "What kind of a joke is this?" Fortunately, there are usually a few people who will see the promise and potential of the new idea. They embrace it, help make it more reliable, and find ways to maximize its benefits.

Many businesses that fail to embrace a new technology will often go further than just not encouraging its adoption. They may actually take steps to even prevent or discourage people from using it. Those who might see promise in the technology are put on other projects or punished for wasting time and effort on the new system.

This does not mean that you should heartily embrace every new idea that appears. You do need to evaluate the cost effectiveness and potential of new ideas. Go after those that have promise. Reject those that don't make financial sense. You will have to take risks. But not taking technological risks will set your company up for obsolescence.

To solve the problem of mechanical reliability, the tank developers made continual upgrades and refinements to engines, transmissions, suspensions, tracks, and other vital parts of the machines. Within a year or so, the British team had developed and tested five different improved models. By late 1917, the Mark V, the first somewhat reliable British tank, was deployed in France. At least half of the tanks could now make it to the front without breaking down.

The French likewise solved the problems with their early tanks. They evaluated what had happened with their early tanks and decided that a radical redesign was necessary. They dropped their initial large box-like designs and opted instead for a small two-man tank with a rotating turret on top. This way, the gun could aim in any direction. Their new tank, the FT-17 (French Tank, model 1917) started to reach the front in numbers in early 1918.

Tank Tactics

The British were also fortunate to have one of the few people to emerge from World War I with the moniker "military genius." He would develop the methods on how to use the new weapon successfully. J. F. C. Fuller was a thin bald guy with a big pointy nose. He came up with the tactics that rightfully earned him the title of "Father of Mechanized Warfare."

Up to late 1917, World War I battles typically started with days, if not weeks, of massive artillery bombardment. Then waves of men climbed out of trenches and tried to make it across no-man's land. Massive casualties among these attacking soldiers then caused them to retreat back across no-man's land and return to the relative safety of their trenches.

Fuller worked out how the tanks should work together with the infantry, supporting artillery, and aircraft. He taught the infantry how, and why, to stick close to the tanks. This was easy as the tanks could barely move at walking speed. By sticking together, the tanks and infantry would mutually protect each other. The infantry could stop the enemy from crawling up next to the tanks, and they could point out other dangers. The tanks, using nearby soldiers as their eyes and ears, would know what to shoot at. The combination of improved tanks and Fuller's tactics would allow the British to break away from the ineffective tactics they had been using.

Fuller's tactics would free the artillery from the job of trying to blow up all of the barbed wire in no-man's land during the preliminary bombardment. After all, the artillery was not destroying it: they were just re-arranging it and adding shell holes as additional obstacles in the process. Tanks would now crush the barbed wire into the ground as they ran over it, creating paths for the infantry. Artillery could now concentrate on enemy positions with a short but very intense bombardment and then fire a curtain barrage in front of the tanks and troops as they advanced. Aircraft would support the attack by bombing enemy headquarters and disrupting the flow of fresh troops to the battlefield.

Fuller tried to dissuade the British High Command from starting the Battle of Passchendaele. The ground there was so swampy that even if the tanks didn't break down, the ground itself would swallow them up. Tanks and Fuller's tactics were therefore of no use at Passchendaele. Once this disastrous battle was finally over, Fuller pitched his bosses the idea of a tank-centered attack against the Germans near the city of Cambrai.

Tanks Unleashed

The British had expended most of their resources in the protracted battle at Passchendaele, so Cambrai would be a much smaller affair. Most of the British general staff viewed the operation as an experiment, but they provided the experiment with the backing Fuller asked for. In fact, they increased the scope of the battle from the raid Fuller had first proposed, to a modest attack of six divisions supported by almost four hundred tanks. Old ways of thinking had not yet died out, so four cavalry divisions were positioned to exploit any rupture made in German lines.

The first inkling the Germans had of an attack is when they heard hundreds of tank engines close to their lines. It was only then that the British artillery started to fire in support of the tanks. Almost everywhere the German lines collapsed. The only unsuccessful British units were those commanded by a general who continued to order his men to stay away from the lumbering machines. Yet Fuller's operation was an outstanding success. They had achieved a complete breakthrough of the enemy trench lines.

The tanks had overrun German lines in the first day at Cambrai. Now the vast majority of them were broken down. There were not enough working tanks available to continue pressing forward with the attack. The few troops in the area and lack of reserves meant there was little else to do other than hold on to the gains of the first day. The cavalry was ineffective, yet again, because of the horse's difficulty in crossing no-man's land and because a single German with a machine gun could easily stop them.

The Cambrai experiment worked beyond everyone's expectations, except Fuller, of course. From now on, the British were completely sold on the tank. From this point forward, they would insist on including hundreds of tanks in all of their offensives

The gains at Cambrai were short-lived. The Germans reacted to the breach of their lines swiftly. Within a couple of days, they had more troops in the area than the British. Some of the newly arrived German units were elite shock divisions. They counterattacked the British only ten days after the tank breakthrough. The Germans regained most of the ground that they had lost and even made advances into previously British held territory.

ANALOGY 2: IGNORING DEVELOPMENTS

The story of the tank is an excellent illustration of what can happen when you ignore the potential of a technological innovation. By the time they realized the dramatic impact of tanks, it was almost too late for the Germans to catch up. Even when they tried, they made the same initial development mistakes as their competitors. The German failure to embrace the tank's potential was a major factor in their losing the war. You cannot allow the competition to get the jump on you technologically because something new has teething troubles and does not immediately live up to its promise. You must continually stay abreast of technological developments. Quite a few of them will be useless. But you need to analyze their potential before jumping to any conclusions. You can only ignore new developments at your own peril.

The final results only reconfirmed German opinions that they could deal with tanks through their own new tactics. They believed they could continue to deal with tank attacks and that any breakthroughs would only be temporary. Some Germans thought they should develop their own tanks, but they did not have much support. The Germans did build some tanks in 1918, but they were plagued by the same problems the British and French machines had in 1916; they were too big and tended to easily break down. The Germans had fallen behind their competitors in an important technological advance, and they weren't trying very hard to catch up.

Tanks, But No Tanks

The first tank concept vehicle was not designed by someone with either the British or French Armies. Nor was it first designed by a German or American either, which is what many might guess. The first true tank design is displayed in the Austrian Military Museum in Vienna. The first true tank was actually designed before World War I ever started, by a junior officer in the Austro-Hungarian Army.

ANALOGY 3: REJECTING IDEAS FROM UNACCEPTABLE SOURCES

You might think, "What difference does it make who comes up with the idea?" But, unfortunately, most organizations *do* care about who comes up with something new, enough to reject innovations that don't come from an acceptable source. Those bold enough to bring up their ideas find their lack of status prevents consideration of their ideas. This results in the stifling of many new ideas. In such an organizational culture, most people won't voice their ideas to their superiors. They feel they will get the same treatment as the young Austro-Hungarian officer. All of this reinforces the belief that no one wants innovation. Any company with such a culture will find itself increasingly unable to deal with changes in the marketplace. It is quickly out of ideas on how to adapt, and it dies.

This young Austro-Hungarian officer designed a tank that included many innovations that the British and French were slow to adopt, like the rotating turret. This design, had it been accepted and produced, would have turned the tables. It would have put the Austro-Hungarians and their German Allies way ahead of the British and French in tank development and use. It could have changed the outcome of the war. The design was rejected and discarded by the Austro-Hungarian military bureaucracy. The young designer's superiors quickly dismissed his ideas. No one would listen to him, and, thoroughly discouraged, he gave up. Of course, senior officers in the Austro-Hungarian Army did not see the upcoming need for a new weapon like the tank. But they also had other, more insidious reasons for quashing the radical new ideas of the young designer. The problem for them was not so much the new idea, but where it came from. The young designer was someone who, in their eyes, had little experience. He also occupied a relatively inconsequential post. Who was he to propose a radically new weapon design? The innovation met not only with disapproval, but with scorn and derision as well. It is little wonder that the designer decided it would be in his best interest to drop the whole thing.

Failure to Embrace New Technology

Viable battlefield tanks were available to the British starting in 1917. Rather than make the new technology the centerpiece of the next major offensive, the British High Command opted to use the old techniques, equipment, and ideas at Passchendaele. They even managed to pick an area where they couldn't use the new technology effectively even if they wanted to. No tank could have done much in the quagmire of Passchendaele. Only when the old ways failed again did the British put tanks to the test. They didn't have much left over for the attack at Cambrai because they had already lost so many men and expended so much ammunition at Passchendaele. As a result, when the tanks broke through German defenses, there was not enough infantry to pour through the opening. For a couple of days, until the German reinforcements arrived in the area, they had the opportunity they had wanted for years. If they could exploit their Cambrai breakthrough, they might possibly unhinge much of the German defense of northeastern France. But all the British could do at that point was to hold on to modest gains of the first day, and they could only do that temporarily. They had a magnificent opportunity. They failed to take advantage of it. They were incapable of utilizing the full potential of the new weapon.

The British weren't the only ones to fail to fully exploit the potential of a new technology. There is an even earlier example. Only this time it was the Germans that failed to take advantage of the opportunity created by a new weapon. The first major use of this weapon exceeded all expectations, but the Germans did not have troops available to exploit its success.

Poison Gas

The Germans had taken a different route. While the British and the French turned to mechanical technology to find a solution to the problems of deadlocked trench warfare, the Germans turned to chemistry. This played to their strengths. At the time, Germans were the world's best chemists. The new weapon they developed was poison gas. Many had predicted the eventual development of this ghastly weapon. Prewar treaties even banned research on such weapons. The Germans did not allow this to stand in their way.

The Germans developed many different poisonous gases during the war. The first effective one was chlorine gas. Chlorine gas does not kill you right away. On exposure, it mixes with the moisture in the eyes and the lungs, turning into hydrochloric acid. The effect of chlorine gas is like having someone spray acid into your eyes and breathing acid vapor into your lungs. The near-term effects are blinding and choking. The blinding is often permanent. It often took weeks for someone who had inhaled this gas to die. It is a horrible and painful death.

The first chlorine gas used went to the front lines in large cylinders. These cylinders looked and worked just like the ones welders use. The plan was to dig the cylinders into the ground of no-man's land, not far from German trenches, in relative secrecy. The Germans would then simultaneously open a long line of thousands of dug-in cylinders. The gas would spray out and form a cloud. Wind conditions had to be correct, or this cloud would not move toward the enemy. If the wind blew the wrong way, the poisonous cloud could blow back over the German's own trenches. This could be disastrous in the first uses, since the Germans were using gas before they had invented and fielded an effective gas mask for their own troops.

The Germans had enough chlorine gas by the early spring of 1915 for effective battlefield use. General Falkenhayn decided on using the gas as part of an operation in April that year. At the time, Falkenhayn needed to withdraw troops from the western front for his upcoming offensive against the Russians. To mask the troop withdrawal from the western trenches, Falkenhayn planned a feint attack against the French and British holding the Ypres salient. His idea was to keep the French and British busy reacting to a German move. Falkenhayn thought this would prevent them from exploiting temporary German weakness on the Western Front.

The Germans partially buried between five and six thousand chlorine gas cylinders in front of their trenches outside of Ypres. They opened the cylinder valves in the morning on a day when the weather conditions were right. The gas formed a cloud almost four miles across. The wind slowly pushed the cloud over French trenches.

Technology

> ## ANALOGY 4: WASTING THE GOLDEN OPPORTUNITY
>
> Buying and using new technology is costly and risky, so most businesses are quite wary. They want to wait and see results before they take the plunge and spend money on the new systems. They want to see proof that it works before they commit. They also don't want to deal with the chaos of introducing new systems into their company unless they know it will pay off in the end. These attitudes can seriously hinder the acquisition and effective use of new technology.
>
> Neither the British use of tanks at Cambrai, nor the German use of gas at Ypres was the first use of the new weapons. The British had tried out the first tanks during the battle of the Somme in late 1916, and again at Arras in 1917, both instances well before Cambrai. The Germans tried out gas for the first time a few months before Ypres against the Russians. A trial run in realistic real world conditions is necessary. The point is that the greatest opportunity for dramatic results is in the first mass use of an innovation, especially if you can do it before your competition develops effective countermeasures. At both Cambrai and Ypres, the higher ups were still insisting on further testing and definitive proof of new weapon effectiveness. By doing so, they lost the ability to truly exploit the stunning successes of the new weapons during their first mass use.
>
> Many companies find the first real use of an innovation produces phenomenal results. Yet, because of the probationary nature of the use, they are not prepared to exploit those results. The company finds itself shocked by the achievements. Because they were still testing out the innovation, there is no follow-up plan. There are no additional resources available to quickly add into the stunningly successful project. The company fails to quickly take advantage of the sudden opportunity. And by the time the company scrapes together the resources necessary for the follow through, the competition has already closed the window of opportunity. And the long, slow process of a business war of attrition, where no company can gain a clear advantage, continues.

The French soldiers quickly felt the effects of the gas. Those not blind and choking panicked and fled. Entire units ran to the rear trying to stay ahead of the deadly cloud. The only people left in the trenches were the incapacitated. The gas had opened up a gap more than four miles wide in the French lines. The Germans advanced about two miles through this gap. And there they stopped.

A nearby Canadian division got the credit for stopping the German advance. The gas also inflicted horrible suffering on the Canadians. Yet they did not stop the Germans. The Germans only penetrated two miles because they were in no position to exploit the breach. This was, after all, a feint. It didn't matter if the attack worked or not; the primary purpose was just to divert British and French attention away from events elsewhere. The Germans had no reserves available to throw into the breach. Their army was moving everything it could east to attack Russians. The gas attack at Ypres was only a diversion. The Germans only advanced forward to points they could easily defend. There was no one available to push on farther.

The chance to exploit this huge opportunity was soon gone. The French and British quickly discovered the true nature of the poisonous cloud. By the next day, troops were protecting themselves by wearing goggles and stuffing soaked bandages in their mouths. While obviously temporary stop gap measures, these methods did provide enough protection for troops to stay at their posts when attacked. The opportunity to gain a dramatic victory by using poison gas came one day and was gone almost the next.

Innovation in the Air

The airplane also saw its first real use in World War I. It was invented barely a decade before the start of the conflict. Although the airplane was an American invention, European inventors quickly took the lead in developing newer and better aircraft. This happened because the Wright brothers spent most of their time trying to protect their patents instead of developing newer and better airplanes, but that is another story. The European developments ensured each major power had reasonably effective scouting planes at the start of the war.

At first, opposing pilots could do little more than wave at each other. The first warplanes did not have machine guns mounted on them. No one had figured out how to shoot through the propeller arc without shooting off the propeller blades. Two solutions were found to the problem. One was to redesign the aircraft to put the propeller behind the cockpit, to push the plane forward instead of pulling it. Unfortunately, these planes were not very maneuverable. The other solution came from an ingenious French pilot with a very radical idea.

Roland Garros heard of a technician experimenting with steel deflectors. Garros had such devices installed on the propeller of his aircraft. He also installed a fixed, forward firing machine gun. The deflectors would protect the propeller and most of the machine gun bullets would get through while the propeller blade was not in the way. Of course, some bullets would hit the deflectors and bounce off in random directions. This sounds unbelievably silly, but it actually worked. With his new invention, Garros shot down five German planes before he crashed behind German lines due to engine trouble. Garros became a great hero. There is even a tennis stadium in Paris named after him. And to this day, a fighter pilot has to shoot down five planes to become an "ace."

The Germans developed a much better solution to the "Oh no, I shot off my propeller" problem soon after Garros. Their invention was an interrupter gear. A cam attached to the propeller shaft prevented the aircraft's machine gun from firing whenever the propeller blade was right in front. The Germans fitted this invention to a new nimble airframe. The new German aircraft could attack and shoot down opponents. The French and British quickly copied the invention, as they recovered examples from crashed German planes. Within a year of the start of the war, the added dimension of air combat existed over the European battlefields.

The Air War

The image you might have of World War I air combat is of huge clusters of biplanes flying around each other, guns blazing. Every now and then an aircraft falls out of the sky burning and crashes into the ground. This picture is actually pretty accurate. What is not accurate is the idea that losses in these dogfights were pretty even. They weren't.

The French and British together produced more than 125,000 aircraft during the course of the war. Compared to this, the Germans produced only slightly more than 47,000. The French and British together lost more than 88,000 planes, while the Germans lost about 28,000. In the middle of 1918, the last phase of the war, the British and French, reinforced by Americans, had about 8500 frontline aircraft available on the western front. The Germans at the same time had less than 3000.

These numbers tell us that the French and British outnumbered the Germans in the air by a ratio of almost 3 to 1. But while seriously outnumbered in the skies, the Germans managed to shoot down three times as many of enemy aircraft than they lost themselves. The German Air Force in World War I was shooting down three allied aircraft to each one that they lost and doing it while outnumbered by three to one. The Germans were three times more effective in the air than their adversaries were, and they were doing it with a third as many aircraft.

You might think the Germans were more effective in the air because they had better aircraft. This was not the case. During some time periods, the Germans did have a slight technological edge, but at other times, the French and British did. Both sides continually developed better and better aircraft during the course of the war. The planes became faster and more maneuverable. In this developmental race, one side had a slight edge only to lose it when the other side came out with better models. This cycle continued throughout the war. So while the Germans did indeed have fine aircraft like the Fokker Triplane, Fokker D7, and Albatross Ds, the British had the Sopwith Camel and SE-5a and the French had Spads and Neiuports. Overall, neither side possessed clear technological advantages over the other. The German success was not due to better equipment. Instead, it was due to two other significant factors, better pilot training and better aircraft tactics.

Source of Advantage

Pilots of the British or French Air Forces barely had an hour's flying time before they went to the front. They showed up at their squadrons barely able to take off or land their aircraft. Most only lasted a week or so before they were dead. Those who survived learned what they needed to know through their own on the job experience.

Training for German pilots was a very different experience. They trained their pilots intensively before sending them anywhere near the front. The best German pilots were sent back to train others, even when their presence was demanded at the front. German pilots were not left to their own devices, like so many of their British and French counterparts, when they arrived at their squadrons. Instead, they were assigned mentors. The experienced pilots taught them further lessons on how to stay alive and be effective in aerial combat. Top German aces like Boelke and Richtofen were not just good fliers; they embraced the roles of teacher and mentor as their most important responsibility.

The Germans did more than just train their pilots better. They also trained leaders in the proper uses of massed aircraft. The French were actually the first to form squadrons. The concept was to have all squadron aircraft operate together under the squadron commander's direction. The Germans saw how effective this was for the French during the battle of Verdun. They copied the squadron concept, as did other armies. But the Germans did more than just copy the idea. They went further by developing tactics for aircraft squadrons.

Organizing for Success

The French and British squadrons belonged to specific ground armies. The commanders of these armies were very insistent on having control over their own airplanes. Each army commander received an allotment of aircraft squadrons. This spread out French and British aircraft all along their lines. It also meant that the ground force commander also commanded the aircraft, even though he and his staff had no experience with aircraft and did not know how to use them properly or how to exploit their capabilities. This wasted a lot of the efforts and abilities of French and British airmen.

The Germans separated their squadrons from their army's command structure. The German squadrons were under the operational control of seasoned airmen. The trained air commanders ensured the most effective use of the aircraft at their disposal. A German Army commander could not stop squadrons from moving outside of the sector he controlled. Independent of the ground forces, German squadrons moved quickly to where they were needed most.

In the air, the Germans made the most of what they had. They had better trained pilots. Their use of squadrons concentrated their aircraft into the most vital sectors. This is how they were effective even though their enemies had three times the resources. Their methods were copied by everyone else in preparation for the next war.

ANALOGY 5: TRAINING PEOPLE TO USE TECHNOLOGY

You don't become successful just because you buy the latest technology. Technology, in and of itself, doesn't produce results. People have to know how to use it. They need training, not just as competent operators, but also in how to take advantage of the technology. Just sending someone to learn what buttons to push is not adequate. This is the same as just training pilots to take off and land before sending them off to the front. The people who are going to use the new technology must also know how to exploit it.

Don't just train your people on the new equipment. Provide for mentors and coaches to help people put their training to the most effective use. Insist that those who have figured out how best to use new technology share their knowledge and insight with others. This is the only way to quickly exploit the learning and experience of your best people. This way, you don't just have a couple of individual aces, but whole squadrons of effective people. This way your entire enterprise will be able to exploit the advantages of the new technology.

Training individual users is just the first phase. Just as important is making sure that you put the new technology under the control of people who have faith in it and who know how to get the most out of it. Do not place control of new technology under the direction and supervision of people who do not understand it, or who are pessimistic about its success. Such people might even undermine the technology in attempts to be able to say, "I told you it wasn't going to work."

Don't dilute your investment in new technology. Most of your company's departments will want to have the latest toys. This is just like the French and British Army commanders wanting little Air Forces for their sector of the front. If you dilute your new resources, you may not have enough to concentrate on critical projects during the initial window of opportunity. Put all that you need into use on projects that create your breakthrough. Be prepared to back up the success to exploit your competition's disarray.

CONCLUSIONS

The stories of the tank, poison gas, and combat aircraft show that most organizations have great difficulty in taking advantage of the full potential of promising new technological developments. The French and British successfully developed the tank, yet it took them years to employ them effectively. The Germans failed to see the tank's potential. They mistakenly believed their early experiences proved the tank was a failure. When they changed their minds, they were too far behind to catch up.

Both the British with tanks and the Germans with poison gas failed to exploit the success of their new technology on the battlefield. The enemy quickly came up with countermeasures that nullified the advantages created by the use of new the new weapons. Failure to plan for success meant ultimate failure.

In the air, only the Germans effectively trained their pilots and used their aircraft to the greatest effect. Even while greatly outnumbered, they were more successful than their adversaries were. All of these stories make for good business analogies. The most important include:

- **Failing to embrace new technology**

    The main reason for failing to embrace new technology is skepticism. New technology usually has teething trouble. It has reliability problems. People don't use it properly. Yet these issues do not mean the problems are insurmountable. When you look at new technology, you can't look at it in terms of "What can this do now?" Instead, you have to think about "What *will* this be able to do?" Failing to take advantage of new technology will make you and your business fall behind. And as you try to catch up, your company will have to learn lessons your competition has already mastered.

- **Why innovation is often dismissed**

    Sometimes people don't listen to important ideas just because of who is doing the talking. They are more concerned with the source than the merits of those ideas. Rarely do executives listen to those who have little influence or who hold minor positions in the company. Few, if any, think these people are capable of coming up with any great ideas. So dismissing their ideas is already a foregone conclusion.

You and others in your company must be willing to listen to everyone. You need to seriously consider all ideas, even those proposed by people in humble circumstances. What matters is the idea, *not* the source. Too often, the solution to a problem or a great idea is there all along; it's just that no one is listening.

- **Failing to exploit technological advances**

    Most companies fail to use new technology effectively because they adopt a "wait and see" attitude. They wait for multiple cases of proven results. Even then, will they use it under controlled conditions where there is little chance of failure. This setup has little chance of stunning success either. Too often, we fall into the trap of continuing to go with old methods because these are what we are comfortable with, even when those methods are not producing results.

    To be truly innovative, you have to accept the risk of using new ideas and new technology before they are completely proven. It may be that your success is what will prove the new developments, and in the course of doing so, you will leave your competition far behind. The window for such success is usually small. Have plans to quickly exploit any success. But remember, if you wait too long, the opportunity for stunning success will pass as everyone climbs on the bandwagon.

- **Training to effectively use new technology**

    It does little good to introduce new technology into your company if your people don't know how to use it. You need to train them not just on how to use it; you also need to train them on how to use it effectively. This means you have to do a lot more than just buy the technology. You also have to develop methods and practices to maximize the new technology's benefits. Then you have to teach your people to adopt those new methods and practices. If you don't, you will lose most of the new technology's advantages.

ACTION FILE

HOW TO MAKE THE MOST OF NEW TECHNOLOGY

 BAD IDEA #1—Wait for others to prove it works.
You would think that most businesses by now have figured out that you have to keep up technologically with your competition. But there are still some that don't get it. Eventually it will get them. Technology continually provides ways to improve communication, increase worker productivity, reduce costs, and generate revenue. If your competition improves in these areas while you are stagnant, it will spell your company's doom.

Even if you do eventually adopt new technology, waiting until the last minute will mean that your people are behind the learning curve. They will need time to learn how to use it. They need time to integrate it into their work processes. They will need to familiarize customers and suppliers with these new processes. All of this will take up time and energy your competition doesn't have to spend because they already did this when they adopted the new technology earlier. This puts your company at a distinct disadvantage.

Waiting also prevents you from creating breakthrough types of successes. You won't be in a position to offer your customers something your competition doesn't have. You won't be able to name your own price for an innovative product or service. You will be following the lead of others.

 BAD IDEA #2—Get it before determining potential payoff.
This problem is going too far in the other direction. You buy the latest thing the moment it is available. It's bad to wait for new technology to fully mature before getting it. It's also bad to acquire the latest thing before you know if it will make economic sense.

Do your homework. Don't believe all the promises made on behalf of technology that no one is using yet. Have your technical people look into what is under development, what the problems are, and what the probability is that the developers can solve these problems.

Look at how you might be able to use the new technology. Look at cost versus potential payoff. You have to take risks with new developments, but make sure you base those risks on sound judgment. Don't just jump on the bandwagon because others are buying it. If you buy something that doesn't work out, you've just wasted a lot of money, not to mention tying up your people with toys they will soon stop using. Let your competitors waste their time, efforts, and money.

BAD IDEA #3—Buy the latest stuff for everybody.

Even when you decide to buy new technology, do so carefully. Everybody at your company will want the latest equipment, the latest software, and the latest toys. Buying it for everyone costs a lot of money. Buy it only for those areas that need it and will put it to productive, revenue-producing use.

Most people can barely use the technology they have now. You would be surprised how many people, top executives included, barely know how to run basic devices and software. Don't waste your money buying technology. Make sure that the investment makes sense. Make sure you are buying it for people who will know how to use it and that you will end up making more money because you got it.

Now the real dark side: a lot of money you spend on technology is actually counterproductive. This means that you are spending your money on making your people *less* productive. Sometimes it is because you are buying something like software that has serious flaws, like crashing a lot. Other times, it is because people will use the technology to goof off. Many organizations are in almost complete denial about what people are doing with their computers and the Internet.

GOOD IDEA #1—Continually study new technologies.

You need to always be on the lookout for good ideas that you can put to use in your company. You should actually have a group of people who investigate new technology. They need to look into the new idea's realistic probability of overcoming development problems. They need to research potential uses and potential markets. They need to see if it would make economic sense that would result in a good return on your investment.

When you find things that make sense for your company, get them, not just to test them, but to get an edge over the competition. Put more than just tentative backing behind projects using the new stuff. Prepare for and then execute your breakthrough. Plan for, and be ready to exploit, success.

 GOOD IDEA #2—Use new technology judiciously.
Never go on spending sprees. You want to make sure that you are always spending your money wisely. Even if you are convinced that a new technology will give you a definite advantage, buy what you need, and then only for the people who actually need it. You don't want your business to become a toy store for your people, but you do want to ensure that people have the tools they need to be as productive as possible.

Study where putting new technology makes the most economic sense. You want to make reasonably sure that you will make more with the technology than you will spend on it. Always use this as the purchase criteria. Don't just buy technology because it would be cool to have.

When you do buy it, put it in the hands of people who will use it most effectively. Don't just give it to people who want to have it. There needs to be a valid justification. Give it to people who can show you they will use it. Make sure that their superiors will also support them in using it. You don't want to give new and costly technology to people whose bosses don't understand it and who will actually hinder its effective use.

You must spend money on technology wisely, but you need to provide people with the tools they need to be productive. There is nothing wrong with buying older technology when it is all that some people need. If all someone needs is a computer to do word processing and look at e-mail, then that is all you should buy.

GOOD IDEA #3—Train to maximize productivity.

It is not enough to just buy the technology. You have to properly train people how to use it. Believe it or not, a lot of people have a hard time learning how to use something by reading the manual. They need hands-on training that includes practical applications.

Initial training is just that, the starting point. It takes more than that to make your people truly effective with new technology. They need to know how to put it to the best use. They need to learn the tactics that will allow them to get the most out of the new tools. Everyone involved needs this kind of training, even those who are not personally using it. Managers need to know what it can and cannot do, and how to rearrange or redesign work processes to maximize its benefits to the company. There may be new supply or maintenance or other requirements that change with the technology. Those involved in those areas also need to know what adjustments they need to make.

Demand results from training. You want to ensure that the time and money you spend on it results in people actually being more productive. Test to see if people can use the technology. Make sure they can demonstrate that they can use it just like they would on the job. You cannot assume that just because someone went to a class that they actually learned everything they need to know.

Do more than just provide training. Identify people as mentors. Have them help the people that have just returned from initial training. Many of the tricks of the trade are unwritten. Mentors need to pass these on to those they mentor. You cannot allow people to try and safeguard their positions by withholding information and knowledge. Penalize people who do this. They are costing your company a lot. Reward those who embrace the role of mentor and help raise the productivity of others.

CHAPTER 12

VICTORY OR DEFEAT

Systems and Processes in Times of Drastic Change

INTRODUCTION

IN 1918, the stalemate between the armies facing each other across no man's land would end. New methods and technology would break the old patterns. New armies were available to both sides. The war could go either way. Both sides would have a chance to win and end the war on their terms. As the story of 1918 unfolds, the following important points will come into play:

- Dangers of rigid command and control
- Strength of low level decision making
- Listen to ideas without judging the source
- Myth of the "perfect way to do things"
- Importance of long-term goals even in a fluid environment
- Accepting risk by failing to take risks
- Danger of fixation on a particular project
- Dangers of incompetents
- The need for continual improvement

HISTORICAL CASE AND BUSINESS ANALOGIES

The Trench Problem

In 1914, at the start of World War I, the opposing armies crossed open fields as they maneuvered for position. It was common for them to advance twenty miles a day then. This was certainly not the case during the battles of 1915, 1916, and 1917 on the Western Front. During these three years, the front lines were relatively static. The opposing armies dug deep into the ground and solidified their defenses. Neither side had the strength or means to expel the other from their trenches. In the mid-war period, gains on the battlefield were measured in mere yards.

The opposing trench lines were roughly a hundred yards apart, often in plain sight of each other. The area between the lines was no-man's land, as neither side controlled it. Both sides constructed dense barbed wire obstacles in this area. Infantry could not make it through the wire entanglements without being shot to pieces by machine guns.

A typical mid-war battle began with an intense and prolonged artillery bombardment. The idea was to destroy the barbed wire and to kill as many of the entrenched enemy as possible. This bombardment lasted days, often more than a week. It involved thousands of artillery pieces firing literally millions of shells. When the bombardment stopped, all the attacking infantrymen would climb over the top of their trenches and then move across no-man's land toward the enemy.

The bombardments didn't work. The shelling didn't destroy the barbed wire; it just rearranged it. Also, the barrages created all kinds of destruction and obstacles that further hindered movement across no-man's land.

The shelling didn't work very well on the enemy, either. It didn't destroy the defending infantry nor did it reduce their will to resist. Soldiers quickly realized their trenches were inadequate protection against an intense bombardment, so they dug shelters into their trench systems. These shelters were reinforced concrete bunkers buried deep in the earth. When an intense bombardment started, the troops moved down into the shelters. When it was over, they came back out and manned their weapons in the trenches.

Unsuited Tactics

In many of the mid-war battles, when the attacking infantry climbed out of their trenches, they formed up into battle lines. Their officers arranged them in almost parade-like formations of lines abreast. These lines were supposed to walk across no-man's land together. The idea was to arrive at the enemy trench at the same time. This way, they would have the strength in numbers to storm and take the enemy trench. It just never worked out that way. At the start of the Battle of the Somme in July 1916, at the end of a ten-day bombardment, the British Army lost sixty thousand men just on the first day. Forming up into lines to walk across no-man's land was disastrous.

The whole idea of lining up and walking across no-man's land shoulder to shoulder seems pretty naive. However, back then, it was an accepted practice based on thousands of years of military experience. All the way back to Alexander the Great, army units set up in formations their leaders could watch and control. This is how organized armies conquered vast barbarian hordes. The barbarians fought as unorganized and uncontrolled mobs. Formations allowed military leaders to oversee, control, and direct everything their army did.

The problem was that this entire system of command and control was obsolete even before World War I started. This was not just because of the lethality of new weapons, but also because of the sheer magnitude of the armies involved and the vast size of the battlefields. In the First World War, the battlefields were so large, the numbers of troops so vast, that generals could no longer see the majority of their troops, nor could they control them once they left their trenches.

The armies continued to teach their obsolete pre-war doctrines to their new officers. The officers followed their training and formed their troops into straight, parallel lines, and then tried to move across the battlefield. When they failed, their superiors told them to do the same thing over again, just try harder. The generals made all kinds of excuses for the failures. They complained there was not enough artillery, nor were there enough shells for the guns they did have. They griped about their new soldiers not having proper training. They insinuated that too many people back home were defeatists, and were contaminating the fighting spirit of the soldiers. They did little to develop new battlefield tactics.

> ### ANALOGY 1: PROBLEMS DUE TO RIGID CONTROL
>
> Some businesses lock themselves into a system of rigid command and control practices. The people in these companies are not trusted to think for themselves. The company watches its people closely. The employees get specific directions on what to do and how to do it. The bosses feel that their people do not have the experience to know what to do. They are certainly not to make decisions on their own. Only the trained and trusted leadership is supposed to do that. The people in companies like these are just supposed to carry out their instructions, no matter what.
>
> There is no questioning of methods, even when situations arise where the prescribed procedures do not work. Instead, those in charge assume failures are due to people not properly carrying out their instructions. They do little or nothing to determine the true cause of problems. They never question their decision-making process and their rigid command and control system. They certainly never call into question their own wisdom and actions. Such businesses continually repeat their failures. In the end, their rigid and untrusting corporate culture undermines and dooms the company.

Capitalizing on Defensive Advantages

On the Western Front from 1915 to 1917, the Germans were usually on the defensive. They figured out rather quickly that they needed to develop the best possible defensive tactics. They needed to minimize their own losses while maximizing enemy casualties. This way, they could best retain the ground they had conquered in 1914. They called the system they developed "defense in depth."

Prior to defense in depth, the defender placed the vast majority of his troops in a single trench line at the very edge of no-man's land. Troops in this trench had the unfortunate habit of frequently being shot or blown up by the enemy. The enemy could directly observe this front line and easily target it with his weapons. It wasn't just that the front line trench was a dangerous location. If the enemy should breach this line, they could wreak havoc on the vital and yet unprotected rear areas.

Defense in depth used not one, but three trench lines. Only a few soldiers manned the trench on the edge of no-man's land, the one the enemy could actually see. These troops were to fire off flares if the enemy infantry started moving en masse across no-man's land. They were also to man their machine guns to kill as many of the enemy as possible before they were overrun. This most forward trench was just a warning line, a deadly speed bump to an enemy attack. It was not expected to hold out if the enemy reached it in strength.

Defense in depth put the majority of defending troops in a parallel second trench line, well behind the forward line. This second line was the "Main Line of Resistance." This is where most of the fighting would take place. This line was behind the crest of a ridge wherever possible. This way the enemy could not see it and could not target it directly.

The real problem for the attacker was taking this second trench. By the time they reached the first trench, the attacking infantry would already have heavy losses. In moving from this trench to the main line of resistance, they were not advancing across no-man's land. Instead, they were moving across ground the defender owned. The defenders had an intricate knowledge of this area, while the attackers had probably only seen it from aerial photographs. As they continued to move forward, coordination between the attacking infantry and their supporting artillery was much more difficult. Without radios, they would have to communicate across the fractured landscape of no-man's land. The attacking army's commanders could not see where their forces were, and this made it difficult for them to decide where to send their reserves. All of these problems worked together to make the attack on the second trench line incredibly difficult. Attacks on the main line of resistance usually failed miserably. If not, the Germans still had a third line of trenches that they could fall back to.

The Germans would usually counterattack after defeating the assault on their main line. The Germans would reinforce the main line with reserves moved up from the safety of the third trench line. They would then attack and throw back what was left of the assaulting forces all the way back across no-man's land to their initial starting point.

The German's defense in depth doctrine allowed them to hold their lines even when greatly outnumbered and outgunned. Even if the French and British were somehow able to get through the three lines, by that time the Germans would have brought fresh troops into the area by train. These new troops would dig more trench lines and continue the defense in depth of the area.

Finding the Solution

A lot of thought and work went into solving the problem of how to conduct a successful attack. Some went off to find technical solutions like the tank or poison gas. Others started to question the time-honored attack methods. By mid- to late-1916, everyone on the western front had experienced serious setbacks with massive attacks. The French had failed in their large 1915 offensives. In 1916, the Germans failed at Verdun, and the British attacks on the Somme fared even worse. People with experience in these failed attacks gained insight into what worked and did not. With this knowledge and understanding, they began to develop new processes and procedures on their own.

The Germans were the first to put new attack tactics into practice. They called their new methods infiltration tactics, but this name is misleading. "Infiltration" brings to mind images of people in trench coats sneaking through the woods, and that's certainly not the new method. Clearly, no army was going to sneak tens of thousands of men across no-man's land.

Decentralized Control

There were two underlying principles to German infiltration tactics. The first was an acknowledgement that senior commanders could no longer control in detail what happened on the battlefield. Since this was not possible, they allowed low-level junior leaders to decide where to go and what to do to. Small groups were responsible for creating their own success. Their generals would no longer try to tell everyone what to do and how to do it.

The second principle behind infiltration tactics was that attacking strong enemy positions like machine gun bunkers head-on was not smart. Instead, the German infantry teams would bypass enemy strong points and do their best to get into the enemy's rear areas. They would then mop up bypassed strong points after they were isolated and surrounded.

These new tactics were very different from the old system of lining people up to walk together towards enemy trenches. Instead, small teams would move in short spurts across sections of no-man's land, carrying only essential equipment with them. They would look for weak spots in the enemy line. They would avoid enemy machine gun nests instead of charging them. The team leaders would make quick decisions as to where and when to try to breach the enemy lines. The groups were to find their own opportunities and then exploit them. Under this new system, the general was responsible only for the big picture, allocating resources of men and munitions to most decisive locations.

Resistance to Change

There was resistance in the German Army to adopting these new tactics. Most of the resistance was due to the demise of the control system used for millennia by senior military leadership. The new methods meant that generals had to give up control over exactly who did what and went where in the course of a battle. The generals would be responsible for massing the troops and guns for the attack, and for publishing the intent of the battle, but the troops would be largely responsible for creating breakthroughs themselves.

ANALOGY 2: SUCCESS THROUGH TEAMWORK

The infiltration tactics developed by the German Army are actually the first widespread use of what today's business literature calls "teaming." The new methods discarded the obsolete system of leaders making all of the decisions and attempting to control everything and everybody. The German methods were a breakthrough in the organizational way of doing things. The new methods empowered people at low levels to make decisions. They decided for themselves how to best use the assets available to their teams. Since they were out in front, they could use their first hand knowledge of the current situation to attain their organization's goals.

There was resistance to new methods, the same kind of resistance you will face in any company that moves away from top-down decision making. Most of the resistance surfaces due to the misguided belief that only top executives know what to do and that only by following their instructions will the company succeed. This resistance will only subside when leaders see and acknowledge that old ways don't maximize business results. Once they make this realization, once they are willing to move into a new mode of leadership, the entire business will be more effective, more productive, and more profitable. The people in the business itself will find and act on the ideas that will produce successes not currently attainable.

Millions died in the course of World War I because their leaders would not consider changing the accepted way of doing things. Nor would they give up any of the control they wielded over their soldiers. The generals did not consider the junior officers and sergeants capable of making proper battlefield decisions. Shortsighted leaders condemned their armies to continued and repeated failures. To the end of the war, many armies would still form up into lines before moving across the deadly ground of no-man's land.

The exact origins of the new infiltration tactics are rather murky. It is not exactly clear who developed the first ideas on what to do and how to do it. One accepted version of events states that Germans developed the new system based on enemy reports captured at Verdun. A group of junior French officers wrote these reports, which contained compilations of operational data that showed what was working in the field and what was not. The reports also contained proposals for changes to French tactics. The French Army never listened to the ideas of these junior officers and did not make the proposed changes. The Germans, on the other hand, translated the reports and studied both the data and the proposals. Their own people probably had voiced similar ideas, but the fact that the competition was thinking about such things really intensified official interest.

ANALOGY 3: SEEING PAST THE SOURCE

Stories about the origin of breakthrough ideas are the same today. People at the lowest levels too often face impenetrable barriers when they come up with radical ideas, even when data and experience on what works and what doesn't support these ideas. Management has an all-too-frequent habit of shooting these ideas down without further investigation. They say the proposed changes are "too simplistic," or "It could lead to breakdowns in other processes," or "It doesn't take the big picture into account." These quick retorts leave little or no chance to the implementation of the new idea.

However, if corporate leaders find out the competition is thinking about making the very same changes, their attitudes change radically. Top executives now are all excited and very interested. Maybe the new reaction is due to fear the competition may get ahead by using the new ideas. Maybe it is because they don't see the people who came up with the ideas at the other company as ignorant no-bodies. In any case, the old saying about "A prophet is not accepted in his own country" is certainly true. Most companies reject radical ideas from their own lower levels, but embrace those coming from the outside.

This behavior is bad not just because new ideas are lost. It does all kinds of damage to workforce morale. If new ideas are shot down too quickly, if people don't think anyone will use their improvement ideas, they will just keep their mouths shut. Innovation will not exist, and the company can only follow its competitor's lead. This is a horrible position to be in for any company.

Centralization of Critical Resources

The German Army did more than just develop new infantry tactics while redesigning their operating processes. They also came up with innovative artillery tactics. These new artillery methods did away with long bombardments that did little other than inform the enemy of the location of the next big attack. Instead, the new method used bombardments only lasting a few hours. In the past, the guns fired huge numbers of shells into every square mile the enemy occupied. Under the new procedures, they would only shoot at specific targets, and then only with a number of shells prescribed for that kind of target. This would maximize the damage per shell and would do so relatively quickly. This type of bombardment would be much faster and much more effective than older methods.

The new artillery tactics also called for the mass centralization of all of the guns available in the battle area. Previously, the senior artillery officer within each unit had control over the unit's own guns. Each unit had a sector of the front line, and its guns would only fire into that particular sector. This methodology diluted the artillery's firepower across all of the different sectors. The new system required all units involved in an attack to release control over their artillery assets to a central authority. This new high-level staff controlled the targeting and firing of all of the artillery available for a specific large-scale attack.

Different Paths to Success

What's extremely important to note here is that two different branches of the army, the infantry and the artillery, took very different paths to improve their performance. For the infantry, decentralization of control and delegation of decision making to lower levels produced greatly improved performance. The artillery went in the opposite direction. Their improved performance resulted from increased central control and decision making by a central authority. The success in each area came from two diametrically opposed management philosophies. Yet, in both cases, performance dramatically improved by looking at the data about what worked, what produced results, and what did not, and then by making serious changes to accepted policies, practices, and procedures.

> ## ANALOGY 4: THE SOLUTION DEPENDS ON THE SITUATION
>
> There is no one-size-fits-all solution for maximizing performance in any business. The historical examples show that the best control and decision-making methodologies are situation dependent. You have to look at the data that shows what is working and what is not. You have to do this in each area of your business. You will need to find ways to change accepted methods so that you can produce results not possible with the old practices and procedures. In some cases, that may mean reduced control, low-level empowerment, and more flexible planning and execution guidelines. In another area, it may mean increased centralized control, restrictions on lower level decision making, and stricter planning and execution guidelines. This is not some kind of paradox. What works best for one particular area in a particular situation is not necessarily what is best for another.
>
> There are plenty of experts who say a company has to be organized in some specific way to be successful, or who say that a business has to operate a certain way to get the best results. What history shows is that the best organization and operating methods depend on what produces results and what fails. For different parts of even a single large organization, there may be very different paths to success.

> You won't find the best changes, the ones that will dramatically improve your business's performance, by blindly accepting some management theory. You must accurately assess current performance and accept input from those out front on what works and what doesn't. Then, be open to suggestions for improvement from any source, even if those suggestions fly in the face of accepted ways of doing things. Only when you have all of this kind of information out on the table, and only when you are open to making any kind of change necessary, will you be able to identify what you need to do. The ability to do this is what repeatedly produces breakthrough successes. Failure to do this will lock you and your company into the self-defeating behaviors exemplified by most of the armies and generals of World War I.

German Window of Opportunity

By mid-1917, the Russian Army began to disintegrate as their country fell into revolutionary chaos. The Tsar was deposed. The first civilian government was unable to assert control. Then the Bolsheviks took over. The new Bolshevik leaders sued for peace at any price. Russia surrendered. The German Army was now free to redeploy their armies from Russia to the Western Front. They could attack with numerical superiority for the first time since the opening of the war in 1914. But, they would only have this advantage until the Americans, who recently entered the war, arrived in France in telling numbers.

Ludendorff worked out the plan for the 1918 German offensives. Instead of a large single effort, his plan involved a series of attacks against the British Army. His idea was that multiple, smaller attacks would shake the entire British front, causing a collapse at one or multiple points. But here the plan stopped. Since Ludendorff could not tell where the British front might open up, he made no definitive follow-up plans. When senior members of his staff asked Ludendorff what the ultimate objective of the offensives was, he responded, "We will make a hole, and the rest will take care of itself." There was not even a fuzzy end goal, such as "surrounding the British in France."

The lack of even a temporary long-term plan, a flexible one that they could change due to new developments and circumstances, led many senior German generals to lose faith in their leadership. The army itself did not know what its long-term goals were. In 1914, German soldiers put forth amazing efforts in the belief that Paris was their goal, and the city's capture would mean success, victory, and the end of the war. In 1918, they did not know where they were going, what the desired results were, or if what they were doing would win the war.

ANALOGY 5: LONG-TERM VISION

You need to be flexible. You and your company will need to make changes to your long-term goals as new opportunities arise. But you still need long-term goals. You can't dispose of them in efforts to be even more flexible. Without long-term goals, your company will have numerous serious problems. People in any company expect their leadership to have a plan, to have an idea of where the business is going and how to get there. Long-range goals are how you communicate your vision of the future to the entire company. If they know where you want to go, they can help you to get there. If they don't know where you want to go, they will stop every time there is a problem. You don't want people to do this. You want them to keep marching on to the goal. This is impossible if they don't know what the goal is.

Without long-range goals, people will lose faith in their leadership. Your business needs and wants executives with specific ideas on how to beat the competition. No one wants to hear something like "We will gain shelf space and everything will take care of itself." You always need a rallying cry that motivates others to reach specific goals and objectives.

Ludendorff knew that Germany could not hope to win the war if the early 1918 offensives failed. The massive influx of Americans meant the Germans would lose their numerical advantage by mid-1918. Already, the German economy was collapsing. Civilians were starving due to the British blockade of German ports. This situation made Ludendorff risk-averse. If he gambled on one great attack, and it did not work, he would fail. So instead of one great attack, he opted for a number of smaller attacks. By reducing the risk associated with a single attack, Ludendorff merely accepted a different kind of risk. Now, he would need multiple successes from the smaller attacks for his plan to succeed.

> ## ANALOGY 6: RISK AVERSION IS ALSO RISK
>
> Failing to take risk is also accepting risk. If you don't take chances, you accept the risk that you are passing up the chance for a stunning success. You guarantee that you won't have breakout successes if you don't accept risks. You just won't have the opportunity. Failing to take risks, not trying to do something at the limits of your company's ability, means the business is just "trying to get by." You do this whenever you consciously choose only "safe" paths and options, or when you try to hedge your bets by trying multiple options at once, and each only with limited resources. In all of these risk-averse situations, you are pursuing a strictly survival strategy. You aren't trying to win, you're just trying to stay in the game longer. How many businesses with survival strategies stay ahead in the marketplace? Not many. In fact, few even manage to survive for long. To stay in the game and succeed, you and your company must repeatedly be willing to take significant risks.

The Tide Turns

On the other side of no-man's land, the British Army was making plans of its own. The losses at Passchendaele did not deter Haig from planning new attacks for the spring of 1918. German reinforcements from Russia were arriving daily. The huge increase in German strength did not dissuade Haig in the least from his attack planning. There was little effort to improve British defensive positions during the winter of 1917–1918. The British Army only contemplated more of their own attacks.

Ludendorff's plan commenced with two separate attacks on the British. The first was against the southern part of the British line, near the boundary between the British and French armies. The second attack would take place a couple of weeks later, at the northern end of British lines. After that, Ludendorff would play it by ear, attacking where he could best to exploit weaknesses caused by these first two actions.

Three different German armies supported by over seven thousand pieces of artillery would conduct the first German offensive. They would attack on a front of about fifty miles. The three German armies involved were the Seventeenth under Below, the Second under Marwitz, and the Eighteenth under Hutier.

The attack's main thrust was towards the city of Arras, spearheaded by Below's Seventeenth Army. [Fig 39]

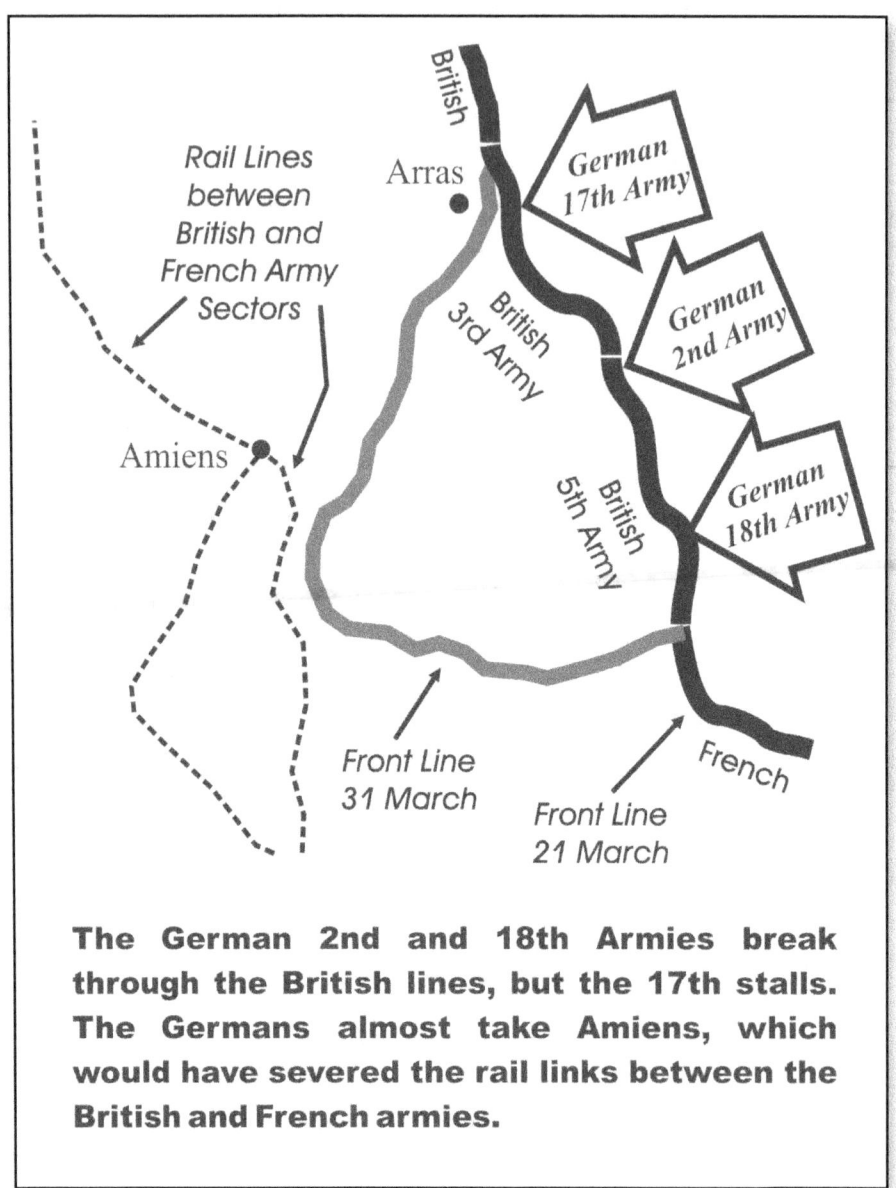

Figure 39. The March 1918 German Offensive

The Germans attacked on March 21, 1918, after a six-hour bombardment of nine million shells. A dense fog that hung over the battlefield in the morning hours greatly aided the Germans. Units of the Second and Eighteenth Armies were completely through British lines by the end of the day. The Seventeenth Army had captured forward British trench lines, but could not get much further. The next day, the German Second and Eighteenth Armies poured through the holes they had cut through the front lines and into British rear areas. The Seventeenth Army failed to make much additional headway. Hutier's and Marwitz's armies advanced forward at rates not seen since 1914. They came close to utterly destroying the British Fifth Army, and were advancing almost unchecked to the west. Below, whose army was supposed to be the one making the biggest gains, was hardly advancing at all.

Failure to Embrace Change

There were reasons Below's army didn't make much headway. It was attacking a more heavily defended area. But this was not the main reason for the lack of progress. The root cause of the problem was the attitude and actions of Below's senior staff during the preceding months, while their army converted over to the new infantry and artillery tactics. While many eagerly adopted the new methods and techniques, Below's subordinates did not. They preferred the old methods and decided to continue to use them. During the great attacks of March 1918, the men of the Seventeenth Army climbed out of their trenches, formed into lines, and marched shoulder to shoulder across no-man's land toward the British. And they were slaughtered just like everybody else who did this.

The senior leadership of the German Army should have known about the resistance to the new tactics by the Seventeenth Army. They did not, because like so many others who rise to the highest levels of command, Field Marshals Ludendorff and Hindenburg became isolated from reality. They lost touch with what was really happening out in the field. The two ensconced themselves in their headquarters. Ludendorff sent out reams of memos and directives to his subordinates, but did little to observe first-hand conditions. He did not go out to visit the units that would actually execute his great plans for victory. Hindenburg left most things up to Ludendorff. He had little to do with the day-to-day military operations due to his increasing involvement in political and social circles. Both of them refused to accept the validity of reports contrary to their own views and opinions. Neither of them took action to ensure the adoption of the new tactics. They just assumed their subordinates would follow their orders.

> ## ANALOGY 7: DEALING WITH RESISTANCE
>
> Too many companies are incapable of changing. They are unable to adopt new practices and procedures that would significantly increase their productivity, effectiveness, and profitability. They can't because of the resistance of mid-level managers. While many parts of the company may embrace some changes, those who refuse to go along with the new methods seriously hinder the business as a whole.
>
> Few people will tell their boss outright that they are not going to follow instructions. Instead, they will just nod their heads and keep their mouths shut. You cannot assume that the lack of an outright refusal means that someone will carry out their instructions and implement desired changes. What typically happens is that those who disagree won't say anything; they will just fail to make the changes. They will even prevent others, especially those who report to them, from making changes too.
>
> You need to have personal relationships with your subordinates. You need to discuss not only what your instructions are, but also the why and how. It is critical for you to impart to others your own conviction of the importance of the changes. You need to give them reasons to accept and execute the changes. You will have to work to draw out any hesitancy that may exist and rationally talk through any resistance others may have. You cannot just dismiss others' misgivings outright. You must deal with it. You have to be the salesperson for the changes, selling others on the change's urgency and importance. You cannot underestimate the importance of this almost emotional appeal to get others to break out of the comfortable habits they have concerning old ways. This is how you excite others and motivate them about the advantages of the changes and how they can improve things for everyone involved. If you rely on memos, directives, and e-mails, you will miss this important opportunity to inspire others to accept changes. You won't overcome mid-level resistance to doing things differently, and your business will fail in its efforts to evolve and improve.

Attempting to Redeem Failure

Ludendorff didn't just make a mistake by not knowing that Below's army wasn't using the new tactics. Below's lack of progress was apparent enough in the first few days, and Ludendorff certainly did know about this. Apparently, the issue for him was that in his plans he wanted Below to make the biggest advance. But Below's army was going nowhere. Yet at the same time, the other two attacking armies were far outstripping their objectives. Ludendorff failed to seize the opportunities the successful commanders presented him.

In military science, there is a respected principle that you should use your reserves to exploit success, not to try to redeem failure. Ludendorff certainly knew this theoretical advice. He chose not to follow it. He funneled his available reserves to Below's army, even though Hutier and Marwitz had overrun British defenses. The German High Command expected Hutier and Marwitz to continue to produce stunning successes without reinforcement. They began to slow down as they reached the limits of their available strength to push on. Meanwhile, Below continued to fail in efforts to break through.

ANALOGY 8: FIXATION ON A DESIRED OUTCOME

Some people want a particular project to be successful so much so that they fail to see and capitalize on successes elsewhere. They continue to pump resources into their favorite project, the one they have lofty aspirations for, even when it appears to be going nowhere. When other opportunities arise, they will even starve them of needed resources in order to keep their preferred project going. The result is not just a failed project. It is missed opportunities that could have produced the success they were looking for. They will miss out on success they could have had, if they had but properly exploited the ignored opportunities. Do not be blinded by the desire to have a particular project succeed. Be willing to change direction to exploit whatever produces success.

Opportunities don't always come from expected directions. Ludendorff's plan was to punch a hole in the British lines. When that happened at unexpected points, he literally looked the other way. He tried to force an opportunity to happen where he wanted it to. At the same time, he failed to reinforce stunning success in what he viewed as only supporting operations. The result was they missed out on the biggest chance Germany had for winning the war since the opening battles of 1914.

Lost Opportunity

The German attacks ran out of steam right outside of the important rail junction of Amiens. If they had taken this town, the Germans would have severed the rail links between the British and French armies. If this had happened, the British would have almost certainly evacuated Flanders through the Channel ports. It would have been a decisive victory for the Germans. The Germans tried to take Amiens later, but by then the situation was different. The other side was not blind to Amiens' importance. Both the French and British sent substantial reinforcements to the area. Amiens was briefly within the German's grasp, but they failed to seize it. Now they had to look elsewhere to try to create another opportunity.

The success of the German's March 1918 offensive brought the French and the British to the brink of disaster. Many senior military and government officials of both countries came close to panic. Many thought the German breakthroughs had cost them the war. Obviously, the British suffered a major defeat.

Ludendorff's plan called for multiple blows against the British. The next effort was a more modest attack against the northern portion of the British line. Ludendorff reasoned that the British would have weakened their northern lines to shore up their punctured southern defenses. Attacking in early April, the Germans again had stunning initial success. But the gains were not as dramatic as the time before. The Germans advanced about ten to twelve miles, not much compared to the March offensive's thirty- to thirty-five mile penetration. The northern British line held, even though they lost possession of battlefields made famous in the last three years of fighting. While the British had another good scare, that's all it was. Meanwhile, the Germans suffered even more irreplaceable losses.

The French greatly assisted the British this time by moving substantial reserves into British sectors. Ludendorff was fixated on beating the British. But now the French were helping them. Therefore, Ludendorff planned his next action to tie up those French reserves. This way, he could go back to defeating the British. The intent of the next German attack was to pressure the French just enough to pull their troops back from supporting the British Army.

Failing to Learn from Others

The Germans picked a spot to attack along French lines that was even less prepared than the British were in March. The Germans directed their efforts against the French Sixth Army, commanded by General Duchene. His only qualification for an army level command was his influential big-shot brother-in-law at French General Headquarters.

Duchene's army consisted of both French and British divisions. The British divisions were veterans of the March battles. Depleted, they were sent to the French Sixth Army in return for fresh French divisions sent north to help the British.

The British divisions in Duchene's army had first hand experience with the new German tactics. They knew what to expect the next time. Their officers begged General Duchene to allow them to deploy in depth, just like the Germans did, across multiple lines. They had learned this was the only way to slow down the Germans. Duchene would have none of this. His army was crammed up into the front line, the same way it had always deployed.

ANALOGY 9: TRUE DANGER OF INCOMPETENCE

Here's an example of someone who owes their leadership position almost solely to family connections. He ignores advice from experienced people on how to best handle the situation in favor of traditional methods. In most cases, incompetent leaders do this out of insecurity. They know themselves they are incompetent. They just don't want everyone else to know. And by this deluded reasoning, they think that if they accept suggestions from others, people will discover their inadequacies. This is delusional thinking because everyone already knows. They are hiding nothing. They are a serious impediment to the part of organization they are supposed to lead. Worse yet, they may even place the entire business in mortal danger.

> When a disaster does begin, they try to cover it up. They downplay the magnitude of what is happening and try to deal with it with whatever they have available. They don't raise the alarm and ask for assistance. Again, they think this will expose them as incompetent. Instead, they allow things to get even further out of control, creating an even bigger disaster.
>
> The danger here is not people who owe their positions to family connections. The danger is the person who will not listen to sound advice based on recent experience. Those unwilling to listen, to contemplate new ways of doing things, can ultimately cause organization-wide failure.

The Germans attacked at the end of May. They again achieved massive success. The British and French troops packed in the front line were sitting ducks for the intense German bombardment. Those who survived were bypassed and surrounded by the German storm troops. The Germans created a huge breach in the French front lines and poured through. Duchene panicked. He sent small groups forward straight from railroad stations to meet the German onslaught. He withheld information on the magnitude of the disaster from his superiors.

The French High Command soon got word as to how bad the breach was. The French Fifth Army moved over to cover the eastern flank of the German penetration. Forces previously sent to help the British hurried back. The French also pleaded with General Pershing, the new American commander, to rush his recently arrived units into the fray.

German Difficulties

The Germans were having difficulties of their own. They failed to capture the important rail and road junctions at Rheims. This meant resupply difficulties for the entire salient their breakthrough created. They continued to take casualties as they moved forward, and they had the additional task of defending the flanks of new salient.

All of these factors combined to stop the Germans. As their attacks started to lose steam, they ran into Americans coming to aid the French. Running low on supplies and fresh soldiers, the Germans stopped to deal with American and French counterattacks. Once again, the immediate danger of the German attack passed.

Germany was rapidly running out of soldiers, food, and supplies. Their allies were out of patience. Even if German leadership could not see the writing on the wall, the smaller countries tied to Germany's fate could. They knew the German Army needed to win decisively in early 1918. If it did not, the war was lost. The Germans knew their allies were wavering. Their leaders were also under intense pressure from their own starving citizens. This pressure kept the Germans on the offensive.

To continue aggressive action, Ludendorff decided on a small attack to even out the front lines between the two great bulges created by the March attack against the British and the May attack against the French. [Fig 40] The idea was to shorten the length of the front line, freeing up troops for additional attacks.

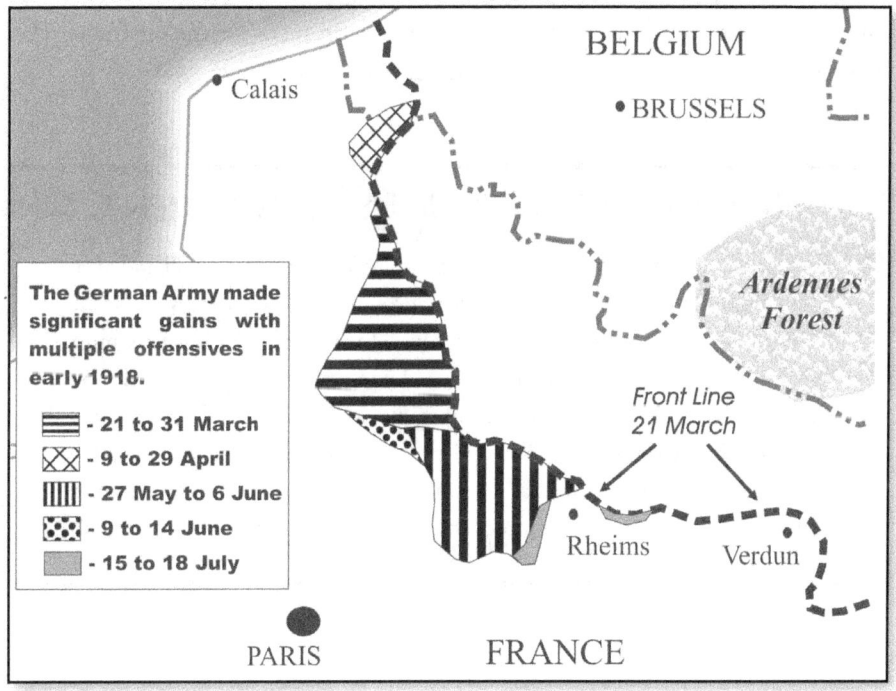

Figure 40. German Advances in 1918

Learning from the Competition

This time the defenders were not all crammed into the forward trenches. They adopted the German scheme of "defense in depth." Furious counter attacks by the defenders sealed off any German penetrations. The attack achieved very little. The French and British had changed their practices as they adapted to thwart the German attack techniques.

Ludendorff tried once more to improve the position of his troops who were now defending ground gained in the previous attacks. He launched a concerted effort to take the important road and rail junctions at Rheims. He was also still trying to tie up French reserves so they wouldn't be available to help elsewhere. His intention was to follow up the capture of Rheims with more attacks against the British.

The French were even better prepared this time. They anticipated the artillery tactics by moving their own guns back, outside of the German's range. They were ready for the German infantry as well. The French front lines were thinly held, and they positioned troops in the rear to counter-attack any German penetrations. The mid-July German attack barely made a dent in the French front lines. But the failure to break through was not the only problem for the Germans. The French were finally ready to launch major attacks of their own.

ANALOGY 10: CONTINUOUS IMPROVEMENT

You won't continue to be successful by doing the same thing over and over. The competition will learn. They will make adjustments and even drastic changes as they try to catch up with you. This is why your business must continually improve. Take what you are doing well and expand on it. You cannot rest on your laurels. You cannot think "we have got it all figured out." Because when you do, the competition catches up with you and possibly passes you. You must continually evaluate how you are doing. You need to continually change, to make improvements, to stay on top.

Americans Tip the Scales

While the Germans were fully engaged outside of Rheims, the French prepared to attack them in the bulge created by the attack against Duchene's army. This was now possible for three reasons. First, the Germans had very little extra strength left. Second, the Germans had abandoned the strong defensive positions they had occupied in 1917 as they advanced. The trenches of the new front lines were rather new and were not as sophisticated as the defensive lines now farther to the German rear. Third, the Americans now had hundreds of thousands of troops ready for action on the Western Front. Some of the Americans would participate in the attacks, while others freed up experienced French units by taking over quiet sectors.

The French and Americans attacked on July 18. With his goal of taking Rheims now unattainable, Ludendorff wrote off most of the May gains. The Germans pulled back in the face of attacks coming at them from three directions. This was the last swing in the changing tides of war. The Germans had lost the initiative. From this point on, they could only react to the latest attack. Only days after the French and American attacks ended, the British attacked.

The British had used the time while the Germans were preoccupied with the French to ready their own offensive. The gathered over four hundred tanks and prepared to attack without a preliminary bombardment. The British had worked out tactics to improve cooperation between the tanks, accompanying infantry, and rolling artillery barrages. Their attacks on August 8 completely routed entire German divisions. It became known as the "Black Day of the German Army."

Repeating the Competition's Mistakes

Many senior German generals foresaw what was going to happen even before the start of their first offensive in March. They thought if the British and French could not break through on the Western Front after numerous offensives over three years, why should Germany gamble everything in the belief it could? Instead, they argued for staying on the defensive in France and attacking elsewhere with the troops made available by the Russian surrender. They proposed taking care of all of the little fronts. This would eliminate pressure on their smaller allies. They wanted to knock Italy out of the war with another big attack. They also wanted to finish off the Romanians, who continued to fight even after Russia collapsed. They could also take care of the British and French in their Greek enclave around Salonika, propping up their ally Bulgaria in the process. In addition, they could do something to keep the Turks in the war. Let the British, French, and Americans pound their heads against the wall of the Hindenburg Line. The citizens of the democracies would tire of the endless casualties and a negotiated settlement would be possible.

Instead, Hindenburg, Ludendorff, and the Kaiser rejected these opinions and gambled everything on victory in France. The manpower made available by the collapse of Russia died in the spring offensives. The German lines were elongated by the territory conquered in the big attacks. As the German Army moved forward, it abandoned the strong positions of the Hindenburg line. Exposed, weary, short of supplies, and overextended, the German Army reached its breaking point.

The End

From July 18 on, the allied powers of Great Britain, France, and the United States would keep up the attacks on the German Army. First one salient and then another were attacked and eliminated. The Germans fell steadily back. They were out of resources, out of soldiers, and no longer possessed the national will to continue the war. Their allies began to desert them. Their navy mutinied, and revolutions broke out in German cities and within the German Army. The Kaiser was forced to abdicate, and the new German government sued for peace. The war was ended by an Armistice on November 11, 1918.

CONCLUSIONS

This chapter discussed the new tactical methods developed by the Germans, and their use in the great 1918 offensives. While some were initially very successful, all the German attacks were eventually thwarted. Ludendorff, responsible for the planning and execution of the attacks of the German Army, made great gambles. He fixated on the war turning out as *he* wanted it to. The attacks bled the German Army white and facilitated victories by the allied nations of Great Britain, France, and the United States. From the account of how this happened, there are a number of significant lessons, including:

- **Dangers of rigid command and control**

  Your people are better than machines. They are the best at finding innovative ways of doing things, of solving vexing problems, of identifying and implementing effective changes for the better. Rigid command and control practices demean people by treating them like machines. Such methods deny people the latitude to think about, develop, and deploy effective changes. Without this kind of help from your own people, things will never improve that much.

  Rigid command and control systems also assume that your own people cause your company's problems. These systems start punishing people before you really know what the true source of the problem is. Effective problem solving within such systems is usually too little, too late.

- **Strength of low-level decision making**

  Don't get caught in the ego trap. Don't start to believe that because you were selected to be in charge, that you know more than others. Don't think that you are the only one capable of making proper decisions. This is the road to disaster. You stop listening to others. You retain too much decision-making authority because you think others are not as capable as you are. This mindset reduces your effectiveness and that of any group you lead.

  You need to push decision making to the lowest levels possible. This includes eliminating as many review and approval steps as you can. Trust your people to do the right thing. If you don't trust your own people, your business has little hope of success.

- **Listen to ideas without judging the source**
  You must constantly seek out information from people on the front lines. Work with people from all levels to evaluate this information together. This is how to identify what works and what is failing. This process will enable your business to find paths to improved performance and success. You should never care where an idea comes from. Judge an idea on its merits, not its source. So many great ideas have humble origins. But you have to evaluate them fairly. When you dismiss good ideas, you can't take advantage of them. Worse yet, your competition might.

- **Myth of the "perfect way to do things"**
  There is no "one size fits all" solution in the business world. Solutions are culture, department, and individual specific. You have to fit solutions to your problems. Analyze the problem and develop the right solution for the particular situation. You cannot issue blanket edicts about "how things will be around here" and expect to have optimal results.
  What works in one area may actually be the worst possible idea for another area. In fact, you may have areas within your business with diametrically opposed ways of finding success. As long as their processes produce optimal results, there is nothing wrong with that!

- **Importance of long-term goals even in a fluid environment**
  No matter how fluid your business situation is, no matter how fast things are changing, people still need a good idea of where they are headed and why. Vague goals like "whatever makes more money" are not enough. You need to have long-range strategic goals for your business. People need to know what these are. If they don't know where they are going, they are certainly not going to get there.
  It is okay to change your strategic goals. Just don't do so too often. If you change them too frequently, your company will lose its direction. Bring people together to discuss the implications and alternatives before making such major changes. Make them if you need to; just make sure that everyone understands the change and why you are making it.

- **Accepting risk by failing to take risks**

    If you don't take risks, you are actually accepting another one. You are taking the risk that a super-conservative approach will win. No matter what you do, you are taking some risk. This is especially true of trying too many different things at once. When you do this, you are putting a fraction of your resources behind multiple projects. You may not have put enough into the projects to allow them to succeed. Instead, you may have dissipated your efforts.

    Sometimes you do need to put a lot more than you may be comfortable with into a single project. This is the only way to achieve big breakthroughs. Just don't do this lightly or base it on gut feel. Weigh current information and critical projections. But don't do so alone. Listen to the debate of ideas and make the best possible informed decision. Just don't wait too long.

- **Danger of fixation on a particular project**

    We all have activities we want to see succeed. This is a good thing. What is not good is when we want something to succeed so badly that we pass up better opportunities to stick with a project we really want to succeed. Be flexible enough to move to the project with the higher chance of ultimate success.

    Always reinforce what is working. Don't reinforce failure. Put your resources where they will do you and your business the most good. Put them where they will be most productive. Don't try and redeem a project by throwing more money and people at it. Don't allow yourself to get too emotionally attached to a particular idea or endeavor.

- **Dangers of incompetents**

    Incompetents are not just dangerous because they don't really know what they are doing. Sure, that is bad, but it's usually not disastrous. There are two things that incompetents do that tend to lead to disasters. Both actions are rooted in their attempts to cover up the fact that they don't know what they are doing. The first is not listening to sound advice. They don't take the advice because they think that if they do, others will think that they themselves don't have good original ideas. They would rather pass on a good idea than risk confirming their incompetence to others. The second problem is even worse. They often try to hide their incompetence by hiding the truth, so they don't tell superiors when they have a big problem. As they attempt to cover up the problem, their delays allow the problem to get much worse. Often, by the time the truth comes out, you have a real disaster on your hands, a disaster that could easily have been avoided had others only known about it.

- **The need for continual improvement**
  You can never sit still. You can never think that just because you have found a breakthrough methodology that you can rest on your laurels. The competition is always going to get better. They will eventually copy you and do even better than you have. If you relax, they will pass you up. You have to continually improve, continually find ways of doing better. The end result of failing to evolve is extinction. And this can happen rather quickly in the business world.

ACTION FILE

HOW TO FIND THE BEST WAY OF DOING THINGS

 Bad Idea #1—Believe a formula works every time.

Every couple of months, there seems to be a new management fad, the latest and greatest way to business success. Every couple of years, one of these fads really takes off, and it seems that everyone rushes to embrace it. Companies train their entire workforce in the methodology. With their new skills, they are supposed to overcome all problems and achieve breakthrough corporate performance. There is usually some benefit, but far short of the promised results.

People recognize when they are involved in a management fad. They realize this fad won't solve many of their problems. They lose faith in their leadership. The fad wastes a lot of their time and effort, because they have to deal with training and implementation. The end result is the fad costs the business time and money it doesn't have. The fad even delays true problem solving and breakthrough-approach development.

There is no cookie-cutter universal approach guaranteed to produce business success. There is no method that will produce optimal results every single time. You have to find the appropriate methodology for each case. This means investigating what is working and what is not in a particular situation. You need to take long, hard, and detailed looks at business processes, costs, personnel issues and revenue production in that situation. Then develop changes suited to that situation together with the people involved. This is how you will optimize results and deal with recurring problems and issues related to the specific situation you are dealing with.

 Bad Idea #2—Believe you no longer need to improve.

When your business is highly successful, when you are far more successful than your competitors, it is easy to become complacent. It is very tempting to believe that you have found the perfect way of doing business. You might even believe that you no longer need to waste time and money on improvements.

Such complacency results in stagnation. As you stop improving, your business's current performance becomes the attainable goal of others. They will continue to improve while you sit still. They will soon overtake you. There is only one way to avoid this. No matter how far in front you may be, you still need to continue to improve your own performance.

You can never rest on your laurels. You need to continually motivate your people to do better, even when things appear to going along just fine. Wouldn't it be great to make a breakthrough without the threat of imminent disaster? Don't wait until your business is in danger of failing to question your methods and practices. Work on improvements while you have time and resources. This is the best way to stay ahead.

 Bad Idea #3—Move between extremes.

Companies often move between extremes in desperate attempts to find solutions. One extreme may be total centralization of control and decision making. Under this extreme, there are controls for doing everything, and only the highest levels of the company have decision making authority. The opposite extreme is almost total decentralization. There are almost no controls, and everyone can decide for themselves what to do. In desperation, a company may adopt one such extreme, and then switch dramatically to the other when the first one doesn't work.

These radical changes happen because the business's leadership thinks dramatic change is necessary. This is a poorly thought out, knee-jerk reaction to serious problems. It is a manifestation of leadership panic. The company is literally trying something completely different, just because it is completely different from current practices. There is no study of what needs fixing and what is working well. The newly adopted methods are just the opposite of the current ones. The company actually discards many practices that actually work well in their hurry to embrace extreme change. The result is chaos and disaster.

Good Idea #1—Adopt changes to specific situations.

Treat each department, each group, each process as a specific situation. What works for designers may not work for the marketing group. What is best for accounting processes may not be the best for manufacturing processes. You need to look at the particulars of each specific situation. Design changes and adopt practices based on what will work best for a particular case.

Do not begin the change process with prejudices or predispositions. Don't think that you already know what the answer is. Base any changes on the facts. The facts will tell you what is productive and what is not. The facts will tell you things like how long parts of the process actually take. The facts will show you what is providing your company a good return and what is wasting your money. Use this information to make appropriate changes.

It is perfectly fine to make different changes for different situations. You can make one kind of change in one area and a completely different change in another area, and they can both dramatically improve performance. This is not a contradiction. What works for one group may be detrimental to another. And what is a bad idea for one group may be a great idea for another. It all depends on the people involved and the particulars of the situation. Give yourself, your people, and your company this flexibility.

 Good Idea #2—Continually review and improve.

Your organization should always be looking for ways to do better. Continual improvement is continually necessary. There is always a better way. You need to find improvements before your competition does.

Always plow some of your profits, some of your down time, back into development. Use your resources to help you find new venues and approaches to increased productivity and profitability.

Constantly review what you are doing. Ask your customers to help you in this. Continually look for new products and services that you could provide. Continue to develop opportunities to exploit in the future.

Good Idea #3—Learn from others and yourself.

Improvement is driven by learning. Your business needs to learn both from external and internal sources. Externally, you need to learn from competitors and other companies who face similar situations. Conduct benchmarking or use similar methods to identify other businesses' best practices. Modify these for your own use. Study how others are dealing with difficulties and try to make analogies to your own situation. Overcome the tendency to think of your situation as unique. Never give in to the temptation to think that you know it all.

Internally, encourage everyone to participate in coming up with new ideas. Ensure that you are all sharing information on the current situation and the particulars of troublesome issues. Evaluate ideas based on their merit, never on their source. Further encourage ideas by properly rewarding innovation.

Help the different parts of your company to work together on learning what is best for the business as a whole. Each area needs to learn from the others, to see how it fits in, to see how it impacts the other parts of the company. You need solutions that will help the entire business, not just one part.

SUMMATION

FINAL THOUGHTS

"Use the Lessons of the Past to Influence the Future"

PEOPLE love to hear stories. We remember stories. Stories teach us and inspire us. And the best stories are about things that really happened. True stories.

Everything you have just read is a true story. These events actually happened. They shaped the world we live in today. The stories told of real people making difficult choices in the most difficult of situations. Some succeeded. Many failed. And the stories tell us *why*. The analogies tell us how the stories apply to us *today*.

While the stories came from military history, their focus is on human problems, problems common to every age and every endeavor. The stories of the past are eerily similar to situations in any business today. The stories delved into both the good and the bad. They can show you both what *to* do and what *not* to do if you want your company to be successful.

All of the stories are similar to situations you find in any business. The causes of problems and the repercussions of actions are the same. The stories are so similar to business situations because the business environment is so similar to military conflict. Both are high pressure and fast paced and both deal with the highest of stakes. The stories compare the situations in military history to the business environment of today. They show that history is very much a repeatable experiment. The same inputs and the same conditions continue to yield the same results.

Of course, the modern world is different from the past. But most of the differences are due merely to technology. The point is that while technology changes, human behavior, and the reasons for that behavior, does not change. We might think that we are much more sophisticated, intelligent, and in most ways better than those who came before. The reality is that we are not very different from them. We make the same kinds of mistakes they did and for the very same reasons. The stories and analogies are familiar to the workplace each of us deals with every day. The people in the stories are no strangers to us. They acted just like our bosses and coworkers do today. History does indeed repeat itself.

The point of this book is to help you avoid mistakes and to greatly increase the probability of your own success. To do that, you need to learn from the past. Why repeat their mistakes if you don't have to? Learning from their mistakes allows you to avoid the serious problems, if not disasters, the stories described. This allows you to focus on behaviors, programs, and actions that have proven time and again to lead to personal and organizational success.

Most of the issues and problems described by the stories resulted from leadership problems. The tendencies and decisions of those in charge have colossal impacts on the organizations they lead. This is just as true for businesses today as it was for the armies in the stories.

The primary lessons of the stories are to avoid self-defeating behaviors and to do things that allow you to use your organization's own strengths to achieve significant breakthroughs. You need to be constantly critical of your own motivations and actions. Compare yourself and your organization to the stories. Ask yourself whose example you are following. Is it a good example or a bad one? Use the stories and their outcomes to allow you to see what the potential end results of your actions and decisions will probably be. Make drastic corrections if necessary to avoid predictable pitfalls and put yourself and your business on the right track.

In a grand sense, the stories provide optimism for the future. The best practices do indeed result in improvements, in business, in technology, and in society as a whole. Things can, and usually do, get better. The point is that you want to avoid the rough patches in getting there. You want to avoid the disasters of the past. Use the stories as a guide to what works and what doesn't. This will put you and your business on the path to success.

ANALOGIES

Chapter 1

1 - Inherited Subordinates 17
2 - Discounting the Competition 19
3 - Organizational Alignment 21
4 - Problems with the Limelight 25
5 - Long Term versus Short Term 26
6 - Emotions and Errors 28
7 - The Leader or the Team 29
8 - The Rose-Colored Glasses 31
9 - "Now I'm in Charge" 32
10 - Prestige versus Success 32
11 - Organizational Arrogance 34
12 - Organizational Arrogance continued 35
13 - Know the Limits 36

Chapter 2

1 - The Revenge Strategy 48
2 - Single Minded Strategy 49
3 - Compliant Thought 50
4 - Failure to Admit Failure 52
5 - Failure to Learn From Others 54
6 - Need for Rapid Change 57
7 - Accepted Assumptions 59

8 - The True Risk Taker 61
9 - The True Hero 62
10 - Insecurity 64
11 - Departmental Myopia 68
12 - Leadership Optimism 70
13 - Making Leadership Changes 71
14 - Strategic Inflexibility 74
15 - Listening To Subordinates 75

Chapter 3

1 - Popular Programs 89
2 - Aura of Success 92
3 - Elitism 93
4 - Pitfalls of Joint Partnerships 95
5 - Predestination 96
6 - Limits to Professionalism 97
7 - Undefined Leadership 99
8 - Finger-Pointing 101
9 - Difficult People 105

Chapter 4

1 - The Need to Continually Learn 121
2 - Political Promotions 125
3 - Unacceptable Risk 129
4 - Letting Others Fend for Themselves 130
5 - Exploiting Success 132
6 - Self-Fulfilling Prophecy 134
7 - Adjustment 135
8 - Regression in Crisis 137

Chapter 5

1 - Short-Term Temptations 150
2 - Understanding Success 156
3 - Continuous Improvement 158
4 - Organizational Feudalism 160
5 - Success is Mine, Failure is Yours 164

Chapter 6

1 - Something Completely Different 181
2 - Slack in the System 182
3 - The Dumping Ground 183
4 - Reality Check 186
5 - Merger Problems 187
6 - Financial Folly 188
7 - Impending Doom 192
8 - The Training Deficit 193
9 - Class Distinctions 194
10 - Conflicts of Interest 196
11 - Limits of Delegation 197
12 - Performance Management 198
13 - Feuding Departments 201

Chapter 7

1 - The Road to Ruin 219
2 - Which Way to Go? 221
3 - Strategic Vacillation 223
4 - Executive Deception 224
5 - Political Intrigue 225
6 - Leadership Blackmail 226

7 - Self-Preservation Gamble 231
8 - Myth of the Special Few 233
9 - Control of the Selfish 235

CHAPTER 8

1 - "That's Not My Job" 249
2 - Refusal of Help 250
3 - Swallowing One's Pride 251
4 - Task Feedback 253
5 - "That's Not My Job" part 2 254
6 - Stealing Other's Laurels 256

CHAPTER 9

1 - The Moving Target 275
2 - Fleeting Opportunity 276
3 - Common Complaints 279
4 - Foundation for a Good Relationship 281

CHAPTER 10

1 - When to Pull the Plug 297
2 - Too Good to be True 301
3 - Similar Background Myopia 302
4 - The Matrix 305
5 - "Prerequisite Disaster" 307
6 - Judging by Appearances 308
7 - Know the Battlefield 309

Chapter 11

1 - Seeing Potential Over Problems 322
2 - Ignoring Developments 325
3 - Rejecting Ideas from Unacceptable Sources 326
4 - Wasting the Golden Opportunity 329
5 - Training People to Use Technology 334

Chapter 12

1 - Problems due to Rigid Control 344
2 - Success through Teamwork 347
3 - Seeing Past the Source 348
4 - The Solution Depends on the Situation 350
5 - Long-Term Vision 352
6 - Risk Aversion is also Risk 353
7 - Dealing with Resistance 356
8 - Fixation on a Desired Outcome 357
9 - True Danger of Incompetence 359
10 - Continuous Improvement 362

SELECTED BIBLIOGRAPHY

Asprey, Robert B. *The German High Command at War*. New York: William Morrow & Co, 1991.

Austrian Bundesministerium für Landesverteidigung. *Österreich-Ungarns letzter Krieg, 1914-1918*. 8 vols. Vienna, 1929-35.

Conrad von Hötzendorff, Franz. *Aus meiner Dienstzeit, 1906-1918*. 5 vols. Vienna: Rikola, 1922.

German Reichsarchiv. *Der Weltkrieg, 1914 bis 1918*. 14 vols. Berlin: E. S. Mittler, 1925-1944

Gray, Randal, with Argyle, Christopher. *Chronicle of the First World War*. 2 vols. Oxford: Facts on File, 1990.

Horne, Alistair. *The Price of Glory*. New York: St. Martin's Press, 1962.

Joffre, Joseph Jacques Césaire, Mott, Thomas Bentley, and Lowe, Sydney Joseph. *The Personal Memoirs of Joffre*. 2 vols. New York: Harper & Bros., 1932.

Stone, Norman. *Eastern Front 1914-1917*. New York: Scribner, 1975.

Toland, John. *No Man's Land*. Garden City, N.Y.: Doubleday, 1980.

Tuchman, Barbara W. *The Guns of August*. New York: MacMillan & Co, 1962

INDEX

accomplish, 17, 21, 42, 81, 82, 106, 169, 185, 203, 204, 207, 213, 215, 235, 250, 257, 305
accomplishment, 31, 198, 212, 241, 249, 256, 258
accountability, 112, 114
accuracy, 30, 43, 44, 163, 198, 224, 238, 253, 268, 314, 317, 331
acquire, 158, 196, 207, 337
acquisition, 18, 187, 204, 329
adapt, 50, 74, 76, 110, 119, 121, 147, 167, 168, 326, 361
adhere, 142, 211
adjust, 107, 260
adjustment, 80, 81, 135, 204, 340, 362
admit, 27, 28, 38, 43-46, 52, 62, 77, 125, 144, 145, 194, 211, 255, 256, 297, 298
adversary, 259, 281, 287, 332, 335
advice, 64, 89, 271, 278, 357, 359, 360, 367
agenda, 17, 21
Aisne, 272, 273
Albrecht, Field Marshal Duke, 18
Alexander the Great, 343
align, 17, 21
alignment, 21, 37, 133
allegiance, 176, 288, 289
alliance, 8, 12, 49, 87, 88, 90, 110, 118, 123
ally, 12, 15, 49, 98-100, 103, 122, 123, 158, 159, 178, 218, 220, 234, 300, 326, 332, 360, 361, 363-365
Alsace, 12, 15, 22, 23, 48, 50-53, 73, 219
ambition, 25, 47, 76, 214, 215, 235, 239
America, 233

American aircraft, 331
American Army, 295, 351, 352, 360, 362, 363
American Navy, 119
American Civil War, 233, 303
Amiens, 358
analogy, 8, 9, 17, 19, 21, 25, 26, 28, 29, 31, 33-37, 48-50, 52, 54, 57, 59, 61, 62, 64, 68, 70, 71, 74-76, 84, 89, 92, 93, 95-97, 99, 101, 105, 109, 121, 125, 129, 130, 132, 134, 135, 137, 139, 150, 156, 158, 160, 164, 166, 181-183, 186-188, 192-194, 196-198, 201, 203, 219, 221, 223-226, 231, 233, 235, 249-251, 253, 254, 256, 257, 275, 276, 279, 281, 297, 301, 302, 305, 307-309, 322, 325, 326, 329, 334, 335, 344, 347, 348, 350, 352, 353, 356, 357, 359, 362, 372-374
anarchy, 160, 219, 236
anticipate, 20, 56, 79, 80, 81, 144, 149, 150, 156, 180, 181, 362
appearance, 23, 25, 28, 64, 144, 155, 193, 219, 225, 240, 241, 250, 255, 272, 297, 308, 313, 321, 322, 357
aristocracy, 118, 195
aristocrat, 104
armistice, 364
Arras, 329, 354
arrogance, 34, 35, 51, 84, 158
artillery, 53, 73, 92, 119, 120, 153, 161, 186, 199, 200, 247, 249, 254, 266, 269, 271, 274, 276, 293, 298, 300, 303, 310, 319-321, 323, 324, 342, 343, 345, 349, 350, 353, 355, 362, 363

assess, 147, 156, 157, 166, 240, 242, 351
assessment, 156
assist, 12, 17, 35, 66, 74, 75, 87, 90, 94, 99, 123, 126, 132, 135, 154, 209, 223, 241, 250, 251, 252, 263, 312, 358, 360
assume, 17, 19, 25, 32, 34, 41, 59, 110, 134, 148, 155, 156, 166, 169, 206, 212, 213, 238, 241, 248-251, 253-255, 258, 259, 280, 289, 308, 311, 315, 320, 340, 344, 356, 365
assumption, 34, 35, 41, 59, 92, 185, 248, 294, 317
attribute, 171, 241, 305, 308, 312
attrition, 220, 229, 245, 247, 269
Austria-Hungary, 15, 158, 175-180, 182, 184, 187, 188, 192, 202, 203, 218, 220, 227, 232, 300
Austrian Military Museum, 326
Austro-Hungarian Army, 158, 159, 161, 175-178, 182-195, 197-200, 202, 203, 227, 230, 231, 326
    Austrian Reserve Army, 187, 192
    Austro-Hungarian First Army, 189, 190
    Austro-Hungarian Second Army, 189, 190
    Austro-Hungarian Third Army, 189, 190
    Austro-Hungarian Fourth Army, 189, 190, 197
    Croatian Reserve Army, 187
    Group A, 178, 180, 185, 189
    Group B, 178, 180, 182, 185, 189
    Group Balkan, 178, 180
    Hungarian Reserve Army, 187
Austro-Hungarian generals, 195-197
Austro-Hungarian Headquarters, 196
Austro-Hungarian officers, 192, 194
Austro-Hungarian railway, 178, 180, 182
authority, 21, 30, 62, 64, 99, 133, 165, 168, 214, 226, 238, 278, 290, 349, 350, 365, 370
averse, 140, 352, 353
aversion, 353

avoid, 7, 9, 10, 29, 30, 42, 45, 64, 85, 104, 117, 137, 139-141, 164, 190, 225, 237, 242, 247, 249, 281, 287, 322, 346, 368, 370, 374
aware, 21, 44, 80, 110, 165, 170, 199, 243

background, 92-94, 104, 105, 109, 235, 240, 241, 262, 286, 293, 301, 302, 311, 312
backstabbing, 167
Balkan wars, 54
Balkans, 177, 178
bankrupt, 219, 236
barbed wire, 254, 303, 320, 323, 324, 342
barrier, 207, 291, 348
battle, 8, 9, 14, 19, 25, 27, 29, 32, 35, 67, 68, 70, 72, 77, 82, 99, 102, 103, 106, 107, 118, 119, 126, 128, 132, 137, 138, 149, 152, 153, 155, 157, 161, 163, 165, 220, 221, 229, 230, 245-247, 252, 257, 265, 269-271, 276, 293-301, 303, 309-311, 322-324, 329, 333, 342, 343, 347, 349, 358, 359
battlefield, 104, 155, 195, 200, 247, 284, 298, 299, 309, 310, 316, 320, 321, 324, 327, 328, 331, 335, 342, 343, 346, 348, 355, 358
Beer Hall Putsch, 236
behave, 97
behavior, 17, 42, 46, 62, 64, 70, 100, 105, 110, 117, 125, 137, 140, 164, 170, 175, 195, 196, 224, 225, 235, 237, 249, 256, 258, 280, 349, 351, 374
Belgian Army, 19, 20, 34, 52
Belgian fort, 22, 152, 247, 248
Belgium, 13-16, 22, 23, 25, 32, 34, 52, 53, 56-59, 64, 72, 87, 94, 98, 101, 117, 147, 219, 294-296, 300
belief, 39, 40, 52, 54, 86, 92, 94, 105, 120, 121, 145, 187, 204, 267, 271, 284, 302, 303, 320, 326, 347, 352, 363
believe, 12, 14, 18, 31, 32, 38, 43, 49-56, 58, 70, 73, 82, 85, 101, 112, 120, 123, 139, 143, 156, 162, 163, 172, 187,

Index 383

199, 204, 220, 221, 226, 231, 232, 240, 247, 267, 268, 271, 272, 275, 284, 286, 296, 297, 300-303, 315, 325, 335, 337, 340, 365, 369
Below, Gen. Otto von, 353-355, 357
benchmark, 86, 372
Berlin, 132, 152, 154, 224, 225
best practice, 86, 187, 372, 374
Big Bertha, 22, 247, 248
blackmail, 217, 226, 238, 241
blame, 57, 61, 74, 96, 100, 102, 127, 134, 135, 147, 163, 164, 167, 170, 201, 205, 236, 270, 303
blind, 38, 48, 50, 76, 79, 186, 321, 328, 329, 357, 358
blockade, 13, 352
Boelke, Capt. Oswald, 332
Boer War, 90, 91, 303, 306
bombardment, 249, 271, 276, 293, 299, 303, 310, 323, 324, 342, 343, 349, 355, 360, 363
border, 14, 15, 23, 25, 48, 52, 53, 73, 94, 123, 126, 128, 129, 134, 147-150, 153, 178, 180, 182, 184, 185, 189, 221
borrow, 188, 279
Bosnia, 176, 177, 178, 179
Brandis, Lieut. Cordt von, 255, 256
British aircraft, 331, 332, 333
British Army, 25, 27-29, 55, 58, 60, 66, 72, 87, 90, 92, 94, 97-102, 104, 106, 107-109, 220, 221, 230, 231, 234, 270-272, 276, 293-303, 308, 311, 324-328, 330, 334, 343, 345, 346, 351, 353, 355, 357-363
   British Expeditionary Force (BEF), 87, 90, 92, 94-109, 298, 301
   British Fifth Army, 355
   British Tank Corps, 298, 299
British general, 90, 95,
British High Command, 95, 97, 295, 311, 324, 327
British tank, 320-323, 325-327, 329, 335
Brusilov, Gen. Alexei, 197, 200, 230, 232
Brusilov Offensive, 200

budget, 160, 167, 175, 186, 187, 203, 207-210, 250, 289, 297
Bulgaria, 363
Bülow, Gen. Karl von, 17, 18, 20, 22, 25, 27, 28, 29, 30, 31, 69
bunker, 198, 342, 346
business environment, 7, 57, 105, 122, 130, 142, 309, 373
business plan, 19, 79, 80, 81, 301
bypass, 40, 125, 270, 272, 346, 360

Cambrai, 324, 325, 327, 329
Canadian Army, 330
Carpathian, 184, 191
casualty, 22, 119, 184, 220, 270, 323, 344, 360, 363
caterpillar tractor, 321
cavalry, 91, 92, 94, 95, 104, 107, 108, 119, 120, 136, 293, 301-303, 306, 324
centralize, 142, 187, 188, 269, 349, 350, 370
Chancellor, 235, 236
change, 11, 15-17, 20, 23, 25, 27, 28, 30-36, 38, 39, 44-47, 49, 50, 52, 53, 55, 57, 59, 70-78, 80, 81, 85, 86, 89, 105, 109, 110, 112, 120-122, 125, 126, 139, 144, 147, 150, 158, 167-169, 171-173, 175, 180-182, 185, 187, 189, 203, 204, 207, 209, 233, 234, 237, 260, 274-276, 278-280, 283-285, 290, 295, 298, 311, 315, 316, 319, 320, 322, 326, 335, 340, 341, 347-353, 355-357, 361-363, 365, 366, 369-371, 374
Chemin des Dames, 272
Chief of Staff, 16, 18, 151, 155, 306
China, 118, 119
chlorine gas, 328
civilian, 26, 58, 182, 219, 220, 235, 351, 352
class, 7, 58, 59, 113, 175, 193-195, 199, 204, 262, 286, 287, 340
class culture, 286, 287
class warfare, 175, 204, 287
coach, 17, 41, 42, 105, 110, 134, 140, 198,

199, 334
codebook, 128
colonies, 11
combative, 87, 105, 110
command and control, 341, 343, 344, 365
committee, 172, 198, 307
communicate, 19, 106, 133, 135, 155, 171, 245, 248, 253, 257-262, 316, 337, 345, 352
compare, 33, 118, 123, 208, 210, 267, 295, 305, 331, 358, 373, 374
comparison, 9, 221, 295
compete, 81, 223
competence, 89, 101, 182, 193, 226
competition, 7, 8, 11, 12, 19, 35, 37, 59, 74, 78, 79, 81-84, 86, 94, 110, 125, 139, 140, 142, 156, 158, 167, 181, 201, 205, 223, 275, 276, 284, 287, 288, 301, 311, 313, 325, 329, 334-337, 339, 348, 349, 352, 361-363, 366, 368, 371
complacent, 369, 370
complain, 128, 207, 210, 250, 279, 343
complaint, 207, 210, 278, 279, 291
concentrate, 10, 76, 82, 112, 117, 137, 148, 221, 227, 267, 324, 333, 334
concentration, 82
condition, 8, 70, 74, 85, 92, 133, 140, 147, 167, 185, 188, 195, 197, 277, 278, 287, 293, 299, 300, 309, 311, 328, 329, 336, 355, 373
confidence, 20, 22, 28, 47, 62, 69, 70, 77, 96, 169-173, 185, 219, 225, 271
conflict, 54, 87, 88, 91, 94, 97, 110, 175, 196, 199, 201, 204, 212, 215, 219, 259, 330, 373
confront, 52, 104, 277
confrontation, 21, 105, 106
Conrad von Hötzendorf, Field Marshal, 158, 159, 161, 178-182, 184, 185, 188-192
consensus, 17, 21, 181, 223
consolidate, 132, 237
contact, 11, 20, 31, 35, 60, 63, 80, 96, 99, 102, 130, 136, 142, 144, 190, 195, 197, 261, 262, 315, 316
continual improvement, 341, 362, 368, 371
contract, 195, 196, 284
control, 12, 16, 62, 64, 72, 88, 90, 99, 105, 108, 110, 120, 133, 161, 168, 187, 188, 195, 206, 208, 224, 227, 229, 235-237, 239, 248, 250, 252, 333, 334, 336, 342, 343, 344, 346-351, 360, 370
cook, 183, 278
cooperate, 21, 34, 49, 90, 94, 95, 97, 98, 102, 103, 104, 106, 124, 126, 134, 157, 199, 271, 273, 321, 363
coordinate, 20, 21, 22, 37, 72, 90, 101, 102, 107, 124, 126, 128, 129, 131, 134, 139, 152, 155, 187, 266, 345
Cossack, 25, 182
credit, 74, 145, 157, 163, 164, 170, 245, 255, 256, 258, 330
crisis, 26, 27, 47, 57, 68, 77, 110, 117, 136, 137, 140, 179, 182, 188, 196, 212, 225, 296
culture, 18, 53, 55, 85, 86, 92, 101, 118, 125, 142, 160, 176, 187, 188, 194, 249, 261, 286, 326, 344, 366
cutback, 289

d'Espérey, Gen. Louis, 72
damage, 17, 28, 36, 46, 50, 71, 89, 97, 101, 113, 137, 168, 170, 192, 203, 219, 230, 235, 239, 256, 296, 298, 300, 306, 349
data, 238, 299, 348, 350
debate, 69, 152, 153, 222, 261, 367
debt, 175, 186, 188, 204
decentralize, 346, 350, 370
deception, 224, 314, 316
decide, 14, 15, 19, 22, 23, 25, 28, 29, 33, 40, 43, 49, 57, 67, 72-74, 87, 88, 90, 96, 99, 103, 106, 114, 118, 119, 128, 133, 151, 157, 167, 168, 180-183, 195, 196, 222, 223, 232, 233, 248, 254, 255, 257, 267, 273, 295, 309, 316, 321, 323, 327, 328, 338, 345, 346, 347, 355, 361, 370

Index

decision, 7, 8, 17, 18, 28, 30, 43-46, 61, 64, 69, 77, 78, 88, 92, 94, 95, 99, 109, 112, 121, 128, 139, 142, 151, 172, 184, 185, 191, 197, 205, 208, 222-224, 232, 237, 238, 240, 241, 266, 290, 296-298, 302, 308, 311-315, 317, 341, 344, 346-348, 350, 365, 367, 370, 374
decision maker, 8, 45, 94, 223, 241, 302
decision making, 7, 8, 99, 238, 341, 347, 350, 365, 370
defense in depth, 274, 344, 345, 361
defensive, 23, 24, 48, 53, 148, 184, 185, 266, 271, 274, 344, 353, 362, 363
delegate, 37, 197
delegation, 197, 305, 350
delude, 85, 112, 183, 225, 359
delusion, 192, 211, 359
demoralize, 36, 53, 70, 104, 133, 157, 169, 172, 192, 267, 295
department head, 21, 130, 160, 250
depose, 219, 351
Der Tag, 12
desert, 364
desertion, 198, 300
develop, 8, 13, 53, 55, 128, 178, 271, 309, 319, 320, 323, 325, 328-333, 335, 336, 343, 344, 346-349, 365, 366, 369, 371
development, 7, 151, 178, 234, 305, 312, 320, 325, 326, 328, 330, 335-338, 351, 369, 371
dialog, 38, 281, 282, 285, 290, 291
dictator, 236
difficult people, 105
dilute, 26, 82, 208, 334, 349
diplomacy, 15, 177
diplomatic, 49, 176, 178
direction, 11, 17, 21, 29, 38, 41, 49, 52, 77, 82, 89, 103, 109, 121-123, 132, 148, 149, 161, 162, 172, 182, 213, 214, 226, 236, 258, 260, 262, 269, 280, 298, 323, 331, 332, 334, 337, 344, 350, 357, 363, 366
disagree, 142, 356

disagreement, 99, 143, 270
disaster, 21, 22, 31, 53, 58, 68, 69, 76, 94, 113, 133, 136, 153, 154, 170, 190, 197, 209, 232, 247, 256, 258, 278, 286, 302, 307, 308, 314, 358, 360, 365, 367, 368, 370, 374
discipline, 93, 197, 198, 277, 280, 295
discount, 11, 19, 31, 37, 52, 53, 172, 299
discourage, 322, 326
dishonest, 224
dislike, 97, 124, 130, 243, 282
disseminate, 86, 289
dissent, 121
dissipate, 367
doctrine, 50, 270, 274, 343, 345
dog and pony, 251, 316
doom, 7, 41, 74, 76, 192, 314, 337, 344
Douaumont, 247-249, 251, 252, 254, 257, 267, 268, 270-272
Duchene, Gen. Denis, 359, 360, 362
dumping ground, 175, 183, 203

East Prussia, 25-27, 123, 124, 126, 129, 130, 132, 133, 135, 137, 139, 148-153, 155, 159, 161, 163, 166
Eastern Front, 117, 219-221, 225, 227, 229, 234
economy, 235, 352
Edward VII, King of England, 306
effective, 19, 47, 50, 57, 77, 78, 82, 86, 112, 121, 122, 147, 156, 157, 163, 166, 167, 185, 199, 206, 207, 209, 210, 213, 215, 225, 251, 253, 275, 277, 282, 284, 285, 316, 319, 321, 322, 327-330, 332-336, 339, 340, 347, 349, 356, 365
ego, 28, 33, 43, 45, 77, 145, 212, 215, 245, 251, 257, 365
Eisenhower, Gen. Dwight, 233
élan, 49, 55, 56, 58, 267, 270, 272
elite, 87, 93, 94, 105, 109, 110, 240, 288, 308, 325
emotion, 28, 48, 170, 172, 219, 305, 356, 367
empower, 347, 350

encircle, 14, 23, 27, 28-31, 33, 65, 72, 102, 130, 152, 190
engineer, 92, 297-299, 307
English Channel, 51, 90, 95, 221
entitle, 240
environment, 7, 8, 50, 57, 87, 92, 109, 223, 287, 317, 319, 320, 341, 366, 373
error, 28, 101, 176, 193, 240, 248
escalate, 36, 137, 236
evaluate, 46, 78, 86, 199, 307, 311, 322, 323, 362, 366, 372
evaluation, 45, 78, 205
evidence, 75, 85, 114, 121, 122, 210, 229, 260, 279, 303
execute, 7, 17, 19, 22, 25, 32, 34, 37, 53, 74, 80, 81, 101, 117, 129, 142, 144, 151, 158, 203, 227, 252, 257, 280, 305, 309, 311, 339, 350, 355, 356, 365
executive, 32, 80, 87, 97, 110, 117, 139, 169, 170, 195-197, 217, 221, 224, 225, 231, 238, 281, 289, 290, 308, 313, 335, 338, 347, 349, 352
expectation, 17, 41, 97, 106, 140, 156, 210, 287, 325, 327
experience, 7, 8, 15, 18, 39, 47, 53-56, 71-73, 77, 79, 81, 84, 85, 94, 101, 113, 11-122, 124, 128, 134, 136, 139, 143, 145, 158, 181, 184, 187, 192, 233, 235, 239, 240, 243, 244, 261, 271, 272, 274, 277, 278, 281, 283, 286, 289, 302, 303, 305, 307, 312, 314, 316, 327, 332-335, 343, 344, 346, 348, 359, 360, 363
exploit, 7, 8, 57, 109, 117, 132, 133, 140, 156, 166, 209, 257, 276, 301, 319, 324, 327-330, 333-336, 339, 346, 353, 357, 371
extreme, 7, 36, 97, 144, 204, 212, 278, 280, 300, 305, 370

failure, 7, 10, 42, 43, 47, 50, 52, 54, 57, 69, 73, 74, 76-78, 86, 101, 117, 119, 121, 124, 135, 140, 143-145, 150, 156, 158, 160, 164, 166, 167, 169, 170, 173, 175, 203, 210, 213, 217-219, 223, 245, 250, 252-254, 258, 276, 284, 295, 303, 311, 320, 325, 327, 335, 336, 343, 344, 348, 351, 355, 357, 360, 362, 367
faith, 49, 50, 51, 56, 69, 72, 77, 96, 100, 101, 104, 134, 226, 244, 270, 278, 301, 334, 351, 352, 369
Falkenhayn, Gen. Eric von, 165, 219, 220, 222, 224, 225, 227, 229, 231, 232, 234, 235, 245, 328
family, 17, 71, 169, 195, 279, 280, 303, 306, 308, 359, 360
fantasy, 293, 311, 314
farm, 53, 195, 267
fashion, 9, 145
feedback, 40, 45, 205, 214, 215, 253, 258, 260, 290
feelings, 12, 70, 71, 113, 114, 171, 281
feint, 59, 82, 328, 330
feldgrau, 55
feud, 101, 201, 251
feudal, 160, 167
finance, 188, 193, 196, 204, 279, 289, 290, 322
finger-pointing, 87, 101, 110, 147, 164, 167, 201, 205
fire, 18, 32, 39, 40, 53, 64, 71, 108, 112, 119, 120, 135, 142, 143, 169, 212, 247, 249, 254, 266, 270, 274, 276, 278, 280, 293, 299, 303, 310, 319, 320, 324, 331, 342, 345, 349
firepower, 267, 349
fixate, 48, 72, 279, 358, 365
fixation, 341, 357, 367
flame thrower, 320
Flanders, 358
flawless, 80, 81, 311
flexible, 144, 161, 178, 181, 209, 227, 350-352, 367, 371
flip-flop, 217, 237
fluid, 341, 366
focus, 17, 19, 22, 76, 134, 135, 137, 139, 141, 156, 161, 164, 188, 201, 203,

205, 207, 240, 247, 249, 250, 271, 287, 288, 295, 302, 305, 373, 374
Fokker, Anton, 332
folly, 28, 36, 75, 89, 144, 175, 188
food, 88, 128, 136, 183, 185, 278, 279, 283, 360
foreign policy, 88, 90, 235
formula, 7, 129, 369
fort, 22, 23, 27, 62, 119, 132, 160, 194, 195, 229, 245-257, 266-268, 270-272
foundation, 41, 212, 281
France, 12-16, 23, 25-28, 31-33, 48, 49, 51, 52, 58, 61, 64, 67, 69, 73, 74, 87, 90, 92, 94, 95, 99-101, 103, 104, 107-109, 117, 118, 122-124, 137, 138, 147, 148, 165, 182, 188, 219-222, 229, 245, 246, 248, 267, 268, 270-273, 277, 278, 298, 323, 327, 351, 363-365
François, Gen. Herman von, 153, 155, 161, 162, 163
Franz Ferdinand, Archduke of Austria-Hungary, 15
French aircraft, 331, 332, 333
French Army, 12, 15, 22-25, 27-29, 32-36, 47-60, 62, 63, 65-67, 69-74, 76, 87, 90, 94, 95, 97-104, 106, 107, 165, 220, 221, 229, 230, 234, 245-248, 252, 257, 265-272, 276-278, 280, 283, 284, 295, 296, 298, 300, 326-328, 330, 334, 345, 346, 348, 353, 358-363
    French Army Group of the Rupture, 276
    French First Army, 51, 52, 55-57, 62, 73
    French Second Army, 52, 55-57, 62, 73
    French Third Army, 52, 56, 62
    French Fourth Army, 52, 56, 60, 62
    French Fifth Army, 25, 52, 57-60, 62, 65, 66, 72, 90, 97-100, 102, 360
    French Sixth Army, 62, 64, 65, 102, 359
    French Ninth Army, 62
French forts, 27, 48, 62, 245
French general, 47, 53, 63, 72, 98, 99, 104, 251, 265, 268, 277, 284,
French government, 63, 74, 271
French General Headquarters, 359
French High Command, 247, 250, 271, 360
French tank, 320, 321, 323, 325, 326, 335
friend, 71, 72, 90, 112, 113, 115, 178, 192
friendship, 77, 112, 148
Fuller, Gen. John F.C., 323, 324, 325
funds, 89, 160, 186, 188, 192, 196
future, 9, 12, 24, 41, 42, 44, 45, 48, 76, 77, 80, 81, 83, 84, 122, 143, 145, 157, 158, 163, 164, 167, 169-172, 178, 187, 223, 224, 226, 242, 278, 279, 285, 317, 352, 371, 373, 374

Galicia, 184, 185, 189-192, 194
Gallieni, Gen. Joseph, 63, 64, 66, 67, 74
gamble, 14, 34, 129, 192, 218, 219, 229, 231, 232, 236, 238, 250, 352, 363, 365
Garros, Roland, 331
gas mask, 320, 328
Gates, William, 308
Genghis Khan, 17
genius, 32, 226, 323
German aircraft, 331, 332, 333
German Army, 11-17, 19, 20, 22, 23, 25-29, 31-34, 36, 47, 48, 51-53, 55, 56-67, 69, 73, 74, 76, 87-90, 94, 99-102, 106, 107, 117, 119, 123, 124, 126, 129-139, 147-155, 157-163, 165, 166, 182, 186, 190, 197, 198, 202, 219-221, 227, 229-232, 234-236, 245-249, 254, 255, 257, 266-277, 294-296, 299-301, 303, 305, 310, 311, 324, 325, 327, 328, 330, 333, 344-349, 351-353, 355, 358-365
    German First Army, 16, 17, 20, 29-31, 65, 67, 100, 106, 107
    German Second Army, 16, 18, 20, 30, 65, 67, 69, 106, 355
    German Third Army, 16, 18, 20

German Fourth Army, 16, 18, 22
German Fifth Army, 16, 18, 22
German Sixth Army, 16, 18, 22, 23
German Seventh Army, 16, 22
German Eighth Army, 147-152, 154, 155, 157, 163
German Seventeenth Army, 353-355
Schlieffen Plan left wing, 14-16, 18, 24, 25, 32-36
Schlieffen Plan right wing, 13, 15-20, 22-25, 27-32, 34-36, 53, 57-59, 73, 74, 87, 99-101, 137
German fort, 132, 147
German general, 14
German General Staff, 13, 15, 148, 225, 245, 351, 363
German High Command, 20, 26, 29, 30, 52, 117, 156, 182, 234, 237, 247, 357
German Navy, 88, 89, 90, 296
German tank, 320
Germany, 12-15, 18, 19, 22, 24, 25, 27, 32, 48-50, 57, 87-90, 94, 117, 118, 123, 124, 126-129, 131, 134, 137, 148, 155, 158, 160, 165, 166, 178, 179, 217-222, 231, 232, 236, 237, 246, 255, 272, 295, 296, 320, 352, 358, 360, 361, 363
glory, 23, 130, 212
goal, 8, 11, 17, 19, 21, 28, 33, 36, 37, 38, 41, 42, 44, 46, 48, 50, 54, 61, 70, 72, 73, 76, 79-81, 95, 101, 113, 134, 144, 151, 161, 182, 192, 198, 203, 204, 207, 208, 212-215, 229, 235, 250-252, 257, 261, 262, 282-285, 289, 294-296, 311, 341, 347, 351, 352, 363, 366, 370
golden opportunity, 74, 132, 329
Golden Path, 307
Golden Rule, 289
goodwill, 286, 289
Gorlice, 227, 229
Grant, Gen. Ulysess S., 233
Great Britain, 12, 87, 88, 89, 90, 94, 101, 295, 364, 365
greed, 242

Grierson, Gen. Sir James, 95
guideline, 117, 129, 140, 350
Gumbinnen, 126, 129, 132, 134, 136, 149, 150, 152, 153

Habsburg, 176
Haig, Field Marshal Sir Douglas, 102, 108, 109, 298, 300, 301, 302, 303, 304, 306, 308, 309, 353
handsome, 306, 308
Haupt, Capt., 255
Hausen, Gen. Baron Max von, 18, 20, 25
headquarter, 20, 22, 30, 31, 38, 63, 64, 102, 124, 127, 133, 135, 136, 150, 152, 196, 255, 260, 268, 271, 285, 298, 309, 310, 314, 324, 355
hedge, 353
help, 7, 9, 10, 20, 22, 24, 27, 28, 33, 39, 41, 42, 44, 52, 64, 72, 74, 75, 78, 80, 84, 100, 105, 114, 122, 123, 130, 132-135, 137, 140, 145, 152, 155, 156, 158, 159, 171, 172, 193, 195, 201, 208, 209, 212-215, 235, 245, 250, 252-254, 257-259, 261-263, 272, 283, 285, 289, 296, 306, 308, 309, 322, 334, 340, 352, 358-360, 362, 365, 371, 372, 374
hero, 62, 104, 155, 225, 255, 256, 270, 272, 331
high-pressure, 8
Hindenburg, Field Marshal Paul von, 151-153, 155-157, 160, 161, 163, 165, 166, 219-222, 224-227, 229, 231, 232, 234-237, 355, 363, 364
Hitler, Adolf, 236
hoard, 147, 160, 167, 242
Hoffmann, Gen. Max, 152, 153
Holland, 13, 15
hourly employee, 194, 204
howitzer, 22, 120, 247, 276
Hutier, Gen. Oskar von, 353, 355, 357
hydrochloric acid, 328

idea, 17, 20, 21, 23, 33-35, 40-42, 44, 53, 55, 61, 63, 64, 73-76, 82, 86, 89, 92,

Index 389

95, 109, 121, 122, 140, 145, 161, 170, 182, 193, 196, 212, 217, 219, 222, 223, 226, 231, 237, 254, 261, 272, 278, 284, 285, 290, 301, 306, 321, 322, 324, 326-328, 330, 331, 333, 335, 336, 338, 341-343, 347-349, 351, 352, 361, 366, 367, 369-372
identify, 39, 47, 78, 80, 85, 156, 206, 209, 225, 233, 290, 305, 307, 340, 351, 365, 366, 372
ignorance, 43-45, 314
ignorant, 37, 349
ignore, 26, 40, 44, 97, 122, 137, 139, 186, 212, 213, 235, 240, 270, 315, 325, 357, 359
implement, 55, 86, 183, 290, 356, 365
implementation, 290, 348, 369
improve, 10, 20, 32, 41, 44, 49, 71, 80, 81, 85, 112, 114, 117, 120, 122, 139, 158, 161, 166, 167, 171, 196, 197, 199, 201, 205, 206, 209, 235, 278, 283, 284, 302, 320, 323, 337, 350, 351, 353, 356, 362, 363, 365, 366, 368-371
improvement, 71, 72, 81, 85, 86, 114, 121, 158, 164, 281, 282, 290, 322, 349, 351, 362, 369-372, 374
improvise, 49, 305
incompetence, 64, 70, 90, 176, 359, 367, 368
incompetent, 8, 9, 52, 56, 104, 113, 124, 135, 148, 183, 192, 200, 201, 221, 266, 341, 359, 360, 367
indecision, 70, 172
infantry, 53, 56, 92, 95, 120, 199, 200, 247, 248, 254, 266, 271, 293, 301, 302, 303, 310, 321-324, 327, 342, 343, 345, 346, 349, 350, 355, 362, 363
infiltrate, 346-348
inflexible, 47, 74, 76
inform, 121, 128, 170, 186, 206, 215, 257, 258, 296, 349, 367
information, 8, 19, 31, 32, 43-46, 52, 53, 55, 70, 81, 100, 121, 122, 135, 139, 143, 152, 157, 166, 169, 184, 209, 214, 224, 235, 238, 242, 243, 251, 260-262, 268, 281, 282, 284, 289, 290, 309, 311, 313-317, 340, 351, 360, 366, 367, 371, 372
initiative, 32, 44, 47, 61, 63, 72, 79, 117, 142-145, 151, 189, 257, 258, 266, 290, 299, 363
innovate, 50, 74, 80, 265, 271, 275, 284, 336, 337, 349, 365
innovation, 121, 143, 271, 319, 320, 325-327, 329, 330, 335, 349, 372
innovator, 122, 269, 321
insecure, 64, 137, 359
insight, 7, 8, 17, 31, 38, 84, 122, 257, 278, 282, 284, 285, 290, 312-316, 334, 346
inspire, 42, 54, 172, 196, 204, 265, 285, 356, 373
instruct, 21, 22, 94, 97, 201, 253, 258-260, 315, 344, 347, 356
interaction, 261, 262, 282
interest, 29, 101, 122, 143, 164, 168, 169, 175, 195, 196, 204, 205, 209, 215, 231, 235, 327, 348, 349
internet, 57, 338
intervene, 31, 96, 97, 180, 199
intervention, 87, 104, 160, 197, 259
intrigue, 139, 225, 235
investigate, 145, 156, 158, 171, 198, 261, 283, 338, 369
investigation, 156, 171, 198, 267, 348
Italy, 176, 178, 363

Japan, 54, 118-120, 124
Japanese Navy, 119
Jilinski, Gen. Grand Duke, 127, 133-136
Joffre, Marshal Joseph, 50, 53, 55-64, 66, 67, 69-75, 98, 102, 106, 254, 266-268, 270-272
judge, 71, 293, 308, 313, 341, 366
judgment, 28, 255, 308, 313, 338
junior officer, 30, 50, 195, 197, 326, 348

khaki, 55
Kiggell, Gen. Sir Launcelot, 309
Kitchener, Field Marshal Earl Horatio Herbert, 90, 92, 94-97, 102-106, 108, 306
Kluck, Gen. Alexander von, 17, 18, 20, 22, 25, 27, 29, 30, 65-69
knowledge, 10, 84, 120-122, 143, 286-288, 309, 313, 316, 334, 340, 345-347
Konigsberg, 132, 161
Korea, 118, 119
Kovno, 124, 126
Krakow, 191
Kunze, Sgt., 254-256

labor relations, 283
Lanrezac, Gen. Charles, 58-63, 72, 74, 97-100
last minute, 175, 181, 182, 203, 337
Le Cateau, 102
lead, 9, 17, 18, 28, 33, 39, 40, 41, 43-46, 56, 65, 70, 72, 82, 90, 94, 105, 110, 121-124, 126, 130, 136, 145, 157, 166, 168, 169, 184, 194, 196, 199, 203, 204, 210, 212, 219-221, 224, 227, 230, 232, 233, 235, 239, 241, 243, 248, 254, 255, 257, 259, 260, 266, 267, 268, 270-272, 282, 285, 286, 293, 297, 298, 300, 305, 307, 312-314, 316, 321, 330, 337, 348, 349, 351, 359, 365, 367, 374
leader, 8, 9, 16, 17, 19, 21, 25, 28, 29, 31, 33, 37-39, 41-44, 46, 52-54, 56, 61, 62, 64, 68, 70, 71, 74-77, 80, 87, 89, 92, 93, 96-99, 105, 106, 109, 112, 113, 115, 119, 121, 122, 126, 130, 134, 137, 139, 140, 145, 150, 151, 155-157, 160, 164-172, 176, 185, 186, 188, 192, 193, 195, 198, 199, 203-205, 207, 212-214, 233, 237, 239, 240, 242, 243, 250, 252, 254, 256, 260, 266, 272, 277, 278, 281, 282, 285, 297, 301, 302, 305, 306, 311, 313, 314, 320, 332, 343, 346-349, 351, 359, 361

leadership, 8, 10, 14, 17, 20, 28, 31, 32, 38, 41-44, 47, 48, 50, 53-55, 59, 64, 69, 70-72, 76, 77, 81, 87, 92-95, 97, 99, 101, 106, 109-112, 115, 117, 120-122, 125, 126, 128, 136, 139, 147, 150, 151, 155-157, 160, 164, 166, 169-173, 175, 176, 182, 188, 192, 196, 197, 203, 207, 214, 217, 218, 221, 223, 226, 233, 234, 237, 238, 240-243, 253, 256, 259, 265, 266, 268, 278, 281, 283-285, 289, 293, 295, 297-299, 302, 303, 305, 306, 308, 311-313, 344, 347, 351, 352, 355, 359, 361, 369, 370, 374
leadership assessment, 156, 293, 312
leadership attribute, 117, 139
leadership change, 71, 265
leadership optimism, 70
leadership practice, 283
leadership style, 266, 268, 281, 284
learn, 7, 10, 45-48, 54, 55, 60, 64, 77, 84, 85, 104, 119, 121, 122, 129, 137, 139, 141, 145, 157, 158, 167, 187, 193, 233, 260, 261, 274, 278, 284, 285, 309, 332, 334, 335, 337, 340, 359, 361, 362, 372, 374
leave, 18, 29, 36, 64, 77, 82, 94, 102, 125, 140, 141, 157, 192, 198, 238, 253, 277-280, 283, 288, 303, 336, 348
liability, 279
Liege, 22, 152
limelight, 25
limit, 36, 76, 86, 89, 97, 110, 121, 144, 150, 178, 188, 197, 198, 203, 211, 219, 227, 229, 233, 237, 238, 240, 243, 267, 268, 270, 322, 353, 357
limitation, 186, 187, 279, 293, 312
Limoge, 266, 270
line of march, 18, 25, 57, 130, 136
listen, 26, 40, 75, 85, 98, 122, 136, 152, 194, 206, 209, 255, 260, 261, 268, 277, 278, 282, 290, 301, 326, 335, 336, 341, 348, 360, 365-367
Lloyd George, Prime Minister David, 300
loan, 188, 195, 196

long-range, 26, 223, 352, 366
long-term, 12, 26, 57, 150, 158, 166, 169, 171, 223, 235, 237, 257, 279, 341, 351, 352, 366
Lorraine, 12, 15, 22, 23, 48, 50, 52, 73, 219
loser, 40, 41
low-level, 224, 225, 280, 346, 350, 365
loyal, 112, 171, 196, 283, 288, 289
luck, 49, 74, 79, 158, 254
Ludendorff, Gen. Erich, 151-153, 155-157, 160, 161, 163, 165, 166, 219-222, 224-227, 229, 231, 232, 234-237, 351-353, 355, 357, 358, 361-363, 365
Luxembourg, 13, 15

machine gun, 53-55, 119, 254, 255, 271, 293, 302, 303, 310, 319-321, 324, 330, 331, 342, 345, 346
Mahan, Adm. Alfred, 88
main line of resistance, 345
manage, 12, 107, 120, 141, 184, 199, 205, 217, 224, 238, 255, 327, 331, 353
management, 43, 47, 59, 77, 193, 194, 198, 199, 206, 232, 243, 249, 265, 279, 285, 287-289, 297, 307, 348, 350, 351, 369
management fad, 369
management practice, 279
managing earnings, 217, 224, 238
Mangin, Gen. Charles, 277
manipulate, 282
Marne, 29, 32, 35, 67, 68, 72, 103, 106, 107, 138, 165, 220, 246, 266
Marwitz, Gen. Georg von der, 353, 355, 357
Masurian Lakes, 148, 161, 163
matrix, 293, 303, 305, 312
meeting, 8, 31, 41, 82, 101, 104, 105, 128, 133, 181, 182, 206, 214, 261, 262, 278, 282, 283
mentor, 140, 332, 334, 340
mercenary, 288
merchant shipping, 88, 295, 296
merger, 175, 187, 204

messenger, 19, 44
meteorologist, 298, 299
method, 9, 17, 19, 41, 50, 54, 84, 106, 109, 120, 122, 135, 142, 158, 167, 207, 212, 236, 238, 253, 275, 281, 283, 284, 305, 319, 323, 330, 333, 336, 341, 344, 346, 347, 349, 350, 355, 356, 359, 365, 368-370, 372
Meuse, 268
Michel, Gen. Victor, 53
micromanage, 137
military governor, 248-250
militia, 148, 198
mislead, 43, 314, 317, 346
mistake, 7-10, 27, 28, 36, 38, 39, 43, 45, 47, 52, 54, 64, 69, 74, 79, 81, 89, 112, 126, 128, 135, 139, 145, 155, 156, 158, 161, 163, 166, 193, 203, 208, 214, 233, 235, 242, 245, 248, 252-257, 270, 298, 319, 325, 357, 363, 374
mobilize, 15, 16, 25, 51, 95, 178, 180, 182, 184, 185, 188
modern, 7, 8, 52, 76, 109, 118, 120, 139, 176, 192, 203, 223, 303, 319, 373
Moltke, Field Marshal Helmuth von, 15, 16, 20, 22-28, 30-34, 36, 148, 150, 151, 161, 165, 219
Mons, 99, 100, 101, 103
morale, 49, 55, 73, 77, 110, 171, 172, 223, 230, 278, 279, 281, 283, 289, 349
Morocco, 188
motivate, 8, 9, 42, 114, 171, 258, 260, 285, 352, 356, 370
motivation, 9, 17, 113, 169, 171, 173, 195, 204, 231, 242, 266, 284, 288, 374
Mulhouse, 53
mutiny, 276, 277, 278, 280, 295, 296, 300, 364
myopia, 59, 68, 158, 243, 302
myth, 120, 233, 238, 239, 341, 366

Napoleon Bonaparte, 15, 48, 176
naval power, 88
Nazi, 236

negative, 42, 57, 113, 117, 125, 130, 139, 144, 151, 166, 169, 192, 196, 223, 242, 288, 289, 322
negotiate, 219, 236, 363
neutral, 13, 14, 88, 94
Nivelle, Gen. Robert, 265, 266, 270-278, 281, 283, 284, 295

obedience, 142
obey, 97, 153, 315
objective, 8, 37, 73, 113, 133, 144, 164, 220, 227, 229, 243, 261, 262, 267, 272, 294-296, 305, 309, 351, 352, 357
observation, 198, 205, 209, 260, 314, 316
observe, 85, 119, 260, 344, 355
office, 38, 117, 124-126, 139, 260, 282, 285, 306, 308, 313, 314
office politics, 117, 124-126, 139, 306, 308
on the job experience, 332
one size fits all, 366
open-book, 289
opportunity, 7, 23, 29, 35, 41, 46, 48, 55, 57, 64, 66, 69, 73, 74, 76, 107, 109, 118, 132, 133, 143-145, 157, 163, 166, 177, 209, 213, 237, 263, 279, 282, 290, 308, 315, 327, 329, 330, 334, 336, 346, 351-353, 356-358, 367, 371
oppose, 8, 56, 118, 130, 136, 152, 160, 184, 189, 219, 221, 222, 226, 267, 298, 330, 342, 350, 366
opposition, 23, 34, 73, 132
optimism, 70, 172, 272, 299-301, 311, 314, 374
organizational model, 58
Ostend, 295
Ottoman Empire, 177
outcome, 9, 17, 25, 54, 57, 80, 101, 105, 126, 144, 151, 155, 169, 191, 214, 219, 283, 301, 320, 326, 357, 374
oversight, 213, 214
Oxford, 303, 304

pad, 175, 181, 203
panic, 26, 52, 69, 70, 117, 137, 147, 150, 151, 159, 166, 170, 182, 234, 267, 268, 305, 312, 329, 358, 360, 370
paradox, 350
Paris, 12, 14, 23, 27, 29, 31-33, 36, 62, 64-67, 74, 87, 102-105, 107, 138, 277, 331, 352
particulars, 371, 372
partner, 95, 110, 131
Passchendaele, 293-301, 309-311, 324, 327, 353
path to success, 49, 302, 350, 374
payoff, 166, 337, 338
Pearl Harbor, 119
peer, 18, 21, 33, 37, 52, 91, 97, 110, 130, 207, 212-214, 254, 262, 267, 272, 287, 307
performance, 17, 36, 40-44, 71, 79, 81, 96, 97, 104-106, 110-115, 122, 125, 168, 175, 192, 194, 196-199, 202-205, 235, 240, 243, 250, 266, 267, 283, 284, 290, 302, 308, 350, 351, 366, 369-371
performance evaluation, 199
performance management, 40, 175, 198, 199, 205
performance problem, 105
Pershing, Gen. John, 360
personal ambition, 33, 38, 168, 217, 239
personal difficulty, 97
personal goal, 37, 38, 94, 130, 236
personal success, 11, 38, 114, 130, 217, 237, 242
personality issue, 21
pessimism, 70, 300, 334
Petain, Field Marshal Henri-Philippe, 265-270, 272, 278, 280-284
philosophy, 47, 49, 50, 52, 55, 76, 85, 122, 302, 319, 350
physically attractive, 241, 308, 313
pitfall, 87, 95, 110, 293, 313, 374
plan, 11, 18, 19, 22, 23, 25-27, 31, 32, 34-38, 42, 47, 49, 52, 59, 62, 72-74, 79-82, 87, 89, 90, 97, 98, 100,

101, 109, 122-124, 126, 128, 129, 131-135, 139, 142, 144, 147-153, 155, 158, 161-164, 166, 176, 178, 180-186, 189, 191, 203, 217, 219, 220, 222, 223, 229, 237, 245, 247, 270, 272, 273, 275-277, 284, 293-296, 299-302, 305, 306, 309, 311-313, 317, 328, 329, 335, 336, 339, 350-353, 355, 357, 358, 365
Plan R (Austrian), 178, 180
Plan S (Austrian), 11, 178, 180
Plan XVII (French), 47, 49-51, 53, 55, 57, 59, 63, 69, 73, 90, 99, 101
Plumer, Gen. Sir Herbert, 95
plunder, 288
poison gas, 319, 320, 328-330, 335, 346
Poland, 123, 176, 227
policy, 17, 86, 88, 139, 140, 188, 204, 224, 225, 265, 283, 284, 287, 288, 322, 350
politics, 17, 18, 118, 125, 126, 139, 185, 225, 226, 231, 232, 235, 236, 266, 267, 278, 355
pool, 217, 238, 239, 243
popular, 87-89, 109, 155, 225, 236, 256, 320
Port Arthur, 118, 119
potential, 12, 37, 77, 86, 97, 109, 128, 129, 205, 214, 257, 297, 321, 322, 325, 327, 335, 337, 338, 374
Potiorek, Gen. Oskar, 184
power, 11, 49, 55, 60, 84, 88-91, 99, 112, 118, 119, 122, 164, 172, 175-178, 180, 185, 186, 196, 207, 221-223, 226, 231, 235-238, 278, 289-291, 303, 330, 364
practice, 17, 53, 54, 57, 61, 64, 76, 80, 86, 120, 122, 139, 140, 147, 157, 167, 183, 187, 215, 238, 265, 271, 281, 283, 284, 288, 296, 319, 322, 336, 343, 344, 346, 350, 356, 361, 365, 370, 371
predestine, 96, 117, 140
prerequisite, 49, 94, 233, 239, 243, 244, 293, 304, 307, 312

pressure, 7, 18, 23, 26, 27, 36, 59, 60, 63, 64, 69, 70, 98, 123, 124, 127, 131, 132, 134, 136, 137, 140, 147, 148, 150, 159, 163, 166, 185, 206, 267, 295, 297, 359, 361, 363, 373
prestige, 11, 33, 164, 165, 183, 192, 226, 231, 246, 247
price control, 195
pride, 29, 49, 52, 62, 145, 251, 297, 298
Prittwitz, Gen. Max von, 26, 148, 150, 151
privilege, 18, 194, 195, 287
problem, 7, 9, 19, 20-22, 25-27, 30, 36, 39, 43-45, 52, 54, 58, 64, 68, 72, 77, 80, 81, 84, 85, 87, 89, 92-94, 96, 97, 101, 102, 104-106, 109, 110, 114, 125, 126, 128-130, 135, 137, 140, 144, 145, 148, 158, 163, 166, 171, 172, 175, 178, 182-185, 187, 188, 192-194, 197-199, 201-205, 208, 209, 212-215, 221, 222, 225, 235, 238, 243, 249, 250, 253, 257, 259-261, 266, 270, 277-284, 286-288, 296, 298-301, 303, 311, 312, 315-317, 320-323, 325, 327, 330, 331, 335-338, 342-346, 352, 355, 362, 365, 366, 368-370, 373, 374
problem solving, 110, 365, 369
procedure, 43, 57, 80, 86, 139, 162, 188, 201, 204, 253, 322, 344, 346, 349, 350, 356
process, 15, 23, 44, 45, 81, 85, 125, 126, 142, 184, 187, 193, 201, 238, 240, 241, 253, 290, 305, 307, 319, 324, 329, 337, 340, 341, 344, 346, 348, 349, 363, 366, 369, 371
procrastinate, 78, 114
productive, 77, 89, 139, 168, 208, 213, 214, 240, 283, 287, 338-340, 347, 367, 371
productivity, 41, 46, 85, 169, 173, 192, 196, 199, 206-209, 214, 279, 281, 283, 285, 287-289, 337, 340, 356, 371
professional, 18, 93, 97, 100, 110, 192, 212, 288

profitable, 48, 194-196, 204, 290, 291, 347, 356, 371
program, 44, 88, 89, 262, 278, 290, 297, 374
promote, 50, 64, 95, 96, 105, 112, 125, 135, 139, 142, 145, 157, 167, 205, 212, 215, 242, 243, 256, 261, 262, 266, 267, 270-272, 278, 286, 306, 307, 312
promotion, 45, 49, 93, 94, 110, 125, 126, 205, 240, 241, 308
proof, 44, 73, 145, 271, 290, 308, 317, 329
prophecy, 40, 134, 200
prophet, 349
proposal, 23, 25, 27, 152, 153, 155, 222, 223, 273, 348
prove, 50, 96, 104, 145, 151, 164, 168, 180, 199, 201, 205, 207, 214, 288, 290, 335, 336, 337
Prussia, 26, 27, 123, 124, 130, 137, 148, 151, 152, 166
Przemsyl, 194
punish, 15, 44, 62, 143-145, 180, 184, 213, 315, 322, 365
purchase, 339

quality, 175, 278, 279, 283
question, 9, 10, 28, 45, 52, 54, 55, 57, 74, 89, 96, 97, 104, 139, 182, 195, 206, 226, 277, 282, 297, 298, 300, 303, 317, 344, 346, 370

radical, 323, 326, 330, 348, 349, 370
radio, 19, 135, 136, 152, 155, 162, 345
Radtke, Lieut., 255, 256
railroad, 15, 90, 95, 123, 124, 126, 130, 161, 163, 178, 180-183, 185, 269, 358, 360, 362
react, 11, 32, 47, 68, 69, 82, 89, 130, 166, 315, 316, 325, 328, 363
reaction, 11, 19, 37, 68, 81, 279, 349, 370
reality, 28, 34, 38, 42, 59, 69, 71, 73, 74, 76, 100, 120, 121, 130, 148, 150, 160, 186, 190, 211, 243, 252, 303, 309, 314, 355, 374

reallocate, 25, 31, 206, 207, 210
reassign, 31, 206, 297
rebellion, 278, 283
redeem, 357, 367
reduce, 26, 32, 38, 55, 82, 90, 164, 193, 199, 204, 210, 226, 227, 234, 242, 243, 253, 275, 279, 284, 296, 300, 302, 337, 342, 350, 352, 365
reduction, 208, 209, 303
refusal, 250, 356
refuse, 29, 43, 44, 53, 120, 121, 153, 186, 208, 209, 224, 245, 250, 257, 261, 275, 277, 295, 355, 356
regress, 136, 137, 140
reinforce, 24, 66, 73, 105, 114, 124, 171, 189, 271, 277, 285, 303, 326, 331, 342, 345, 358, 367
reinforcement, 25, 27, 73, 137, 161, 167, 189, 191, 255, 271, 310, 327, 353, 357, 358
reject, 73, 85, 102, 120, 322, 326, 349, 363
rejection, 113
relation, 89, 113
relationship, 17, 71, 72, 97, 112, 113, 115, 126-128, 193, 204, 261-263, 265, 281, 285, 291, 356
religion, 93, 240
Rennenkampf, Gen. Pavel, 124, 126-134, 136, 137, 161-163
report, 22, 30-32, 39, 52, 54, 55, 58, 59, 69, 70, 101-103, 136, 150, 162-164, 198, 209, 214, 224, 225, 248, 253, 255, 260, 267, 268, 276, 277, 279, 298, 309, 313, 314, 348, 355, 356
reserve, 25, 27, 52, 58, 59, 62, 80, 161, 187, 192, 193, 197, 203, 230, 231, 271, 274, 276, 300, 303, 324, 330, 345, 357, 358, 362
resign, 40, 217, 225, 226, 238, 241
resist, 34, 73, 315, 342
resistance, 17, 20, 22, 25, 27, 28, 34, 44, 81, 208, 272, 315, 345, 347, 355, 356
resolution, 218
resolve, 114, 172, 215, 281
resource, 21, 24-26, 28, 31, 34, 35, 48,

Index

57, 59, 61, 76, 80-83, 89, 95, 110, 130, 135, 144, 147, 151, 157, 160, 166, 167, 178, 180-182, 186, 203, 206-211, 214, 218, 219, 221, 223, 231, 237, 242, 250, 257, 276, 277, 298, 301, 306, 309, 322, 324, 329, 333, 334, 347, 349, 353, 357, 364, 367, 370, 371
responsibility, 37, 41, 61, 93, 94, 99, 105, 134, 137, 140, 141, 151, 156, 164, 197, 199, 204, 209, 214, 233, 237, 240, 242, 249-251, 266, 279, 286, 287, 307, 311, 312, 332
responsible, 32, 43, 101, 113, 128, 133, 155, 164, 175, 176, 178, 183, 226, 249, 252, 254, 255, 298, 315, 346, 347, 365
result, 9, 12, 17, 19, 40, 41, 44, 48, 50, 53, 56, 59, 74, 77, 79-81, 84, 86, 88, 92, 94, 99, 105, 112, 114, 118, 128, 133, 134, 136-140, 143, 144, 150, 157, 158, 163, 164, 166, 169, 170, 171, 173, 181, 183, 192, 196, 203, 205, 208, 210, 219, 220-224, 235-238, 240, 242, 243, 248, 250-253, 256, 257, 260, 261, 266, 270, 282, 283, 285, 289-291, 295, 297, 301, 303, 306, 308, 313, 317, 325-327, 329, 334, 336, 338, 340, 347, 350, 352, 357, 358, 366, 368-370, 373, 374
retreat, 23, 27-30, 35, 53, 61-64, 67, 70, 72, 100-103, 107, 147, 150, 151, 154, 163, 165, 190, 191, 220, 224, 266, 273, 323
revenge, 12, 47, 48, 50, 76
review, 31, 64, 114, 198, 288, 365, 371
revolt, 277, 280, 295
revolution, 277, 300, 364
Revolutionary War, 233
reward, 41, 42, 110, 112, 114, 126, 144, 145, 157, 167, 171, 197, 205, 210, 214, 215, 226, 256, 267, 286, 290, 340, 372
Rheims, 360, 362, 363
Rhine, 48, 50

Richtofen, Capt. Manfred von, 332
rigid, 341, 344, 365
risk, 15, 34, 35, 37, 46, 47, 61, 62, 77, 95, 109, 110, 117, 129, 130, 131, 140, 142, 143, 145, 150-152, 169, 170, 181, 203, 204, 217, 223, 229, 231, 236, 238, 322, 329, 336, 338, 341, 352, 353, 367
Roman Empire, 160
Romania, 176, 232, 234
Royal Navy, 13, 88-90, 295, 296, 300
ruin, 36, 48, 74, 150, 219, 237, 251, 283, 314
rumor, 70, 170, 268
Rupprecht, Crown Prince of Bavaria, 18, 22-25, 27, 28, 32, 33, 35, 62
ruse, 82
Russia, 12-15, 49, 54, 118-120, 122-124, 126, 127, 148, 178-180, 184, 186, 192, 220, 222, 300, 351, 353, 363
Russian Army, 15, 16, 25-27, 55, 90, 117-120, 123, 124, 126-131, 133, 135-139, 147-156, 158, 160-163, 166, 178, 182, 184, 185, 189-192, 194, 197, 220, 221, 224, 227, 229-231, 300, 328-330, 351
Russian First Army, 124, 126, 127, 129, 132, 133, 137, 138, 149, 152, 153-155, 160, 161, 163
Russian Second Army, 124, 126-136, 138, 149, 150, 152-155, 160, 163, 220
Russian Third Army, 189
Russian Fourth Army, 189
Russian Fifth Army, 189
Russian Eighth Army, 189
Russian Ninth Army, 189
Russian Northwest Front, 124, 127, 133
Russian general, 221, 230,
Russian Navy, 118
Russo-Japanese war, 55, 128

saber, 90, 120, 178
sacrifice, 112, 140, 157, 239, 242, 278, 285

salary, 194, 204
salespeople, 42, 356
Salonika, 363
Samsonov, Gen. Alexander, 124, 126-137
Sandhurst, 304
Sarajevo, 179, 184
Schlieffen, Field Marshal Alfred von, 13-15, 18, 19, 23, 24, 32-35, 148, 218
Schlieffen Plan (German), 11, 13, 15-20, 23, 24, 25-28, 32-37, 50, 89, 94, 137, 148, 151, 165, 217-219, 222
secret, 7, 157, 169, 276, 282, 289, 328
self preservation, 231
self-improvement, 45
selfish, 160, 235, 237, 242, 285
self-optimization, 72
self-serving, 29, 168, 196, 235, 242
sell, 41, 42, 172, 260, 282, 288, 325, 356
Serbia, 15, 122, 176, 178-180, 182, 184-186, 189
Serbian Army, 184
servant, 283
service, 31, 81, 88, 151, 187, 194, 217, 239, 266, 316, 337, 371
share, 23, 70, 71, 76, 87, 95, 100, 118, 122, 157, 166, 169, 208, 212, 221, 255, 261, 262, 278, 285, 290, 302, 316, 334, 372
shareholder, 26
shell, 120, 200, 220, 247, 293, 299, 300, 303, 310, 321, 324, 342, 343, 349, 355
short-term, 26, 147, 150, 166, 223, 235, 237, 279
Siberia, 315
siege, 119, 246
Sir John French, Field Marshal, 72, 90-92, 94-109, 298, 301, 306
situation, 7-13, 15, 20-22, 26, 27, 30, 38, 40, 43, 45, 48-51, 54, 58, 64, 68-70, 72, 76, 77, 79, 80, 84, 85, 92, 96, 98-101, 103, 106, 114, 121, 122, 130, 132-135, 139, 140, 150, 151, 154, 166, 169-172, 176, 178, 186, 188, 194, 206, 210, 213, 214, 218, 219, 231, 232, 249, 250, 257, 259, 266-268, 270, 275-277, 279, 281, 283, 284, 295, 300, 301, 314, 316, 344, 347, 350, 352, 353, 358, 359, 366, 369, 371-373
skepticism, 272, 300, 335
skill, 17, 18, 61, 81, 93, 94, 105, 110, 118, 121, 124, 126, 139, 199, 214, 233, 240, 243, 244, 287, 307, 308, 312, 313, 369
slack, 180, 182, 209
Slav, 122, 178
Smith-Dorien, Gen. Sir Horace, 95-97, 102, 108, 301
social barrier, 262
solution, 13, 20, 44, 46, 50, 94, 137, 178, 205, 257, 260, 283, 312, 320, 321, 327, 330, 331, 336, 346, 350, 366, 370, 372
Somme, 230, 232, 270-273, 276, 298, 329, 343, 346
source, 31, 64, 86, 101, 122, 135, 139, 166, 182, 187, 190, 195, 229, 242, 243, 281, 288, 298, 303, 314, 326, 332, 335, 336, 341, 348, 351, 365, 366, 372
South Africa, 90, 91
special few, 233
special privilege, 194, 196
spending spree, 339
sport, 240
stagnate, 370
stalemate, 221, 341
steal, 256, 258
stockholder, 150, 226
story, 8-11, 36, 37, 47, 53, 54, 61, 76, 84, 89, 109, 117, 156, 166, 175, 192, 226, 233, 243, 245, 254-257, 261, 265, 268, 278, 282, 284, 293, 309, 311, 325, 330, 335, 341, 348, 373, 374
strain, 22, 69, 70, 182, 269
strategic, 12, 13, 26, 72, 74, 82, 83, 87, 109, 110, 150, 217, 223, 295, 301, 317, 366
strategy, 35, 47-49, 57, 73, 74, 76, 82, 87,

Index 397

109, 122, 123, 150, 152, 187, 204, 217, 223-225, 227, 229, 237, 238, 275, 290, 293, 302, 306, 311, 353
Straub, Gen. Johann, 180, 182
study, 84, 86, 147, 156, 166, 206, 267, 284, 338, 339, 348, 370, 372
stupid, 34, 35, 79, 180, 194
submarine, 295, 296, 300, 320
subordinate, 11, 16, 17, 20-22, 29, 31, 37-42, 62, 64, 70, 72, 74, 75, 90, 93, 96, 97, 102, 106, 133-135, 137, 140-142, 152, 153, 155, 163, 164, 168, 197, 199, 205, 226, 249, 259, 262, 270, 287, 299, 309, 313, 316, 355, 356
success, 7, 10, 11, 22-24, 26, 31-33, 36-39, 48, 51, 52, 67, 69, 71-73, 75-77, 80, 82, 83, 85, 91-93, 95, 97, 109, 112, 114, 117, 121, 122, 129, 132, 133, 135, 139, 140, 143-145, 147, 150, 155-158, 160, 163, 164, 166-172, 184, 188, 215, 221, 223, 224, 226, 229, 237, 242, 243, 247, 248, 252, 261, 262, 266-268, 271, 272, 275, 276, 278, 284, 286, 296, 297, 302, 309, 311, 312, 320, 324, 327, 329, 332-337, 339, 346, 347, 350-353, 357, 358, 360, 365-367, 369, 374
Sudan, 306
Sukhomlinov, Gen. Vladimir, 119-121
superior, 17, 39, 49, 61, 63, 96, 97, 100, 101, 104-106, 110, 112, 113, 143, 144, 152, 163, 190, 193, 207, 225, 262, 267, 269, 279, 287, 326, 339, 343, 360, 368
surprise, 8, 59, 79, 82, 95, 117-119, 137, 149, 162, 197, 253, 279, 281, 309, 316, 338
surround, 23, 28, 29, 53, 61, 107, 118, 123, 132, 136, 137, 147, 152, 155, 161, 166, 220, 254, 272, 346, 351, 360
swamp, 148, 161, 298, 299
Switzerland, 51, 221
syndrome, 245, 252, 254, 257, 261

tactics, 9, 49, 53, 55, 57, 76, 92, 122, 207, 223, 267, 274, 275, 278, 323-325, 332, 333, 340, 343, 344, 346-349, 355-357, 359, 362, 363, 365
tank, 298, 299, 319-327, 329, 335, 346, 363
Tannenberg, 136, 155-158, 160-163, 190, 220
target, 17, 53, 55, 86, 123, 167, 247, 254, 255, 275, 299, 302, 344, 345, 349
Tarnow, 227, 229
task, 40, 42, 132, 141, 172, 197, 205, 249, 250, 253, 257, 309, 360
team, 29, 60, 110, 114, 156, 171, 212-215, 222, 283, 297, 310, 311, 323, 346, 347
teamwork, 101, 212-215, 245, 251, 257, 347
technology, 7-9, 253, 302, 307, 319-322, 327, 329, 334-341, 373, 374
telegraph, 19, 128, 135
telephone, 310, 314
temper, 104, 105, 110
temporary, 133, 140, 166, 208, 209, 245, 250, 257, 279, 325, 328, 330, 351
temptation, 140, 147, 150, 166, 204, 372
territorial, 58
theoretical, 150, 151, 166, 357
theory, 61, 89, 94, 120, 235, 236, 267, 272, 351
think, 17, 19, 22, 23, 25, 28, 29, 31, 33, 34, 39, 40, 42-47, 50, 52, 54, 59, 64, 70, 76, 77, 80-82, 84-86, 89, 93, 96, 105, 109, 110, 112, 121, 126, 133, 134, 140, 143, 144, 158, 164, 169, 183, 194, 199, 207- 210, 212, 219, 225, 231, 233, 235, 238, 240, 241, 257, 258, 260, 263, 272, 279, 282, 286-288, 291, 300-303, 308, 314, 317, 324, 326, 332, 335-337, 344, 348, 349, 359, 360, 362, 365, 367, 368, 370-372, 374
thought, 12, 22, 25, 26, 33, 34, 50, 52-54, 56, 59, 89, 107, 117, 133, 144, 151, 154-156, 161, 162, 180, 182, 183,

185, 219, 220, 232, 236, 251, 255, 261, 270, 278, 290, 299, 300, 303, 306, 311, 322, 325, 328, 346, 358, 363, 370, 373
threat, 12, 13, 32, 62, 65, 67, 69, 74, 82, 88, 89, 96, 120, 123, 126, 129, 134, 137, 148, 161, 163, 178, 200, 217, 226, 227, 238, 241, 300, 370
threaten, 12, 28, 49, 88, 107, 122, 123, 132, 137, 158, 161, 163, 179, 225, 226, 241, 322
thrust, 25, 73, 82, 275, 302, 354
top down, 262, 290
training, 7, 8, 18, 27, 39, 95, 123, 127, 130, 141, 148, 153, 154, 178, 180-183, 185, 186, 189, 192-194, 212, 214, 278, 280, 287, 290, 295, 305, 319, 332-336, 340, 343-345, 369
transfer, 39, 206, 224, 266, 280
trench, 7, 74, 94, 120, 198, 221, 248, 250, 268, 271, 274, 276-278, 282, 293, 295, 302, 303, 309, 310, 320, 321, 323, 324, 327, 328, 330, 342-346, 355, 361, 362
trust, 72, 81, 93, 142, 208, 290, 291, 314, 344, 365
Turks, 119, 176, 177, 184, 363
turnover, 39, 284
turret, 254, 323, 326

U-boat, 295, 296
unacceptable, 129, 170, 326
undefined, 99
understand, 9, 10, 17, 38, 41, 42, 84, 106, 115, 130, 140, 156, 169, 171, 194, 240, 242, 253, 258, 277, 281, 288, 289, 334, 339, 346, 366
unexpected, 18, 19, 25, 81, 144, 161, 193, 357
uniform, 53, 55, 56
unique, 54, 77, 85, 188, 372
United States, 295, 364, 365

vacation, 196, 197, 279, 287
vacillate, 222, 224, 237

vacillation, 185, 223
valid, 8, 46, 58, 75, 86, 94, 139, 209, 229, 272, 297, 302, 312, 317, 339, 355
venture, 95, 314
Verdun, 229, 230, 232, 245-248, 250, 257, 265-272, 274, 276, 277, 295, 333, 346, 348
Versailles, 12
victorious, 124, 148
victory, 10, 11, 15, 20, 23, 27, 30, 32, 56, 58, 69, 74, 82, 109, 130, 136, 147, 154-158, 160, 163, 188, 190, 191, 220, 221, 224, 225, 229, 248, 271, 272, 330, 341, 352, 355, 358, 363, 365
Vienna, 326
vision, 41, 42, 80, 308, 352
visit, 20, 22, 31, 184, 196, 268, 278, 315-317, 355
Vistula, 150, 151
voice mail, 253
Vosges, 51

wait, 66, 72, 78, 80, 86, 106, 114, 126, 128, 129, 132, 133, 136, 153, 166, 182, 209, 210, 257, 258, 284, 303, 329, 336, 337, 367, 370
war of attrition, 220, 221, 227, 329
Warsaw, 124, 126-128, 135, 158, 160, 161
Washington, Gen. George, 233
waste, 9, 39, 40, 82, 164, 168, 187, 201, 205, 219, 278, 282, 322, 329, 333, 338, 369, 371
weak, 12, 22, 34, 56, 73, 101, 106, 132, 137, 151, 183, 218, 237, 271, 276, 301, 346
weaken, 25, 27, 29, 39, 191, 230, 358
weakness, 8, 276, 328, 353
Western Front, 161, 165, 218, 220, 221, 224, 227, 229, 230, 234, 235, 245, 293-296, 300, 328, 342, 344, 351, 363
Wilhelm, Crown Prince of Germany, 18, 255, 256

Wilhelm II, Kaiser of Germany, 12, 49, 88, 89, 118, 179
working relationship, 41, 96, 117, 139, 251
World War II, 9, 233, 295
Wright Brothers, 330

Zeebrugge, 295

www.ingramcontent.com/pod-product-compliance
Lightning Source LLC
Chambersburg PA
CBHW051416290426
44109CB00016B/1320